Bottom Line's

Smart Consumer

How to Get the Best Deals

Anytime, Anywhere

Bottom Line
Books
www.BottomLineSecrets.com

Contents

1

How to Be a Savvy Consumer

Secrets of Smart Shopping

Become an educated consumer—you'll get the best value for your buck and extend the life of your budget. Here's how it's done.

Make a Checklist

Decide what you need and how much you want to spend *before* you enter a store. If you have a checklist, it won't be so easy to fall into the trap of impulse buying, which leads to purchasing what you don't need and spending more than you planned.

Shop Around

Do some research before you make a purchase. Don't be in a hurry. Try to compare the cost of the same item in at least two stores (the more the better). Many times stores will sell you an item at a competitor's lower price if you bring in an advertisement showing that the same item is being sold for less.

Best Free Sources of Consumer Help

Many nonprofit consumer agencies and resource groups can help you find the best value for the product, service or investment you're considering.

- Call the **People's Medical Society** (610-770-1670) for guidance in getting the best medical care for the best price.

- Call the **National Committee for Quality Assurance** (202-955-3500) for information on managed-care organizations, so that the health insurance you purchase is an educated investment.

- Call the **Certified Financial Planner Board of Standards** (888-237-6275) for free brochures, information materials and services that will help you choose a reputable certified financial planner and make wise investment purchases.

Buy Quality

Buy the best the first time and you'll save yourself the expense of repeat purchases. *Example:* If you have to replace a TV every year or two, you can wind up spending twice what you would have for a quality set that would have lasted much longer. The same is true of clothing—if your shirt falls apart after the second washing, you'll have to buy a new one. If you'd bought one of better quality it may well have lasted for years. *Good idea:* To learn more about determining quality, consult a consumer service such as Consumer Reports (www.consumerreports.org) or the many free government information sources such as the Consumer Information Center (888-878-3256).

Shop Sales

Most sales occur at the end of a season. *Example:* beach chairs and towels are the least expensive after Labor Day, and fur coats cost less in the spring and summer.

Free Advice for Better Buying

Organizations—federal, state and private—supply consumers with advice, information materials and guidance on staying healthy and spending wisely. Here are some government and nongovernment agencies you can contact:

Federal Trade Commission (FTC) (877-FTCHELP; www.ftc.gov) provides free consumer education publications. For free consumer brochures on scams (how they work and tips for recognizing and avoiding them), call the FTC's Public Reference Branch (202-326-2222).

US Department of Education (800-872-5327; www.ed.gov) offers free guidance and information on college financial aid.

USDA Forest Service (202-205-1706; www.fs.fed.us/recreation) supplies free information on forest activities nationwide.

Food and Drug Administration (888-463-6332; www.fda.gov) provides free information on food and drug benefits and hazards.

National Fraud Information Center (800-876-7060; www.fraud.org) operates a consumer hot line to provide service and assistance with filing complaints against fraudulent businesses.

Council of Better Business Bureaus (703-276-0100; www.bbb.org) gives consumers free information on how to spend their money wisely and safeguard against scams—as well as provides reliability reports on businesses.

Department of Health and Human Services (877-696-6775; www. hhs.gov) gives free information on health, medicine and health products.

Privacy Rights Clearinghouse (619-298-3396; www.privacyrights. org) supplies information on how to control and secure your personal information, such as your Social Security number and medical records.

State Consumer Affairs Offices

When you've tried everything you can think of to settle a dispute with a company, and your complaints and protests of unfair treatment are still being ignored, it's time to take advantage of the consumer affairs department in your state.

The consumer protection division will file a complaint against the business and attempt to remedy the situation through mediation. If enough complaints are filed against the business, the matter goes to the attorney general and further action is taken.

Alabama
Office of the Attorney General
Consumer Affairs Division
Montgomery, 205-242-7334
(800-392-5658 in Alabama)

Alaska
Better Business Bureau
Anchorage, 907-562-0704

Arizona
Office of the Attorney General
Consumer Protection Division
Phoenix, 602-542-5763
(800-352-8431 in Arizona)

Arkansas
Office of the Attorney General
Consumer Protection Division
Little Rock, 501-682-2341
(800-482-8982 in Arkansas)

California
California Department of
Consumer Affairs
Sacramento, 916-445-1254
(800-344-9940 in California)

Colorado
Office of the Attorney General
Consumer Protection Unit
Denver, 303-866-5189

Connecticut
Department of Consumer Protection
Hartford, 860-713-6050
(800-842-2649 in Connecticut)

Delaware
Division of Consumer Affairs
Department of Community Affairs
Wilmington, 302-577-3250

District of Columbia
Department of Consumer and
Regulatory Affairs
Washington, 202-442-4400

Florida
Department of Agriculture and
Consumer Services
Division of Consumer Services
Tallahassee, 850-488-2221
(800-435-7352 in Florida)

Georgia
Governor's Office of Consumer Affairs
Atlanta, 404-651-8600 or 404-656-3790
(800-869-1123 in Georgia)

Hawaii
Department of Commerce and
Consumer Affairs
Office of Consumer Protection
Honolulu, 808-586-2636

Idaho
Office of the Attorney General
Consumer Protection Unit
Boise, 208-334-2424
(800-432-3545 in Idaho)

Illinois
Office of the Attorney General
Consumer Protection Division
Chicago, 312-814-3000

Indiana
Office of the Attorney General
Consumer Protection Division
Indianapolis, 317-232-6330
(800-382-5516 in Indiana)

Iowa
Office of the Attorney General
Consumer Protection Division
Des Moines, 515-281-5926

Kansas
Office of the Attorney General
Consumer Protection Division
Topeka, 785-296-3751
(800-432-2310 in Kansas)

Kentucky
Office of the Attorney General
Consumer Protection Division
Frankfort, 502-696-5389
(800-432-9257 in Kentucky)

Louisiana
Office of the Attorney General
Consumer Protection Section
Baton Rouge, 225-342-9638

Maine
Office of the Attorney General
Consumer and Antitrust Division
Augusta, 207-626-8849

Maryland
Office of the Attorney General
Consumer Protection Division
Baltimore, 410-528-8662

Massachusetts
Department of the Attorney General
Consumer Protection Division
Boston, 617-727-8400

Michigan
Office of the Attorney General
Consumer Protection Division
Lansing, 517-373-1140

Minnesota
Office of the Attorney General
Consumer Services Division
St. Paul, 651-296-3353

Missouri
Office of the Attorney General
Division of Consumer Protection
Jefferson City, 573-751-3321
(800-392-8222 in Missouri)

Montana
Consumer Affairs Unit
Department of Commerce
Helena, 406-444-3494

Nebraska
Consumer Protection Division
Department of Justice
Lincoln, 402-471-2682

Nevada
Commissioner of Consumer Affairs
Department of Commerce
Las Vegas, 800-326-5202
(800-992-0900 in Nevada)

New Hampshire
Office of the Attorney General
Consumer Protection and Antitrust Bureau
Concord, 603-271-3641

New Jersey
Division of Consumer Affairs
Newark, 973-504-6200

New Mexico
Office of the Attorney General
Consumer Protection Division
Santa Fe, 505-827-6060
(800-678-1508 in New Mexico)

New York
Office of the Attorney General
Bureau of Consumer Frauds and Protection
Albany, 518-474-5481

North Carolina
Office of the Attorney General
Consumer Protection Section
Raleigh, 919-733-7741

North Dakota
Office of the Attorney General
Consumer Fraud Section
Bismarck, 701-224-3404
(800-472-2600 in North Dakota)

Ohio
Office of the Attorney General
Consumer Frauds and Crime Section
Columbus, 614-466-8831
(800-282-0515 in Ohio)

Oklahoma
Office of the Attorney General
Consumer Protection Division
Oklahoma City, 405-521-4274

Oregon
Financial Fraud Section
Department of Justice
Salem, 503-378-4732

Pennsylvania
Office of the Attorney General
Bureau of Consumer Protection
Harrisburg, 717-787-9707
(800-441-2555 in Pennsylvania)

Puerto Rico
Department of Consumer Affairs (DACO)
Santurce, 809-721-0940

Rhode Island
Office of the Attorney General
Consumer Protection Division
Providence, 401-274-4400
(800-852-7776 in Rhode Island)

South Carolina
Department of Consumer Affairs
Consumer Fraud and Antitrust Section
Columbia, 803-734-4200

South Dakota
Office of the Attorney General
Division of Consumer Affairs
Pierre, 605-773-4400

Tennessee
Office of the Attorney General
Division of Consumer Affairs
Nashville, 615-741-4737

Texas
Office of the Attorney General
Consumer Protection Division
Austin, 512-463-2070

Utah
Division of Consumer Protection
Department of Commerce
Salt Lake City, 801-530-6001

Vermont
Office of the Attorney General
Public Protection Division
Montpelier, 802-828-3171

Virginia
Office of the Attorney General
Antitrust and Consumer Litigation Section
Richmond, 804-786-2116

Washington
Office of the Attorney General
Consumer Protection Division
Olympia, 206-753-6210

West Virginia
Office of the Attorney General
Consumer Protection Division
Charleston, 304-558-8986
(800-368-8808 in West Virginia)

Wisconsin
Division of Trade and Consumer Protection
Department of Agriculture
Madison, 608-266-9836
(800-422-7128 in Wisconsin)

Wyoming
Office of the Attorney General
Cheyenne, 307-777-7874

Pocket Protection: Easy Ways to Safeguard Your Wallet

Two of the best ways to safeguard your wallet are asking questions before you make final decisions about a purchase or investment and registering a complaint if you have any problems with a purchase or service you have received.

Inquire About Future Sales

Before you make a significant purchase at full price, ask if the item is going on sale anytime soon. If so, find out when, and consider waiting until then to make your purchase. Ask if the salesperson thinks the item will still be available by sale time. If you are unsure about the salesperson's response, ask his/her boss.

When you enter a store, it's always a good idea to question managers or salespeople about where to find sale items. Many stores have permanent areas devoted to sale merchandise, but if you don't ask where these areas are, you may lose out.

Keep in mind that all types of stores have seasonal sales. If a store can't tell you when the next sale is, think about when the season ends and consider waiting to do your shopping then.

Take Advantage of Customer Service

If you have any problems with or questions about a purchase or services you've received, call customer service. That's what it's for.

You can ease your dissatisfaction by asking customer service to help you receive a refund, locate a product you can't find or solve a service problem with a store. If you've been wronged by a store or salesperson, customer service should help you get what you paid for.

Many chain stores have toll-free customer-service numbers. You can find a store's number by calling toll-free information (800-555-1212) or by calling a local store and requesting the number.

If you can't find a customer-service number, or the store is not helpful, consider asking the company's corporate office to help you or guide you to assistance.

Request a Refund If you aren't satisfied with a product or service and feel you deserve a refund, it's important to make a formal complaint. Customer satisfaction is a top priority to most reputable companies.

Many times, contacting a store's customer service department or corporate office will get you a refund plus a discount coupon on future purchases or services, a free gift or a brand-new replacement product or free repeat service.

What to Ask Before You Buy

- What's the store's return policy: Full refund, credit, how many days, do you need the receipt and original packaging?
- What happens if you are not satisfied with the service you receive? Do you get a repeat service free of charge or do you get nothing?
- Is there a warranty or insurance included? Does it have an extra fee attached?
- Does the store have a repair policy? Are there any contracts to sign? (Make sure you read the small print.)
- Did the salesperson seem knowledgeable about your questions?
- Are you comfortable with the price and quality of the item?
- Is this service something you can do for yourself or is it really essential to hire some help?

Best Way To Deal with Unwanted E-Mail

E-mailed newsletters, press releases and bulletins typically contain directions for how to stop them from being sent.

For E-mails that don't contain a way out, SpamCop (www.spamcop.net) will report unwanted E-mail (spam) to the right sources for free in an effort to get the sender kicked off its Internet service provider.

SpamCop also offers two other services—one that enables you to filter out spam and one to help you resolve problems if you were unfairly reported for sending spam.

Nancy Dunnan, a financial adviser and author based in New York. Her recent book is How to Invest $50–$5,000 *(HarperBusiness).*

Words that almost always work when dealing with unsatisfactory answers from customer service: "Please call your supervisor." Usually, supervisory personnel have authority to overrule decisions based on general policies in exceptional situations. If this still doesn't work, try going directly to the chief executive officer of the firm.

If you want to make sure that you get your money's worth, it's important to voice your dissatisfaction when it occurs, and keep a record of your complaints.

Cash-Back Complaining Strategies

Often, the best way to complain is to write a letter. Here are some tips on the best ways to write a complaint letter that will get results:

- Find out to whom you should be writing. Start with the store manager, and consider sending a duplicate to the owner. If you're dealing with a larger company, send letters to the director of consumer affairs or the chief executive officer.
- Describe your problem calmly and carefully. Be polite but firm, and don't include obscene language or wild accusations.
- Get the correct names of everyone involved. Give times, dates and locations of any conversations, and include serial or model numbers of products.
- Include copies of any receipts, invoices and warranties involved, including those for any repairs you had to pay for on your own. Keep the originals for your files.
- Mention anything you tried to do to remedy the situation yourself.
- Send the letter return receipt requested so that you have proof that it was received and the name of the person who signed for it.
- Keep copies of any letters you send. Also get the full name of anyone you speak with on the phone or in person, and jot down the dates, times and details of your conversations.
- If you fail to get a satisfactory response, contact your local Better Business Bureau, state attorney general's office or department of consumer protection. Send one of these agencies a brief explanation of the problem and your attempts to resolve it, plus copies of any letters you sent to the company. Send a duplicate of this explanation to the offending company and you may receive results before the public agency even gets a chance to respond. Most companies would rather settle without government intervention.

- Comment on how you would like the problem to be corrected. If you were a victim of fraud, you may be interested in regaining the money you lost. If you bought a defective product and can't get the company to repair or replace it, you may want your money back, or may be satisfied with a store credit.

Remember, if you complain when you've been a victim of fraud or negligence, you may help prevent someone else from being victimized.

Instantly Stop Telephone And Mail Solicitations

If you've ever ordered from a catalog, donated to a charity, used a credit card or subscribed to a magazine, your name has been put on a variety of mailing and phone lists. These lists are sold to direct marketers who hope to sell you their products. If you're tired of junk mail and telephone solicitations, you can do something about it. Here's how:

No More Calls During Dinner To be placed on a do-not-call list for telephone solicitors, send your name, home address and home telephone number (including area code) to the Telephone Preference Service, Direct Marketing Association, Box 9014, Farmingdale, NY 11735-9014. Telephone solicitations should decrease about two months after your name has been entered into the file. *Warning:* The Direct Marketing Association does not guarantee that calls will stop completely.

No More Junk Mail If you want to decrease the amount of commercial and nonprofit mail you receive, send your name and address and a request to be placed on the removal file to the Mail Preference Service, Direct Marketing Association, Box 9008, Farmingdale, NY 11735-9008. You should see a decrease in the amount of unsolicited mail you receive within three months after your name is entered into the file.

The Direct Marketing Association takes only postal requests, so you can't call in your request. If you move, remember to send in new instructions.

How to Avoid Phone Scams

❑ Don't ever give your credit card number or checking account number for any reason other than making a purchase.

❑ Know the company you're dealing with. If you have questions or doubts about a company, check with your state or local consumer protection office, or the Better Business Bureau where the company is located before you make a purchase.

❑ Keep a record of your transactions, including the name, address and telephone number of the company, and the purchase cost and date.

❑ Always ask if there are additional fees for shipping, handling, sales tax or insurance.

❑ Ask about refund and exchange policies.

❑ Know the total cost of the merchandise before you buy.

❑ Don't be pressured to act on impulse. Take time to understand an offer and talk it over with someone you trust. Reliable offers don't expire at "midnight tonight."

Stop! When You Hear These Words

When you hear words like these, chances are the person on the other end of the line is trying to scam you:

- You must act now or the offer won't be good.
- You've won a free gift or prize—but you must pay a small fee.
- You must send money, give your credit card or bank account number or have a check picked up by a courier immediately.
- You don't need to check out our company with anyone like the Better Business Bureau—we're legitimate.
- You don't need any written information or referrals about our company.
- You can't afford to miss out on this offer.

If you want information about spotting or stopping fraud, or you want to report a scam, contact the **National Fraud Information Center** (800-876-7060, www.fraud.org).

What to Do When Toll-Free Isn't *Free*

Many companies that provide entertainment or information services charge you for calls to 800-, 888- and other toll-free numbers. They're supposed to follow the Federal Trade Commission's (FTC's) 900-number rule, which requires companies to inform consumers of their service charge and method of billing before they provide the service (called a pre-subscription arrangement). But sometimes this law is broken.

Here's what the FTC suggests you do to minimize the risk of unauthorized charges on your next telephone bill:

- Remember that dialing a number that begins with 888 is just like dialing an 800-number. Companies are prohibited from charging you for calls to these numbers unless they set up a valid pre-subscription agreement with you first.
- Recognize that not all numbers beginning with 8 are toll-free. For example, the area code 809 serves the Dominican Republic. If you dial this area code, you'll be charged international long distance rates.
- Make sure any 800- or 888-number you call for entertainment or information that costs money provides security devices—including PINs—before you enter into a pre-subscription agreement.
- Check your phone bill for 800, 888 or unfamiliar charges. Calls to 800- and 888-numbers should be identified. Some may be mislabeled as "long distance" or "calling card" calls and are easy to overlook.
- Dispute charges on your phone bill for an 800- or 888-number if you don't have a presubscription arrangement. Follow the instructions on your billing statement.
- Know that if the telephone company removes a charge for an 800- or 888-number call, the entertainment or information service provider may try to pursue you through a collection agency. If this happens, you may have additional rights under the Fair Debt Collection Practices Act.

How to Avoid the Latest Scams

Scams pop up at any time by phone, mail or on the Internet. Be suspicious of all out-of-the-ordinary offers—for anything. Here are the best ways to fend off scam artists.

Telephone Scams

More than half of the $40 billion each year that telemarketing fraud rakes in comes from senior citizens, according to AARP. *Common telephone scams:*

Free Prize Offers If you're asked to do something, buy something or give your credit card number in order to get your prize, it's a scam.

Bogus Charities Phony charities have clever names that make them seem legitimate. The problem is that they take all the money you send. Nothing will go to charity.

 To check on the legitimacy of a charity: Go to the IRS Web site at www.irs.gov…or contact the Better Business Bureau Wise Giving Alliance at www.bbb.org or 703-276-0100.

Cheap Travel Packages A low-cost vacation offered over the telephone may end up costing more than a legitimate travel package. *Worse:* The tickets may never materialize.

Useless Health Products You'll end up paying hundreds of dollars for products worth little. What's more, you probably don't need them.

Get-Rich-Quick Schemes They promise little risk but high returns and include deals involving rare coins, precious metals, art, gemstones and other such "investment opportunities." In most cases, they're worthless.

Recovery Scams The victim of a scam is told he/she can get his money back, for a fee. He gets nothing for his fee. In most cases, even government agencies and the police can't help scam victims.

Mail Scams

Sending money in response to an unusual mail solicitation is a good way to lose money…

Foreign Lottery Tickets and Bonds You'll never get them. It's illegal to sell foreign lottery tickets and bonds by mail in the US.

Inheritances A "locator" offers to help you claim an inheritance— for a fee. *Reality:* Fees charged by legitimate law firms to track down beneficiaries are paid by the estate—not the beneficiary.

Nigerian Letter Scam This letter typically says that a Nigerian official needs to place millions of dollars in the US…and, if you let him use your bank account, you'll get to keep 25% of the money. But there's a catch. The official needs money up front to cover taxes and expenses before the funds can be wired. *Reality:* There is no money. If you send the up-front fee, you'll never see it again.

 If you get such a letter, fax it to the Secret Service Financial Crimes Division at 202-406-5031.

Lowdown on Internet Scams

Today's most popular Internet scams— and how to avoid them—are explained at the new **Dot Cons** Web site of the **Federal Trade Commission (FTC)**.

 Covered: Scams involving Internet auctions, investments, credit card fraud, health-care products and services, travel offers and more. You can also file a complaint with the FTC through their Web site. Visit www.ftc.gov/dotcons.

 Self-defense: Learn if any complaints have been lodged against the vendor's Web site by visiting www.fraudbureau.com…learn more about safe on-line shopping by visiting www.safeshopping.org, an educational resource of the American Bar Association.

 Eileen Harrington, assistant director of marketing practices, Federal Trade Commission, Washington, DC.

Spot Travel Scams

Bargain travel packages may be more than you bargained for. The most common travel fraud is a mail or telephone offer—you're presented with an unbelievably good travel opportunity that changes in price as soon as you give your credit card number.

Usually, telephone scam artists offer you a deal that they couldn't possibly deliver. They will ask for your immediate decision, and tell you if you don't act now you'll lose out. Also, they'll skirt any questions or concerns you present to them. And you won't know you've been scammed until you receive the confirmation of your deal. The confirmation rarely bears any resemblance to the offer you thought you accepted. Once you see the deal in writing, you'll notice lots of hidden fees, terms and costs that were not disclosed over the phone.

Bogus Promissory Notes Investors are offered a guaranteed fixed rate of return on money they lend to a company. They can't lose, they're told, because they'll get a promissory note signed by the company. They advance the funds, but their interest checks never show up. The promissory note is bogus. The investors have no hope of ever getting their money back.

Internet Scams

On-Line Auctions Shady auctions are the number-one Internet scam. You send off your money and never receive the goods.

Even if you know the Web site is legitimate, you can't be sure of the person you're dealing with through the site.

Self-defense: Use an on-line escrow company such as www.escrow.com to hold your money until you receive the goods.

Investments You're promised quick profits based on inside information. The promoter uses words like "guarantee," "high return" and "risk free." Usually the scammer isn't registered with the SEC …or your money is sent abroad.

Self-defense: Avoid investments that sound too good to be true.

To Protect Yourself

- Ask for written information about any company trying to sell you something. Get references.
- Check out unfamiliar companies with the Better Business Bureau, the state attorney general, the National Fraud Information Center (see below) or your local consumer protection agency.
- Take your time before making a decision. A legitimate company won't pressure you.
- Discuss any investment offers with your financial adviser or attorney.
- Don't respond if you cannot understand the offer. Ask questions until you have all the details.
- Never give out your credit card or bank account number—or send cash, a cashier's check or money order—to an unfamiliar company or charity.
- Even if you do telephone business with a legitimate company, don't give information to the person who called you. Instead, call the company back.

Helpful Resources

For information about consumer fraud or to file a complaint, contact the Federal Trade Commission (FTC) at 877-382-4357, www.ftc.gov or www.consumer.gov/sentinel.

John Featherman, president of Featherman.com, a Philadelphia-based consumer privacy protection firm.

Charitable Scams

If you donate money to charities, it's important to be sure that your money is actually going to benefit the people and organizations you want to help. Unfortunately, there are fraudulent solicitors for charitable contributions that you need to be aware of. The best way to ensure that you are supporting an actual charity is to follow these guidelines recommended by the Federal Trade Commission:

- Before you give to a charity, ask for written information, including the charity's name, address and telephone number. Legitimate charities will be able to send you information on their goals and how they use donations, as well as proof that your donation is tax deductible.
- Call the charity to make sure that the solicitation was authorized, and that the solicitor you spoke with wasn't a fraud.
- Watch out for charities that have similar-sounding names to ones that are highly respected and legitimate. This may be a sign that the solicitation is a fraud.
- Look out for professional fund-raisers. Some charities find it more efficient to pay professional fund-raisers (rather than use staff or volunteers) to handle large-scale mailings, telephone drives and other solicitations. Professional fund-raisers, however, keep a portion of the money they collect. If you're solicited for a donation, ask if the caller is a paid fund-raiser and what percentage of your donation the fund-raiser will keep. If you're not comfortable with the amount, you may want to consider other options for donating (such as contacting the charity directly).
- Make sure the money you're donating goes toward activities which makes it legally tax deductible. Donations to a division that runs politically-motivated advertisements might not be deductible, while donations to other divisions of the same charity are.
- Be wary of organizations that use meaningless terms, such as "tax-exempt charity."
- Don't rely on an invoice that tells you to "Keep this receipt for your records." It doesn't mean your donation is tax deductible.
- Be on alert for calls and invoices thanking you for a pledge that you don't remember making. Keep records of your donations so that you're not falsely convinced that you've donated to a charity when you haven't.
- Specify how you want the money you donate to be used.

If you are unsure of the legitimacy of a charity, call one of the following organizations for help:

- **BBB Wise Giving Alliance,** Council of Better Business Bureaus (703-276-0100, www.give.org)
- **The American Institute of Philanthropy** (773-305-0414, www.charity watch.org)

Look Out for Counterfeit Goods

Counterfeit goods almost always have a price that's too good to be true. If you're looking for the real thing, such as a Rolex watch or Gucci handbag, know whether what you're buying is worth the money you're spending.

Counterfeit goods are sold by street vendors or small, questionable-looking stores. Quality products are sold by established merchants at fixed locations. A product without a manufacturer's label, wrapped in flimsy packaging and lacking a warranty is most often a fake.

Unfortunately, once you buy a counterfeit product, there's not much you can do. A manufacturer of the genuine article won't be able to help you. The only way to get your money back is to find and confront the original seller, which is usually next to impossible.

Be Wary of Prizes

The most important thing to know about prize scams is that if you have to give any money to receive your prize, it's not a prize. If you receive a letter or phone call telling you that you've won a prize, be skeptical. Here are some ways to make sure that a prize is really a prize:

- Don't be lured by official or urgent-looking letters.

- Always read the letter carefully, especially the small print. Look for fees or special requirements involved in receiving the prize.

- Find out the odds of winning the prize before you enter a contest. Winning a prize usually has very slim odds.

- Be cautious of 800-numbers that direct you to call a 900-number. Charges for 900 telephone calls are usually very expensive.

- Never give your credit card or bank account number to a company you're unfamiliar with.

- Check out the agency awarding the prize with the Better Business Bureau or your local consumer protection office.

- Read all contracts or agreements very closely before you sign anything, because once you sign your name, you're obligated.

Mail Theft Self-Defense

Postal theft is on the increase nationwide—and much more is at stake than just your mail. According to inspector Molly McMinn, criminal investigative arm, US Postal Inspection Service, Washington, DC...

- Criminals who have obtained your Social Security number or other personal information can establish and use credit in your name.
- Crooks who find out your checking account number can print phony checks.
- An intercepted check can be *washed*, leaving the signature but making it payable to a different person for a greater amount.

How to Protect Yourself

- Do not use an unsecured mailbox, such as an out-box at a hotel.
- Incoming mail should go into a front-door slot or a locked mailbox.
- Hand outgoing mail to a letter carrier...use collection boxes... or bring it to the post office.
- Know when you should be receiving bank/brokerage statements, blank checks and other valuable mail. Contact the sender if your mail is delayed.
- Check your credit rating at least once a year by calling one of the big three credit bureaus—Equifax (800-997-2493, www. equifax.com)...Experian (888-397-3742, www.experian.com)... Trans Union (800-916-8800, www.transunion.com).
- Don't write your Social Security number or other personal information, such as your driver's license number or account number, on checks.
- Protect yourself from *dumpster divers* by shredding all pre-approved credit card and loan offers, discarded bills, etc.
- When it is an option, consider paying bills electronically—through your financial institution...US Postal Service, www.usps.com...the on-line giant Quicken, www.quicken.com...or another service.

How to Protect Your Identity...Your Assets... And Your Life

Keeping personal information private helps protect you from frivolous lawsuits...identity theft...and unwanted sales calls. It could even derail a stalker or someone else looking to do you physical harm.

How far you should go to protect your privacy is a personal decision. But I believe these steps make sense for just about everyone:

Birth Date

While most people are careful with their Social Security numbers, many of us give out birth dates without a second thought. If someone wants to track you down—a private investigator, a con man, an ex-lover—you have just made it much easier for him/her.

Most people are listed in thousands of databases compiled from medical records, divisions of motor vehicles, credit agencies, employment records, court records, Internet companies, etc. Not all of these records are secure.

If it is just your name in a database, it doesn't mean much—there are probably many people who share your name. But combine that name with a date of birth, and the pool shrinks by more than 99%—enough for any competent private investigator to find you.

Safer: Don't provide your date of birth. When you cannot avoid it, consider making some minor alteration to the date that can be called an innocent error if it is picked up later.

Example: Suppose your birth date is December 4, written 12/4. In most countries other than the US and Canada, this is written as 4 December—or 4/12.

Obviously, if your date of birth is after the 12th, this won't work. Then you might "mistakenly" enter the month and date of a family member. But be honest on government forms, loan applications or anywhere else that it is likely to be checked.

The personal information that is already in databases is there for good. The only "solution" is to move…get a new phone number…and never again allow your true name to be coupled with your true address, thus leaving only the old information in the databases.

Providing ID

When someone insists that I show identification, I show my passport. Unlike a driver's license, it does not provide my home address.

This strategy is particularly useful for women who might be asked for identification at a bar—and then get an unwelcome visitor later. *Exception:* When the police ask for a driver's license, that is what you must provide.

Telephone

Anyone who wants privacy should get an unlisted phone number and *caller-ID blocking.* Then people you call can't find out your number, even if they have caller ID. Fees for this service vary by provider—usually a few dollars per month. *Note:* Caller-ID blocking does not work when you call toll-free or 900 numbers…or when you call many US government offices. Calls to 911 will show your street address and phone number.

Protect Your Personal Data on The Internet

Web site "clones" can entrap the unwary. They look legitimate, but are used by hackers to steal personal data.

Example: One criminal cloned the site of an Internet Service Provider (ISP) and sent out E-mails asking customers to visit their ISP to confirm credit card data. Each E-mail contained a link to the phony site, where the hacker stole credit card numbers.

Self-defense: Check a domain name using the WhoIs program, www.nsi.com. Type in the site's Web address to see who operates it. If details do not match those of the legitimate site you wanted to visit, stay away.

Jonathan Rusch, head of Internet Fraud Initiative, US Department of Justice, Washington, DC, quoted in *Forbes*, 60 Fifth Ave., New York 10011.

Magazine Subscription Scams

Magazine subscriptions are frequently sold by phone. Unfortunately, there are fraudulent telemarketers who will sell you a subscription that's much more expensive than the regular rate.

- Never accept a subscription to a magazine without fully understanding the total cost. If a seller won't divulge this information, hang up the phone. Also, be careful of sales pitches that tell you the subscription amount only in dollars per week. Some deals sound great until you add up the yearly cost. You can wind up paying more than twice the regular subscription rate.

- Make sure that you have cancellation rights before you accept a deal. Some states mandate that you are legally required to pay for a subscription once you verbally accept the deal.

- To safeguard yourself from scams, ask for a written copy of the contract before you agree to make a deal. Read the contract very carefully and figure out the cost of the entire package.

- And finally, be very careful who you give your credit card or bank account number to, because it may be used to debit your account without your permission.

If you are serious about not being tracked down, an unlisted phone number is not enough. Instead, get an unlisted number under a *different* name. Then no one will be able to trace that number to you.

Use a prepaid phone card at a pay phone for calls that require extra security.

Prepaid *cell phones* also are now available. While any cell-phone call can be intercepted, prepaid cell-phone calls can't be tracked to you...and no one can run up a huge bill on your account.

US Mail

More than 100,000 residential mailboxes are burglarized every day. Unsecured mailboxes make a tremendous amount of personal information available to anyone who cares to know it. In addition to your name and address, your mail could provide someone with:

- Signed checks that can be easily altered. A $20 check could become $2,000.
- Account numbers from bank, credit card and investment statements.
- Preapproved credit card solicitations.
- Social Security and other personal information from government forms.
- A profile of your interests and shopping habits.

To keep your mail private...

Outgoing Mail Use *indoor* mailboxes located at the post office or other public areas.

Incoming Mail Consider using a commercial mail-receiving agency, such as Mail Boxes Etc. (800-789-4623, www.mbe.com) or Post-Net (800-841-7171, www.postnet.net).

Post-office boxes are another solution, although they can't be used for deliveries by private shipping companies.

These are imperfect solutions because all these services require identification to open a mailbox. Many people have arranged to receive mail through their real estate agents, accountants, lawyers or other advisers.

E-Mail

E-mail sent via your work computer is not protected by personal privacy laws—so your employer can "spy" on you.

To keep your E-mail private: Consider sending messages via an "anonymizer" Web site, such as www.lokmail.com. This free service encrypts messages to assure that only the intended recipients can read them. The encryption will work only if the sender and the receiver both use LokMail addresses.

Banks

If someone is considering a lawsuit against you, the first thing that he/she will do is ask a lawyer if he has a case. The first thing the lawyer will do is call a private investigator to find out if you have the money to make it worth his while.

A private investigator will subpoena the records of all the banks in your town—and perhaps the surrounding towns—looking for accounts. Most banks insist they would not provide such records, but a good investigator can get the information.

Self-defense: Move all but a small amount of cash to a bank *outside* your immediate region—at least in another state—or a national investment company, such as Fidelity (800-343-3548) or Merrill Lynch (800-637-7455). A lawyer will then be less likely to find your assets.

Bonus: US Treasury money market accounts at investment firms offer better returns than bank accounts, with low risk and similar services—including checking.

Garbage/Recycling

It is perfectly legal for anyone to snoop through your garbage or recycling stack once you put it at the curb. A paper shredder is an inexpensive way to deter invasion of your privacy for any personal or financial documents.

A standard shredder ($30 to $40) is enough for most people. If you have serious privacy concerns, a cross-cut shredder (about $100) leaves documents so diced that they can never be put back together.

J.J. "Jack" Luna, an international consultant to individuals interested in protecting their identities. www.howtobeinvisible.com. He is author of *How to Be Invisible: A Step-by-Step Guide to Protecting Your Assets, Your Identity, and Your Life* (St. Martin's).

Florist Scam

If you love to send flowers, you should be aware that there are unscrupulous telemarketing firms that pose as local florists, charge you high fees for your order, and take business away from the legitimate florists in your town.

How It Works

The telemarketer takes out a fake listing in the white pages of your telephone book using a local town name to make consumers believe it's a neighborhood store. When you call the number, you're unknowingly forwarded to an out-of-town telemarketing operation. Your order and credit card information are taken, and the information is forwarded to an area florist. The telemarketer pockets a processing fee and usually a percentage of the sale. But the real scam occurs when you receive your credit card bill with higher than expected charges from an out-of-town company. You may also learn that the flowers weren't delivered as ordered or were never delivered at all.

Better Safe than Sorry

To safeguard yourself from florist scams, ask neighbors, family, friends and coworkers for florist recommendations. Deal only with shops that list a street address with their phone number. If you get a number from directory assistance, ask for the street address, too.

And finally, ask for an itemized bill from the florist. You may be charged an unusually high delivery fee or too much tax for an order.

2

Don't Shop Retail:
Money-Saving Alternatives

Thrift Store Secrets

Thrift stores sell used clothing, housewares and other items at extremely low prices. They are usually run by not-for-profit organizations such as The Salvation Army, Goodwill or local charities and hospitals, and can charge low prices because they get their merchandise for free. Usually it is donated by people who no longer want the items. Any profits go to the organization that operates the shop.

Two Styles of Pricing

There are usually two types of pricing used in thrift stores. One is individual pricing of each item, and the other is straight pricing. An example of straight pricing is when all jackets cost $3. Thrift store prices usually change frequently, so if something looks too expensive one week, go back the next week. Chances are it will cost less.

Most thrift shops are located in the less fashionable parts of town or in suburban strip malls.

Thrifting Like an Expert

Don't mix thrift shopping with regular shopping. Regular stores will look over-priced, and thrift stores may look dirty and faded. Thrift shopping should be an event in and of itself.

A good day's thrift shopping could center around five or six stores. Saturday is an ideal day to shop because most of the merchandise that has come in during the week is on the floor. Note that many shops are closed on Sunday.

When you enter a thrift store, begin by scanning the racks. Walk up each aisle and look for colors or styles that interest you. Don't be afraid to run your hands along the clothing. If the clothing feels good to your fingers, it will probably be a comfortable item to wear. If you find something you like, check for obvious defects. If you see any, decide if they are things you could fix for very little cost. If you don't sew, keep looking. Most thrift shops have lots of clothes to choose from.

Many thrift stores lack dressing rooms, so be careful about buying items you can't try on. There is a no-return policy at most thrift stores, so if an item doesn't seem like it will fit, don't buy it.

Thrift Tips

- Don't buy things you don't like just because they are cheap. A bargain is only a bargain if you'll use it.
- Bring friends who look more than they buy. They may help you restrain yourself and give you an objective opinion.
- If you know seasoned shoppers, ask if you can tag along with them. They will have researched the best places for bargains and can teach you the tricks of the trade.
- Look for Thrift Shop, Consignment Store, Resale Store and Flea Market listings in your *Yellow Pages* under their respective titles. Consignment Stores are sometimes listed under Thrift Stores and vice versa.
- When you travel, look for thrift shops in the area you're visiting. The Salvation Army, Goodwill, churches and not-for-profit organizations have stores in many towns and cities.
- When you're considering an item, it is best to carry it around with you. If you don't hold on to it, chances are it won't be there when you've made your decision.

An Eye for Quality

One advantage of buying used clothing is that if an item has been worn, yanked, washed and dried several times and it still looks good, it will probably keep looking good for a long time to come. Remember, though, that thrift shop clothes aren't always a perfect fit, since the clothes have already had a life before you. The real question is whether or not it's a fit that you can handle.

And finally, always wash the clothes you buy from a thrift store before wearing them. A lot of stores clean the merchandise before they put it on the floor, but it is safest to wash it again anyway.

Uncovering Consignment and Resale Bargains

When shopping in consignment or resale stores, it is important to keep these guidelines in mind:

- Look for well-organized stores. They tend to have better merchandise.
- Check whether the store launders or cleans the clothes before displaying them. Most stores do, but don't be afraid to ask.
- Pay special attention to cuffs, collars, pockets, armpits and crotches for stains and wear and tear.
- Make sure the garment has all necessary parts, such as zippers and buttons.
- Check for moth holes if the clothes are made of wool.
- Find conveniently located stores so that you can stop by frequently, since new merchandise is always coming in.

When you find a store that carries brands you prefer, ask the owner or manager to call you when new items of interest arrive. That way, you'll get first crack at the things you're interested in.

The Differences Between Consignment and Resale Stores

Consignment and resale stores sell expensive clothes at rock-bottom prices. Although the terms resale and consignment are often used interchangeably, there are a few differences between them.

Consignment Selling

Consignment shops accept merchandise from individual owners to be resold. They then pay a percentage of the selling price, often 40% to 60%, to the owner after the item has been sold. Haggling over price is not as easy as it is at a garage sale, because there is more than one party involved in the pricing.

Consignment stores may be a great way of reselling your own unwanted clothing as well as buying what other people want to sell. Ask the shop owner or manager what the buying procedures are. And, be prepared to wait for your items to sell.

You may want to research which stores have a fast turnover. Stopping by as a buying customer a few times may help you identify a store that moves its merchandise quickly. If you don't think the salesperson you talk to seems professional or knowledgeable, ask to speak with someone else. If you are not confident that you can trust the store or that your clothes will sell, continue your search.

If you do decide to use a consignment shop, it is important to keep track of what you give and to whom. Keep your receipts and check in regularly with the stores to see if your things have sold.

Resale Buying and Selling

Resale stores buy items outright from previous owners. Resale stores also specialize in selling clothing from medium-priced department stores or very high-end department stores and boutiques. Most of the clothing you will find is secondhand, but you can also find brand-new merchandise with the original tags still attached.

Many resale stores also carry manufacturer samples and last season's clothing from retail stores. Shopping resale for children's clothing can really be a bargain, since kids tend to outgrow their clothes before they're worn out.

While prices at resale stores are less expensive than at retail stores, don't expect thrift store savings. Since resale stores pay for the clothes they sell, they have to charge enough to make a profit. But this also means they tend to have a more upscale selection.

A Quick Guide to Discount Shopping

Specialty chains, general merchandise stores, off-price stores and outlets are all good places to look for inexpensive apparel. *Remember:* Discount shopping doesn't mean lower quality, just lower costs.

Specialty Chains and General Merchandise Stores

You can save up to 50% or more when you shop at a specialty chain or general merchandise store. These no-frills stores sell brand-name products at discounted prices and have multiple locations at the national, state or city level. You can telephone the national headquarters of a store for a list of local locations. Also, check your local *Yellow Pages* under General Merchandise stores.

Types of Discount Stores Specialty chain stores, such as Burlington Coat Factory and Sally Beauty Supply, typically focus on one type of merchandise. In contrast, general merchandise stores like Wal-Mart and Target carry a whole range of different products including clothing. Both types of stores carry a variety of manufacturers and designers, and new products arrive daily and weekly. It pays to drop in often. If you see something you like, it is wise to buy it because not every item comes in every week. If you find an item at a good price, buy it, too. It may not be there on your next visit.

Return Policies Return policies are usually liberal in these stores, but you should check the policy at each store you visit. There may be limits on the amount of time you have to return or exchange an item, and you'll probably need to have a receipt to get your money back.

Outlets May Be Your Best Bets

Outlets may be the most cost-effective clothing and accessory sources around. Most brand-name, high-fashion designers have at least one outlet store. By shopping in outlets, you can dress in expensive styles but pay discounted prices.

Outlets carry overstock, preseason styles and irregular items at prices 20% to 70% off retail. Often, you can call an outlet to find out if they carry a particular item that you saw in a retail store. You probably won't be able to purchase the item over the phone, but some stores may hold the item for you until you can go in. Many experts advise you to stop buying at designer retail stores until you have explored the outlet option.

Tips for Shopping Outlets When you are shopping for outlet bargains, you need to remember some smart shopper techniques.

High Quality for Low Prices

When you hear that a store is off-price, don't assume that the merchandise it carries is damaged or made from lesser quality materials than what you can buy at a department store or designer boutique.

In fact, the definition of an off-price store is one that sells only brand-name, nationally known labels. The only difference between the items you buy at an off-price store and those at a fancy boutique is the price. So if you're looking to get the best buy without compromising fashion or style, off-price stores may be one of your best options.

At an off-price store, you can find designer, brand-name items marked 40% to 70% below retail prices. Off-price stores buy their merchandise from the same manufacturers as department and designer stores, and negotiate pricing so that they can then sell the garments to consumers at a discount.

Preseason shopping is about the only thing you can't do at an off-price store. As part of their contract with manufacturers, off-price stores, such as **Syms** and **Burlington Coat Factory**, don't receive the new designs until the season begins. Designer-label shoppers know that you can buy fall apparel in traditional retail stores as early as June, sometimes even in May. But if you're willing to wait a few weeks, you can find the same styles for less at an off-price store.

Off-Price Chain Store Listings

- **Bed, Bath and Beyond**
  212-255-3550
  www.bedbathandbeyond.com
- **Burlington Coat Factory**
  800-444-2628
  www.coat.com
- **Clothestime**
  877-825-3266
  www.clothestime.com
- **DSW Shoe Outlet**
  800-477-8595
  www.dswshoe.com
- **Famous Footwear**
  800-403-2668
  www.famousfootwear.com
- **Loehmann's**
  800-366-5634
  www.loehmanns.com
- **Marshalls**
  800-627-7425
  www.marshallsonline.com
- **T.J. Maxx**
  800-926-6299
  www.tjmaxx.com
- **The Men's Warehouse**
  800-776-7848
  www.menswarehouse.com
- **Sally Beauty Supply**
  800-275-7255
  www.sallybeauty.com
- **Syms**
  201-902-9600
  www.syms.com
- **Target**
  800-800-8800
  www.target.com
- **Wal-Mart**
  800-925-6278
  www.walmart.com

- Before you buy, find out the outlet's return policy. Ask if you can return an item, and if you'll receive cash or a credit. Some discount outlets have an all-sales-final policy.
- If you are searching for a particular item, perhaps shoes for a suit, take a fabric swatch with you.
- Look in the back of the outlet store. Many stores have a table or rack with clearance merchandise priced below the everyday discount prices.
- Don't forget to check the size of the clothing carefully. Tags get lost and mismarked all the time, so it's best to try on any item of clothing before you decide to buy.
- If you buy merchandise marked "irregular," make sure that the irregularity is something you can live with.
- Carefully check every item for faults before you pay. If a button is missing or there's a frayed seam, talk to a salesperson or cashier. Sometimes an outlet or discount store will give you a further markdown on the already discounted price.

For Your Comfort On a more personal note, always dress comfortably when you outlet shop. Sturdy, comfortable shoes are advisable, because chances are you'll spend more time than you expect on your feet. Be prepared for a crowd (although during the off-season, outlets may not be any more crowded than retail stores).

Off-Price Chain Stores and Clearance Centers

At off-price chain stores or clearance centers, you can find brand-name merchandise at greatly reduced prices. Many nondiscount stores and retail chains also have their own clearance centers. Check with your favorite department store to see if it has a clearance location. Many do.

Generally, all the unsold products from all of the company's stores go to one location to be sold at a discounted price. The items sold include seconds, slightly damaged goods, returns, floor models, previous season's stock and mismatched goods.

Outlet Centers and Stores Across America

Belz Factory Outlet World (901-260-7348, www.belz.com/factory) has five outlets near major thoroughfares in Florida, Montana, Nevada, Tennessee and Puerto Rico.

Champion Outlets (800-999-2249), located nationwide, has sweats and other athletic clothing.

Charter Oak Partners (888-SHOP-333, www.charteroak.com) has 12 outlet centers in 11 states. Call for their coupon book.

Chelsea GCA Realty (973-228-6111, www.chelseagca.com) has 19 outlet centers in 11 states. Ask about their coupon book.

FAC Realty Trust (800-SHOP-USA, www.factorystores.com) has 36 outlet centers in 21 states. Call for money-saving coupons.

Hosiery Outlets (800-831-7489) has more than 200 factory outlet stores selling L'eggs, Hanes, Bali and Playtex hosiery nationwide.

Prime Outlet (800-980-SHOP, www.primeoutlets.com) has 47 outlets in 27 different states. Call for a free brochure listing outlet centers, store names, maps and area attractions.

Tanger Outlet Centers (800-4-TANGER, www.tangeroutlet.com) has 31 centers in 23 states. Call for a free coupon book.

VF Factory Outlet (800-772-8336, www.vffo.com) sells items at half off the lowest ticketed price on Vanity Fair, Lee, Healthtex and Wrangler products at 53 stores in 25 states.

For Kids Only

OshKosh B'Gosh (800-282-4674, www.oshkoshbgosh.com) has 140 outlet stores that sell top-quality children's clothing at 30% below retail prices.

Carter's Childrenswear has outlet stores in more than 30 states nationwide. Contact Outlet Bound (888-688-5382, www.carters.com) for the Carter's outlet closest to you.

Hanna Andersson (800-222-0544, www.hannaandersson.com), a high-quality children's catalog company, has three outlet stores, in Oregon, New Hampshire and Chicago. You can find clothes at 20% off catalog prices, and get irregular and off-season clothing at big markdowns.

Guide to Outlet Shopping Centers And Factory Stores

Your best bet in finding what outlets are available and where you can find them is to call **Outlet Bound** (800-336-8853). Outlet Bound provides free information, brochures and VIP vouchers for 300 outlet centers and 1,700 factory stores across the country, as well as directions on how to reach them. The vouchers can be redeemed for specific store coupons at each outlet center.

And if that's not enough, Outlet Bound publishes an annual nationwide guide for $14.45 (price includes $4.50 for shipping), which includes a discount coupon you can use at any one of the outlet store locations.

If you're on-line, check out their Web site at www.outletbound.com, where you can search for stores by brand name, location or outlet center name.

Mail-Order Bargains

Shopping by mail usually saves you time and can also save you money if you do some research before you buy. Always compare the mail-order price with the retail price of each item you're considering.

If the price is right, verify shipping and handling costs. They can make buying by mail more expensive than you think, especially if you order just one or two items at a time, or if the company uses an expensive delivery service and doesn't offer a more economical alternative. One strategy is to compare the shipping and handling costs printed in several different catalogs to figure out what's typical.

Also check return policies. You want to be able to get a full refund on any item you send back, including the cost of return

Shop Factory Outlets for Men's Shoes

Are there holes in the soles of your shoes? Almost every major men's shoe brand has an off-price outlet store. Each of them sells first-quality, in-season shoes at almost 40% off, and some sell irregulars at almost 80% off.

Irregulars are slightly damaged shoes that were never sent to the retail stores, or were returned for being imperfect. Damages usually consist of a slight stitching mistake, color error or size irregularity, but most often the imperfections are invisible to an untrained eye. Call to find the nearest location of these outlet stores.

- **Bally** (800-825-5030)
- **Cole-Haan** (800-633-9000)
- **Timberland** (800-445-5545)
- **Florsheim** (800-808-1356)
- **Rockport** (800-762-5767) (factory irregulars only)

shipping. Some, but not all, companies arrange to have their delivery service pick up your returns or provide postage-paid return receipts. Ask before you order.

Most of the information you need will be printed in the catalog, and most mail-order companies have customer service departments and toll-free numbers. Don't hesitate to call and ask questions.

Extra Savings

If you're looking for extra savings, check the pages near the order form, usually in the middle of the catalog. Companies frequently list their clearance items there. If no clearance or sale items are listed, ask the sales representative you order from if there are any discounted items available. But be sure to check sale prices against the regular prices in the catalog so you'll know whether or not you're really getting a good deal.

Many catalog companies publish clearance catalogs as well as their regular catalogs. If you're on their mailing list, you can order the items you want as they go on sale.

Tips for Better Mail-Order Shopping

- Comparison shop. Compare similar items in different catalogs and with items in retail stores to make sure that you get the best price available.
- Read product descriptions carefully. Don't rely on photographs which may falsely represent the items. But remember that sometimes text can be as deceptive as pictures.
- Find out about the company's return policy before you order.
- Keep a photocopy of every order form you mail and date it for easy reference if there is a problem.
- Never send cash with an order.
- Use a credit card if you can. You can delay payment until any problems are resolved.
- If you order by phone, write down what you ordered, the total cost of the order and the reference number (which the phone representative should give you).

Best Mail-Order and On-Line Sources

There is no reason for shoppers today to wait for great sales on selected items at retail stores. You can buy almost anything you need at wholesale prices right now if you know where to go.

The companies below offer products and services starting at 30% below suggested retail prices. Ordering in large quantities can get you as much as 90% off...

Bed and Bath Textiles

Bates Mill Store Sturdy cotton bedspreads and blankets sold direct from this 1850s Maine mill—no middleman to up the prices. *Bargain hunters take note:* Bedspread seconds are marked down here an additional 40%. 800-552-2837…or www.batesbedspreads.com.

J. Schachter Corp. Down-filled luxury comforters and pillows. Buy a high-end comforter—$700 at top New York department stores— for at least 40% less. 800-468-6233.

Cameras/Photo Services

Owl Photo Corp. Photofinishing and video transfer are cheaper than at any other mail-order photo lab. 580-772-3353.

Porter's Camera Store Photographic and darkroom equipment and supplies. The prices on cameras, video equipment and optics are slashed by about 60%. 800-553-2001, www.porters.com.

Children's Clothing

Basic Brilliance 100% cotton everyday wear for infants, children and mothers—all at 30% to 50% off. 360-385-3835, www.basic brilliance.com.

Gohn Bros. Manufacturing Co. Low-cost, high-quality, brand-name children's clothing, underwear and outerwear. 219-825-2400.

Food and Beverages

Gibbsville Cheese Company Wisconsin cheeses, specializing in cheddars, Colbys and Monterey Jacks. Sausages, too. Ships October through April. 920-564-3242, www.gibbsvillecheese.com.

Jaffe Bros. Natural Foods Organic dried fruits—Fuyu persimmons, Black Mission figs, kiwis—and nut butters. 760-749-1133, www. organicfruitsandnuts.com.

Home Appliances

ABC Vacuum Cleaner Warehouse Top brands and models up to 70% off. Free shipping on many items. 800-285-8145, www.abc vacuum.com.

EBA Wholesale Save hundreds of dollars on appliances and pluggables—from TVs and video equipment to refrigerators. Nationwide delivery. 800-380-2378, www.shopeba.com.

Lawn and Garden

Butterbrooke Farm Seed Co-Op Very low prices on vegetable seeds. For a free price list, send a self-addressed, stamped, business-sized envelope to 78 Barry Rd., Oxford, Connecticut 06478.

Take Your Time And Save

A good way to avoid overspending when you catalog shop is to mark the items that you like, and then put the catalog down for a couple of days. If you still like the items and feel they're a good buy when you look at them again, place your order. But if you change your mind, you have avoided buying something you may not really need or want.

The same holds true for store buying. Put an item on hold, and if you still like it when you go back to the store, you know you won't be wasting your money.

Best Free Catalogs

Catalogs can cost you, but they don't have to. Some companies, (such as **Victoria's Secret**), charge you for catalogs if you want to pick one up at the store. Instead, ask for the company's 800 number. Often, you can order the same catalog for free over the phone.

Many freebie web sites, such as the **Smart Shopper Super Site** (www. smartshop1.com), **Catalog Link** (www.cataloglink.com) and **Catalogs Across America** (www.catalogsusa. com) allow you to order free catalogs on-line. Or you can always call toll-free information (800-555-1212) for the customer service number of a manufacturer, and order a catalog directly.

Le Jardin du Gourmet Offers 30-cent sample seed packets of lemon balm…German chamomile…spearmint…and hundreds of culinary herbs. Flat-rate shipping charge of $2. 802-748-1446.

Prentiss Court Ground Covers Save 50% on more than 50 varieties of live ground cover plants…ornamental grasses…and more. 800-577-9778.

Van Dyck's Exhibition-quality Dutch flower bulbs and perennials at 40% below retail prices. 800-248-2852, www.vandycks.com.

Health and Beauty Products

AARP Pharmacy Service You don't have to be a member of AARP to make use of this full-service drugstore. Generic medications at half the cost of the brand-name items. And an on-duty pharmacist is available to answer questions via phone six days a week. Honors most prescription insurance plans. Flat-rate shipping charge of $1.50. 800-456-2277, www.rpspharmacy.com.

American Health Food Vitamins and health supplements up to 33% off retail—60% if you buy the company's brand. Flat-rate shipping charge of $3.95. 800-858-2143, www.amerhealth.com.

Perfumania Up to 50% off suggested retail prices on fragrances for both men and women. 800-927-1777, www.perfumania.com.

Kitchen Equipment

Cook's Wares Discounted gourmet ingredients, cookware and cookbooks. A Cuisinart Pro Classic listed at $240 costs $155. 800-915-9788, www.cookswares.com.

Kitchen Etc. Up to 50% off on tableware from Lenox, Mikasa, Pfaltzgraff and Wedgwood. 603-773-0020, www.kitchenetc.com.

Luggage and Leather Goods

Santa Maria Discount Luggage First-quality travel and business bags and cases. A Samsonite 29" Oyster hardside listed for $200 costs $69.97. Buy five pieces of luggage and get an additional 10% off. 888-832-1201, www.luggageman.com.

Luxury Items

Bennett Brothers Corporate gift catalog with dress and casual watches at 40% off retail, including styles from Seiko, Geneve and Jules Jurgensen. 800-621-2626, www.bennettbros.com.

Evergreen Farms Cut fresh flowers. 30 stems of snapdragons or 15 stems of Asiatic lilies cost just $29.95 plus $12 overnight shipping. *Phone hours:* 8 am to 5 pm CST, Monday through Friday. 877-868-6985, www.evergreenfarms.com.

House of Onyx Investment-quality, imported gemstones and jewelry at wholesale prices—50% to 60% less than you would find elsewhere. 800-844-3100, www.houseofonyx.com.

Office Supplies/Equipment

Affordable Photocopy Top brands of photocopiers, faxes and printers at 60% off suggested retail prices. Free shipping on business-grade machines. 888-293-8071, www.photocopiers.com.

Factory Direct Furniture Office furniture and institutional equipment. Discounts of 50% off retail are common here. Additional discounts on orders over $1,000. 800-972-6570, www.factorydirect furniture.com.

Recycled Software Used IBM-compatible software at 50% to 90% off retail. Thousands of titles available. Orders include all original manuals and disks—virus free. 800-851-2425, www.recycledsoft ware.com.

Pet Supplies

Omaha Vaccine Company Prescription and nonprescription medications, grooming supplies and accessories for all animals—at up to 50% off retail prices. Many veterinarians buy here. 800-367-4444, www.omahavaccine.com.

That Pet Place Huge discount pet supplier for birds, fish, reptiles, dogs and cats. 717-299-5691, www.thatpetplace.com.

Printing and Stationery

Brown Print & Co. Custom-designed business cards, stationery, invitations and more. Proprietor works one-on-one with every client. Prices are competitive with those of large chains. *Samples and price list:* $2. 626-286-2106.

Tools and Hardware

Harbor Freight Tools Save up to 70% on tools, hardware, camping equipment and lawn and garden machinery. Free shipping for orders over $50. 800-423-2567, www.harborfreight.com.

Gail Bradney, consumer bargain expert, Woodstock, NY, and author of *Wholesale By Mail and On-Line 2000* (HarperCollins).

Catalog of Catalogs

Say good-bye to in-store shopping. *The Catalog of Catalogs: The Complete Mail-Order Directory (6th edition)* by Edward L. Palder (Woodbine House) offers access to more than 15,000 mail-order companies in approximately 800 different categories catering to every interest. Chances are, your favorite brand or store has a catalog which will give you access to special sales and extra savings.

Personal Recommendations From America's "Black-Belt Shopper"

Shopping by mail is more than just a convenience—many of my favorite items are not sold in local stores. These winning catalogs offer value-and-price-conscious products...with smart designs...and unusual and/or high-quality materials. Customer service is knowledgeable and friendly...and they have overstock and end-of-season bargains.

Travelwear

Travel Smith (800-950-1600, www.travelsmith.com) specializes in wrinkle-resistant, lightweight, packable and fast-drying "miracle" fabrics in versatile styles. Outfits for travelers wanting easy-care clothing. *Fabrics to look for:*

CoolMax (wicks away moisture)...*Microfiber* (suede-like polyester)...*Supplex* (cotton-finish nylon that dries quickly)...*Tencel* (rayon-like and wrinkle-free).

Everything Useful

Vermont Country Store (802-362-8440, www.vermontcountrystore.com) is like a stroll back in time. Useful, hard-to-find, old-fashioned merchandise, ranging from home remedies to underwear. When was the last time you saw oilcloth tablecloths? Yankee wisdom is scattered throughout the pages.

Outdoor Equipment

Campmor (800-226-7667, www.campmor.com) is for campers, hikers, cyclists, etc....or bargain hunters who love superior activewear, travel gear or sunglasses—all cheap.

Underwear/Activewear

One Hanes Place (800-300-2600, www.ohpcatalog.com) sells hosiery, pajamas, activewear, underwear (bras are a specialty)—all at 40% off list price. Items for women, men and children.

Natural Fibers

Garnet Hill's (800-622-6216, www.garnethill.com) products are made from cotton, wool and silk—in classic good taste, delightfully comfortable and at fair value. They range from bed, bath and home furnishings to clothes for kids, expectant mothers and women.

Leisurewear for Men

The Territory Ahead (800-882-4323, www.territoryahead.com) clothing is for the rugged male trekking across the countryside… or an urban cowboy dressing down at the office. *Note:* Its women's items don't have the same styling.

Pain Relief

FeelGood (800-997-6789, www.feelgoodfast.com) sells products to comfort back, neck, feet and joints as well as magnetic therapy devices, exercise equipment, foot inserts and supports.

New York Delicacies

Zabar's (800-697-6301, www.zabars.com) is New York's best-loved gourmet market, known for its smoked fish and meats, breads and bagels, imported cheeses and exotic foods. Plus there are great buys on kitchenware and appliances. Offers overnight shipping.

Susan Dresner, president, Ways & Means, wardrobe-management and retail consulting firm, New York. She was voted "The Nation's Black Belt Shopper" by *Money* magazine and is author of *Shopping on the Inside Track* (Gibbs Smith).

Super Money-Saving Catalogs and On-Line Deals

Jewelry, Silver, Crystal

Alan Marcus and Company (800-654-7184) specializes in name-brand watches…fine jewelry…crystal…flatware…fine pens. Rolex… Cartier…Waterford, etc. Many products up to 50% off retail.

Home Accessories

The Blair Shoppe Catalog (800-458-2000) carries a large array of accessories for the home—including bedding…pots/pans…linens… towels…and some men's and women's wear. Call for daily specials.

Plus Sizes/Women

The Lane Bryant Catalog (800-248-2000, www.lanebryant.com) offers large discounts on sale items, which appear in every catalog.

Home-Office Furniture

Reliable Home Office (800-869-6000, www.reliablehomeoffice.com). Name brands include Riverside…Sauder…Herman Miller office accessories.

Best Prices On-Line

Use shopping *bots* or *aggregators* for on-line price comparisons. Go to a bot site such as **MySimon**, www.mysimon. com, or **Yahoo! Shopping**, http:// shopping.yahoo.com, and enter information about what you are looking for.

MySimon, an independent site, searches 2,600 on-line retailers. The Yahoo! aggregator searches more than 10,000 retailers, including national chains, such as **The Gap**, **Macy's**, **Saks Fifth Avenue** and **Target**.

For secondhand merchandise: www.biddersedge.com. It tracks about 200 auction sites and lets you know when what you want is for sale.

Dana Blankenhorn, Internet consultant, a-clue.com, Atlanta.

On-Line Shoppers Take Note

Don't count on free shipping. Many Web sites used to offer free shipping to set themselves apart from real-world stores. Few do now. Some even add handling charges to shipping costs—an extra profit source for the sites.

Better way: Use a price-comparison site, such as www.mysimon.com, to find the true cost of an item, including shipping, when purchased from various merchants. www.freeshipping.com maintains a list of 1,200 on-line retailers offering good deals on shipping.

Check out the return policies and warranty coverage before buying anything on-line. Some Web stores allow you to return items to their brick-and-mortar locations. If you return a Web purchase via mail, you may have to pay postage—unless the problem was the vendor's mistake. And...some heavily discounted electronic items that are offered on-line are sold without any manufacturer warranties.

Rob Turner, staff writer, Money, *Time-Life Bldg, Rockefeller Center, New York 10020.*

Pet Supplies

New England Serum (800-473-8872, www.neserum.com) has a wider selection of well-priced products for dogs and cats than most retail pet stores.

Gardening Supplies

Park Seed (800-845-3369, www.parkseed.com) offers more than 2,000 items—including flower and vegetable seed...bulbs...and gardening supplies.

Athletic Shoes and Apparel

Road Runner Sports (800-662-8896, www.roadrunnersports.com) is one of the largest mail-order companies for running shoes, specialty footwear such as hiking shoes and brand-name athletic wear. Road Runner sells post-season styles and current season overstock items at prices up to 60% off retail.

Ann Fox Chodakowski and Susan Fox Wood, identical twins who write about their money-saving strategies. They are coauthors of Living on a Shoestring *(Dell).*

Here's the Right Way To Get Outstanding Deals On-Line

The World Wide Web has become one of the easiest ways to shop. You can order directly from your favorite brand-name or catalog company, or shop in a number of on-line malls.

What's easier than being able to price and product compare without leaving your home? Prices are competitive because there are lots of choices on the Web.

But if you're going to shop with your computer, there are things you should know before you pass your buck over the wire.

A Few Words About On-Line Security

Unsecured information sent over the Internet can be intercepted by an unwanted third party. This is why it is best to consider using a browser that will scramble purchase information.

Two protocols that comply with industry standards are Secure Socket Layer (SSL) or Secure Hypertext Transfer Protocol (S-HTTP). Most often they are included with your Internet connection services.

If you don't have the software to assure the security of your transaction, consider calling the company's 800-number, faxing your order or paying by check or money order instead of com-

pleting the order on-line. If you do decide to send your credit card information into cyberspace, then it is good to know that you are partially protected by the Fair Credit Billing Act.

You should always avoid using established numbers for your password, such as your birth date or a portion of your phone number or Social Security number. Try to be as original as possible in creating your password, and use different passwords to access specific areas on the Web. And never share your Internet password with anyone.

Shop Smart

Here are some valuable tips for shopping on-line:

- Buy from on-line companies that you know and would shop with off-line. If you want to try new merchants, ask them to mail you a catalog or brochure to get a better sense of their merchandise and services.
- Always find out a company's return policies before you place an order.
- Pay attention when you are filling out the order form on your screen. You don't want to order 100 hats instead of 1, or a size 16 when you want a 6.
- Always check what the shipping charge will be and that all of your charges are calculated correctly. You usually have different shipping options, and if you're not in a hurry to receive the item, it pays to have your purchase sent for the lowest cost.
- The same laws protect you whether you shop by phone, mail or cyberspace. If a company does not state how long it will take for you to receive your merchandise, you can expect to receive it within 30 days. Otherwise, they must notify you so that you can determine whether you still want the items.
- Always remember to print out a copy of your order and confirmation number for your records.

A Word of Warning

Always be cautious if anyone on-line asks for you to supply personal information, such as your Social Security number, to conduct a transaction. It is rarely necessary and should be taken as a warning sign. Scams are spreading very quickly on the Internet and as a smart consumer, you'll want to safeguard yourself.

On-Line Auctions: Secrets of Better Buying and Selling

hether you're buying or selling, whether you're going on-line or working the traditional auction-house circuit, here's how to gain more with less pain:

Government Auctions

Have you ever considered contacting the federal government to buy jewelry? The **U.S. Customs Service** holds auctions to sell jewelry and other valuables that have been confiscated. You can buy valuable gems at greatly reduced prices, but it isn't always easy to determine which auctions to attend.

You can contact the U.S. Customs Service directly by looking in the blue pages of your local telephone directory for the number. Often you can look at the merchandise the day before the auction is scheduled. It is best to check out an item before you make a bid.

TV Home-Shopping Traps

Home-shopping channels often prey on lonely viewers. People who feel alone or alienated can fall victim to sweet-talking order-takers, who may lure them to buy more than they could ever need.

Be careful of buying junk as well. Some channels sell low-quality jewelry, carpets and other accessories worth even less than the low price you pay.

Don't be fooled by shiny garbage. If you'll never use or need it, it is definitely not a bargain.

On-Line Auctions

On-line auctions give you access to items from all over the world. Bidding is fun. But there are problems involving security, lack of direct contact between buyer and seller and the hard-to-regulate nature of the on-line auction process. *If buying or selling on-line:*

- **Focus on large sites with heavy traffic.** You're more likely to find what you want and you may do better price-wise than you would on a smaller site.

Run a search at www.BidFind.com to see where the most auction traffic is for the item you wish to buy or sell. This company tracks auctions on more than 250 sites.

- **Check various auction sites.** Person-to-person auctions, such as those on eBay and Amazon.com, have the greatest diversity of items for sale.

On commercial sites, such as uBid.com, companies sell their goods in an auction format.

- **Don't overlook real-time Webcasts.** These are live auction "netcasts." Buyers bid from the auction room or from the Web. Several traditional auction houses, such as Butterfields, run Webcast auctions. There are even sites that will do the bidding for you. *Examples:* www.leftbid.com and www.icollector.com.

What Makes a Good Site

In addition to heavy traffic, look for:

- **A secure link whenever credit card information is entered.** You'll know the site is secure if you see a padlock symbol at the bottom of the screen. Some sites run the line, "This is a secure site."
- **Clearly defined dispute policy.** eBay, for example, outlines the precise procedure to follow in the event of a dispute.
- **Fraud protection.** Does the site reimburse you for some of your loss in the event of fraud?
- **A rating system for sellers and buyers.** That way, you'll know the track record of the person you're trading with.
- **Clearly stated fees and commissions.** Selling on-line is inexpensive because buyers pay no fees. Sellers should expect to pay *two* fees—a per-item listing/insertion fee (usually from 30¢ to about $3) and a final value/completion fee that varies depending on the amount of the winning bid (typically up to 5% for items to $25, 1.25% for items over $1,000).
- **Access to escrow services.** For a small fee, a third party—the escrow agent—holds the payment from the buyer in trust until the seller sends the merchandise. The fee runs from $2.50 for items up to $100 to 4% for items up to $25,000.

Using an escrow service protects the seller against credit card fraud and insufficient funds. It also allows the buyer to inspect the goods before the seller is paid.

Better Selling

Selling at an on-line auction is easy, but to get the most for your items, keep the following in mind:

- **Write a clear, concise description of your item.** Be specific. In headlines, use key words that will appear in the site's search engine.
- **Post digital pictures of your item.** Buyers are more likely to bid on items with photos.
- **Set your opening bid as low as possible.** Also, price your items "off-dollar." Buyers respond better to $19.99 than $20.
- **Research the price of the item.** At www.bidxs.com, you can search prices at 300 auction sites.
- **Set a hidden "reserve" price for the item.** This is the price below which you won't go.
- **Schedule your auction to attract the most bidders.** *Best:* Allow it to run over two weekends. Most bidding takes place in the last three hours.
- **Be honest about damage to items.** This will turn off some bidders but save you headaches on having to accept returns and refund payments.

Better Buying

Check out the seller's rating. Note any negative feedback from other buyers. Also important:

- **Not all auctions offer bargains.** Be a wise consumer—investigate retail valuations.
- **Carefully check the item's description and photographs for any damage.** At commercial sites, determine if the goods are used or refurbished.
- **Set a maximum bid and stick to it.** With the ease of on-line bidding, it's easy to get seduced into paying more than you are comfortable with.

Traditional Auctions

Auction houses are the primary source for quality pieces. Traditional firms—such as Sotheby's (www.sothebys.com) and Christie's (www.christies.com)—use their departmental specialists (who cover categories from Aboriginal art to Russian icons) to share their expertise with collectors.

The world of the auction house is quite different from the world of on-line auctions. Although low-end sales (less than $20,000) occur at Sotheby's Arcade auctions and elsewhere, most items are sold for top dollar and where "trophy collecting" or buying an object for sale at any price is common. For buyers:

- **Get a copy of the sales catalog.** It will contain pictures and descriptions. Make sure you understand the "conditions of sale" and "terms of guarantee."

Reality Check on Infomercials

Infomercials—program-length commercials on TV, sometimes identified as paid programming in TV listings—are solely designed to sell you something.

Tip-offs that what you're watching is an infomercial: The show's content and its commercials are similar; the program provides ordering information for a specific product; one product is labeled "better"; when what seems to be a real TV program only has commercials from one sponsor.

Self-defense: Question a promise too good to be true; be skeptical of experts or testimonials endorsing a product (they may be paid to do so); avoid accepting promises of free money or low-interest government loans; check with the Better Business Bureau before you buy.

For more information: Better Business Bureau, Publication 021 (www.bbbsouthland.org/topic021.html).

The Good Housekeeping Institute did a reality check on 15 infomercials. Although none lived up to all promises that were made, a few offered products that were worth the money—The Ronco Showtime Rotisserie & BBQ, Aero Extra Bed In a Minute (inflatable guest bed), Telebrands Rotato (a vegetable peeler for gadget-happy people), Egg Wave (an omelet maker for novices). Details at Good Housekeeping (http://goodhousekeeping.women.com/gh/buysmart).

Good idea: Look for the item in a retail store before you buy. The price might be lower and there's no shipping charge.

Beware of Untrained Property Appraisers

Appraisers of personal property (such as antiques, jewelry, Oriental rugs, etc.) are unregulated and unlicensed, so anybody can call himself/herself an "appraiser."

Trap: Of all the self-described appraisers in the US, only 10% have professional training. And many of those who have professional certification are minimally trained.

Of the four largest groups that provide professional credentials to appraisers, only one, the American Society of Appraisers, requires its members to pass tests in specific areas of appraisal expertise—for example, Oriental rugs, silver, jewelry, paintings. *To find an accredited appraiser:* 800-272-8258 or www.appraisers.org.

Best: If you need an appraisal for a specific reason (such as estate-planning purposes), get a referral to an independent appraiser from another professional (such as an estate lawyer).

Never depend on an appraisal from a dealer who wants to buy or sell the item being appraised.

Malcolm Katt, an antique dealer and owner of Millwood Gallery, which specializes in Nippon and Pickard porcelain, Box 552, Millwood, NY 10546.

- **Examine items carefully in person, if possible.** Items are sold "as is," so be sure to attend the auction preview. Upon request, a specialist can provide a condition report if you can't attend in person. The best advice a specialist can give you is what *not* to buy.
- **Understand the buyer's premium.** This is what you owe the auction house and can be as high as 17.5% of the purchase price.

For sellers:

- **Find out if the auction house specializes in your type of item.** If you're selling rare stamps, for example, you might check out Robert A. Siegel Auction Galleries (http://siegelauctions.com).

To find auctions and auctioneers worldwide, visit www.auctionguide.com. For auctions by category, try www.internetauctionlist.com.

- **Research what your item may yield at auction.** An estimate is only a guide for prospective bidders. It should not be relied upon as a prediction of actual selling prices. A reasonable estimate encourages bidding.
- **Understand the auction process.** It can take two to three months or more from the time your item is consigned to the house—for research, cataloging and photography—until the actual auction. It can take about 30 days after the sale to receive your proceeds. An on-line auction, on the other hand, typically takes only a week or two.
- **Understand the seller's commission.** It can run 10% to 15% of the sale price, plus possible charges for insurance, illustration, restoration and shipping.

Harry L. Rinker, a syndicated columnist who writes about antiques and collectibles in Emmaus, PA. He is author of more than a dozen books, the latest of which is *The Official Rinker Price Guide to Collectibles* (House of Collectibles).

Expert's Guide to On-Line Auction Traps

Buyer Traps

Succumbing to Auction Fever Protect yourself by using the *Maximum Bid* feature offered on many auction sites. This lets you privately indicate—in advance—the highest amount you will pay for an item. If someone outbids your initial offer, the system automatically raises your bid in predetermined increments up to your limit.

Dealing With Sellers Who Accept Money Orders Only Sending a money order is the same as paying with cash. It is impossible to stop payment if something goes wrong. Although most sellers cannot be expected to accept credit cards, there's no excuse for their not accepting personal checks. Waiting for a check to clear adds only

a few days to the process and gives the buyer proof that the item was indeed paid for.

Not Asking About the Seller's Return Policy Many legitimate sellers allow at least three days after receipt of an item to notify them that you're returning it for a refund.

Helpful: Ask sellers to send you an E-mail outlining their return policy. If the seller reneges on the deal, you can complain to the post office's fraud division—if the package was sent via the United States Postal Service (USPS). Make a complaint to the auction site as well.

Worrying Too Much About Snipers These are buyers who make bids moments before a session closes. Some sites offer a five-minute delay. This extends the bidding deadline whenever a bid comes in within five minutes of close. If you use a site without this feature, don't get too upset if you get sniped. You can probably find another of the same item.

Seller Traps

Getting Too Fancy Avoid large, complex photos, animated graphics, background music and other fancy effects when putting together a page featuring the item being auctioned. These features increase the time it takes to download the page. Photograph items against a plain background.

Important: Don't skimp on descriptive copy. Text downloads quickly.

Not Using an Escrow Service When Selling Pricey Items Many potential buyers don't bid because they worry about being cheated. Use a third-party escrow service. Once the buyer approves the item, the money is released to the seller, less a commission of up to 6%.

A reputable escrow service: www.escrow.com.

Not Taking Shipping and Insurance Into Account Buyers generally pay shipping and insurance costs, but you must mention this in your listing. Calculate these costs in advance either by going to the post office or visiting the Web sites run by the USPS, www.usps.gov ...United Parcel Service, www.ups.com...or Federal Express, www.fedex.com.

Not Packing Fragile Items Correctly Sellers are usually responsible for items damaged in transit.

Use crumpled newspaper for protection. After you pack the box, shake it gently. If you hear or feel the item move, reopen it and pack in more filler. For an especially fragile item, pack the item in one box and then pack that box inside another, larger box filled with more crumpled newspaper.

Alternative: Use a professional packing service—but expect to pay twice as much for shipping.

What You Should Expect to Pay at a Garage Sale

If you're new to garage sale shopping, you probably have no idea what items usually go for. Is $1 for a paperback book a good deal or a ripoff?

Here are some common garage sale items and their typical prices:

Cassette tapes	50¢ to $2
Coats	$10 to $30
Compact discs	50¢ to $4
Designer clothes	under $100
Furniture	$5 to $100
Glassware	10¢ to $1/piece
Hardcover books	50¢ and up
Paperback books	5 for $1
Rugs/Carpets	$15 to $80
Silk blouses	$4 to $15
T-shirts	25¢
Toys	under $10
Trousers	$2 to $10

When It's Garage Sale Time

- Signs should say only TODAY— even if the sale is on for several days. You don't want customers to postpone coming or think items were picked over the day before.

  Critical: Make signs simple…big… and legible so people can read them as they drive by.

- Price used items at 10% to 25% of retail value…50% or more of retail if never used.

  Strategy: Attach a retail flyer or page featuring your item to show the bargain you are offering.

- Set up one hour ahead of time, so you are ready for early birds.

- Display items between knee- and eye-level.

- If you are selling clothing, prop a full-length mirror nearby. *Also:* Hang blankets to create a "dressing room." Hang a ladder horizontally, and display clothing on hangers from rungs.

Cindy Skrzynecki, Minneapolis-based author of *50 Ways to Make the Most Money Having a Garage Sale* (available from the author, Dept. T, Box 23448, Minneapolis 55423).

Not Confirming Delivery Ask for a *Return Receipt* from the post office. *Cost:* Only $1.40 in addition to postage. Or get a tracking number to trace packages when using other delivery services.

Reyne Haines, founder of Just Glass, a collectible glass on-line auction site, www.justglass.com, and a columnist for *AntiqueWeek* magazine.

America's Most Amazing Deals: US Government Sales

Just about every day, a government office is selling valuable assets, from fine jewelry to office equipment—all at great prices.

Department of Defense The Defense Reutilization and Marketing Services (DRMS) gets rid of excess military property. Thousands of items are available each day, including tents and air conditioners. National sales are held in Battle Creek, Michigan—but local sales are held throughout the country.

Information: 888-352-9333. Ask for a DRMS kit that lists its offices. *For detailed property information:* www.drms.com.

Department of Justice The US Marshals' Service sells property that has been forfeited by law. Everything from commercial real estate to art and antiques is sold through auction as well as sealed bids.

Information: Check the Consumer Information Center's Web site, www.pueblo.gsa.gov, and search for the National Sellers list by clicking on "Search CIC."

General Services Administration (GSA) GSA's Federal Supply Service sells boats, cameras, communications equipment, hardware and office equipment that is no longer needed by the federal government.

Information: www.pueblo.gsa.gov. Click on "Federal Programs" and then "How You Can Buy Used Federal Personal Property" for a free list of GSA offices. Or order the list by phone for 50¢. 888-878-3256. Contact the office nearest you to find out about current sales.

US Postal Service The Postal Service sells items that have been un-claimed or lost in the mail. Merchandise includes clocks, televisions, radios, jewelry, tape recorders, VCRs and clothing.

Information: For personal property sales, look up the office closest to you in the *GSA Guide to Federal Government Sales.* It is available free at www.pueblo.gsa.gov or for $2 by phone. 888-878-3256.

Nancy Tyler, broadcast manager of the federal government's Consumer Information Center, which offers free and low-cost publications, Washington, DC.

Remote Control Shopping

H ave you ever tried the convenience of home shopping? You can find some unique and interesting items right from your living room.

Some TV networks, like Home Shopping Network (727-872-1000) and QVC (800-345-1515), offer clothing, jewelry and household and gift items at prices that are often as much as 40% below the cost of comparable items from a retail store. Sometimes they offer special deals of the day, so look for them when you tune in, or ask about special sales when you call.

How You Can Save

Home shopping can be cheaper because it cuts out the middleman who tends to increase cost. If you want to shop at home, but you aren't sure of what's offered, ask the shopping station to send you a schedule of times when particular items are sold.

Be a Smart Shopper

It's important to beware of the ease of home shopping. Don't let an enthusiastic host convince you to buy low-quality merchandise, especially if you don't need it.

When you shop from home, it is best to use your credit card, because you are then guarded by a consumer protection policy. If there is a problem, contact the Consumer Protection Agency in your state.

Television shopping's return policies are similar to those at traditional stores. They usually offer a 30-day full-credit refund policy and refunds for damaged goods.

Shop on Board

Shopping aboard cruise ships can be just as cost-effective as shopping in ports—and more convenient. Many onboard shops stock more items than you find onshore, including some from ports that your cruise doesn't visit. Shops are open long hours and accept credit cards, traveler's checks and cash.

Herbert J. Teison, editor, *Travel Smart*, 40 Beechdale Rd., Dobbs Ferry, NY 10522.

Flea Markets, Tag Sales & Antique Finds

B ringing home bargains from flea markets, antique shows and yard sales is very satisfying, but negotiating prices can be intimidating for many people.

Vendors, on the other hand, expect haggling. It is a time-honored tradition in markets throughout the world. Prices are padded for haggling. I find bargaining a lot of fun—a dance of wills and knowledge.

Using these strategies will help you feel more in control during the trading process:

Don't Get Carried Away

Don't be swept away by the flea market experience. If an item you're considering doesn't seem like a bargain, chances are that it's not. Some merchants choose to sell in flea markets because they know consumers think they'll get a deal. Junk is junk no matter what the price, and just because merchants have wholesale quantity, doesn't mean they're selling at wholesale prices. The only true bargain is a smart buy.

Bargaining Basics

- **Make a quick circuit of the area to see if anything is of interest, no matter the price.** If nothing "tugs at your heart," leave. There will always be another opportunity with a better payoff for your time and money.
- **Calculate your price.** If you spot a *must-have*, mentally calculate the most that you would be willing to pay to acquire it. Consider the item's value in the real world...what you think the vendor will want for it...and its value to you.

Scenarios: You spot a battered World War II medal. In better shape, it might go for $50, but the way it has been just tossed in a pile of costume jewelry, the seller might accept $10. You decide you would love it for your collection even if you had to spend $15.

If you do not know an object's worth: Compare prices around the market for similar pieces...or bid at another time, after you have done some research.

- **Engage the vendor.** First, hang around the vendor's stall to watch how the vendor operates. Does he/she set firm prices? How far does he budge from his asking price? Is he pleasant? Knowledgeable? Or scattered and careless?

Once you have sized up the situation, eye the object you want. Pick it up. Examine it carefully for defects. Look for a manufacturer's mark, which makes it more desirable, etc. The vendor will notice your interest, and the courtship game begins.

The Dialogue of Trade

For those embarrassed or intimidated by the thought of bargaining, here's how a typical bargaining session progresses. Use it as a basic script to guide you through the process:

You make eye contact with the vendor and eye the object to acknowledge you are interested in a deal.

How much? you ask casually. He responds firmly with a dollar amount. You examine the object again, taking your time.

If you decide to continue, make a counteroffer—usually one-half to one-third lower than the initial price. Say hesitantly, *I don't know. I don't really need it. How about $____?*

The vendor might communicate *nothing doing* by shaking his head or muttering something like, *It's worth more to me to just cart it away.*

If the vendor appears unwilling to play (he walks off or doesn't respond), move on.

If, on the other hand, he studies you and/or the item and maybe relates a tale about it, you might then ask, *What's your best price?*

For good measure, suggest that you may sell it to someone else. Doing so drives home the point that you need a competitive price. At this juncture, you rejoin with, *My absolute ceiling figure is $____.* Choose a number that is just a bit lower than your real limit...or wait for the vendor's final offer.

Closure

While the bargaining process might seem confrontational, closure should be a win-win situation.

Once you agree on a price, handshakes, a joke or two and smiles all around are in order. As the vendor wraps your prize, tell him how much you love the object and what a treasure trove his stall is. Along with your cash, this cements the deal and opens the door for future trading.

Bargaining Savvy

Not all outdoor markets are the same. Modify your tactics for where you are and what is being sold.

Roadside Flea Market A regularly held market where anybody can sell anything—soap, household gadgets, handmade items, baked goods, old books, etc.

Prices are marked, but bargaining is expected. If you buy two or more things from a dealer, always get a special deal.

Make sure you want what you buy and are not just swept up in the "high" of trading. This year's prize can land in *your* garage sale next season.

Outdoor Antique Show For serious collectors of old postcards, quilts, antique furniture, etc. Trade publications, which can often be found in antique stores, and Web sites, such as www.openair.org or www.collectors.org, post details about these fairs.

Arrive before the show opens (admission fees may be higher at that time) when antique dealers are searching for finds.

Estate Sales The contents of an upscale property must be disbanded. The sales are often professionally run. Find out about them from local newspapers or roadside signs.

Offerings can range from antiques and rugs to linens and kitchen items. My best deals have come from these.

Example: A green-painted armchair, for which I paid $25, turned out to be a 19th-century mahogany piece worth $800—once the finish had been restored and the seat re-covered.

Prices are marked, but negotiations are always in order. At the end of the tag sale or flea market, things fly out at unbelievable bargains.

Garage Sales/Yard Sales Basically offer other people's "junk." Chances to mine "diamonds in the rough" improve when you confine yourself to nicer neighborhoods.

Heirlooms picked up for a song can be sought-after antiques… and throwaway doodads can be transformed into treasures for your home—with some imagination.

Susan Dresner, president, Ways & Means, wardrobe-management and retail consulting firm, New York. She was voted "The Nation's Black-Belt Shopper" by *Money* magazine.

Flea Market Buying Tips

- ❏ Come prepared with a list of items you want to buy.
- ❏ Don't assume everything is a bargain.
- ❏ Be wary of fakes when shopping for brand-name items—some imitations are hard to spot.
- ❏ Know when to bargain. Don't assume that the first price you see or hear is final, even if it's written on the price tag. Always offer a lower price because vendors are interested in moving their goods.
- ❏ Carry cash. Many vendors offer better deals for cash payments.
- ❏ Beware of pickpockets.
- ❏ Dress for comfort and convenience. Wear comfortable shoes and keep your hands free.

What's Hot…What's Not At Flea Markets

Flea markets and antiquing have soared in popularity as more people realize the money-making potential in their attics… and enjoy finding bargains on eclectic home furnishings.

Crafts & Collectibles

Lithographed Tin Banks From the 1940s Through the 1970s Those shaped like children's books, globes and houses are very popular.

Price: $30 to $100. Registering banks—which have a coin-counting mechanism—can be worth several hundred dollars.

Collector's edge: Look for banks made by J. Chien & Co, a well-known East Coast toymaker that produced 65 different designs from 1903 to 1977. An Uncle Wiggily Chien rabbit bank recently sold for $440. A "Save for War Bonds and Stamps" Chien bank shaped like a bullet shell sold for about $600.

Flower/Plant Prints from the US Patent Office. This is our favorite undervalued find. In the early 1930s, the US government began issuing patents on new varieties of flowers and plants. These official photographs and chromolithographs of patented roses, geraniums, etc. are showing up at flea markets for just $10 to $20 a print. They'll be worth much more when people realize what they are.

Czechoslovakian Pottery From the First Half of the 20th Century The most popular of old Czechoslovakian pottery has either brightly colored flower designs or airbrushed designs.

Price: $50 and up.

Collector's edge: Don't be fooled by new reproductions. Look inside pitchers and cups where the handle joins the body. New pottery looks smooth. Older stuff is slightly dented.

Home Furnishings

Reproduction Colonial American Furniture from the 1930s Copies—yes, copies—of famous makers such as Chippendale, Hepplewhite and Sheraton have modern touches, such as patterned veneer tops. You can get especially good bargains on dining-room sets and coffee tables.

Example: A dining-room table with six chairs goes for between $500 and $1,000.

Navajo Wool Rugs Made between 1920 and 1970, many from Navajo reservations in Arizona and New Mexico.

Price: $800 to $3,000.

Look for: Rugs made from homespun, vegetable-dyed wool rather than slicker commercial yarn…intricate and centered pattern …undamaged corners…no bleeding of colors.

Political Memorabilia

Protest/Political Bumper Stickers, Posters and Buttons Anti-Vietnam War items start at $5 and go up to several hundred dollars. Be careful—fake war memorabilia are common.

Collector's edge: White-painted buttons weren't used until after 1972...buttons with yellowish or pinkish rust may be knockoffs that were "aged" to look valuable. Natural rust is reddish-brown.

WW I- and WW II-Era Satin Pillows Featuring military camps or ships, sought by decorators on both coasts for use in vacation homes.

Price: $25 and up. A pillowcase featuring a WW I navy ship sold recently for $145.

Silverware

Victorian-Era Serving Pieces Created between 1850 and 1900, these usually have a very ornate and eclectic look. Sterling silver from Gorham or Tiffany is quite expensive. Silver-plated pieces, such as asparagus servers or soup ladles, go for a reasonable $50 to $100 per piece. The gaudier and more elaborate the design, the better.

Toys

1960s Dolls Most popular include Chatty Cathy/$150 to $250... Nancy Ann Storybook/$100 to $200...Toni dolls with a "permanent wave" kit/$250 to $300.

Collector's edge: A doll in its original box would be worth twice as much.

Wind-Up Toys Disney character memorabilia always fetch good prices. German- or Japanese-made tin windups from the 1950s and 1960s are especially in demand.

Price: $300 and up. For example, a 6" Mickey Mouse playing a xylophone recently sold for $385.

Electronics

1960s Transistor Radios American models from General Electric, Philco and Zenith go for between $30 and $125. Japanese-made radios from Hitachi and Sony sell for up to $600.

General Trends

Use these flea market trends to your advantage when buying collectibles...

Trading Over the Internet This has flooded the market with certain items, greatly cooling off the prices that you can get.

Most affected: Antique and rare books...World's Fair handkerchiefs, tablecloths and other textiles and pennants...souvenir spoons from the 1950s and 1960s.

Blue, White And Red-Hot Collectibles

Americans have collected patriotic memorabilia since Revolutionary days. Flags...Uncle Sam banks...red, white and blue dolls are not just good investments. They're also ways to remember and honor our nation's past.

Demand for Americana often rises in times of crisis. And interest in this collecting category has indeed surged since September 11, 2001.

Ralph and Terry Kovel, Cleveland-based experts on collectibles. Their TV show is *Flea Market Finds with the Kovels.* They are authors of many books on collecting, including *Kovel's Antiques & Collectibles Price List 2002* (Three Rivers).

Attract Customers To Your Yard Sale

If you have a lot of an item, say so. *Example:* "Lots of baby clothes." Give clear directions to your home in the ad. Capitalize important words, such as GREAT BARGAINS. End the ad with a phrase like "and much, much more" to be sure people know you have more than what is listed.

Cathy Pedigo, Colorado Springs-based author and publisher of *How to Have Big Money Garage Sales* (available from the author, 800-841-4248).

Mix-and-Match Sets Huge in the 1950s, they are back now. Using unmatched cups, saucers and plates from different periods, you can put together place settings for $10 a set. You can do the same with chairs around your kitchen table.

Oversized Furniture Is In New homes tend to have large rooms and high ceilings. Decorators are combing flea markets for large pieces—tall beds, armoires and grandfather clocks.

Evaluating Your Stuff

If you think you've uncovered a hidden treasure, the following auction houses will appraise it free. Print an estimate-request form off the Web site, and mail it along with several photographs. Allow at least four weeks for a response:

- **Butterfields Appraisals** (415-861-7500, www.butterfields.com)
- **Sotheby's Appraisal Department** (212-606-7000, www.sothebys.com)

Ralph and Terry Kovel, Cleveland-based experts on collectibles. Their TV show is *Flea Market Finds with the Kovels.* They are authors of many books on collecting, including *Kovel's Antiques & Collectibles Price List 2002* (Three Rivers).

Open-Air Bargain Shopping

You can find listings of garage, yard and lawn sales in the classified section of your local newspaper or shopping guide. Check under headings such as Auctions and Sales or For Sale by Owner. Also, look for street signs advertising them.

Most garage sales are held outside. Early spring to summer is a great time to start garage sale hunting, and you should find good shopping until the weather turns cold.

Garage Sale Buying Strategies

Here are a few basic guidelines to help you get the best deals at garage sales:

- Get a detailed map of the area where sales are scheduled and plan your route to save time.
- Arrive early so that you have your pick of the best items before too many other people arrive. If you're late, you may get lower prices, but the selection of merchandise will be more limited.
- If you want to haggle, bring small bills. If you think the price is fair, don't bother to haggle. You could lose out on the item altogether if you try to make a great bargain better.
- Don't forget to check your merchandise for faults. Plug in all appliances if there's an outlet available. A bargain is only as good as the quality of the item.

Holding Your Own Garage Sale

Garage and yard sales can be great ways to clear out your family's old clothes, and make some cash to buy new ones. Holding a sale can be a very trying business, though, so make sure that you want to invest the time and energy required to make the sale worthwhile.

Where to Hold It

The first rule for a successful sale is to hold it in a populated area where you know other yard sales have flourished. If your best friend's neighborhood is a better area for a sale, ask her about doing a combined sale. More stuff could mean more customers. You should only need an advertisement for your sale if you live off the beaten path.

When to Hold It

The best time to hold your sale is on one of the first sunny spring weekends. Do not hold a yard sale on a holiday weekend when most people are away. It is possible that your town may require a license. Check with town hall before you start the sale. You don't want to do all of the work and then find out you can't hold the sale.

How to Advertise

Post signs advertising the location of the sale. Place them at all of the intersections near your home, out as far as the main road.

Stencil or write the words "Yard Sale" three to four inches high on a piece of cardboard and write the date and location in the middle of the sign. Put an arrow at the bottom showing which direction to turn.

You can use spray paint to save time, but you will have better control with a thick, waterproof marker.

On the day of the sale, make the merchandise as attractive as possible: Large items tend to stop cars, so put those near the road. Hang up as much clothing as possible, and lay out clothing for children according to size. Group similar items together.

What to Charge

Remember, your primary purpose is to get rid of your old stuff, so price everything so it will go.

Consider pricing everything at one-third of the price it would cost new. If someone wants an item but you aren't ready to lower the price, ask them to come back later. Save your negotiating for the end of the day, when you really want to unload any leftovers.

Finding the Best Merchandise

You'll usually find better quality merchandise in affluent areas, though you may have to spend more money to get the items you really want.

Prices are generally cheaper at church or other not-for-profit sales than at people's houses, but donated items may not be of high quality.

Group sales may offer a wider selection of merchandise.

Little Helpers

Yard sales can be a great way to teach your children or grandchildren about consumer buying and selling. If you have your kids work at the sale, let them keep the money they make.

You should only hold things if a customer pays you first. If you hold an item that isn't paid for, and the customer doesn't return, you will lose profit from someone else.

Always guard the money you make at a sale. Keep it in your pocket or in a lockable box.

When It's All Over

Don't forget to take down all yard sale signs immediately. There are always stragglers who will ignore the date and time of a sale. If you still have items left, put them back in a box for next year.

3

Get Good Deals on Just About Anything

Finding Free Stuff

The world is full of free stuff! Finding free—or almost free—products begins with knowing where to look and being persistent about asking for them.

Advertisements Many companies and organizations offer consumers the opportunity to read about or sample products before making a purchase or other commitment. *Tip:* Sometimes brand-name companies will offer perks. *Examples:* Free recipes, rebate coupons or how-to brochures to consumers who buy their product lines. These freebies are usually publicized through advertisements, so be sure to read the small print.

Toll-Free Numbers Quite often there's a customer service or customer comment toll-free number on a product label, coupon or advertisement. You can call these numbers and ask about any unadvertised perks the company may be offering.

Coupons and Labels They sometimes offer good deals, especially on new products. *Warning:* If you get a coupon or read a label

Size Matters

When you order free samples, keep in mind that they can vary greatly in size. Some free samples are quite generous, while others are only good for one use (and sometimes not even that). It's possible to receive a hand lotion sample as small as a packet of sugar, or one that will last you a month. Sometimes you may get only a 50¢ coupon and other times you may get over $5 worth.

that offers a rebate requiring you to mail in a receipt and proof of purchase, be sure the offer is worth your time and the cost of the stamp.

Junk Mail Don't automatically throw out product mailers that sometimes seem to overwhelm your mailbox. Many mailers include ways to receive free samples and information.

Act Fast...

When you find a freebie, you want to be sure to order it immediately because most offers expire quickly.

...But Be Ready to Wait

When you call or send away for free stuff, remember that immediate delivery is not guaranteed. It may take up to two months to receive the item you requested.

A Complaint or Compliment May Get You Something for Free

By voicing your opinion, either positively or negatively, you may receive a free sample, rebate or discount coupon for your next purchase of a product.

Check the Small Print

If you read the small print on the packaging of products you buy, you'll see there's frequently a manufacturer's phone number or address included. Consider taking advantage of this contact information to let a company know what you think.

If a toll-free number is not available, a letter to a company's customer-service supervisor can get the same response. In your letter, explain your disenchantment or satisfaction with a product. Include the label, date and store where you purchased the product, and let the company know exactly why you are writing the letter. Companies will do a lot to keep their customers satisfied, and to let satisfied customers know that they appreciate their business and loyalty.

Get Satisfaction

Many times a customer's dissatisfaction with a product warrants a rebate or replacement of a damaged product bought in a store. And many companies will reward a customer's satisfaction and loyalty to a product line with a coupon toward their next purchase or a sample of a new item in the product line.

Ask for a Sample

If there's a new item you'd like to try, but you don't want to buy an entire box or jar (only to find you don't like it), call the comment line and ask the customer-service department if a sample is available. You won't know what you can get for free until you try.

Fly for Less

If your flight with an airline isn't up to par, your complaint may get you money off of your next trip. Many airlines provide disgruntled customers with coupon vouchers (sometimes for as much as $50) for future flights. Contact the customer service department by letter, on the phone or in person, and explain your frustration and disappointment in the service you had. A freebie can ease the stress of a bad trip.

Big Bargains in Your Backyard

Take a close look at what your community has to offer. You'll find the programs available are varied and that they usually cost very little, if anything.

Take Advantage of Your Local Library

Libraries offer some of the highest quality, least expensive entertainment values around. *Tip:* If you live in or near a city, check out the calendar of events for the central library as well as your local branch.

Movie Night Many libraries show movies on a weekly or monthly basis.

Concerts Look for concert nights when you can enjoy free music by local musicians.

Home Videos They are available for loan and may even be free.

Audios You'll find a selection of compact discs, cassette tapes and records. *Reminder:* Listening to a book cassette is a great way to pass the time on a long drive.

Internet Access You may be able to explore the World Wide Web at no cost.

Newspapers and Magazines You'll probably find a large selection. *Saving:* You won't have to buy a copy for that one article you want to read.

Reading Groups Ask about joining an existing group or starting a new one focusing on your own particular interests.

Special Discounts For Seniors

More than 50,000 discounts for people age 50 and older are available at www.seniordiscounts.com. Discounts on hotels, restaurants, entertainment, travel, medical expenses and more can be searched by category or location.

The site includes a free weekly E-mail newsletter announcing new discount opportunities.

English Tutoring A program where volunteers work with other adults to improve their reading and writing skills.

Children's Programs Watch for children's reading hours, holiday parties, after-school activities and a lot more.

Try the Y

Christian and Jewish Y organizations offer a variety of activity choices at a fraction of the price charged by private recreational facilities. Check out the YMCA, YMHA or JCC (Jewish Community Center) nearest you. Programs are usually open to all faiths.

Exercise Facilities Many Ys are equipped with swimming pools, weight rooms, tracks and exercise rooms. They may also offer classes in stretching and yoga, as well as weekly basketball games.

Entertainment Activities These may include plays, concerts, dance recitals, tours and travel opportunities.

Educational Programs You may find classes in parenting, reading and writing, self-help and personal growth, to name but a few.

For Kids Many organizations offer low-cost day care and summer camps for children.

Libraries On-Line

You can access the catalogs (and other resources) of the world's libraries from your home computer. One of the best places to start is LibWeb (http://sunsite.berkeley.edu/libweb). This enormous directory contains 6,100 pages listing the home pages of almost every library in the world. Just click on a listing and you will be connected to a treasure trove of the world's academic, public, school and special libraries. A very small sampling of what you can find:

United States
- **Air Force Research Laboratory** (www.wrs.afrl.af.mil/library/)
- **American Antiquarian Society** (www.americanantiquarian.org)
- **Archives of African American Music and Culture** (www.indiana.edu/~aaamc/)
- **Berklee College of Music** (http://library.berklee.edu)
- **Black Film Center/Archive** (www.indiana.edu/~bfca/)
- **The University of California** (www.lib.berkeley.edu)
- **University of Chicago** (http://www.lib.uchicago.edu/e/index.html)
- **Folger Shakespeare Library** (www.folger.edu)
- **Goddard Space Flight Center** (http://library.gsfc.nasa.gov)
- **Harvard University** (www.harvard.edu/museums)
- **Library of Congress** (www.loc.gov)
- **Lunar and Planetary Institute** (www.lpi.usra.edu/lpi.html)

- **Marine Biological Library/Woods Hole Oceanographic Institution** (http://mblwhoilibrary.mbl.edu)
- **National Archives** (www.nara.gov)
- **National Library of Education** (www.ed.gov/nle)
- **The New York Public Library** (www.nypl.org)
- **Smithsonian Institution** (www.sil.si.edu)
- **Orion System at UCLA** (www.library.ucla.edu)
- **Yale University** (www.library.yale.edu)

Foreign

- **National Library of China** (www.nlc.gov.cn/etext.htm)
- **Danish Centre for Information on Women and Gender** (www.kvinfo.dk/bible.htm)
- **The Egyptian Library Network** (www.library.idsc.gov.eg)
- **National Library of France** (www.bnf.fr)
- **Russian State Library** (www.rsl.ru/defengl.asp)

Other sources for libraries include:

- **American Universities** (www.clas.ufl.edu/CLAS/american-universities.html)
- **United Kingdom Public Libraries on the Web** (http://dspace.dial.pipex.com/town/square/ac940/weblibs.html)
- **Westchester (New York) Public Library System** (www.wls.lib.ny.us)

Free E-Mail

Many sites, and even some search engines (such as Yahoo and AltaVista), provide World Wide Web users with free Web-based E-mail addresses. They can afford to do this because they put ads on your E-mail page.

Most of the time, you can access your free Web-based E-mail account from any computer, which is appealing for people who have an account they can only access from one station.

Some services you may want to look into are:

- **Bigfoot** (www.bigfoot.com)
- **Yahoo** (www.yahoo.com)
- **Hotmail** (www.hotmail.com)
- **Lycos** (www.mail.lycos.com)
- **Alta Vista** (www.altavista.com)

Cut the Cost of Your Long-Distance Service

There are many options beyond staying with your local phone company. Its basic long distance rates can be cut dramatically. First, check with AT&T, MCI and Sprint. All offer discount programs and/or perks such as frequent-flier miles.

Other sources to check:

Small, Nationwide Providers For example, Qwest Communications, www.qwest.com, offers discounted rates and has a special deal with American Express card holders.

Dial-Around Services They provide an access number to bypass your current carrier. If you only make one or two calls a week, their low by-the-minute fees allow you to save money without changing your present carrier. 10-10-345 (AT&T) is an example of a dial-around service.

Services that help you compare rates:

- **The Telecommunications Research & Action Center (TRAC)** provides a chart of 18 patterns of long-distance telephone use that shows what each pattern would cost using 35 different calling plans

Cut Your Local Phone Bill

Examine your phone bill:

• **If you're charged for inside wiring:** Problems with wiring rarely occur. Tell the phone company you'll assume responsibility for repairs of wiring. It's cheaper to call an electrician or a moonlighting telephone repair person.

• **If you have two lines:** Consider getting distinctive-ring service instead. This provides two telephone numbers with different rings on one line. You'll avoid charges for second-line basic service plus additional expensive surcharges.

• **If you use a dedicated line for a fax:** Buy a fax switch instead and attach it to your regular (voice) line. It recognizes the difference between a voice call and a fax call.

• **If you want better rates:** Check an alternative local carrier's rates. In most areas of the country, your phone company is required to list competition for its local services in its phone directory.

from seven different companies. Send a stamped self-addressed envelope with $5.55 to TRAC, Box 27279, Washington, DC 20005 (202-263-2950). Free service via Internet (www.trac.org) compares your current phone bill with more than 20 plans.

• **Consumer Action** provides a free long-distance survey comparing 14 different companies for different times of the day and three different calling volumes. Send a stamped self-addressed envelope to Consumers Action, 717 Market St., Ste. 310, San Francisco 94105 (www.consumer-action.org).

Shrewd idea: After you do your homework, go to your current provider and tell it about the best rate you've found. It's cheaper to keep a present customer and they may offer you a better deal.

DVDs: Best Time To Buy One

Prices are almost in free fall for the latest crop of DVD players. So here are our recommendations for what and when to buy one.

What a DVD Player Is DVD players, like CD players, use optical media. A DVD looks like a CD, but can contain far more content. DVDs are also used in computers, but these use different incompatible formats.

What You Get Now Superb picture quality when compared to a VCR; ability to play standard audio CDs; one DVD can play a full two-hour-plus movie with a six-channel Dolby Digital or DTS soundtrack and all sorts of additional extras, including multiple languages, onscreen commentary by the directors, etc.

Catch: Stand-alone DVD players designed for home use, unlike VCRs, cannot yet record. Also, if you record your own CDs with your computer, many current DVD players won't be able to read them. DVD *recorders* exist, but there are three DVD recording formats fighting for dominance in the marketplace: DVD-R/RW, DVD+RW and DVD-RAM. *Smart move:* Wait until the dust settles if you plan to buy a DVD player to *record* as well as play DVDs.

Note: If you intend to use your DVD player with an older TV that only has an antenna input, you'll need to buy a special converter.

Time to Say Yes to Satellite TV?

There are two kinds of home satellite systems—big dishes (C-band) and small Direct Broadcast System (DBS) antennas. Either system provides far more channels—close to

500—than cable television…and significantly better picture and sound quality.

Which system you buy depends on what and how you want to watch. To decide what's right for you:

Big Dishes

A C-band dish (typically 7½" to 10" in diameter) is for someone who selects programs in advance and stays with them. Drawbacks:

- Only one channel at a time can be seen in the *entire* household.
- It can take several minutes to move from satellite to satellite for signals, so channel surfing is difficult.
- Snow in the dish may cause you to lose the signal temporarily.
- Homeowners' associations can prevent you from installing a C-band dish. Municipal codes might require a backyard location, even if reception would be better elsewhere.

Cost of a basic large-dish system: About $1,100, including installation. With a standard system, you buy programs from the providers and pay "a la carte."

Example: If all you watch is CNN and the Discovery Channel, you can buy both for just $2.50 a month.

A more sophisticated system with a digital-plus-analog receiver runs $2,500, installed. You get a lot more programming with the C-band digital receiver—about 500 viewing channels, plus thousands of music, news and other feeds, for about $12 a month.

Your savings from cheaper program fees versus cable television rates should pay for the C-band equipment within three years.

Small Dishes

Minidishes—about 18" in diameter—collect microwave signals from one to three satellites. They sit in a fixed position on your roof or windowsill. DBS is best for people who like a lot of channel choices and an easy-to-use system. Minidish owners view as cable subscribers do—they can channel-surf, and every TV in the house can be tuned to something different if a receiver is purchased for each TV.

Drawback: If you get heavy cloud cover or a downpour, you'll temporarily lose the signal.

Costs: There's a lot of competition among minidish suppliers. Typically, either the installation or the hardware (dish, receiver, remote) is free. Either bonus is worth about $100. Hardware and programs are purchased through a single service. Packages average $240 a year.

Want News? You Lose!

Depending on where you live, you might not be able to get local programming—such as local news—via a satellite system. For these programs, you would still need a cable connection or a rooftop antenna.

Jim Scott, editor, *Satellite TV Week*, 140 S. Fortuna Blvd., Fortuna, CA 95540.

Best Deals on Phone Service

Get the best deals on phone services via a free Web site. Enter your area code, telephone exchange and type of service desired to anonymously request customized quotes from competing service providers in your area. Services include long-distance, wireless, data and Internet.

Details: www.simplexity.com or call 866-327-2226.

Directory Assistance Is Free On-Line

Directory assistance costs for long-distance calls have gone up significantly. Most services now charge $1.49 to $1.99 per request, even if the number you want cannot be found.

Self-defense: Use the free long-distance telephone directories on the Internet, such as www.anywho.com... www.555-1212.com...and http://people.yahoo.com.

Dori Perrucci, writer, *Good Housekeeping*, 959 Eighth Ave., New York 10019.

Where to Get the Best Deals on Office Supplies

Nickels and dimes and dollars spent on Scotch tape, staples, copy or laser paper, scissors, etc. can add up to real money. (The average office worker uses about $500 worth of office supplies a year.) However, office supplies can be a controllable expense, even if your office is in your home.

Shop Smart Local stationery stores rarely have the ability to compete on price. Loading a shopping cart at your local office supplies superstore is a waste of time when you add up travel time, wondering aisles and waiting on line. Except in dire emergencies, buy from a catalog of a national discounter of office supplies, or buy from an on-line discount vendor. Better yet, superstores such as Staples (www.staples.com) or Office Max (www.officemax.com) have on-line catalogs. The on-line vendor Quill (www.quill.com) is owned by Staples, but it has different buying offices and different pricing. Shipping is usually free from catalog or on-line stores if total purchases exceed $50. Next-day delivery is featured from some on-line merchants, including Quill.

Warehouse Clubs? They sometimes offer great bargains if you buy in bulk, but they have a very limited selection. Again, do you have the time?

Trap: Falling for a loss-leader from any merchant. Before you buy, make sure that other items you intend to buy at the same time are competitively priced. It's always worthwhile to spend a few minutes comparison shopping, and it's especially easy if you do it using the Internet.

If you can, it's smart to buy reasonably large quantities. Purchasing inventory for six months or a year (if you have the space) is shrewd. For example, buying laser paper in 10-ream cartons can save 10% to 20% over single-ream purchases. If you buy from a store that offers free shipping for orders exceeding $50, for example, it makes sense to buy in bulk or put off buying until you can order several items at once.

Great Gifts that Don't Cost a Bundle

To give memorable gifts, you don't have to spend a lot. You must simply personalize what you give so the recipients feel how much you care.

Every year, Myvesta.org, a national, nonprofit organization dedicated to helping people get out of debt, invites consumers to submit their most creative ways to save money on gift giving for birthdays, anniversaries and other special occasions. Recent winners:

- **Special-interest kits for the recipient's favorite activity.** If your dad loves to fish, his kit might include adhesive bandages, beef jerky, candy, sunglasses, matches and his favorite steel leader hooks.
- **Framed photographs** of your loved one's home during each of the seasons.
- **Address boulder.** Get a large rock at a local quarry. Paint the recipient's house number on it with fluorescent paint. He/she will remember you every time he drives up to his home.
- **Trade in frequent-flier miles** for magazine subscriptions and other gifts, such as home appliances or luggage. Many airlines now send out gift brochures with items costing as little as 500 miles.

Gifts for Kids

- **Personalized picture.** Use heavy paper and crayons or markers to write adjectives for each letter of a child's name.

Example: Jenna—*J* is for *Joyous...E* is for *Exciting...N* is for *Neat*, etc.

- **Coupon gift book.** Each book contains 14 coupons—one for each month plus Valentine's Day and a birthday. Make each coupon redeemable for whatever you choose. The front of each coupon has your favorite saying or advice...the back has space for a thank-you note.

To redeem the coupon, the child must present it to you each month, recite the saying or advice and tell you what it means. He/she must also fill out the thank-you note on the back.

Steve Rhode, president and cofounder, Myvesta.org, nonprofit financial services organization, 6 Taft Ct., Rockville, MD 20850. 800-680-3328.

Beautiful Savings

The best way to save money on cosmetics is to stop buying designer products. For a quarter of the cost, drugstore cosmetics are much better buys. Well kept secret: Revlon and Covergirl use the same basic ingredients in their products as many high-end designers, but they sell them in plainer packaging at a fraction of the cost. For bigger savings: Buy the drugstore's own brand. It's often made by the same company that makes the brand name.

Buy More than One

Most drugstore items cost less, sometimes as little as half the price, when you buy the larger sizes. *Save even more:* In many instances, drugstore chains will also have manufacturers' specials—promote

Personal Toll-Free Numbers

Personal 800 numbers are available on many long-distance telephone plans. Calling toll-free makes it easier for family members to check in because they can call from anywhere and don't need change to call from a pay phone.

Good news: Calls are usually billed at the normal long-distance rate, and by shopping around you can eliminate the $5 monthly fee.

Fred Voit, consumer communications analyst, The Yankee Group, Boston.

Cellular-Phone Contracts

Cellular-phone contracts are hard to avoid. Most plans require you to sign at least a one-year contract. If you terminate early, you can be penalized, sometimes hundreds of dollars.

Self-defense: If you must sign a contract, make sure you can switch calling plans without penalty during the contract period.

Important: Get everything in writing.

Samuel Simon, Esq., chairman and founder, Telecommunications Research and Action Center (TRAC), Washington, DC.

brand name products at large discounts—and that's the time to buy more than one.

Gender-Blind Savings

Women can easily save 20% on toiletries such as deodorants and disposable razors by purchasing products targeted at men. The ingredients are usually the same, although the scents or colors may be different.

Bargain Beauty Supplies

Sally Beauty Supply (800-275-7255, www.sallybeauty.com), a chain that has 1,550 stores in 46 states, specializes in low-cost beauty needs, from cotton balls to hair dryers and shampoo. They will match competitors' prices.

The Beauty Boutique Catalog (440-826-1712) offers fragrances, cosmetics and skin care products from a number of major brands, including Estee Lauder, Elizabeth Arden and Yardley of London, at up to 90% below retail prices.

The American Association of Retired Persons Pharmacy Service offers more than 10,000 drugstore items, including moisturizers and fragrances, at almost 40% less than drugstore prices. The service is available to anyone, but AARP members are eligible for additional discounts. Call 800-456-2277 for a catalog.

Deals on Cosmetics and Toiletries on the Internet

There are a large number of on-line vendors offering discounts of up to more than 70% off retail prices on everything from cosmetics to fragrances to toiletries and other beauty and bath needs. *Our favorites:*

FragranceNet.Com (www.fragrancenet.com) claims to beat any discounter's competitive price by at least 5% on brand names—and they guarantee no imitations or knock-offs of men's and women's fragrances.

Drugstore.Com (www.drugstore.com) is a huge on-line drugstore selling everything from toiletries and perfumes to prescriptions at excellent discounts.

Catalogcity.Com (www.catalogcity.com) sells just about everything, including a full range of bath and beauty products at significant discounts. Go to their "Outlet Center" for blowout deals.

Perfume Mart (www.perfumemart.com) discounts their merchandise and offers a free sample with every purchase. They also offer free shipping.

Sweet Savings

When you buy perfumes at a department store fragrance counter you spend up to 50% more than when you buy them at a drugstore or discount chain.

When to Use Department Stores

Department store perfume counters come in handy when you want to test a new fragrance. And department stores may be your only option if you want to receive free samples of fragrances. *Travel tip:* Easy to pack, sample-size vials are great to use while on the road.

Shop Duty-Free

You can cut fragrance costs significantly when you shop duty-free at shops in international airports or on some international flights. They tend to sell fragrances at 20% off department store prices, though selection may be limited, especially on the planes. Plan to buy duty-free items on your trip home, so you won't have to carry your purchases for your entire vacation.

Consider a Copy

Like many items that carry designer names, perfumes are cheaper when you purchase knockoffs, or copies, that smell the same as name brands. Essential Products in New York City (212-344-4288) offers duplicate men's and women's colognes at up to 90% off their designer-name prices. If you have a particular scent in mind, call to see if it's available. Chances are, they'll have it.

For All-Around Savings

Perfumania (800-927-1777) sells brand-name manufacturers' scents at up to 70% below retail prices. Call for a location near you. And don't forget to check designer outlet stores. In addition to savings on clothing, they offer designer-name scents at reduced prices.

Buy the Big Size

Buying a larger-sized bottle is another way to save money on fragrances. You'll pay 20% to 40% less per ounce when you buy more ounces of a scent. For example, a 200-milliliter bottle that costs $50 is a better deal than a 100-milliliter bottle of the same scent that costs $35.

Thinking About a New Cell Phone?

Here is what to do if you're in the market for a cell phone or service provider:

- Pick a service plan before you pick a phone. New cell-phone designs are so seductive that many people sign up with providers only if they carry the phones they want. That can leave you with excessive calling charges.

  Consider before signing up:

- The number of minutes you'll likely be on the phone each billing cycle.
- How often you'll use your phone outside your local region. Long-distance "roaming" charges are expensive.
- Phone size and options you prefer.

  Also, most people are unaware that if they decide to switch service providers, they will have to buy new phones.

  Reason: While service providers sell identical-looking phones built by the same manufacturers, in most cases, each phone is designed to access the network of one carrier—and one carrier only.

- Don't sign a service contract that lasts longer than one year. Some firms offer two- and three-year deals with what appear to be attractive rates. But considering how far prices have fallen and how much cell-phone technology has improved in the past three years, any contract today will be a terrible deal three years from now. Also, any phone will be obsolete in three years.

  Mike Feazel, managing editor, *Communications Daily*, a magazine for the telecommunications industry.

Get Connected To Government Information

A very helpful site is www.FirstGov. gov. It links you not only to state and local governments, but also to information on hundreds of topics such as starting a business, college loans, Medicare, Customs regulations and even the US budget.

You can get weather, reserve space in a national park...and yes, there's a link to instructions for filing your taxes on-line.

It's probably easier to access filing information at the IRS Web site at www.irs.gov by clicking on "Electronic Services."

Nancy Dunnan, a financial adviser and author whose latest book is *Never Short a Stock on Wednesday and 300 More Financial Lessons You Can't Afford Not to Know* (HarperBusiness).

Bargain Diamonds and Watches

Here's how to get the best deals on jewelry—real or otherwise. Anyone can get jewels fit for a king and a queen on a pauper's income.

Costume Jewelry

Costume jewelry may be one of the best accessory bargains around. You can get jewelry that looks like the real thing—for a fraction of the price.

Save yourself even more money by buying costume jewelry in its off-season. Summer accessories, such as pearls and pastel-colored jewelry, are cheapest in the fall and winter, when you can save up to 30%. Dark-colored jewelry, such as imitation rubies or emeralds, can cost 30% less in the spring and summer.

Providence, Rhode Island, is considered the costume jewelry capital of the world. You can find savings of 50% to 90% off retail prices by visiting the wholesale shops there. For more information, call the state's visitor's bureau at 401-274-1636.

The Real Thing

The best advice in buying real jewelry is to stay away from the mall. Mall stores may charge 20% to 50% more than a discount jewelry warehouse. It's a lot smarter to shop at a discount jewelry store, but you need to be aware of what you are buying. Gems are expensive and you want to make sure that you get what you pay for. When you shop at a discount or other off-price jewelry store, make sure you get a certificate of replacement. This certificate is an appraisal letter, or guarantee, that allows you to return the jewelry if it turns out to be worth less than what was promised.

Jewels of the Season Summer months, like July and August, are the best times to buy real gems. Avoid Christmas time and the pre-wedding season in the spring if you are looking for jewelry markdowns.

Hunt for Wholesale Look in your *Yellow Pages* for a jewelry wholesaler. Wholesalers don't typically sell retail, but some may steer you to a low-cost jeweler, or sell you a stone you can take to a jeweler to have set. The gem is 90% of your cost for a piece of jewelry.

Pawnshop Treasure Many jewelers sell secondhand jewelry at 25% less than the price of a new piece. However, pawnshops often have the best deals on jewelry. You can save 30% or more when compared to buying new jewelry wholesale. But there's no guarantee about quality.

Estate Sales Estate sales are another great place to check for jewelry bargains. Most pieces of jewelry are marked well below their original value. Look in the classified section of your local newspaper for listings of sales near you.

Watches

If you want to buy an everyday watch, your best bet is to head to a discount chain store that carries lines like Seiko and Timex, and sell them for about 20% less than retail watch dealers.

While Christmas and graduation may be the worst times to find a deal on watches, just after these events, in January and July, may be the best time to get a discounted price.

For designer-brand watches at discount prices, call for the Tourneau catalog (800-348-3332, www.tourneau.com). Tourneau carries 45 brands of new Swiss watches as well as some pre-owned designer brands such as Rolex and Piaget.

Compare good deals on the Internet. If you know exactly what you're looking for, you can shop for the best deal by searching for the watch and model number directly via engines such as www.google.com or www.yahoo.com and directly compare prices without leaving your home. If you're not quite sure, and enjoy window shopping, visit these three highly rated on-line stores. Each offers a large selection of fine watches at discounted prices.

Ashford.com (www.ashford.com) Its discounted selection of new and vintage watches ranges from Auguste Remond to Zenith and includes such stars as Bvlgari, Breitling, Cartier, Rolex, Baume & Mercier and Omega. Its "Outlet Center" features special deals (usually discounted at least 50%).

Bluenile.com (www.bluenile.com) A good place to browse through a good selection of medium-priced watches as well as some higher-end watches such as Baume et Mercier and Alfex and others.

Watchzone.com (www.watchzone.com) You'll find most of the familiar brands including Omega, TAG Heuer, Tissot and Wenger.

Let Others Help Pay for Your Wedding

Sponsored weddings allow you to have a lavish wedding without debt. Treat the wedding as a business proposition —and be prepared to shrug off comments about commercialization.

Convince local businesses to supply goods and services—wedding gown, cake, rings, flowers and more—in exchange for advertising on your invitations, in the program and on your wedding Web site...and a display of their products at the reception.

Consensus of people who have arranged sponsorship for their weddings, reported in *The New York Times*.

4

Cheap Eats:
Cutting Costs in the Kitchen

Aisle Aid: Secrets for Supermarket Savings

Shopping at your local convenience store or specialty market may be quick and easy, but ultimately you will lose big by paying consistently higher prices. Supermarkets—retail food centers, which run from midsize to very large—buy food and other household goods in huge allotments, so they have distinct price advantages over small grocers. To take advantage of savings you should understand how supermarkets operate.

Develop Basic Consumer Skills
To really save money when you food shop, you have to know what a good price is. First, you need a baseline cost, or starting point, for each item. Begin by comparing prices of particular food staples such as milk, bread, cereal and meat at several local supermarkets. Bring a calculator and take notes as you go.

You will find that some supermarkets have consistently better prices than others. Some will have better prices on particular items but not on others; others may have higher quality produce or meats or offer a wider selection than their competitors.

Gradually, you will build your own price vocabulary and become better and better at determining what is or isn't a good deal.

Unit Pricing Is There for You

With unit pricing, the price of a specific quantity or amount of a product, such as ounces of spaghetti sauce or number of sheets on a roll of paper toweling, is given on the shelf above or below that product. With that information you can compare costs between one product and another based on a common quantity.

Example: If one bag of potato chips is priced at 10¢ per ounce, and a second is 15¢ per ounce, it's not hard to tell which is the better buy.

Beware: If the price marked on the package with the higher unit cost is lower, it means that the package contains less of the product than the other one.

Unit pricing is now mandated by law in many states. Take advantage of it.

Supermarket Circulars Are for You

Nearly all supermarkets announce food and product sales in weekly circulars, which may also contain coupons for that week. As your knowledge of prices increases, you will quickly recognize which of these offerings are excellent buys.

If for some reason you miss a particular circular, you can pick one up at the supermarket. They're usually stacked near the door. Be sure to ask if you don't see one.

Do Coupons Really Save You Money?

Coupons are paper tickets entitling the holder to a discount, usually cents off, on a particular item. They are issued by manufacturers as well as supermarkets.

Trap: Don't buy an item you neither want nor need just because you have a coupon for it. On the other hand, purchasing a product you often use and want to keep in stock is a very sensible thing to do.

If you have a high-value coupon, it's a good idea to use it to buy the smallest size of that item. It's true that large sizes are usually better buys than small ones, but if you use your high-value coupon, you can get the smaller size item for just a few cents. If it's a double or triple coupon day, you might even get the item for free.

Super On-Line Discounts

On-line coupons can give you discounts on far more products than you find in your local newspaper—plus rebates and freebies.

Try www.coolsavings.com for coupons and www.valupage.com for a list of discounts at your local grocery store. For free product samples, closeout sales and special offers, try www.start sampling.com, www.freesamples.com.

Take a Rain Check

If for some reason your supermarket is out of stock on a sale item, you can usually get a rain check, entitling you to the sale price on that item at a future time. In some states, rain checks are the law. But required or not, most supermarkets are happy to provide them if you ask.

More Coupon Smarts

Double or Triple Your Savings Some supermarkets periodically offer double or triple coupons—they give you two or three times the face value of any coupon. *Bad news:* Many establishments have a $1 ceiling on doubling or tripling.

Organize Your Coupons Coupons sitting in a drawer or crumpled in the bottom of a handbag are useless. Coupons need to be organized and categorized and carried with you when you shop. Small, wallet-sized folders are available with tabbed separators for filling by subject.

Supermarkets Issue and Accept Plastic

Get Your Own Card Supermarkets' cards let you cash checks and give you automated, at-the-register deductions for sale or coupon items (the stores call them clipless coupons).

Credit, Debit and ATM Cards In many supermarkets you may charge your order on your credit card or debit it against your bank account using your ATM card. *Warning:* Hefty additions to your credit card balance will increase your monthly carrying costs and if you don't pay your bill in full, you may be charged transactional fees on your ATM debits.

Timing Is Everything

Avoid shopping just before a meal, when you're hungry. Many things will look delicious, and you'll find yourself purchasing items you might not otherwise consider. Shopping when you're tired at the end of a hard day's work may tempt you to buy expensive prepared food.

Sniffing Out Merchandising Strategies

The goal of any supermarket is to keep the consumer in the store as long as possible, extending a shopper's exposure to displayed goods in the hope of increasing purchases. In contrast, the consumer's goal is to spend as little money as possible in the shortest time. If you familiarize yourself with the following merchandising ploys, you'll be less likely to fall victim to them.

Endcap Sales: Look and Compare

Endcap sales or displays of products at the end of an aisle may not be bargains. They may be displayed before an announced sale begins, so that you end up paying full price because you purchased presale.

Further, these products, though advertised as on sale, may still be more expensive than the competition. The endcap locations, placed some distance from similar products, make it difficult for you to comparison shop.

Endcap products often cost more because supermarkets charge the manufacturer for prime exposure—and those charges are passed on to you.

Look High and Low

Statistics have proven that products displayed on eye-level shelves are purchased much more frequently than those on lower or higher shelves. With this in mind, supermarkets charge food manufacturers to have their products placed in these prime locations.

Better deals for the food shopper are often those brands banished to upper and lower shelves—they don't have added marketing costs to pass on to the consumer.

A Face Isn't Everything

The facing sides of a particular product—such as the front of cereal boxes, displayed in several side-by-side rows—give that product an advantage over a competitor who may have fewer front facings. The more facings a particular product has—five rows of one brand versus two rows of another—the better the product is likely to sell.

Look beyond this marketing technique. Some of the best deals might not be obvious to the eye.

Don't Succumb to Display Trickery

A half-empty shelf doesn't necessarily mean that a product is popular. Supermarkets sometimes remove a few products from a display so you won't think you're the first to buy.

By the same token, loss leaders (large displays of sale items near the door) or other big display sales elsewhere in the store, may be good deals.

Pay Attention to Your Sense, Not Your Senses

Studies have shown that shoppers linger longer and buy more groceries if their supermarket plays background music. The same is true of certain smells. You are more likely to buy cakes and breads if you can smell their fresh-baked aroma.

Be aware that everything from lighting and music to aisle layout and eye-catching displays is carefully planned to encourage impulse spending.

Don't let your senses run your shopping trip. Stick to your list.

Stick to Your List

Be sure to make a shopping list. And don't start it just a few minutes before your trip to the supermarket. Keep a running list in your kitchen. That way, when you discover you're running out of an item, you add it then and there.

Avoid shopping without your list and try to buy only those items you've listed. This will eliminate the danger of impulse buying, one of the most deadly threats to economical food shopping.

Brands Worth Buying

The price differences among brand-name, store-brand and generic foods can range from small to significant, and there are often contrasts in quality as well. When comparing brands, consider both price and ingredients. Read labels and pay attention to the amount of fillers and additives.

Here is some general information on the three basic types of labels you'll find in the supermarket:

Brand-Name Products

Brand-name products are usually the most expensive items in a supermarket. Most consumers believe brand-name products are of the highest quality. Bear in mind, when you buy a brand-name product, you are not only paying for the contents, but also for fancy packaging, store placement and advertising campaigns. However, purchasing a brand name with a coupon or on sale is a good way to get your favorites at lower prices.

Store-Name Products

Store brands usually cost around 15% less than brand names, yet frequently are manufactured by the same company that makes the brand name. But since store brands are not heavily advertised, stores can charge less for them and still make a profit.

Do Generic Products Taste as Good as Brand Labels?

Generic products come in basic, no-frills packaging, usually labeled in black lettering that states simply what the product is, such as dishwasher detergent, sugar or napkins. Generic products are usually the least expensive, but can also be of lower quality or contain additives not found in brand- or store-name products.

You probably won't notice if you switch to generic sugar or chlorine bleach, but you may notice the difference in foods like pickles, pasta sauce and iced tea mix. Still, generics are a great way to save, as long as you're happy with what you're getting.

Packaging Can Fool the Eye

Companies sometimes reduce the amount of a product in a package while maintaining the same size and price. For example, you might find that the five-ounce bag of potato chips you used to buy now contains only four ounces, although the package looks exactly the same.

Manufacturers can trick you into paying the same price for a smaller amount because most customers do not read food labels closely. When your favorite brands come out with different packaging, particularly packaging marked "new and improved," be sure to check the contents weight on the label.

More Supermarket Savvy

The best deals sometimes mean doing a little more work. Following are several ideas to help you be a more price-conscious shopper:

Eye the Scanner

Most stores have scanners that read universal product codes (UPCs). Let the clerk bag your groceries—you watch the register display window to make sure that you are charged the correct amount, particularly on sale items or when you're using coupons. (Some stores give you the product free if you are charged the wrong price.)

Prepare Your Own Food

Be aware that the costliest way to feed yourself or your family is buying prepared foods such as instant pasta with sauce mixes, sandwiches from the deli counter, skinned, boned or stuffed meats, poultry and fish, and salads from the salad bar. With these foods, you are paying for the preparation.

Save a bundle by creating your own meals instead. Plan simple menus. Purchase basic, healthy ingredients such as untrimmed meat, vegetables and fruits, whole heads of lettuce and your own supply of cheeses, eggs, flour, sugar, herbs and spices.

Food Dates that Help You Save

You can sometimes get as much as 50% off a food product that is close to its expiration or sell-by date on the label. Since most items can be safely consumed for a few days after that date, you will be getting an item that may be just as good for half the price.

Skip the Toiletries Aisle

Toiletries, cosmetics and other nonfood items frequently cost more at supermarkets than at discount pharmacies. Supermarkets mark the prices up higher, assuming you won't bother to compare prices or make an extra trip to the drugstore.

Best Bargain Meals for One

Salad Savings
Most supermarkets have salad bars. Although salad bars are expensive for more than one person, they provide a variety of foods from many food groups at a reasonably low cost for singles. And best of all, there's no cooking or waste.

Variety
When you have some time, cook one or two main dishes in large quantities. Freeze what you can't consume in single servings and make a label for each noting what's in it and when it was cooked. If you do this week after week, you will end up with a variety of quick meals to choose from each night.

Think Big to Small
Instead of paying for small and expensive portions, buy foods (particularly meats) in multi-serving packages that can be subdivided and frozen in single servings. Packages of chops, cutlets, beef patties, small steaks or chicken parts cost less in quantities of three pounds or more.

Bulk Buying at Food Warehouse Clubs

Food warehouse buying clubs have sprung up in many parts of the country. These huge, no-frills establishments charge members an annual fee to buy in bulk at discount prices. That usually means large-sized containers, cases or a number of cans or jars packaged together. The markup at buying clubs is

Label Lingo for Smart Shopping

Ingredients on a food label are listed in the order of their volume. This means that a product contains more of the first ingredient on the list than any other ingredient, and the least of the last ingredient.

To determine the best buy, compare ingredients lists on product labels to determine what's inside a jar, package or carton. You may be surprised at the variations you'll find. Take spaghetti sauce, for instance. If the first ingredient in product A is tomatoes and the first in product B is water, product A could be a better deal, even if it costs more.

around 10%, as opposed to 25% at most supermarkets. Warehouse clubs also sell nonfood items, such as appliances, clothes, books and CDs and tapes.

Membership fees range from $25 to as much as $100. Investing this only makes sense if your savings over the year exceed the investment.

Warehouse clubs, such as Sam's, Costco, BJ's and others, rely on high turnover and low overhead to make money.

Rules to Follow

Always Bring a Comparison List Make sure that you can refer to competitive prices from area supermarkets, retail stores, etc. Sometimes the real bargain is your local supermarket. *Tip:* A calculator in your pocket may help you compute the price per can when you consider buying a case of tuna fish.

Always Bring a Shopping List Impulse buying can wreck any savings you find. If you didn't need it when you went to the warehouse, don't buy it.

Buy Only What You Can Store When you buy that case of tuna fish, you should have a place to store it.

Best bets: Look for items you buy regularly, and special sales.

Watch Prices and Merchandising

Don't assume prices are always lower at a warehouse club. Some items may actually cost more than at a supermarket. Compare prices and use your warehouse club as a supplement to, not a replacement for, your regular supermarket.

Like supermarkets, warehouses use clever merchandising to get shoppers to buy on impulse. Loss leaders in bulk are placed prominently at entrances. Free samples of expensive gourmet foods may be offered throughout the store, and multi-packs of books, compact discs, and snack foods are displayed prominently at the ends of aisles.

How to deal with this? Buy only what you can use.

Split Bulk Purchases with Others

If you don't have enough storage space to make buying in bulk practical, think about joining forces with neighbors or friends. Cases of soda or canned goods, or large boxes of paper towels, napkins or toilet tissue, purchased at rock-bottom prices, can be easily divided among several families, resulting in substantial savings for everyone.

Locating a Food Warehouse Near You

Here are a few warehouse chains that have stores around the country:

BJ's Wholesale Club (800-BJS-CLUB, www.bjswholesale.com) has around 85 clubs on the East Coast and one in Ohio. Many stores have their own bakery, meat, produce and deli departments, but most of the food products offered are frozen. The markup on most items is 8% to 10%.

Membership is open to anyone for $40 a year. Stores offer business memberships at $40 (and half-price memberships for up to 99 of the cardholder's associates) but no special business hours. In addition to cash and checks, they accept Discover, MasterCard and Visa. Coupons are also accepted. One-day store passes are available, but there is a 5% nonmember surcharge.

Costco Wholesale (800-774-2678, www.costco.com), incorporating Price Club, has more than 280 clubs in 24 states. A typical store sells an assortment of products from tires and audio equipment to fresh and frozen foods. Some clubs have their own delis, bakeries and produce and meat departments. Costco offers a Double Guarantee—a full refund to any customer not satisfied with membership or any product. Coupons are not accepted.

Costco's membership fee is $45 a year. You can call for an application and directions to the store nearest you. Bring your application and fee to the membership counter at any store or mail them to Costco Wholesale Membership, Box 34535, Seattle 98124-1535. Cash, checks, debit cards and Discover are accepted.

Business memberships are available to owners, managers and directors (plus associates and spouses) of licensed businesses, nonprofit organizations, government agencies and farmers and ranchers. And there are special shopping hours just for business members.

Sam's Club (800-925-6278, www.samsclub.com), owned by Wal-Mart, has more than 430 clubs nationwide. A typical store has more than 3,000 household items in stock. Food sections consist mainly of fresh and frozen meat and produce, but some clubs also have bakery products. The markup on most items is between 8% and 10%, and membership is $35 a year.

Food Label Basics

- Low-fat food has three grams of fat or less per serving.
- Low-sodium food has 140 milligrams or less of sodium…very-low-sodium food, 35 milligrams or less.
- Low-cholesterol foods have 20 milligrams or less of cholesterol and two grams or less of saturated fat.
- Low-calorie food has 40 or fewer calories per serving.
- Reduced-fat food has at least 25% less fat than the original food.
- Light or "lite" food has one-third fewer calories…or one-half less fat than the original food.

Howard Shapiro, DO, whose medical practice specializes in weight control and life management, New York and author of *Dr. Shapiro's Picture Perfect Weight Loss* (Rodale).

Baked Goods: More Bread For Less Dough

The average markup at grocery stores on bread, rolls, cakes and pies ranges from 10% to 50%. At gourmet or private bakeries, the markup can be as high as 75%.

Of course, making your own bread would save you the most money—about 75% off retail prices. But if you don't have the time (or lack the patience) to wait for your bread to rise, here are a few money-saving strategies:

Consider Food Co-Ops

Food cooperatives are small, supermarket-like stores managed and staffed by their patrons. Usually community-based (and sometimes organic), every food co-op operates independently. Products are purchased directly from distributors, resulting in considerable savings for members.

Most co-ops require a one-time membership fee and a commitment to help out periodically as a cashier, shelf stocker or administrator. This is a great way to save cash while getting to know more people in your neighborhood.

To Locate (Or Start) a Food Co-Op Near You
For information on setting up your own grocery co-op, phone the **National Co-operative Business Association** at 800-636-NCBA, or write them at 1401 New York Ave. NW, Ste. 1100, Washington, DC 20005, www.ncba.org.

Twilight Bargains

Consider shopping at night when grocery stores are likely to have completed most of their day's business. In an effort to unload what will be tomorrow's day-old baked goods, many supermarkets and bakeries offer discounts of up to 50% after 5 pm. Day-old bread isn't spoiled. When toasted, for instance, it can be just as tasty as bread straight from the oven. If you don't see these bargains advertised, ask for them.

Thrift Bakeries

Many commercial bakeries collect their unsold products from retail stores and then sell them at greatly reduced prices in their own thrift stores.

Pepperidge Farms operates 86 thrift stores in 23 states east of the Mississippi. The baked goods sold at these thrift stores are either manufacturers' seconds (which fail to meet appearance standards) or market returns (which are approaching their expiration date and have been pulled from retailers' shelves). To locate the Pepperidge Farm thrift store nearest you, call 888-737-7374.

Also try Best Foods Baking Company (800-582-3614), which operates a chain of thrift stores selling day-old products, or Entenmann's (800-356-3314), which runs thrift stores around the country selling imperfect returns and dated goods.

Very Best Deals On Produce

Since good health and nutrition require you to eat a lot of fruits and vegetables, it makes sense to find ways to get the best values at the lowest prices.

Seasonal Fruits

Today, thanks to rapid transport and excellent refrigeration, you can get almost any fruit or vegetable at almost any time of the year. But you pay much higher prices when you buy a fruit or vegetable out of season. You're paying for extensive transportation, frequently from outside the US, and all the middlemen along the way.

Roadside Stands

One of the best ways to get fresh, seasonal fruits and vegetables economically is by shopping at a nearby roadside or farm stand. Open during the local growing season, individual farmers or small growers sell their own produce directly to the consumer.

Prices may be a little higher than supermarket specials, but the extra quality makes it worth every penny. *Trap:* Roadside may be

retail. Occasionally, you will find a roadside stand that is not owned and stocked by a farmer or grower. The proprietor may be an outside retailer who bought the produce from someone else. Or a farmer may be selling, in addition to his own produce, a number of products brought in from elsewhere.

Farmers Market Finds

Farmers markets are a good option for city dwellers and suburbanites to obtain fresh, high-quality fruits and vegetables. Farmers from the surrounding area, as well as some from considerable distances, truck in their produce to one central place, such as a parking lot or a field. They sell their produce right off their trucks or set up portable stands. Because there are usually a large number of farmers involved, shoppers have a wide selection of good, ripened-in-season produce at fair prices.

The best time to shop? If you come early, you get a greater selection. Sweet corn, always popular, may be sold out by mid-afternoon. If you want to get the lowest prices, however, browse through the market during the closing hour. Many vendors are willing to cut their prices and make a smaller profit rather than cart their goods back to the farm. You will sometimes find discounts of up to 50%. To find a farmers market near you, call the US Department of Agriculture's Wholesale and Alternative Markets Program at 202-720-8317 and ask for a copy of *The National Farmers Market Directory*.

At the Supermarket

The supermarket may have some of the best produce bargains around. Particularly early in the day, there will be a good choice of fruits and vegetables in season. And if you choose to pay the price, there will also be a selection of produce from other parts of the country or the world.

Usually, your supermarket will be well-stocked in produce grown in your region or state. And prices for those items nearly always beat farm stands and farmers markets because supermarkets buy more inventory and sell it more quickly.

In New Jersey, for instance, in early summer when blueberries from down-state are in season, blueberries are marketed everywhere. Supermarkets consistently offer the best prices.

The Right Amount

No matter where you buy your produce, if you buy more than you can use before it spoils, you'll lose money.

Shop more frequently and buy only what you can use in a day or two. You will appreciate less crowding in your refrigerator and know that you've gotten the most for your money by consuming your produce in its most edible form.

How to Get Your Produce Super Clean

Much of the produce in your supermarket now comes from outside the US, where health and sanitation standards are not what they are here. For example, 40% of cucumbers in the marketplace come from South America. These crops and many others, such as berries and lettuce, may be irrigated and washed with untreated water carrying E. Coli bacteria.

Wash all produce thoroughly, or you may be putting yourself and fellow diners at risk.

Baby Food

Commercial baby food is expensive and may not be of the quality you wish for your child. But you can easily make your own inexpensive infant food at home by cooking vegetables and starches, and then pureeing them. That way, you can be certain that the ingredients are high quality and you can omit additives such as sugar. All it takes is a good blender and a little extra time.

Use Your Leftovers

You can save money by feeding your baby leftovers if the food is still fresh and appropriately nutritional. Mashed potatoes and squashes, cooked root vegetables such as carrots and beets, small pieces of chicken breast (with a bit of stock added) and soft fruits such as bananas, canned pears or apricots, and apple sauce can be tossed into a blender and pureed.

For recipes: *The Healthy Baby Meal Planner: Mom-Tested, Child-Approved Recipes for Your Baby and Toddler* by Annabel Karmel (Simon & Schuster); *The Well-Fed Baby: Easy Healthful Recipes for the First 12 Months* by O. Robin Sweet and Thomas A. Bloom (Macmillan).

Herbs, Spice and The Best Advice

You don't have to pay high supermarket prices for spices. Try these alternative shopping techniques and create ways to spice up your home-cooked meals for less.

Sources for Seasonings

Many farmers markets carry brand-name, packaged seasonings at prices 25% less than retail stores.

Packaged goods and convenience stores, and even drugstores such as the CVS and Drug Fair chains now sell dried herbs and spices. They offer good selections from lesser-known labels, in convenient jars holding at least twice as much as the usual containers —and the prices are significantly better than at supermarkets.

Share Bulk Buys

Buy in bulk and you might save 70% off the price of smaller bottles of spices. Warehouse clubs and mail-order companies are good sources for bulk herb and spice buys. The San Francisco Herb Company (800-227-4530) sells herbs to the public at wholesale prices. The minimum order is $30.

Remember, however, that open packages of herbs stay fresh for only six months, so don't buy more than you can use or share. A good plan is to arrange with friends and family to buy in bulk, and then divide the herbs into smaller bottles.

Grow, Dry and Grind Your Own

Many herbs are easy and inexpensive to grow. All you need is water, sunlight and care. Chives, parsley and basil are particularly easy to grow, as are tarragon, dill, thyme and numerous others. They can be grown indoors in pots and planters for convenient cooking use, or outdoors, preferably in a place convenient to the kitchen.

Pick your growing herbs throughout the season, bundle them together with rubber bands or string, and hang them in a warm, dry place. Store dried herbs in large, airtight containers and label them with the name and date.

By grinding the herbs you've grown and dried, you'll not only save money but preserve freshness as well. Use a mortar and pestle, coffee grinder or even a pepper mill to grind herbs (and even some spices) just before adding them to a recipe.

Your herbs will be more flavorful and far less costly than those sold prepackaged at any store.

Ethnic Markets

Ethnic markets, most often found in cities where members of ethnic groups tend to congregate and live, are great places to find inexpensive herbs. Asian markets tend to have reasonable prices on all sorts of herbs, from common ginger to the more exotic ginseng. For a market near you, consult your *Yellow Pages* under "Grocers."

Chocolate Values

According to the Chocolate Manufacturers Association, Americans spend nearly $13 billion a year on chocolate and cocoa products, and consume on average about eleven pounds per person a year.

Most people don't plan ahead to buy chocolate, but since many of the best chocolate deals are offered on bulk orders, it often pays to buy in advance.

Holiday Seasons Mean Sales

Good buys on chocolate can be found several weeks before holidays such as Christmas, Easter and Valentine's Day, when chocolate Santas, bunnies, eggs or heart-shaped boxes of chocolates may be as much as 20% off.

However, the best buys of all come immediately after these holidays. Stores must get rid of this specially wrapped and shaped chocolate, just as they have to unload other holiday merchandise, and reductions become drastic. Sales of 50% to 75% are common.

Halloween Competition Lowers Prices

There's no bigger candy-buying holiday than Halloween, when merchants and consumers alike stock up. Pre-Halloween candy specials in both supermarkets and convenience stores, such as CVS and Drug Fair, are widespread because stores count on increased volume and want your business. Competition gets fierce, and you can benefit.

Decide on the candy you wish to offer trick-or-treaters. Then search out the best buys nearest you. Price differences will surprise you, and you can save big.

Buy During the Year

If you're willing to give up the holiday trappings, you can purchase bags of miniature bars and individual chocolate candies any time of year and freeze them.

Hook Up with The Cooks

You might be able to buy cooking chocolate through a local cooking school. Many schools receive discounts for buying in bulk. Check in the *Yellow Pages* under **Cooking Schools**. Your efforts could pay off, particularly if you do a lot of baking at home.

How to Buy Great Coffee

Coffee comes in many different forms and can vary significantly in taste and price. High-quality, gourmet coffee with better beans and extra flavor costs a good deal more than traditional brands.

Freshness Counts

Freshness is as important a consideration as price, since fresh beans make the best coffee. Coffee that has been stored for a long time, although often less expensive, is not necessarily a bargain. Old beans have lost much of their flavor in storage, and the coffee they produce won't taste as good.

Note: Fresh coffee beans can be preserved by storing in your freezer for as long as six months. Grind only what you need directly from the frozen beans. If you grind enough for a few days, you can keep the ground coffee frozen until needed.

Paying for Packaging

Coffee is commonly packaged in one of three ways: Cans, prepackaged or self-service bags, or foil-wrapped bricks. Bricks and cans of coffee tend to sell for the same price, but buying bricks will save you about 10% over cans. That's because most cans contain 11 to 15 ounces of coffee while bricks contain 13 to 16 ounces, costing you less per ounce.

Don't be misled by the rich aroma that comes from self-service coffee grinders at the supermarket. Though the price of this freshly ground coffee is higher than prepackaged, the beans are often of the same quality as those in the cans. Bricks are decidedly the best buy.

Mail-Order Gourmet

Mail-order coffee companies offer some of the best deals in gourmet coffee and some of the most delicious choices. Check the prices at Northwestern Coffee Mills (800-243-5283).

According to Forbes.com, the "best coffee" is produced by Hawaii's Koa Plantation (866-562-5282, www.koacoffee.com). You can join their Coffee Club for regular shipments, with savings, of 100% Kona coffee. Special sales are offered through their Web site. Forbes warns consumers not to buy "Kona blends" that may combine Kona beans with inferior beans from other sources.

Best Low-Priced Wines

The taste and aroma of a fine wine should be complex and mix well. The blend should be smooth so that no one characteristic overshadows another. Poor wine is raw, with obvious, sharp tastes. While it's true that the price of a wine is often an indication of its quality, you can buy some excellent wines for less than $15 a bottle, which is considered a bargain by experts and wine lovers alike.

Bear in mind that tastes are very personal. But if you're willing to taste a number of wines, you can find bargains that you'll enjoy again and again. Here are some suggestions for good quality wines which are reasonably priced.

Bordeaux (red): Chateau de la Cour d'Argent, France; Chateau Ferrande Graves, France; Chateau Tour-Prignac Medoc, France; Chateau Jonqueyres Bordeaux Superieur, France.

Cabernet Sauvignon (red): Hess Select Cabernet Sauvignon, California; Hawk Crest Cabernet Sauvignon, California; Haywood Cabernet Sauvignon, California; Black Opal Cabernet Sauvignon, Australia; Richemont Cabernet Sauvignon, France; Concha y Toro Cabernet Sauvignon, Chile.

Chardonnay (white): Beaulieu Vineyard Chardonnay, California; Napa Ridge Chardonnay, California; Hess Select Chardonnay, California; Oxford Landing Chardonnay, South Eastern Australia; Concha y Toro Chardonnay, Chile; Joseph Drouhin Laforet Chardonnay, France.

Chianti (red): Badia a Coltibuono, Ceta Mura Chianti, Italy; Cecchi Chianti Classico, Italy; Fattoria di Basciano, Italy.

Merlot (red): Forest Glen Merlot, California; Turning Leaf Merlot, California; Heron Merlot Vin de Pays, France; Dulong Merlot Vin de Pays, France; Pravini Merlot Trentino, Italy; Concha y Toro Merlot, Chile.

Pinot Noir (red): Talus Pinot Noir, California; Robert Mondavi Pinot Noir, California; Bridgeview Pinot Noir, Oregon; Joseph Drouhin Laforet Bourgogne Pinot Noir, France.

Sauvignon Blanc (white): Beringer Sauvignon Blanc, California; Canyon Road Sauvignon Blanc, California; Indigo Hills Sauvignon Blanc, California; Martine Sauvignon Blanc, France; Seaview Sauvignon Blanc, Australia.

Kitchen Counter Cost Cutters

- Instead of buying cooking spray, save your butter wrappers and use them to grease your cooking pans.

- Use oven racks as a cheap alternative to cooling racks. Simply place the racks on bricks, cups or anything that works as a prop, and wait for your cookies to cool.

- Use toothpaste instead of silver polish. It's less expensive, but just as effective.

- Stick your sponges in the dishwasher every time you run it. They will last up to a month longer, and you'll kill germs too.

- Divide batter into smaller or shallower pans to reduce baking time and save money on gas or electricity.

- Dough bakes faster in glass than in metal. When using glass cookware, reduce the oven temperature by 25 degrees.

Quality Cookware For Less

For deals on some of the highest quality cookware available, order a free **Chef's Catalog** (800-338-3232), which offers specials throughout the year. Chef's Catalog also has retail stores in Chicago and Highland Park, both of which have sales of 10% to 30% off in March, September and November. www.chefscatalog.com.

Knives: Slicing for a Bargain

Everyone needs a good set of kitchen knives. If you invest in quality, high-carbon stainless steel or forged-carbon knives and take care of them, they should last you a lifetime.

How Many Knives Do You Need?

Don't waste money on a kitchen full of cutlery. Most chefs use only four basic knives: A serrated or bread knife (used for slicing bread and cakes), a paring or utility knife (used for peeling and trimming), a chef's knife (used for chopping vegetables, fruits, nuts and herbs) and a slicing knife (used for carving meat and slicing large fruits and vegetables).

Invest in Quality Names

Quality knives cost more than their cheaper counterparts, but the extra money is well spent. Investing in well-respected brands like Henckels, Wusthof-Trident, Victorinox, Sabatier and Chicago Cutlery will save you money over time because you may never need to buy another knife.

Know Where the Knives Are

Restaurant-supply stores don't sell only to restaurants. Individual customers are frequently welcome and discounts can be up to 70% off department store prices on high-quality knives. Find a supplier in your yellow pages under "Restaurant Equipment and Supplies." Garage sales, estate sales and auctions are other places to look for low-cost, high-quality knives with names you recognize.

Hold Out for the Holidays

The holidays are a great time to buy knives. Discounts are typically 20% off regular prices.

Maintain Your Knives

Buy a wooden cutting board and use it—just make sure to clean it thoroughly with soapy water after each use. Cutting on countertops and stone or plastic cutting boards can damage knives. Store your knives in a wooden block (cutting edge up) or on a magnetic strip on the wall.

Dishy Deals

There is no good reason to ever pay full price for cookware, since sales and deals abound. In April and May—pre-wedding season—department stores offer the year's best savings on cookware and dinnerware. You'll find a good selection for as much as 50% off suggested retail prices.

The Experts Know

Restaurant-supply stores usually offer prices 30% to 60% lower than department stores. Look in the *Yellow Pages* under "Restaurant Suppliers and Equipment" to find a store near you, or ask your favorite restaurants where they buy their supplies.

Restaurant Closings

Over 50% of restaurants close in their first year of business. Many have going-out-of-business sales at which you can buy cookware and dinnerware at rock-bottom prices. Look for signs in your neighborhood, and keep an eye out for public notices or classified ads in the newspaper.

Dinnerware Outlets

Many of the most popular dinnerware brands have their own outlet stores that offer overstocked and out-of-date items at significant discounts. Call these companies for their outlet locations, or look for dinnerware stores at an outlet center near you:

- **Corning/Cornelle** (800-999-3436, www.worldkitchen.com)
- **Crate and Barrel** (847-272-2888, www.crateandbarrel.com)
- **Dansk** (914-697-6400, www.dansk.com)
- **Fitz and Floyd** (800-243-2058, www.fitzandfloyd.com)
- **Mikasa** (800-489-2200, www.mikasa.com)
- **Royal Doulton** (732-356-7880, www.royal-doulton.com)
- **Pfaltzgraff** (800-999-2811, www.pfaltzgraff.com)
- **Vileroy & Boch** (609-734-7800, www.vileroy.com)

Sterling Silver Savings

There are several ways to buy sterling silverware that are less expensive than running out to the local department store. And, although sterling is an expensive investment, once you buy it, it can be passed down through generations.

Buy More for Less

If you're planning on buying your new sterling silver at a retail store, consider waiting until May or November for discounts of up to 40%. And ask if there are discounts for buying larger quantities.

How Much Will You Use It?

If you're planning to invest in a full set of sterling, ask yourself the following questions before you buy:

❑ Will you be inheriting the family silver? If your parents don't use their silver much and are planning on leaving it to you, would they be willing to let you use it now? If not, do you want to buy silver that will match their pattern so you will eventually have a larger matching set?

❑ Will your silver flatware spend most of its life in a drawer in your dining room? Will you use it frequently for formal entertaining such as luncheons or dinner parties? Will you use it to replace your stainless steel for everyday dining?

❑ Do you mind polishing silver? If you hate the idea of polishing, you probably won't bother to use your silver that often.

❑ Would you prefer a second set of stainless steel? If you don't like the idea of polishing and worrying about silver, but want a special set of flatware for holidays and entertaining, consider buying a second set of stainless for more formal occasions.

Affordable Silverware Replacements

Finding replacement pieces for sterling silverware can be expensive and difficult. For affordable replacements, try calling **Replacements Limited** (800-737-5223; www.replacements.com), which has over 90,000 different patterns in stock.

The cost of a place setting often drops 20% if you buy eight place settings instead of six.

Consider Mail Order

Buying your silverware through the mail may save you 20% to 70% off retail prices. Check prices at your local department store, and then call these catalog companies to find out if you can get the same silver for less through the mail (including the cost of shipping and handling):

- **Albert S. Smyth Company** (800-638-3333, www.albertsmyth.com)
- **Barrons** (800-538-6340, www.barronscatalog.com)
- **Gearys** (800-243-2797, www.gearys.com)
- **Michael C. Fina** (800-288-3462, www.michaelcfina.com)
- **Michael Round Fine China & Crystal** (800-752-6622, www.michael round.com)
- **Nat Schwartz & Company** (800-526-1440, www.natschwartz.com)
- **Ross-Simons** (800-556-7376, www.ross-simons.com)
- **Windsor Gifts** (800-631-9393, www.windsorgift.com)

Discontinued Patterns

Stores sometimes offer great deals on discontinued patterns. But consider buying a couple extra place settings, since it may be difficult and expensive to replace lost or damaged pieces in the future.

Secondhand Silver

Secondhand silverware is probably the best deal. Look for place settings and serving utensils at estate sales, auctions, flea markets, secondhand shops and garage sales.

It is sometimes hard to find a complete set, however, and loose pieces tend to cost less than matching sets. So, for an inexpensive and artistic table setting, consider creating your own unique silverware set out of a variety of mixed-and-matched patterns.

Silverware can also be purchased at antique shows. If your pattern is an old and discontinued one, you may be able to pick up some rare serving pieces. Prices will pretty much be the going rate, however, since dealers know exactly what each piece is worth.

How will you know it's the real thing? All American silverware is marked "sterling." If it doesn't say sterling, it could be imported silver which has different markings. But beware of people trying to pass off silver plate as sterling.

5

Dress Well for Less

Bargain Hunting
For Clothes

Building a wardrobe of basics and staying away from trendy apparel are good strategies when you want to make the most of the money you spend. If you want quality without high cost, there are ways to find what you're looking for and not let the cost of clothing drain your budget.

First Things First

Finding bargains begins with knowing how to shop. Think about what you want or need to buy before actually approaching a store. Then make a checklist of the clothes you want to make up your basic wardrobe. If you shop with this list in hand, you will be less likely to buy something you don't need or won't wear.

When considering an item in a store, ask yourself the following questions:

All About Quality

Remember that a low price is not a deal if you aren't buying a well-made item. If your inexpensive shirt falls apart the first time you wash it, for example, you wasted your money. If you want to make sure that the clothes you're buying are well-made, follow this easy checklist:

❑ Tug gently on the zippers and seams to make sure they are sewn on completely.

❑ Be sure all seams are flat and even, with no puckering.

❑ Check for even, small stitching.

❑ Look at the shoulders and armholes of jackets to be sure that they are wrinkle-free.

❑ Examine zippers to be sure they zip, lie flat and are sewn straight.

❑ Make sure the buttons fit into their buttonholes easily.

❑ Try on pants and skirts to make sure you can sit comfortably in them, and try on shirts to make sure that your arms and shoulders can move freely.

- Will it go with anything else in my closet?
- Do I have anything too much like it already?
- Will I wear it more than once?
- Will it wear well?
- Will it soil easily?
- Does it need special maintenance or dry-cleaning?
- Is it within my budget?
- Is it in the right price range for the type of item it is?

Where's the Sale?

Mass-merchandise stores aren't the only places that have sales. Look for sale merchandise in fine boutiques or high-end department stores. And check every time you shop to be sure you don't leave a store without realizing a sale is in progress. It might be one you wouldn't want to miss.

Most major department stores have permanent sale racks or regular areas where they keep sale merchandise, though the sale rack or section may not be in plain sight. Not surprisingly, a store would rather have you pay full price. If a store does not have a sale section or rack, ask when their next sale will be.

A store does not have to have a storewide sale to have sale items. You can find clothes on sale all the time, especially if certain items are overstocked.

Don't be afraid to ask a high-end store if there are any items on sale. Many stores keep the past year's merchandise on sale for a fraction of the original prices. In fact, savings of 50% to 80% off of original (or sometimes off already reduced) prices means that you can wear last season's haute couture for the same price as this season's bargain brands.

The Best Times to Shop

Certain times of the year are better than others for buying various items for your wardrobe. Sales are most prevalent when a new season of clothing is due into the stores. A great sale time is in January, just after the Christmas shopping rush and just before spring apparel arrives. Most department stores and boutiques have preseason sales in July for fall clothing and March for spring fashions. Also, stores tend to hold theme sales during holidays such as Presidents' Day or Mother's Day.

Women's Clothing

Women's clothing goes on sale year-round. During each sale period you can find markdowns of almost 50%.

Dresses December and January are the best sale months for holiday dresses, while February is the month for resort dresses and formal wear. Spring dresses usually go on sale in May, with even further markdowns in June and July. In August you can get big discounts on summer dresses, and October is the sale month for fall designs.

Lingerie Valentine's Day is at the heart of lingerie sales, which run from mid January to mid-February and provide up to 30% savings. Christmas and Mother's Day are also big sale times for intimate apparel.

Victoria's Secret (800-888-8200) is probably the most popular lingerie catalog around. You can receive great catalog savings right after Christmas, and the catalog prices are almost 20% lower than Victoria's Secret retail store prices.

Shoes

Women's Shoes go on sale twice a year, as the new shipments of seasonal shoes arrive. Department stores have preseason sales in July for fall shoes and in February for spring fashions. At the same time, they feature closeouts on shoes from the season that's ending. So, you can find bargains on sandals in July and suedes in February.

Men's Shoes Find great prices in men's shoes twice a year when wholesalers dump their overstock on retailers. June is the time for spring and summer shoes, and October for fall and winter shoes.

Coats and Jackets

The later in the season you shop for coats and jackets, the lower the price will be. After Christmas, discounts on winter coats can be as much as 70% off. And in February and March, you can find great deals on winter sportswear. What's more, you can save an extra 25% on ski jackets if you choose a man-made filling instead of goose or duck down. Man-made fillings will keep you just as warm and are machine washable.

Swimwear

You'll get the best deals on swimwear at the end of the season, and since bathing suits don't take up much space in your closet, you can buy in the fall for the next year. If you look for classic styles, you'll always be in fashion. Buying ahead may not make as much sense if you're shopping for children, however, since it's very difficult to predict the right size 10 months in advance.

If you're shopping by mail, Victoria's Secret offers some great swimwear options for women. And J.Crew (800-562-0258) sells fashionable and affordable swimwear for men and women. Don't forget to check out their catalogs and the catalogs of other sportswear retailers for big end-of-the-season clearance sales.

One advantage of buying from a catalog is that you can return a suit if it doesn't fit right—something you often can't do if you buy a bathing suit in a store.

When Designer Clothes Are Worth the Price

Reasons for buying designer clothes:

❏ Fashion is very important to you.

❏ You discover a particular designer whose work fits you well.

❏ They are often better made than most off-brand clothing (but check carefully before you buy).

❏ They use fabrics and tailoring that drape on the body better.

❏ They command a better resale price when you send them to a consignment shop.

How to Spot A Phony Sale

Sales are so common that we often forget to check whether or not they are really a bargain.

Sometimes a markdown of 50% off is actually just a reduction in an artificially inflated list price. For example, if an item's original price is 150% higher than it should be, a 50% markdown still makes the item overly expensive and not a good deal. Ignore the promise of a discount and focus on the price you will actually pay.

To determine what a good price is, compare prices at different stores that offer sales on the same kind of merchandise. A store that is having a 20%-off sale could have much better deals than one claiming to have a 50% discount. The best way to ensure you're getting a good price is to do your homework by researching prices and proposed markdowns before you buy.

A second advantage is being able to try the bathing suits on at your own leisure. You can order three or four different styles and see which best complements your figure—in the comfort of your own bedroom, not a group fitting room or tiny cubicle with harsh lighting.

Flattering Looks for Hard-to-Fit Men

Too many men overlook the importance of how to wear their clothing. Here's how to look your best:

Shirts

Dress Shirts A cheap shirt makes even the most expensive suit look bad. Use collar stays. Have shirts starched every other time they are laundered.

Choose the right collar: A hefty man should choose pointed collars —ones with a low band height. Spread collars, which usually have high bands, add a chin or two to a man who already has enough.

If you have a skinny neck, choose spread collars.

Casual Shirts Large men should choose shirts with hems that are even at the bottom. Then wear casual shirts untucked.

Suits and Sports Jackets

Smoother Silhouette Don't put anything in outside jacket pockets— and keep jackets closed.

To prevent wrinkling: Buy fully lined garments made of super-100 or 120-wool fabric. These fabrics have a smooth surface and tend to recover the fastest.

Overweight Men Avoid stretch fabrics that cling to the body. Natural fabrics—wool and silk—drape better.

Also: Avoid three-button coats. They are not flattering to portly men. If you want that three-button look, choose a jacket with wide lapels to balance the buttons.

Helpful: Lower jacket buttons…longer jackets…shoulder padding.

Large Behind No vented jackets.

Perspire Heavily Choose natural fabrics. They breathe better than synthetics. Avoid double-breasted jackets—they need to be closed to look good.

Pants

Make Sure the Rise of Your Pants Is Correct Incorrect rise—the distance from crotch to waistline—hinders walking and overall comfort.

Add Extra Crotch Lining It can add to the life of the suit for muscular and heavy men, who often have large thighs that rub together. That wears out the crotch.

Cuff Pants They look neater...hold a crease better...and cling less.

Big-Waisted Men Rigid waistbands and double buttons.

Also buy: Belts at least 1½" wide—to keep the waistband of your pants from rolling over your belt...pleated pants—straight-front pants draw attention to your waist.

Accessories

Shirts and ties are where you should splurge. It is hard to distinguish between a $500 and a $2,000 navy suit. But accessories catch the eye and show your style.

Shoes and Belt Should Match It's basic—but if you forget, you'll look like you dressed in the dark.

Tie Smarts...

- **Right length.** Buy long ties if your neck is 17" or larger to ensure they reach the belt buckle. Never go short.
- **Right-sized knot.** If you have a long, thin neck, stay away from big knots. A simple overhand knot works best.
- **Dimple the knot.** Your tie will keep its shape better. *How:* Place your thumb on the center back portion of the tie after you put the wider part through the loop. When you tighten the knot, press with your index finger in front, applying enough pressure to make a dimple.

Tailoring

Fit comes first—a great designer isn't for you if his/her clothes don't fit.

Look for Stores with Lifetime Alteration Policies Just because something fits today doesn't mean it always will. Clothes stretch...and men's bodies change. If something no longer fits, fix it.

Custom-Made Suits Made-to-measure clothing now takes less than three weeks to make. It's a great option for difficult-to-fit men and costs only a bit more than a quality off-the-rack suit. Custom prices start at around $800.

Michael Duru, a third-generation tailor known as "the difficult fit guru." He is a manager at Rochester Big & Tall Clothing, 1301 Sixth Ave., New York 10019, and a fashion consultant to the movie and television industries.

Women Pay More Unless…

Most women's clothing is more expensive than men's. Many women know the difference exists, they just don't have a solution.

Crossing the Fence
Consider evening the odds by shopping for women's clothes in the men's department. Running shoes and general athletic wear are great items to look for, as are basics such as sport socks and gloves. Oxford shirts and sweaters may be as much as 20% less expensive, and casual slacks will be cheaper.

Clothes for All Sizes
Larger-size women can often find a great selection of slacks and sweaters for a small percentage of the cost of clothing in the plus-size stores.

Petite-sized women may want to consider looking in the young men's or boy's department for smaller clothing that costs even less than in the men's department.

Maternity Wear
The men's department is also a great place to buy inexpensive maternity wear. Men's large shirts and sweatpants, which are roomy and comfortable, can cost 10% less than traditional maternity garments.

Shopping for Shoes

Department stores and discount chains tend to have the lowest prices on shoes. But when you shop for shoes, comfort should be your number-one priority.

Shoes made of synthetic materials, such as plastic or rubber, don't let your feet breathe the way leather does. And poorly made shoes will not wear well. They can even permanently damage your feet or posture.

Your best bet is buying good, medium-priced shoes that are comfortable and classic in appearance (so they won't go out of style for years to come).

Getting the Perfect Fit
Don't damage your feet by wearing a pair of shoes that doesn't fit well. A shoe fits well when your toes lie flat without being squeezed together, your heels fit closely, the sole of your foot rests comfortably on the sole of your shoe and the arch of the shoe is the same as the arch of your foot.

Don't make the mistake of believing that your shoes will stretch to fit if they're not comfortable when you try them on, or that they can be shrunk. If a store doesn't have your size, don't let yourself be persuaded to buy the next bigger or smaller size.

Here are some other useful tips:

- Most people have one foot that is larger than the other, and it's best to buy shoes the size of your larger foot.
- When you go shoe shopping, wear the socks or stockings that you are likely to wear with the new shoes. It's frustrating to find that you can't fit thick, warm socks into your new winter boots.
- Buy your shoes at the end of the day when your feet are a bit larger.
- If you haven't had your feet measured since you were a teen, your next visit to the shoe store is the perfect time. You might find you've been buying the wrong size.
- Be sensible when you buy shoes. Most people have a closet full of shoes, but only one favorite pair they wear all of the time. When you find shoes you live in, buy an extra pair.

Shoes for Seniors
Walking shoes may be the safest shoes for seniors to buy. They provide good support and traction. And shoes that lace up or tie, rather than slip on, are much safer and provide more support. What's more, shoes that lace can be easily fit for orthotics, braces or swollen feet.

People who aren't steady on their feet should avoid wearing slick leather soles on carpets, polished wood or tiled floors—or in the rain. And finally, shoes like slippers or ballet flats provide little support and can lead to falls and broken bones.

What You Can Repair—And What You Can't

Don't waste money by assuming that your shoes or boots have outlived their useful life. The following checklists will let you know if you can revive a favorite pair or if it's time to dispose of them.

Keep shoes and boots if:

- **The problem is a broken zipper.** Most shoe-repair stores can replace broken zippers. And since boots are a little more costly than the average shoe, fixing them is worth the time and cost of getting them repaired.
- **They have a flat, stitched-on sole.** Stitched-on soles can be easily repaired by a shoemaker.
- **Your heel breaks.** Heels, including stilettos, can be reworked by your neighborhood shoe-repair shop.
- **The calf of a high boot has stretched.** Some boots can be altered to fit by a repair shop. Sometimes the store where you bought the boots can send them to their own shoemaker or back to the manufacturer for alterations.

Throw them away if:

- **The fabric covering the inside of the heel is damaged and cannot be mended.** Foot support depends on how securely your heels are held, so don't keep shoes that are too loose.
- **There's a hole in the upper, which is the part of the shoe you see.** Unlike clothing, it is almost impossible to sew a torn shoe.
- **The rubber sole molded to the upper of your shoe breaks.** Rubber cannot be mended easily, and once the foundation of a shoe deteriorates, the rest is sure to go.
- **There's a stain that cannot be removed.** Examples are oil stains from the street, cooking stains and salt stains.
- **Your sneakers still smell even after you have washed them.** Saving smelly sneakers can lead to worse problems, such as the fungal virus called athlete's foot.

How to Buy Comfortable Shoes

- Look for soft, flexible shoes with cushioned insoles. Avoid vinyl or plastic.
- Pick low-heeled, non-spiked shoes.
- Make sure you have enough toe room. You should be able to wiggle all your toes when wearing a shoe.
- Make sure shoes fit your heels comfortably and do not slip.
- Have your feet measured periodically. Sizes can and do change.
- Try on shoes when your feet are not swollen. *Also:* Wear the thickest socks you would use with each pair you are considering.

From: *Mayo Clinic Health Letter*, 200 First St. SW, Rochester, MN 55905.

Hot Tips on Accessories

Like most apparel, accessories are priced lowest toward the end of a season. But you can also find pre-season sales where you can save up to 30% off normal retail prices.

Gloves and Scarves

July is the sale time for chiffon scarves and straw hats. December and January are the times for big discounts on winter accessories such as wool scarves, gloves and hats.

Off-price chain stores such as T.J. Maxx, Syms and Marshalls may offer the largest savings on accessories. But small accessory boutiques are also great places to check for deals. Many boutiques

Extend the Life Of Your Shoes

Follow this easy checklist to make your shoes last as long as possible:

❏ Let your canvas shoes air dry. Drying them in the clothes drier will speed up the aging process.

❏ Don't wear your leather shoes after the roads have been salted in winter. Salt can eat away at the shoes, as well as bleaching or discoloring them.

❏ Always waterproof your suede or leather shoes.

❏ Use a wire-bristle brush to keep your suede or nubuck shoes looking brand-new.

❏ Put rubber soles on the bottom of your leather soles. Rubber will wear much more slowly than leather, especially on hard pavements or city streets.

❏ Don't wait until your heels have worn down completely to replace them. That will be too late.

❏ Use shoe trees to help shoes retain their proper shape.

❏ Keep your shoes in their original shoe box to protect them from dust and scuffing.

❏ Let your leather shoes dry naturally. Drying them on a heater can burn or destroy the leather.

❏ Stuff your wet shoes with paper or cloth so that they will retain their shape.

have frequent sales and offer a wide variety of classic styles. If you stick with the basics for your wardrobe, you are less likely to waste your money.

Socks and Stockings

For slightly imperfect socks and stockings, One Hanes Place offers a variety of styles, sizes and colors at 50% off department store prices. Call 800-522-1151 for a catalog.

Fortunately for men, socks are not a pricey issue. But if you're looking for a deal, try buying socks at one of the many off-price department stores, like Syms, or at mass-market stores like Wal-Mart or Kmart.

You can also buy socks and stockings at warehouse outlets such as Costco, Sam's or BJ's. They carry brand names at reduced prices, though they may feature different brands at different times.

Briefcases, Portfolios and Handbags

The best time to buy briefcases and portfolios is in January and July during the end-of-season clearance sales, when prices are 25% to 50% off. Father's Day and graduation season are also big sale times for briefcases and portfolios, although savings may be slightly less.

Leather products tend to be pricey, but you can find some high-quality, below-retail bags and cases at high-end leather outlet stores such as Coach (800-223-8647) and Bally (800-332-2559). The best prices tend to be on overstock or closeout items, including items in trendy colors.

Consider Man-Made Materials The best alternative to buying a high-priced leather bag is to purchase one in canvas or a man-made material. Durable and generally waterproof, this type of bag is usually available for $50 or less.

For well-made canvas or nylon totes with shoulder straps, Eddie Bauer (800-645-7467 for store locations, 800-426-8020 to order from the catalog) is a great place to shop. Or check out L.L. Bean (800-341-4341).

How to Buy a Handbag Handbags are usually 20% to 50% off during the end of July and August, and just before Christmas, when retailers are trying to make room for new merchandise. Sometimes department stores and specialty stores carry a house brand that costs around 20% less than a designer label. Instead of buying a bag with a name you recognize, look for a no-name version or designer copy.

You'll also want to think about what size bag you need before you buy. The fastest way to destroy a purse is to overstuff it with junk. If you know you carry a lot in your bag, don't buy a cute, petite bag that won't even hold your wallet. Consider buying a backpack or big shoulder bag and save yourself aggravation and money.

Best Finds in Wedding Dresses and Formal Wear

Buying formal wear does not have to be a budget-breaking proposition, even though it tends to be the most expensive clothing there is.

Outlet Stores on the Internet

The best advice for saving money on your fancy clothes is to shop at outlet stores or on the Internet. David's Bridal (800-399-BRIDE, www.davidsbridal.com) is a 38-store chain that stocks wedding gowns, bridesmaid dresses and other apparel the wedding party may need. Sizes range from 4 to 26, and you can save almost 50% off what you might pay at a retail store.

Bridal Bonanza

If you're in the market for a wedding dress, consider planning a February trip to Boston. Filene's Basement (617-348-7934) has an annual blowout wedding gown sale. The sale lasts for only one day, and runs from 8 am to 7:30 pm. Filene's suggests calling at the end of January for the specific sale date.

Merchandise goes fast. The process is basically run and grab. When the store opens on the day of the sale, hordes of women run for the racks, some grabbing 20 gowns or more. Popular sizes go fast, but selection and prices are incomparable.

Used Formal Wear

Consider buying secondhand formal wear if you want to save lots of money. *But beware:* If you're shopping for a special occasion, such as a wedding, you want to make sure that the amount of cleaning and alteration you'll need doesn't cost more than a new dress or suit would.

Renting Clothes

Renting clothes for special events or occasions can be very cost-effective, especially if you need to wear them only once. Renting designer clothes is also an affordable way to wear styles that would normally cost hundreds or even thousands of dollars.

Rental stores specialize in tuxedos, wedding gowns and general evening attire. Check your *Yellow Pages* under "Bridal Shops" or "Tuxedo Rental and Sales" for stores in your area.

Many rental shops also sell off part of their inventory, which means you can get substantial savings. If you find a rental shop that's having a sale, consider buying a used tuxedo. You'll save almost 80% off the price of a new one.

Making Athletic Shoes Last

To save money and get the most from your athletic shoes, air them out for 24 hours after each use. Pull out the insoles and stuff the shoes with newspapers or paper towels. Place the insoles in a well-ventilated area.

Never leave your athletic shoes in the sun or a hot car, and never toss them into a washing machine. Extreme temperatures will reduce their useful life span.

Also, don't try to resuscitate worn-out shoes by adding new insoles. Most shoe breakdowns occur in the midsole, the wedge of cushioning between the outersole and the upper. Insoles are designed to provide support, not replace the midsole.

When Athletic Shoes Can Be Dangerous

Experts believe that some athletic shoes may not be safe in all environments. In fact, some feel that wearing the wrong kind of sturdy shoe can actually increase the risk of falling, especially for the elderly.

Bulky rubber-soled shoes, like some high-fashion sneakers, can be hazardous when worn on carpet. The heavy rubber toes can get caught in the pile and make it easy to trip. Similarly, flat or worn-down athletic shoes can be dangerous on wet surfaces because they increase your chances of slipping.

Returning Without Regret

Don't be afraid to return something you've bought if you find that you don't want or need it. Unless a store clearly states that there are no refunds or exchanges on an item, it is your right as a consumer to be able to return the item for a credit or refund.

Check Out Return Policies

Stores set their own return policies, which tend to vary from place to place. For example, some stores have a "no questions asked, satisfaction guaranteed" approach, while others require evidence of poor quality or damaged goods. Here are some factors to be aware of:

- What the time limit on returns is. It's usually between seven days and six months.
- Whether the store offers a full refund or store credit only. Some stores allow no refunds or exchanges on sale items or clothing that has been worn.
- If the store takes returns only if you have a receipt, or if a receipt is not necessary.

Return policies should be posted at the register or on your receipt, but if you don't see the policy anywhere, ask the clerk to write it down for you. Salespeople and policies change frequently. You want to make sure you have proof of what you were told, so that if you do return the item, there will be no room for disagreements.

A Higher Authority

If you want to return something and are told it's against the store's policy, don't take no for an answer. Ask to speak with the manager. If you offer a good explanation, most stores will go along with your request.

Keep Your Receipts

Keep your clothing receipts to ensure that you'll get back what you paid if you decide to return something. It's a good idea to file them together so they're easy to locate.

If you buy an item at full price and it goes on sale before you return it, you'll need to have your receipt to get a full-credit refund. Otherwise, you'll get back only the sale price amount.

Take Advantage of Customer Service

If you are having problems dealing with a chain store's return policy, you have the option of calling nationwide customer service.

Many companies have toll-free numbers. The company representative may accept a return that the individual store would not.

Care for Your Clothes, And Save a Dime

Your best bet in caring for your clothes may be giving them a vacation from cleaning. Before you decide it's time to launder or clean a garment, air it out for a couple of days and then brush it with a lint removal or pet hair removal brush.

Care Labels and Your Clothes

Best kept secret: If you follow the cleaning instructions on the care label of a garment and it shrinks or the dye runs, you can return the item and ask the store for a replacement, exchange or refund. The Federal Trade Commission's Care Labeling Rule states that manufacturers must tag their textile clothing with at least one safe cleaning method. The label should also provide any necessary warnings about how not to clean the item. Labels are not required on clothing, shoes or accessories made of leather.

Choosing a Dry Cleaner

Experts believe that, like shopping for your clothes, doing a little homework can save you money and time.

- Choose a dry cleaner that has been recommended by someone you trust.
- Ignore stores which claim to be French cleaners. The term is meaningless.
- Find out about the quality of cleaning. Ask whether garments such as fine silks are hand-finished.
- Check out the pricing policy.
- Always check your clothes before removing them from the cleaning facility. A cleaner should redo an item at no charge if it was not cleaned or pressed to your satisfaction.

Help Your Dry Cleaner Help You

If you're bringing stained clothing to your dry cleaner, don't assume all stains will be noticed. Draw attention to the stains yourself. If you've already tried to remove a stain, own up to it. What you've put on the garment may affect what the cleaners can then try to do.

Skipping the Dry Cleaner

A new option for cutting dry-cleaning costs is a home dry cleaning kit. You can find a kit, which includes cleaning supplies for

Wedding Dress Prices Are Negotiable

Competition among bridal salons is high. If you find a gown you like in a bridal magazine, write down the model number. Then call several bridal shops and ask for a price quote. Be sure to let each shop know the lowest bid you've been quoted.

Challenging each store to beat the lowest price can save you as much as 20% off the regular retail price of your dress.

Be Flexible On Fabrics

A pure silk evening dress may be the most luxurious option, but you can save hundreds of dollars by choosing a dress made out of a less expensive fabric.

Consider polyester shantung, a fabric that looks and feels like silk, but costs far less. Polyester is also more durable, more stain-resistant and less likely to snag.

12 garments, in most supermarkets or drugstore chains for about $12. *Caution:* Test the kit's spot-removal process on a like fabric before using it on a favorite garment—it could do more harm than good.

Steam Away Dry-Cleaning Bills

To save money on costly dry-cleaning bills, consider stretching the time between cleanings by using an inexpensive garment steamer.

Steaming your clothing can remove wrinkles and unwanted puckering or creases. It can also help protect your clothing from dry-cleaning chemicals and the wear and tear caused by the cleaning process. *Warning:* You'll need to use dry cleaning to remove perspiration, dirt and stains.

An Alternative to Ironing

Some experts believe that steaming is safer for your clothing than ironing. With a steamer, you aren't placing the extreme heat of an iron directly on your clothing. Therefore, you are protecting your garments from burns and discoloration. Also, irons tend to make sharp creases in clothing that you may not want.

What to Look for in a Steamer

Two types of steamers you may want to consider are the full-sized home steamer and the smaller, easy-to-pack travel steamer.

A full-sized steamer can run from $150 to $300. The amount of money you will save in dry-cleaning bills by using the steamer will save you money in the long run.

A full-sized steamer is what most clothing stores use to remove the evidence of creases from freshly unpacked garments. Placing the head of a steamer in the inside of a shirt can remove all the creases and wrinkles almost instantaneously. Experts say that this type of steamer is the most effective, and some prefer it to ironing.

But you may also want to consider a travel-sized steamer. Travel-sized steamers are small (so they're easy to pack), good for quick touch-ups and cost as little as $30. They can come in handy when you're on business trips or vacation to help cut the expense of hotel dry-cleaning bills.

A Few Steamers Worth Trying

Here are a few steamers, both full-sized and travel-sized, you may want to consider. Prices range from $30 to $200, but you can probably find stores that have them at a discount. Call for local

store information. If you order by phone, remember to ask what shipping and handling charges will be.

- **Rowenta** DA-55 Steambrush (781-396-0600).
- **Rowenta** DA-56 Steambrush, with crease attachment (781-396-0600).
- **Jiffy** Esteem Hand-Held Travel Steamer (800-525-4339).
- **Jiffy** J-2 Jiffy Garment Steamer (800-525-4339).
- **Brookstone** Dual Voltage Garment Steamer for travel (800-846-3000).
- **Brookstone** Pro Garment Steamer (800-846-3000).

Iron Like a Pro

You can save a lot of money by doing your own ironing, both at home and on the road. Most hotels and motels will provide an iron and ironing board if you request them.

Ironclad Ironing Tips

Here are some very basic ironing tips your mother may never have taught you:

- **Always hang items directly after ironing.** This will ensure that wrinkles don't immediately return. Also, if you wear an item after ironing or steaming without letting it air out and cool down, you may increase the amount of puckering and creasing.
- **Starch should be sprayed only on the underside of a garment.** Allow the fabric to absorb the starch before you begin to iron. Consider rolling the garment into a ball to help the absorption process.
- **If the iron sizzles when it touches the fabric,** the iron is set too high.
- **Most irons have temperature gauges** which show the correct setting for certain types of fabrics. Pay attention to what your iron tells you.

  Synthetics and silks should be ironed on low temperatures (approximately 350 degrees), wool should be ironed at medium to high temperatures and cotton and linens should be set at the highest temperatures (approximately 400 to 425 degrees).

Tips from the Experts

Expert pressers suggest ironing sections of your clothes in the following order:

- **Shirts should be ironed starting with the collar,** then the back yoke, then the cuffs, then sleeves and finally the body. Some say you should repeat ironing the collar once the shirt is completed for a fully finished look. And always take a second glance when you're done to make sure there aren't other touch-ups you need to do.

Don't Trust a Dry-Clean-Only Tag

A dry-clean-only tag can be wrong. Sometimes manufacturers place dry-clean-only tags on their apparel as a way of safeguarding themselves against complaints if something goes wrong in the laundry process.

If you are going to take a risk and launder a garment with a dry-clean-only tag, consider first experimenting with one of your least favorite garments made of the same material. Then, if you aren't satisfied with the results, you haven't compromised your favorite sweater.

One caution: Angora and fancy loose-knit sweaters should always be dry cleaned.

Dry Cleaning Can Be Hazardous to Your Health

Some experts advise that wearing your freshly dry-cleaned clothes can be hazardous to your health.

Consider letting your clothes air outside of their plastic dry-cleaning bags for at least 24 hours before wearing them or putting them in your closet. Some experts feel that airing them for at least a few days in a well-ventilated area, such as your garage, is the safest bet.

The solvent perchloroethylene (perc), used in dry-cleaning, is considered a hazardous air pollutant. Experts say if your clothes are returned to you with a strong chemical smell, take them back and insist that your dry cleaner do a better job—or consider finding a different service.

- **Pants should be ironed starting with the pockets,** then the waistline, followed by the inside portion of the legs and ending with the outside portion of the legs. Using an old handkerchief as a "press cloth" can help avoid the shine some fabrics tend to get when ironed.
- **If your clothes tend to get shiny or dulled by ironing,** try ironing them inside out.

Packing Well Can Save You Money

Packing your clothing carefully and logically can save you money on pressing bills. Example: Put your sweaters and jeans on the bottom of your suitcase because they are the sturdiest, and leave your socks and underwear for last so that you can use them to fill empty spaces and kept the rest of your apparel secure.

Choose Your Suitcase Wisely

You may do best with a hardcover suitcase which offers clothing the most protection. Soft luggage will not protect your clothes from wrinkles, although it is more flexible and therefore more convenient.

Consider traveling with a small carry-on case and a garment bag. Most airplanes and trains have room to hold or hang garment bags in their upright position, allowing your clothes to travel wrinkle-free.

Everything in Its Place

The more tightly packed your garment bag is, the tidier your clothes will stay. Try to buy a garment bag that has extra zippered compartments where you can stash shoes, socks and undergarments, and then you will only have to carry one bag.

- **Packing silks, pants, skirts and dresses in plastic** will protect them from creasing.
- **Folding your clothing lengthwise** will not only save space, but protect the clothing from wrinkles.
- **Wrap your toiletries in leak-proof containers.** If you don't have any available, or don't want to buy some just for a trip, put your shampoo and soaps into gallon-sized plastic bags. This way, if an item opens up due to the altitude of a plane or rough rails of a train, your clothes will be protected from spills.

The Many Faces Of Stains

Before you take a stained garment to the dry cleaner or throw it in the trash, make sure you can't remove the stain yourself using products you have around the house.

Here are some insider tips on how to remove the most frequently occurring stains:

Grass Stains Wash the item in hot water with chlorine bleach. If the stain remains, try sponging the spot with alcohol.

Warning: Use bleach only on bleachable fabrics, or you may increase the damage. If the fabric is non-bleachable, omit the chlorine bleach. If you are worried about damaging the color of an item, dilute the alcohol with two parts water.

Bloodstains Soak the stain in cold water and then rub the fabric with detergent and rinse. You can also use unflavored meat tenderizer to break up fresh bloodstains by applying it to dampened spots.

If the stain does not come out of cotton, polyesters, rayons and linens, try applying a drop of household ammonia and rinse. Blood-stains in wool and silk are best treated by the dry cleaner.

Perspiration Stains Use a prewash stain remover or rub with a bar of soap. When perspiration changes the color of fabric, apply ammonia to a fresh stain and rinse. If the stain is old, try applying white vinegar and then rinse.

Stubborn perspiration stains may be effectively removed if you wash the item in hot water with a product containing enzymes or oxygen bleach. Never wash an item in water that is considered too hot for the type of fabric, however. Always remember to check the care label before washing.

Ink Stains Some inks are impossible to remove, and trying to wash the stain out yourself may actually set it in deeper. If you don't know what kind of ink has stained your clothes, but you know the kind of pen it came from, try calling the manufacturer before you attempt to launder the item. The service department should be able to recommend a solution.

If the ink stains don't come from permanent markers, try pretreating the fabric with denatured alcohol or a prewash stain remover and sponging the area around the stain. For removing ball-point pen ink stains, hairspray may be the least expensive solution.

Red Wine Stains Use a thick layer of salt to draw out the stain. Then rinse the fabric in warm water. Red wine stains on wool and silk can be treated with hydrogen peroxide solution, rinsed and then washed.

Cashmere in the Washing Machine

Some fine wool sweaters, even those made of cashmere, come out best when you handwash them in cold water. Cashmere can also be washed in the machine (inside out) and dried flat (not in the drier).

It Pays to Pamper Your Clothes

How you treat your clothes between cleanings will really make a difference. Make sure to blot up spills before they set into your garments. Allow your clothes to air out before you put them away in a drawer or closet. Don't leave your coat or pants pockets full of junk, which will ultimately stretch and ruin the garment.

And don't forget to give your clothes a rest between wearings. It's not smart to wear the same pair of pants three times a week. Rotate your wardrobe.

Chewing Gum Get rid of stubborn chewing gum by freezing it, either in the freezer or with ice cubes in a plastic bag, and then carefully scrape it off with a dull knife. Be careful not to pull too hard and tear the fabric.

Learning to Sew Can Save You a Bundle

Brushing up on your old sewing skills or learning how to sew is a great way to save money on children's clothing. You can also eliminate hefty tailoring bills by learning how to fix your own hems and zippers.

Pulling Your Threads Together

Consider beginning with a sewing class. Sewing classes are frequently given, for minimal cost, at your local high school, community center or fabric shop.

When You Need a Little Help

If you are a beginner or a seasoned sewer who wants to use your skills to make a little extra money, You Can Make It Inc. may be what you're looking for. You Can Make It Inc. is a free referral service for teachers and students of sewing.

For approximately $36 a month, You Can Make It Inc. will set you up with a local sewing instructor who will teach you to sew, help you find appropriate patterns and supplies for your sewing level, and teach you the basics for achieving your sewing goals.

Or, if you would rather work alone, You Can Make It Inc. will supply you with a series of seven different instructional videotapes for $36.95 each (plus $3 shipping and handling).

You Can Make It Inc. works in conjunction with most of the major pattern companies, such as McCalls and Butterick, so you can learn how to make quality clothes at a reasonable price.

Contact You Can Make It Inc. toll-free at 888-576-2739, or check them out at www.youcanmakeit.com.

Buying a Sewing Machine

If you are a beginner, you don't need a Rolls Royce of a machine. Almost any standard machine will have all the bells and whistles you will ever need and won't send your budget into the red. *Money-saver:* Sears Kenmore.

Places for Patterns

There are a number of magazines and pattern companies that provide monthly publications which include sewing tips, free patterns and information on resources.

Butterick (800-766-3619, mail-order division or technical help line) is one of the best-known pattern companies. They publish two pattern magazines, *Vogue Patterns* and *Butterick Home Catalog*, which you can find at your local newsstand or pattern store. You can also call them toll-free for a yearly subscription or for a listing of other publications they offer, like special sewing books and videotapes.

Butterick also publishes two knitting magazines, *Vogue Knitting* and *Family Circle Easy Knitting*, which you may want to look into for making your own sweaters and accessories.

Make It Last

Following these simple tips when you do your laundry can keep your clothes looking like new for many years to come.

Wash It Right

- **Close all fasteners, zippers and buttons** before you wash.
- **Empty pockets** before you wash.
- **Handwash delicates** or wash them separately in the gentle cycle.
- **Separate colors** (whites, brights, pastels and darks).
- **Wash fabrics whose colors may bleed separately.**
- **Wash terry-cloth towels,** robes and other lint-producing materials separately.
- **Wash very dirty garments, such as those covered in mud or lipstick,** in a separate load to keep them from staining other clothes.

Dry It Right

- **Add a couple of clean, dry towels to small loads** to speed up their drying time.
- **Avoid ironing by using the dryer cycle recommended on care labels.**
- **Don't leave clothes in the dryer** after they are dry.
- **If possible, use a dryer with a moisture sensor,** which automatically turns off the machine when your load is dry.
- **Leave enough room for air to circulate** through each load.
- **Use the permanent press cycle** for garments that can be damaged by excess heat.

Store Your Clothes Carefully

Save money by taking proper care of your clothes.

❑ Store clothes in a dark area that is protected from temperature extremes. Choose a closet or chest, not an attic or basement.

❑ When you use cedar chests or wooden hangers, make sure clothes do not touch the wood because it contains oils that can stain fabric. Try to build shelves or racks that let you store clothes at a fair distance (six inches or so) from the walls.

❑ Never starch clothing before storing.

❑ If you're using mothballs, keep them in loosely fastened cloth bags so the chemicals in them do not damage your clothes.

❑ Don't hang clothes in plastic bags because they can mildew. Instead, use an old sheet as a dust cover.

❑ To get rid of pilling that can make jackets and sweaters look old and worn, buy a sweater comb or sweater stone to pull pills off a garment without damaging it. An alternative is masking tape, which can remove many pills. But never use a razor because it weakens fibers and can ruin a garment.

6

Save Money All Around the House

Controlling Your Energy Costs

Here are suggestions on cutting your energy bills without compromising your family's comfort. They cover heating, cooling, appliances and lighting.

Heating/Cooling

Use a Programmable Thermostat to maintain the temperature in your home.

It automatically adjusts the heat or central air-conditioning—which is much easier than trying to fine-tune it manually every night before bed or every time you leave the house.

Cost: $40 to $100 per year.

Potential savings: 20% on heating and cooling bills, which average $2,000 per year for a single-family home located in the Northeast.

Important features: Storage of at least six temperature settings a day...manual override without affecting the remainder of the

daily or weekly preset program schedule...backup battery so you won't have to reprogram the timer after a power failure.

Lighting

Switch to Compact Fluorescent (CFL) Bulbs   They use 80% less energy than standard incandescent bulbs and last up to seven years.

CFLs have shaken their reputation for poor-quality light and limited fit in home fixtures. Now they're readily adaptable to any fixtures and are made by reputable manufacturers.

Cost: $5 to $15 per bulb—but many local utility companies discount them or offer rebates of up to 50%.

Potential savings in energy costs: $50 per bulb over its lifetime.

Halogen Floor Lamps   Replace old floor lamps with floor lamps that are made for compact fluorescents.

Cost: $30 to $50 for bulb and lamp.

Potential savings: CFLs will save you $30 per lamp in electricity annually and are far less dangerous because they generate 95% less heat.

Floodlights   Replace standard floodlights in all recessed ceiling lights and outdoor fixtures with CFLs. If you have a dozen or more lights, you can save several hundred dollars a year.

Appliances

Look for the *Energy Star* Label   Every appliance meets the minimum federal energy-efficiency standards.

Appliances that are awarded the Energy Star certification by the Environmental Protection Agency, however, use approximately 20% less energy than the minimum. Energy Star appliances are not necessarily more expensive, and they pay for themselves in energy savings within five years.

Example: Replacing an old refrigerator with an Energy Star model costs about $600. But you'll save $100 to $150 a year on electricity.

You may be able to receive rebates from your local utility company for using a variety of energy-efficient appliances.

And many stores—including Home Depot—have rebate coupons.

Buy a Front-Loading Washing Machine   These models use 50% less water, require less detergent and reduce wear and tear on clothes.

While front-loading machines cost about 20% more than top-loaders, a family of four can save as much as $150 per year.

Turn Off Your Computer Monitor when you step away. The monitor requires far more energy than the hard drive, and a screen saver won't help.

If you're buying a new computer system, look for a monitor with a sleep-mode feature. It automatically converts to a low-energy mode when not in use, cutting electricity usage in half.

Lights! Savings!

Even though lighting doesn't use as much energy as heating, cooling and refrigeration do, there are still ways to save energy when using lights. The first step is to turn off lights when they aren't needed. Also, don't over-light a room. Try turning off a light or two to see if you miss them.

Keep all of your bulbs, lighting fixtures and lamps clean. Dirt blocks light and increases heat.

When you're away from home, use timers to turn lights on rather than leaving one lit all the time. It's safer and cheaper.

Off Doesn't Always Mean *Off*

Many appliances continue to draw electricity even when turned off. Electric appliances usually go into standby mode, waiting to respond to a remote control or recharging a battery.

Result: Up to 5% to 7% of a household's annual electric bill comes from turned-off appliances.

Self-defense: Except for appliances that need to stay plugged in, such as clocks, use power strips to completely shut off an appliance when you aren't using something.

Alan Meier, PhD, staff scientist, Berkeley National Laboratory, University of California, Mail Stop 90-2000, Berkeley, CA 94720.

Windows/Insulation

Install Low-Emissivity Windows Low "e" glass is coated with a film that doesn't affect your view, but provides greater insulation. Most major window manufacturers carry them now.

Insulate Properly Lay down fiberglass "batts" correctly to realize greater savings.

- **Attics:** Lay down fiberglass between the floor joists (support beams). If existing insulation comes up to the top of the joists, add an additional layer. Purchase batts without a vapor retarder.

  Do not store items on top of insulation—insulation loses effectiveness when it is packed down.

- **Basements:** If unheated, insulate the basement ceiling first, rather than the foundation and the walls.

  Support the ceiling insulation from below by using wire mesh or chicken wire fastened to the joists under the batts.

  If the basement is heated, simply insulate the foundation and the walls in addition to the ceiling—a carpet on the floor, fiberglass batts in the walls.

General

Choose a Low-Cost Energy Supplier More than half the US has deregulated electric and gas companies competing for your business. Get a list of licensed suppliers from your state public service commission. Be sure to get each supplier's *standard offer* or *price to compare*. This is the price per kilowatt-hour (therm) the utility charges.

Even easier: My Web site, *Energyguide.com*, provides comprehensive support for reducing energy bills by helping individuals buy more efficient products and find the best energy suppliers.

Potential savings: $100 to $300 a year for a typical home (two parents, two children).

Get a Free Energy Audit from Your Utility Company Some companies will inspect your home for its energy effectiveness and recommend ways to cut costs—insulating water heaters, repairing weatherstripping, etc.

Other Internet resources to easily compare and save on energy bills:

- **www.lowermybills.com** finds the best deals in nine categories of recurring bills, including energy usage, insurance, mortgages and long-distance telephone service.
- **http://hes.lbl.gov**, sponsored by the EPA and Department of Energy, lets you compute your home energy use based on your detailed input.

- **www.ase.org,** run by Alliance to Save Energy, offers a home energy checkup. You can also order the free booklet "Power-Smart: Easy Tips to Save Money and the Planet" on-line or by calling 888-878-3256.

Harvey Michaels, CEO of Energyguide.com, an on-line resource that helps consumers lower home and business electric and gas costs and includes calculators that show annual savings, Newton, MA. Mr. Michaels has spent the last 20 years in the energy field.

Easy Ways to Save Energy at Home

Here are some reminders of how you can save energy all year round, according to Ralph Cavanagh, Esq., codirector, Energy Program, Natural Resources Defense Council, New York:

- Set your thermostat at 68° F in winter (55°at night) and your air conditioner at 78° in summer.
- Set refrigerator temperature to 37° and freezer to 3°. Check gaskets around doors—they should be clean and seal tightly.
- Clean permanent appliance filters at least once a year. Replace non-permanent filters every month or two of use.
- Contact your local utility to see if it offers free energy-saving materials or home energy-use audits.

More information: Check the Natural Resources Defense Council Web site at www.nrdc.org.

Pretty Ways to Cut Energy Costs

Trees, shrubs and vines all provide valuable shade to cut down on the heat entering your home in the summer. Plants create a cool climate that can dramatically reduce the temperature in their surrounding area.

- **Deciduous trees** (ones that lose their leaves in winter) offer one of the best ways to cut home cooling costs. When selectively placed around your home, they shade the roof, walls and windows from the sun. Plus, when the leaves drop in autumn, they permit the winter sunlight to reach and warm your house.
- **Shrubbery planted a few feet away from the house** will provide extra shade without obstructing air currents.

Compare Utility Prices on the Internet

When competition in the electricity marketplace comes to your area, visit www.wattagemonitor.com or www. energyguide.com. For information on environmentally friendly fuels, try www. greenmountain.com.

Kilowatt marketing companies in deregulated areas buy power wholesale and resell it to customers—generally saving users a few pennies per kilowatt hour.

Jane Bryant Quinn, syndicated personal finance columnist, writing in *Good Housekeeping*, 959 Eighth Ave., New York 10019.

Plants for Shade

Factors to consider when choosing trees and plants include height, growth rate, branch spread and shape. Then think about placement. Experts recommend planting trees between directions. For example, plant a tree on the northeast side of your home, instead of on the north or east side. When selecting a planting site, notice the size and direction of shadows at the site, especially during summer.

- **Vines grown on trellises** can shade windows or a whole side of a home. Set trellises away from the wall to allow air to circulate.
- **Try planting trees or shrubs** to shade the outside portion of window air conditioners and increase their efficiency. Be careful not to obstruct the air flow around the unit.

Are Extended Warranties Worth the Price?

Nearly all appliances and electronic devices on the market today are sold with optional service contracts, which augment the protection of the product's warranty. However, you should carefully consider whether a service contract will actually benefit you.

The Difference Between Warranties and Service Contracts Warranties are included in the purchase price of a product. They cover certain repairs for a period of time. The type of coverage and time period varies from warranty to warranty. Service contracts, even when they are called extended warranties, cost extra and must be purchased separately.

The Value of Service Contracts In most cases, service contracts are not worth the money because they duplicate the same contract period as the manufacturer's warranty or overlap it by only one year. According to consumer sources, problems with new products most likely happen right away, when they are still covered by the factory warranty. This makes the purchase of an extended warranty unnecessary.

Before Purchasing a Service Contract Ask the following questions:

- Does the included manufacturer's warranty sufficiently cover repairs for an extended period of time? If so, a service contract may be a waste.
- What will the service contract cover? It may cover only certain parts of the product or specific repairs. If the contract does not list something as specifically covered, assume that it is not.
- Is the product likely to need the repairs covered by the service contract? If the product is unlikely to need servicing, or if the cost of repairs is very low, a service contract would not benefit you.
- What are the requirements or conditions for obtaining repairs under the service contract?

Best Home Water Filters

With regular news reports about water contamination—even in the best communities—more and more people are using home water filters.

Determine Your Needs

To choose the best filter for you, have your tap water tested.

Larger water utilities are now required to send an annual report to customers with the results of tests for about 80 different contaminants.

If you have well water—or if you don't want to wait for your water company's report—look in the *Yellow Pages* under "Water Testing" or "Laboratories—Testing." Test price depends on what contaminants you look for. The range is wide—between $17 and $800. The most likely contaminant is lead (20% of US households), which can be picked up by the household plumbing system.

Clean Water Lead Testing (828-251-6800) provides a mail-in test that tests water twice (when it is first drawn and after running the water for one minute) for $17. *Warning:* Home testing kits may be unreliable.

Carafe Filters Water flows by gravity, and there's plenty of the filtering medium with which it interacts to remove lead, reduce chlorine by-products and improve taste and smell. Inexpensive (less than $30).

Drawbacks: Slow...holds only two to three quarts...filters must be changed often, generally every 50 to 100 gallons, depending on the level of contaminants in the water.

Top carafe filter: Pur Pitcher CR-500. Half-gallon pitcher uses carbon and an active agent to improve water taste while reducing levels of lead, chlorine, copper and zinc. Safety gauge indicates when filter needs replacing. $20. *Replacement filters:* $8 each. 800-787-5463.

Faucet-Mounted Inexpensive (less than $50)...easy to install and change filters.

Drawbacks: Units are small, and water pressure forces water through the filter too quickly to thoroughly remove all impurities.

Top faucet filter: Pur Plus FM-3000. Removes microorganisms, such as giardia and cryptosporidium, as well as contaminants, including lead, chlorine and mercury. Automatic shutoff stops water flow when filter needs replacing. Filters last for 100 gallons. $30. *Replacement filters:* $15 each. 800-787-5463.

Under-Sink Filter Contains a reservoir so water has more time to pass through the filtering mechanism...long-lasting filters.

Drawbacks: Costs $100 or more...may require a plumber for installation.

Double the Length Of Your Warranty

Approximately 120 million credit cards, including **American Express**, **Optima** and **Visa Gold** cards, automatically double the length of the manufacturer's warranty by adding up to six additional months when you use that card to buy a product.

Check with your credit card companies to see which ones offer this benefit.

Quick Ways to Save on Water Heating

- Do as much cleaning as possible with cold water.
- Repair leaks in faucets and showers.
- Turn the faucet off when shaving.
- Install a low-flow showerhead. They provide an inexpensive way to reduce hot-water consumption by 30%.
- Lower your water heater thermostat. Most heaters are automatically set at 140°, but 120° is sufficient for most household needs. Check your dishwasher first, however. If it doesn't have a booster heater to raise the temperature of incoming water, you should not lower your water temperature.
- For electric water heaters, try installing a timer that will automatically turn the heater off at night and on in the morning.
  Note: If you have special night rates, set your timer to turn off your heater in the morning and on at night.
- Wrap exposed hot water pipes with insulation to minimize heat loss, especially in unheated areas such as basements.
- If you have an electric hot water heater, place an insulation jacket or blanket around it. Insulation is easy to install. Check with your local utility company. It may offer the blankets at a lower price, give you a rebate or even install them at no cost. Installation is more difficult on gas and oil-fired heaters. Ask your local furnace installer for instructions.

Top under-sink filter: Waterpik IF-100A. Dual-filter unit removes lead, chlorine and some pesticides—such as lindane—while improving water odor and taste. Installs easily and comes with extra-long tubing and a movable base for quick filter changing. Filters last for approximately 1,200 gallons. $159. *Replacement filters:* Lead filter/$38.59…chlorine/pesticide/taste and odor filter/$12.49. 800-525-2774.

Whole-House Filter For homes on well water and not connected to a municipal water system.

Contains sophisticated filtering material tailored to meet the home's specific needs—removes hardness…neutralizes water… removes bacteria. Filtered water is supplied to the whole house, including taps, showers and washing machine.

Drawbacks: Expensive ($1,000 to $3,000, installed, plus filtering materials)…requires monthly maintenance—changing filters and/or adding filtering materials.

There is no *best* whole-house system—it depends on your water-treatment goals. Leading manufacturers include Culligan, Flek and Hauge. The company that services your well can provide guidance following a comprehensive water test. Or look in the *Yellow Pages* under "Water Purification & Filtration Equipment."

Richard P. Maas, PhD, professor of environmental studies at University of North Carolina, Asheville. He is codirector of the university's Environmental Quality Institute, a leading center for research on tap water purity.

Nontoxic Ways to Clean Your Home… Cheaper, Too

Here's a laundry list of inexpensive and efficient cleansers from an environmental specialist. Many of these ingredients are probably on hand.

Liquid Cleanser *For cutting grease and cleaning countertops, baseboards and appliances:* In a plastic spray bottle, combine two cups of very hot water, one teaspoon borax, half teaspoon washing soda and half teaspoon Murphy's Oil Soap (or similar vegetable-based detergent).

Antibacterial Spray for Cutting Boards Fill spray bottle with one cup of water and 10 to 20 drops of essential oil of lavender. Spray on surface and leave overnight. Rinse, if desired.

Easy Scrub for Sinks and Bathtubs Combine quarter cup of baking soda and enough liquid soap or detergent to make a frosting-like paste.

Floor Cleaner for Wood, Tile or Linoleum Put two gallons of warm water in a plastic pail, and add one-eighth cup of liquid soap or detergent and half cup of white vinegar.

Oven Cleaner Sprinkle dirty spots with water, then cover with baking soda. Rinse. Repeat, leave overnight, and wipe up grime the next morning. Residue can be removed with liquid soap and water.

Toilet-Bowl Cleaner Pour in one cup of borax, leave overnight and flush in the morning.

Glass Cleaner In a spray bottle, combine half teaspoon of liquid soap or detergent, three tablespoons of white vinegar and two cups of water.

Dusting and Polishing Wood Moisten a cotton cloth in a bowl containing half teaspoon of olive oil and quarter cup of white vinegar or lemon juice.

Air Freshener Put a few slices of lemon, orange or grapefruit in a pot of water. Simmer gently for one hour to fill your house with a citrus scent.

Annie Berthold Bond, Rhinebeck, NY-based author of *Clean and Green: The Complete Guide to Nontoxic and Environmentally Safe Housekeeping* (Ceres) and *Better Basics for the Home: Simple Solutions for Less Toxic Living* (Clarkson Potter).

Smarter Refrigerator Buying

Look for one with a freezer on top or bottom, to save both money and energy. Side-by-side models cost more and use far more energy.

Also: Avoid built-in ice makers. They add about $200 to the refrigerator's cost and $50 to your annual energy bill —and they are the part of a refrigerator most likely to break.

Tightwad Living, Box 629, Burgin, KY 40310.

More Low-Cost Ways to Remove Tough Stains

In the Kitchen

Soap Residue and Hard-Water Stains in the Dishwasher Put a cup or two of vinegar in a shallow bowl, and set it in the bottom rack of an empty dishwasher. Run it through its cycle.

You can also use powdered lemonade mix. Put two teaspoons in the soap drawer, and run the dishwasher through its normal cycle. The ascorbic acid in the mix will brighten up the dishwasher.

Food Spills in the Oven Sprinkle spills with salt immediately after removing food. By the time the oven cools, the paste will be dry. Gently scrape the spill with a sturdy spatula. Wash the area with a mixture of vinegar and baking soda.

Tomato Sauce Stains in Plastic Containers Rub container with a damp cloth dipped in baking soda. Or fill the stained container with water, and drop in one or two foaming denture-cleaning tablets. Wait 20 minutes and then rinse.

More Efficient Freezers

Fill your freezer with gallon jugs of water instead of leaving it only partly full. A full freezer turns on less often and costs less to run. In case of a power outage, the frozen jugs will keep the freezer cold longer and prevent food from spoiling. When you need more space for frozen foods, take out a jug.

Caution: Leave room at the top of jugs when filling them. Water expands as it freezes and will crack a too-full jug.

$avvy Discount$ Newsletter, Box 96, Smyrna, NC 28579.

Wooden Cutting Boards Rub stubborn stains with a mix of baking soda and water, then rinse.

Mineral Deposits Around Faucets Apply vinegar, let sit for 10 minutes, and scrub with a toothbrush.

Countertop Stains *Marble:* Sprinkle a wedge of lemon with salt and rub over the marble. Rinse. *Laminated:* Cover stain with a paste of baking soda and lemon juice. Allow to dry and scrape off with a rubber spatula. Then rinse.

Around the House

White Rings on Wood Tables from Wet Glasses Make a thin paste of vegetable oil and salt. Using your fingers, gently massage this mixture into the ring. Let it sit for an hour or so, then wipe it off with a soft cotton cloth.

Or cover the ring with a thin coat of petroleum jelly and let it sit for a day. Then wipe off.

Wall Smudges that Don't Wash Off Rub the marks with a "gum eraser" —available at most art-supply stores. Or try a piece of stale bread. This works on paint or wallpaper.

For small grease spots, use a powder puff to rub white talcum powder over the offending mark. What the powder puff doesn't rub off will be covered up by the powder.

If the spots are bad, mix cornstarch with just enough water to make a paste. Rub the paste over the spots on the wall and leave for one hour. Then brush off.

Washing the Walls Wash from the bottom up—not the top down. When dirty water runs over a dry, dirty wall, it leaves streaks that are hard to get out. But dirty water will not stain a wet, clean wall.

For textured surfaces, use a piece of burlap or old nylons for scrubbing.

Brick or Stone Floors Use one cup of vinegar in one gallon of water. Scrub the brick or stone floor with the vinegar solution, then rinse it with clean water.

Outdoor Grills If the top of your grill has cooked-on food and grease, first apply some dishwasher liquid or oven cleaner. Then place the grill top in a large plastic garbage bag and let sit overnight. When you take it out, the caked-on dirt should be easy to wipe away.

Mare-Anne Jarvela, assistant managing editor, *The Old Farmer's Almanac 1999 Homeowner's Companion* (Yankee Publishing).

Very Best Buys in Power Tools Don't Cost a Lot

These great tools will get the work done—and done well—and save a lot of money, according to John R. Lewis, 23-year veteran of the home construction and remodeling industry in North Carolina and editor of the on-line magazine *Ubuild.com*:

Cordless Screwdriver/Drill A 12- to 14-volt drill is enough for driving screws and simple jobs. More powerful drills are heavy, expensive and better for large jobs.

Electric Drill Buy the lowest-priced, national-brand, ⅜", variable-speed drill you can find for less than $75. It should give five years of fairly heavy use.

If you build furniture and use a drill often: A higher-quality drill is worthwhile. Purchase the least expensive drill that has a ball bearing shaft.

Table Saw Essential for furniture and rip cuts—long cuts with the grain on boards. A nationally known maker's direct-drive table saw in the $150 range should last a lifetime.

Circular Saw Purchase the least expensive circular saw that has a ball bearing or roller bearing shaft. Such saws make more accurate cuts and will outlast three ordinary circular saws.

Helpful: Carbide-tipped saw blades are better than standard "kerf-cut" blades.

Router Unless you plan to make lots of furniture, stick to a standard router. Few people use a router much, but it is indispensable for certain tasks, such as fancy edge cuts for furniture.

Helpful: Purchase a router with the most powerful motor (as measured by horsepower) you can find for between $60 and $100. It rarely makes sense to pay more than this.

Miter Saw While a table saw's strength is cutting with the grain of the wood, a miter saw cuts strictly across the grain—what is known as a "crosscut."

Purchase the lowest-priced 10" *compound* electric miter saw you can find. The compound feature allows you to make both angle and bevel cuts at the same time.

Alternative: If you can live without a compound miter saw, save a bit by purchasing a noncompound miter saw.

Reciprocating Saw A reciprocating saw can reach where other saws can't, such as flush cuts and tight spaces. Great for cutting through wood with nails and vital if you're building or remodeling a house—but not a must-have in every workshop.

What's in a Name?

Buy sister brands. Major manufacturers often make several virtually identical lines of appliances—and charge more for the one with the manufacturer's name on it.

Alternatives to consider: Frigidaire makes Gibson, Kelvinator and Tappan...Maytag makes Admiral, Magic Chef and Jenn-Air...General Electric makes Hot Point.

Misleading names: Don't be misled by names when you look for energy-efficient appliances. Names such as Energy Miser, Energy Saver or Fuel Saver don't necessarily guarantee savings. The best way to determine energy efficiency is to compare the information provided on **EnergyGuide** labels.

Tightwad Living, Box 629, Burgin, KY 40310.

Garbage Bags That Won't Split

Today's plastic kitchen garbage bags are better than ever. However, although some are stronger than others, you can't judge them solely on the basis of their thickness in mils or their price.

Example: A recent study found that among the top 11 performers, thickness (in mils) varied from .60 to .95. Price per bag (30 to a box) varied from 4¢ to 18¢. Among the best were American Fare with ties (.74 mils, 4¢/bag from Kmart), Hefty CinchSak Twist Tie (.74 mils, 5¢/bag) and Kirkland Signature Drawstring (.85 mils, 5¢/bag from Costco).

www.channel2000.com report on a study appearing in *Consumer Reports* (www.consumerreports.org).

Saber Saw (Jigsaw) For curved cutting and necessary for many projects—the least expensive one works fine.

Band Saw For serious woodworkers, this tool is for accurate, smooth, curved cuts and cutting thick wood. Band saws cut more smoothly and accurately than saber saws.

Downside: Band saws cost much more than saber saws—good ones run $250 to $400—and might not fit large pieces of wood. (Band saw arms generally reach only 10" to 18".)

Belt Sander It is easy to economize too much on a belt sander. You can find them from big-name makers for as little as $45. But these low-end products don't do a great job for medium to heavy-duty wood sanding…and probably won't last five years.

Orbital (vibrator) sanders leave scratches. I go straight from smooth belt sanding pads to hand sandpaper, rather than using an orbital sander as an interim step.

Best Ways to Keep Deer Out of Your Backyard

If you have a problem with deer in your backyard, here are some solutions. Surprisingly, the least costly deer repellants are natural scents that deer dislike:

Bars of Deodorant Soap Leave the wrappers on the bars to protect them from rain. Drill a hole through each bar, and run a long length of string through the hole. Tie a knot at each end of the soap to hold it in place.

Then hang the long string of soaps from the trees at grazing level along the edges of your property. To be most effective, the soap bars should be strung at intervals of about 18".

Hair Cuttings Deer fear the smell of humans. Wrap hair cuttings from a local barbershop or salon in small mesh bags. String the bags from the trees the same way as for the bars of soap.

Commercial Repellents

There are four types of repellents that are made from ingredients that deer find especially distasteful:

- **Chew-Not**—contains fungicides.
- **Bobbex**—made with fish powder and oil.
- **Hinder**—made from ammonium soaps of high fatty acids.

All three of these can be purchased at garden-supply stores. Chew-Not and Bobbex last through rain. Hinder, which also repels rabbits, needs to be reapplied after rain.

- **Milorganite** is a lawn fertilizer made from human waste and is not intended as a deer repellent. But it still works.

Spread milorganite on a lawn surrounding the shrubs you want to protect. Or create a border around the base of the plants.

Deer apparently find the smell unpleasant enough that they avoid it.

These repellents are most effective if they are rotated with each new application. Apply according to package instructions.

Cheryl Merser, contributor to *Garden Design* magazine and author of *The Garden Design Book* (HarperCollins).

Stop Throwing Dollars Down the Drain

Some homeowners spend needlessly when it comes to taking care of their homes. The most common home-maintenance money wasters:

High-End Paint

Repainting is one of the most common home-maintenance jobs. And since time and labor—not the paint itself—are the major expenses, many consumers select high-end paints.

Overspending on paint does not necessarily improve the quality or life of a paint job.

An expensive paint might spatter or drip less—but for most of us, that's not enough to justify paying as much as $40 a gallon, rather than $20 or less.

I'm a big fan of store brands, such as Ace Hardware's. I would certainly think twice before buying any paint selling for more than $20 a gallon.

When repainting the exterior: Certain mistakes mean the whole job will have to be redone. Biggest problems:

- Scraping off loose paint, then failing to coat exposed wood with oil-based primer before repainting.
- Painting when the temperature is below 50°F.

Deck Replacement

I get many calls from homeowners who want to replace decks that are showing their age. At a typical price of $10 to $12 per square foot, installing a new deck can easily cost $1,500 to $3,500.

To make an older deck look great for another 10 years or more, pull out the nails on the flooring and turn over the boards. The wood's underside is rarely as weathered as the top. Have it pressure-washed, sanded and water-treated.

Since nails pull out of wood over time, consider replacing them with deck screws. This is easy with a cordless drill. *Best screws:* Square-drive deck screws 1" longer than the thickness of the deck board.

How to Determine If Furniture Is High-Quality

Look for:

- Oak, mahogany or cherry.

- Solid frame construction—legs, armrests and seat backs should be assembled using wood pegs, glue and screws (not nails or staples).

- Quiet—not squeaky—internal coils that can't be felt when you sit.

- Solid-foam or synthetic-down padding—not shredded foam.

- Tightly woven, evenly stretched fabric, with aligned patterns.

- Well-aligned moving pieces—such as drawers that operate smoothly.

Jack Weber, consultant to consumer and trade groups, based in the Washington, DC, area, and author of Honey, I've Shrunk the Bills! *(Capital).*

New Fixtures

Repairing or reconditioning bathroom and kitchen fixtures is far cheaper than simply replacing them.

Example: Cast-iron tubs eventually chip or fade—or simply no longer match a redesigned bathroom. Most homeowners replace them with modern fiberglass tubs.

A cast-iron tub was most likely installed before the wallboards went in—so walls must be torn apart to remove it. The new tub might cost $300—but the cost of removing the old one and installing the new one could easily tack another $1,500 onto the bill.

Better: Recoat a cast-iron tub through a process called *refinishing*. Your local plumbing store should be able to recommend someone to do this for you. *Cost:* About $300.

Example: Leaky faucets are among the most common kitchen and bathroom problems. A new faucet might solve the problem—but it's likely to cost more than $100, and it may not match the room and the original unit.

Better: Take the leaky valve cartridge to a local plumbing store. Chances are a 59¢ washer will do the job. If not, the plumbing store should be able to replace the whole valve for $8 to $12.

Refurbishing also can be better for kitchens. It costs $8,000 to $30,000 to redo a typical kitchen. But you can refinish cabinets and replace the countertop and the sink for less than $5,000.

If you have solid wood kitchen cabinets, refinishing might be the only way to avoid taking a step down in craftsmanship. Few modern companies make solid wood cabinets. Check with a local hardware store or a trusted contractor for cabinet-resurfacing recommendations.

Relying on Warranties

Warranties are only as good as the companies behind them.

I'm embarrassed to say that this is a mistake I made a number of years back. I was replacing the thermalpane windows on the second floor of my house, and I decided to use a lesser-known brand. I felt safe because the windows came with a long-term warranty.

Seven years later, the windows began fogging up—the most common form of failure with thermalpane windows. When I tried to use my warranty, I found the company was out of business.

Stick with well-known companies. Most established companies have 10-year warranties and supplies to service older windows at a fraction of the cost to replace them.

Roof shingles are another place where people pay extra for long warranties of questionable value. Most roof shingles come with a 25-year warranty. In most climates, you are unlikely to get

more than 25 years on any asphalt or fiberglass shingle. But you can pay up to double to get shingles with a 40-year warranty.

Overcleaning

Some people take their desire for cleanliness too far and damage their homes. Overcleaning can often lead to premature aging of components.

Example: Overscrubbing sinks and tubs with abrasive cleansers is a sure way to wear off the finish.

Better: Head to a plumbing store—or a well-stocked home-improvement store—for a bathroom-fixture coating such as Gel Gloss. This provides a protective coating for both fiberglass and ceramics that lasts six to eight weeks. Water spots can be easily removed with a soft cloth.

Example: Overcleaning carpets. Steam cleaning more than twice a year damages the carpet. If that doesn't provide enough cleaning for you, consider putting inexpensive throw rugs over high-traffic areas.

Also: When replacing carpeting, few homeowners pay attention to the padding underneath. But a poor-quality pad can contribute as much to reducing the life of the carpet as the quality of the carpet itself. I recommend a minimum of six pounds rebound padding—eight pounds is better and should add only $75 to $150 to any job.

High Energy Bills

Everyone complains about high heating bills, yet few homeowners take the simple home-maintenance steps necessary to reduce them.

Mistake: Not putting in enough attic insulation. More heat is lost through inadequate roof insulation than through any other part of the home. Adding attic insulation is an inexpensive and easy job. A professional can blow insulation into ceiling areas for $250 to $750.

Important: Without proper venting, you could get ice damming or attic moisture leading to wood rot. Hardware stores sell Styrofoam baffles that can be slid down into the eaves near where the roof meets the attic floor to ensure the necessary air flow.

Mistake: Using a furnace made before 1980. Old furnaces were only 67% efficient at best—one-third of the fuel they burned was wasted. Modern furnaces are 90% efficient. A new furnace costs $1,500 to $5,000—but with current energy prices, it is money well spent.

Bill Keith, owner of Tri-Star Remodeling in St. John, IN, and a 16-year contracting veteran. Mr. Keith is host of the cable-TV program *The Home Tips Show*, broadcast in the upper Midwest. He has a free remodeling answer service through www.billkeith.com.

Guide to Choosing the Best Mattress for You

It is no accident that buying a mattress is so complex. Manufacturers issue the same mattresses under various model names, making it difficult to compare prices. But there is a way:

Use the manufacturer's name and the mattress type—along with coil count and wire gauge—to make sure you are comparing prices on the same product.

Coils provide support—look for a coil count of 400 or more. Ample padding is important for comfort. A good mattress should last 10 years.

Shopping Secrets

❑ **Stick to the five Ss.** Buy from a top mattress manufacturer—Sealy, Serta, Simmons, Spring Air or Stearns & Foster—to get a decent, affordable mattress.

❑ **Make sure there is a return policy.** Most reputable mattress stores have a 30-day return policy —although it is not always advertised.

❑ **Take your time trying out the mattress.** It takes lying on a bed in one position for five to seven minutes to know if you'll be comfortable sleeping on it.

Brenda Benner, senior editor at *Productopia*, an independent source of product information and buying advice.

Protect Your Home From Disasters...

- **Wildfire:** Create a 30' defensible zone around your house...prune branches near your home to no more than 8" to 10" high...remove dead needles, limbs and debris from roof and gutters.

- **Hurricanes:** Install storm shutters ...reinforce roof with bracing and hurricane straps...bring lawn furniture inside when a watch or a warning is issued.

- **Earthquake:** Secure bookcases, furniture and appliances with bolts... and relegate large, fragile or heavy items to lower shelves...buy earthquake insurance.

- **Flood:** Elevate the main breaker or fuse box and any heating, ventilation or cooling equipment...purchase flood insurance...keep insurance policies, important documents and other valuables in a safe-deposit box ...install check valves in sewer traps to prevent backflow.

Cynthia Ramsay Taylor, spokesperson, Federal Emergency Management Agency, Washington, DC. 800-462-9029...www.fema.gov

Pay Less for Home Repairs

It's up to you to keep your home-repair or renovation experience safe from outrageous cost overruns and shoddy work. Here are some basic rules to follow:

Educate Yourself

Information is your best resource and your best protection. This can range from looking at pictures in home-design magazines to speaking with your local building inspector. Your research goal is to be able to:

- Refine the scope of the job you want done.
- Have a hands-on feel for the products you will be using.
- Determine what types of contractors you need.
- Draft a realistic budget.
- Ask the contractors the right questions.
- Know how to judge workmanship.

Develop a Plan

Think through all the related parts of the job you set out to do. Remember that it will cost less to do it all at once than to hire contractors a few years down the road for another round of work.

Visit showrooms, home centers and lumberyards that sell furniture or materials for the specific room you are working on. While you take in ideas, see if there is a designer on staff who could give you a free consultation.

Relevant government agencies, industry trade associations and manufacturers are all important sources of information on permits and codes, hiring remodelers, products and design ideas. The following organizations provide consumer information such as planning steps, checklists and helpful brochures:

- **National Association of Plumbing-Heating-Cooling Contractors** (703-237-8100, www.naphcc.org)
- **National Association of the Remodeling Industry** (800-611-NARI, www.nari.org)
- **National Kitchen and Bath Association** (877-NKBA-PRO, www.nkba.org)

Establishing Relationships

There are long-term benefits to becoming someone's customer. Once you have found a contractor you are comfortable with, this relationship can benefit you as long as you own your home. You will have access to a network of other contractors, and you will have someone who is already familiar with your home to call in case of an emergency.

General Contractors

Assess your job—do you need one contractor or a team? Often one job requires you to use several different contractors—architect, engineer, plumber, electrician, carpenter, roofer, tiler, asbestos remover, painter. Because the coordination of all of these services can be a full-time job in itself, it makes sense to hire a general contractor if you're doing a substantial building or renovation job. On many jobs, the plumber, electrician or mason doubles as the general contractor.

Finding a Reliable Contractor

The process of working with contractors has a bad reputation—and legitimately so. However, if you educate yourself, use certain screening steps, trust your instincts, and include specific expectations and checkpoints in your contract, you will be fine. Not that the job will go as expected—there are always unforeseen circumstances!

The important thing to remember is that contractors who get through your screening process want the job to go as smoothly and quickly as you do. Happy customers are their most valuable means of getting work in the future—both from you and your friends.

The Screening Process

Your chances of finding a reputable contractor greatly increase if you follow these recommendations:

Find Likely Candidates

- **Get remodelers' names from people who have gone through the process before—friends, family, neighbors.** A personal recommendation is the best reference. If you don't know someone who's recently completed the kind of job you need, names from professional associations are a better bet than from the phone book. If the same names keep coming up, they are the ones to interview first.
- **Interview several contractors on the phone.** Talk over the project in general. Pay attention to their phone manner. Do they have listening skills? Do they return calls quickly? Reject anyone using high-pressure sales tactics.
- **Check references.** Ask for current customers as well as prior customers to get a sense of how the contractor handled the routine parts of the job—as well as the problems. Try to get a feel for what it was like working with the contractor. Examine the work to see if it meets your requirements.
- **Verify that the contractor is licensed to work in your town and carries general liability insurance and workers' compensation.** Write down the contractor's license number.
- **Follow up by calling the Better Business Bureau or Consumer Protection Agency** in your area to ask if the contractor has a good track record.

Rx for Power Failures

A gasoline-powered home generator is a smart buy if your home is prone to lengthy power outages.

A 5,000-watt generator—available at home centers—should keep the refrigerator, heat, lights and even television running until power is restored. *Cost:* $1,800 to $2,700.

Favorite brand: Honda. An electrician will install a manual transfer switch, which changes over power from your usual electric service to the generator. *Cost:* $90 to $150.

Precautions: Start the generator once a month to exercise the motor. Keep some gasoline on hand—in a metal or plastic can outside or stored in a shed. Refill it every three months—gasoline is only good for about 90 days unless you add a stabilizer.

Allen Gallant, master electrician, *This Old House* magazine, and owner of Gallant Electric, 100 Villa St., Waltham, MA 02453.

All About Firewood

Firewood Basics

- Buy wood several months before you plan to use it.

- Stack it in loose piles on wooden pallets—off the ground. Cover the top to protect it from rain and snow.

- Know measurements. A full cord is 128 cubic feet—4' by 4' by 8'. A "face cord" or "fireplace cord" is half a full cord.

Best Woods for Burning

Ash, red or white oak, beech, birch, hickory, maple, pecan, dogwood. All generate high heat...split and burn easily...and produce little smoke.

Firewood from US national forests is available to people living nearby. Find the phone listing for any national forest near you in the US Government section of the phone book under "US Department of Agriculture, Forest Service." *Note:* Permits to obtain firewood are required.

John Dwyer, PhD, associate professor, forest resource management, University of Missouri-Columbia, and Chris Holmes, USDA Forest Service, Washington, DC.

Screening Interview Questions You'll want answers to these questions for all potential contractors:

- How long have they been in business, and at what address?
- How long has the current crew been with them?
- How many other jobs are they doing simultaneously?
- At what number can you always reach the boss directly?
- What's their policy on changing orders—yours and theirs?

Getting Quotes

Here's the standard procedure for the initial appointment:

1. Make an appointment to meet the contractors at the job site to fully explain the job.
2. Be prepared to discuss budget. This is the starting point for design as well as product selection.
3. Don't be surprised if you are asked to pay a consultation fee, to be charged up front but credited to the job if you choose that company. Ask questions. You are paying for their professional expertise.
4. Assess their work habits. Are they on time for the appointment? What is their personal appearance like? Do you sense a mutual respect?
5. As a follow-up to the appointment, contractors will submit their quotes in writing. Pay attention to how long it takes them to get this done. Expect a flat fee for the job.

Dealing with Quotes You should get several quotes to choose from. As you assess them, keep in mind that you are probably not comparing apples to apples. Look at the design and product ranges, and select the one that represents what you want. Remember that it is not always a bargain to go with the lowest quote. Sometimes contractors will lowball a bid to get the job, and it can cost you in service, punctuality and lack of expertise. Discuss what can go wrong and how much more it might cost under a worst-case scenario.

Be prepared to pay a fairly large down payment, perhaps 30% to 50%. This amount can be negotiated, however.

Who Buys the Appliances? Either the homeowner or the contractor could buy appliances. It comes down to the balance among money, headaches and time.

The contractor typically buys an appliance at wholesale, marks it up and passes the cost to you. Yet in this age of discount shopping, a smart shopper can buy appliances for not much more than wholesale. The person who buys the appliances, however, assumes responsibilities of shopping, delivery, coordination as far as fit and compatibility, and returning the appliances if they're damaged.

7

Hobby and Leisure-Time Bargains

Great Starts on Popular Hobbies

Hobbies are a great way to provide low-cost, at-home entertainment for yourself and your family. Here are some ways to get started on some fun activities:

Stamp Collecting

Stamp collecting is a very personal and individual venture that allows you to collect any type of stamp you want. You can collect stamps from the US, Russia or other country. You may even want to focus on collecting stamps of famous people, or a certain time period or style. Or you may just want to collect every stamp that's out there.

Mystic's Guide to Stamp Collecting Get a free beginner's guide to stamp collecting from the Mystic Stamp Company (800-433-7811, www.mysticstamp.com). This guide tells you how to begin collecting stamps, how to identify stamps, how to locate them, how to preserve them and how to tell if a stamp is valuable.

A Bird Lover's Best Bargain

The **National Audubon Society** (202-861-2242 or 800-542-2748, www.audubon.org) is birding's best bargain. You can join the National Audubon Society for as little as $20 a year, or $15 if you're a student or senior. And for $30 you can join for two years.

With a membership to the National Audubon Society you'll receive six issues of *Audubon* magazine, membership in your local chapter and many member benefits, including free or low-cost admittance to all National Audubon activities and events. You'll also receive a monthly newsletter and be invited to a once-a-month program for the entire chapter. The monthly programs are also open to the general public free of charge.

The society offers a wide variety of bird-watching field trips every month, which range in cost from $2 for members to $4 for non-members. Some field trips are even free.

Also ask for Mystic's free *Catalog of US Stamps* (800-433-7811), a 112-page, full-color catalog of United States stamps which is published every year. With more than 3,000 stamps, this catalog helps you get your stamp collecting hobby on its way.

USA Philatelic and **Introduction to Stamp Collecting** These two free books on stamp collecting are available by calling 800-STAMP24 (www.askphil.org).

These guides instruct you in the different types of stamps, such as booklet format or peel-and-stick, and give guidance on how to remove stamps from envelopes, how to organize your collection and stamp-collecting groups you may want to join.

In the back of the beginner's guide is also a listing of free nationwide museums, libraries and displays that focus on stamps and stamp collecting.

Coin Collecting

You can collect a variety of coins at a variety of prices. If you collect old pennies, dimes and quarters, you won't have to spend much money at all, but other types of coins can run anywhere from $10 to more than $100. (Coin collecting encompasses paper as well as metal currency.)

Magazines such as *Coins World* (800-253-4555, www.coin world.com) and *Coins* (715-445-2214) can tell you how to start your collection and where to find worthwhile currencies to collect.

Bird-Watching

Bird-watching associations and community groups have turned bird-watching into a global pastime. There are nationwide birding festivals which can provide you with an active birding education. The National Fish and Wildlife Foundation (202-857-0166) organizes a *Directory of Birding Festivals*. If you have Web access, you can get birding information from the US Fish and Wildlife Service's Web site, www.fws.gov.

Birding festivals are a great way to see new birds and habitats while being guided by local birding experts. Many festivals offer guided field trips that take you to local hot spots. Some provide transportation and self-guided tours.

You can also learn about bird watching by reading or subscribing to birding publications like *Birder's World* (800-446-5489).

Birding on the Web

When it's too dark to go bird-watching, I go on-line instead, says Sheila Buff, author of many books about birding and the outdoors, including *The Complete Idiot's Guide to Birding* (Macmillan). Favorite Web sites:

OWL: Ornithological Web Library With more than 1,100 links to other birding sites worldwide, this is a good jumping-off point. (www.aves.net/the-owl)

Cornell Laboratory of Ornithology Excellent site with great pictures and outstanding bird sounds from the world-famous Library of Natural Sounds. Click on the BirdSource icon for weekly features. (www.birds.cornell.edu)

USGS Patuxent Wildlife Research Center Thorough site with excellent photos and bird sounds and good information on bird identification. Also lots of solid ornithological information on bird migration, banding and other research projects. (www.pwrc.usgs.gov)

The National Aviary in Pittsburgh More than 200 bird species live at the aviary. Excellent photos of exotic birds along with lots of great information about birds in general. (www.aviary.org)

Hummingbirds! Site devoted entirely to hummingbirds. Excellent photos and information about hummingbirds, including how to attract them. (www.hummingbirds.net)

The Virtual Birder An Internet magazine for birders. Interesting features, photo galleries, bird ID quizzes (some content is free). (www.virtualbirder.com)

Birdwatching.com Commercial site with lots of good information and links for birding products and other birding Web sites. (www.birdwatching.com)

Big Days For Birders

If you're a bird lover, there are two **National Audubon Society** events you won't want to miss. One is an annual spring event called **The Big Day**, which is a bird-watching event at the peak of migration. And the second event is **The Christmas Day Bird Count**.

The Christmas Day Bird Count is an annual hemispheric early winter bird census. National Audubon volunteers join forces to count every individual bird and bird species over the course of one calendar day. Representatives from each counting group meet at the end of the day to compile a master list which is then used by the government as the official bird census.

National Audubon Society members not only experience the fun and relaxation of birding, but contribute to the welfare of our environment.

How to Get the Best Deals On Antiques & Collectibles

You can build any kind of collection at discount prices by following a few simple, but very practical, guidelines. Here's how:

Groundwork

Educate Yourself About What You Collect The more you know about your field of interest, the better chance you'll have of discovering authentic bargains. Effective ways of learning include reading, visiting museums and galleries, taking courses, attending shows and building relationships with dealers.

Buy the Book Before the Item A collectibles price guide, that is. This will help protect you from being ripped off. There are standard collector guides for most antiques and collectibles, though some fields have no good reference books.

Shopping for Vintage Goods On-Line

Great Web sites for classic, retro and vintage goods—often sold at lower prices than brand-new items:

- **Formal wear.** Vintage wedding gowns...cocktail dresses...tuxedos ...men's suits...jewelry. Descriptions include waist size and other measurements needed to ensure good fit. **Carla's Vintage Wedding Gowns**, http://hometown.aol.com/gowns4you/index.html.

- **Tableware.** Estate silverware, teapots, china and crystal. **The Silver Queen**, www.silverqueen.com.

- **Home decor.** Furniture, lamps, tabletop items and other furnishings—all handpicked from Beverly Hills estate sales. **Freda LA**, www.fredala.com.

- **Telephones.** Working candlestick phones...novelty and reproduction phones...old parts...etc. **Phoneco, Inc.**, www.phonecoinc.com.

- **Musical instruments.** High-quality vintage guitars...banjos...violins... accordions...flutes...more. **Elderly Instruments**, www.elderly.com.

- **Records.** Vintage and hard-to-find LPs and 45s in all musical categories. **Record-Rama Sound Archives**, www.recordrama.com.

- **Heirloom vegetable seeds.** Open-pollinated (nonhybrid) flower, vegetable and herb seeds from backyard gardens—the same varieties grandmother used to grow. **Heirloom Seeds**, www.heirloomseeds.com.

Gail Bradney, Bearsville, NY–based consumer bargains expert and author of *Buy Wholesale by Mail 2001* (HarperCollins).

Caution: Don't rely on most price guides for the *actual*—or up-to-date—fair value of an item you're considering buying. Prices in the guides are only estimates of what items may sell for.

If you use a price guide to get some idea of price, always use the most up-to-date version. General collector guides:

- *Antique Trader's Antiques and Collectibles Price Guide* (800-258-0929).
- *Kovels' Antiques & Collectibles Price List* (800-571-1555).
- *Schroeder's Antiques Price Guide* (800-626-5420).

Subscribe to Collectors' Publications There are national trade papers that publish prices of items from recent sales. These include:

- *Antiqueweek* (800-876-5133, www.antiqueweek.com).
- *Maine Antique Digest* (207-832-4888, www.maineantiquedigest.com).

Inspect for Flaws, Fakes and Reproductions It's vital that you examine the condition of any item you're considering buying. Some fine collectibles lose 50% of their value with their first dent or scratch.

Also be on the lookout for fakes and reproductions. It's not a bargain if it's not the real thing.

Hunting

The typical collectible changes hands five to seven times as it moves from the original owner to the final collector. Each person who handles the item raises the price.

If the final collector pays 100% of the value, the lower down the ladder you can buy an item, the cheaper it will be. Bargains, though, do exist at:

Thrift Shops These are run by charities and get their merchandise free. An educated buyer can snap up bargains.

Garage and Yard Sales Homeowners make many mistakes in valuing items, so a knowledgeable collector can find good stuff cheap.

Take your time. Cash is king at garage sales. The measure should be how many bargains you can find in a day, not how many garage sales you can visit in a day.

Flea Markets There are thousands throughout the US. Few prices are firm at flea markets. Prices are lower because the dealer's overhead is very low. Shopping strategies:

- **Walk away from ridiculously high prices**...pay the bargain price without haggling...negotiate when in the middle by making your best offer. If the dealer agrees, great. But if not, just move along.
- **Get to the market as early as you can.** Other dealers and pickers usually want the best stuff, so if you really want a particular item, you'll have to get there before they do. Early means when they set up their wares, which at many flea markets may be before sunrise—so bring along a flashlight.

- **If you see an item at a price you like—buy it.** If you walk away and come back later, the piece may be gone.
- **Take one last tour of the market before it closes.** The best bargains are at the end of the day when dealers are packing up.

Major Flea Markets Brimfield, Massachusetts, along Route 20, is the Mecca of the flea market world. It runs Tuesday through Sunday the first full week in May, July and September, and features more than 5,000 dealers.

On the West Coast, visit America's Largest Antiques and Collectibles Show at the Portland, Oregon, Expo Center. It runs Friday through Sunday in early March and mid-month in July and October.

Antique Shops Generalizations are difficult because specialties and skill levels vary. But shop owners make frequent mistakes, especially when they sell outside of their specialty. How cheaply they sell is dependent on their need for cash, how anxious they are to move inventory and what they paid for an item (usually 30% to 75% of retail values).

Almost every antique shop has one good thing priced at less than 10% of fair value.

On-Line Auctions This relatively new trend in shopping for antiques and collectibles allows you to pretty much set your own price. Many auctions, though, have a "reserve" (the lowest price the seller will let an item go for).

Just as at a traditional auction house, you are bidding against others for what you want, so you can get caught up in auction fever and spend far more than you intended. You can be swept away in the last-minute rush when most of the bids come in.

Shopping strategy: Set a limit on what you're willing to pay so you don't overspend.

Both dealers and amateurs sell items on-line, and amateurs usually don't know fair value, so it's possible to get bargains.

eBay is the world's first and biggest on-line trading community (www.ebay.com). You need to register as a member to bid, but that's free. And it's easy to do. You can enter a maximum bid and the service will bid on your behalf up to that limit. You can check on the reputation of the seller, viewing positive and negative feedback left by previous buyers.

Look over carefully what you're bidding on. You are only covered for fraud up to $200 (minus a $25 deductible).

You can use an escrow service for added security—your payment isn't disbursed to the seller until you receive and examine the goods.

Harry L. Rinker, author of Price Guide to Flea Market Treasures *(Random House).*

Better than Videotape

Personal video recorders (PVRs) have replaced videotape with a hard drive to bring computer sophistication to video recording.

Examples: While watching a "live" show you can replay what you just saw, or pause it while you leave the room and resume when you return, as the PVR continues to record...shows can be recorded with commercials deleted...using an Internet-like connection and search engine, you can scan cable and satellite channels for any show you are interested in...selected channels can be blocked from children's viewing. In fact, you can program the PVR to function in a multitude of ways—much like a computer.

Leading products: Replay TV and TiVo. *Cost:* From about $400.

Patricia Robison, chief technology officer, Nekema Inc., 30 Montgomery St., Jersey City 07302.

Buying and Selling Collectibles on the Web

The volume of business on the Internet's collectible auction markets has exploded in the last few years, and for very good reasons. Collectible trading on the Internet gives you:

- Secure, anonymous, cheap and effortless access to collectors all over the world.
- The chance to view pictures of the thousands of items that are for sale in your special field of collecting—no matter how quirky it is.
- The opportunity to make a few extra dollars—or a few thousand.
- A fascinating entrance to the information superhighway—if you're not there yet.
- The possibility of developing friendships through E-mail exchanges with other collectors.

If you're a serious collector, you may have to go on-line. It has been estimated that within the next five years, 50% of all collectible sales will take place over the Internet.

Fact: The world's largest Internet trading service, eBay, was started in September 1995 as a way to help its founder's girlfriend sell her collection of Pez dispensers. (The company went public in September 1998 and the founder is now a billionaire.

Buying and Selling On-Line

eBay (www.ebay.com) is the biggest Internet auction site by far. At last report more than 1.2 million people have used eBay to buy and sell merchandise in more than 1,000 categories—from Beanie Babies to books. Every day there are more than 12 million "page views," that is, viewings by potential buyers checking out wares.

What does it cost? On-line auction companies typically charge an "insertion fee" for listing an item and a commission based on the selling price.

On eBay, the top insertion fee is $2, and the commission is up to 5% when items are sold.

There are several software programs available to help sellers manage on-line selling.

Example: *Auction Assistant 2* by Blackthorne Software provides eBay sellers with low-cost/high-featured software to automate the tasks of listing and maintaining auctions. *Cost:* $39 (www.blackthornesw.com).

To be a buyer on-line: Register at one of the auction sites. Simply fill out an on-line application that includes your name and mailing address. It is not necessary to reveal your Social Security or credit card number. Details:

- You are described on-line only by a code name you have selected.
- The highest bidder is notified by E-mail and contacted by the seller to arrange payment.
- Payment is made directly to the seller by check or money order.

Safeguards

The buyer has the ability to verify the seller's honesty by checking a "feedback" rating. So, you can avoid dealing with individuals whose ratings raise questions.

Sellers receive positive, negative or neutral comments from previous buyers.

On eBay, if a seller has too many negative comments, he/she can be terminated from using the service.

Keep in mind that reputable sellers give the buyer the opportunity to return the item if unsatisfied for a valid reason.

On-line escrow services for expensive items are also available.

There is no fee to view, bid and buy on-line. The seller pays the insertion fee and commission. Buyers typically pay for postage and insurance.

Buyer Beware

Just like written descriptions, a photo seen on a small screen does not always reveal damage or problems that the seller has overlooked.

Remember that buying on-line is no different from buying in person. Often the seller is ignorant of what he is offering or is purposely deceitful. As always, *buyer beware*.

Malcolm Katt, an antique dealer, owner of Millwood Gallery, which specializes in Nippon and Packard porcelain, 50 Shingle House Rd., Millwood, NY 10546.

Smart Tax Planning For Collectors

If you enjoy collecting, tax planning can have a big impact on your personal bottom line when you decide to sell all or part of your collection…or if it is lost in a fire or to theft.

Basic Rules

All income earned from a hobby is taxable and must be reported on your tax return. But special rules apply:

- Gain from the sale of a collectible held for more than one year is subject to a long-term capital gains tax rate of 28%. That is tax-favored if your tax bracket is higher than 28%.

Free Trial Issues Of Magazines

You'll find the most offers for free, no-risk magazine trial issues on the Web, but keep your eye out for magazine inserts and direct-mail advertisements as well.

Magazines offer free trial issues so that consumers can see if the publication is something that they'd like to receive regularly. If you can't find an advertisement for a free trial issue of a magazine you're interested in, call the publication to see if they will send you an issue before you make an annual investment.

Before you request a trial issue, however, consider the drawbacks: You will have to cancel within an allotted time period if you don't want to pay for the full subscription, and there's a chance you'll be mistakenly billed for an annual subscription even if you cancel your order.

Locating Free Trial Offers

To locate magazines with free trial offers, check out the **#1 Free Stuff** Web site at www.1freestuff.com or the **Electronic Newsstand** at www.enews.com. Or go directly to the Web site of the magazine you're interested in to find out about special deals.

You can also locate trial issue advertisements by checking out inserts in magazines at the library.

Remember, it is your responsibility to cancel your subscription if you aren't interested after receiving the first issue. Make sure you cancel before the prescribed deadline.

Free Magazine Subscriptions

Very rarely, but once in a while, you may find a magazine that offers free subscriptions. Sometimes these offers are limited to a certain age category, or are for a limited amount of time (such as one year).

Book Bargains

- **Daedalus Catalog** (800-395-2665, www.daedalus-books.com) offers many categories of books at sale prices. Once you get on their mailing list, you'll receive catalogs throughout the year.

- **The Strand Bookstore Catalog** (212-473-1452, www.strandbooks.com) is one of New York City's largest independent bookstores. They handle new and used books in every category.

- **Edward R. Hamilton Catalog** sends out large catalogs every few months. Write to Edward R. Hamilton Bookseller, Falls Village, CT 06031-5000 to get on their mailing list. They have an on-line catalog at www.edwardrhamilton.com.

Both **Borders** (www.borders.com) and **Barnes and Noble** (www.bn.com) offer discounts at their stores and on their Web sites.

- Expenses incurred while conducting your hobby are deductible up to the amount of income you earn from it. Include these expenses among your miscellaneous itemized expenses. That total is deductible to the extent that it exceeds 2% of your Adjusted Gross Income (AGI).
- Losses from a hobby are *not* deductible. *Included:* Losses from the sale of collectibles and losses in the form of expenses that exceed hobby income.

Keep Records

To minimize tax owed on the sale of items, keep careful records of your total cost for each item. Your taxable gain is the difference between this tax cost (also called *tax basis*) and the selling price. If you can't prove your cost basis, you may owe tax on the item's entire sale price.

When you buy a collectible, your tax cost is the price you pay for it. Tax cost increases when you further invest in items to restore or enhance them—such as the cost of restoring an old painting. Other considerations:

- When you inherit an item, its tax cost is the fair market value on the date of death of the person who left it to you or the alternate valuation date (six months later).
- When you receive an item as a gift, the tax cost from the giver is generally carried over to you.

Lost-Collection Tax Traps

If a collection is lost, such as to fire or theft, you may try to claim a casualty-loss deduction or file an insurance claim. Traps exist here as well:

- A casualty- or theft-loss deduction is allowed only to the extent of the tax cost of the lost property (subject to limitations). So if your tax cost is slight relative to its value—or if it is undocumented—your deduction may be worth little.
- Insurance proceeds generate *taxable gain* to the extent that they exceed your tax cost in the lost property.

Example: Your collection is worth $10,000, and your tax cost is $1,000. If the collection is lost in a fire and you receive $10,000 from insurance, you will have a taxable gain of $9,000.

Self-defense: Defer the taxable gain by reinvesting insurance proceeds in like-kind replacement property. Technical rules and deadlines apply—talk with your tax adviser.

Go Into Business

You may benefit tax-wise by pursuing your hobby as a business. Advantages:

- All expenses in running a business are deductible, without the 2%-of-AGI limitation on hobby expenses.

- Losses incurred from a business are deductible against income from other sources—such as salary. So converting your hobby into a business may greatly increase the deductions you get from it.

To qualify as a business: Your activity must have a profit motive. But you do not have to actually earn a profit. Profit motive can be demonstrated by managing the activity in a businesslike manner.

Caution: Once your collecting actually becomes a business, your collectibles become *inventory*. Gain on the sale of inventory is taxed at ordinary rates. So business status is not worthwhile if you expect to sell items at great profits.

Laurence I. Foster, CPA/PFS, partner, personal financial planning practice, Richard A. Eisner & Co., LLP, 575 Madison Ave., New York 10022.

How to Get the Best from Your Point-and-Shoot Camera

Problem: *Colors don't look rich and vibrant.* Use a slower film—ISO 100-speed or even ISO 50-speed. Just be sure you get close to your subject. These film speeds enhance color and produce more vibrant tones. Other solutions:

- Make sure your subject is the most colorful element in the shot. Avoid surrounding or backgrounding your subject with bright reds or oranges. These desaturate colors your subject is wearing.
- Take photos back to your processor, and ask for a remake if they are not bright enough. Many dull photos are the result of poor-quality printing.

Problem: *People in photos look old or heavyset.* Have subjects protrude their chins toward the camera while keeping shoulders stationary. This creates a slender neckline. Also have them show their teeth when they smile. It makes their faces look brighter.

Problem: *Subjects close their eyes just as the photo is taken.* Make a small, unexpected noise just before you take the photo. This gets people to raise their eyes involuntarily. Professional photographers hide a clicker in one hand—but any noisemaker will do.

Problem: *People come out too dark.* The reason for this problem is that the sun or light source was behind them. Throw more light on the subjects by using your flash, even in bright light.

Problem: *Sunlight makes people's faces look flat or washed out.* They look harsh because sunlight is falling unevenly across their faces.

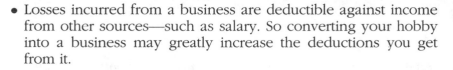

Bargain Books Both Rare And Used

Secondhand books are a great buy and sometimes you can turn up a true treasure. It's not unusual to find a signed first edition if you're willing to take the time and brush away the dust.

The **American Association of University Women** holds sales throughout the country. Watch for their ads in your local paper.

Yearly sales at local libraries are worth dropping in on. At other times during the year, your local library may sell off their old copies. Be sure to ask if they have anything available.

Antiquarian bookstores (you can find them in the yellow pages) are worth dropping in on. Some specialize in particular categories of books while others carry only first editions.

You can shop on-line for used books at **Bibliofind** (www.bibliofind.com) and **Amazon.com** (www.amazon.com).

Get the Best Music For Less

If you're a music buff, discount music catalogs and clubs can save you lots of money. Most discount music catalogs and clubs offer a 25% to 60% discount on retail prices. You can find a variety of music genres, hard-to-find music collections and limited-edition imports at sale prices. As with other mail-order offers, however, don't forget to add in shipping and handling costs when estimating your final price.

Daedalus Music Catalog

Daedalus (800-395-2665, www.daedalus-books.com), also a book catalog, has a discount music selection. It sends out seasonal catalogs with recordings that its editors like and want to recommend. Most of the items are available only on CD. In the catalog you can find classical, opera, vocals, jazz, world music, blues and children's music. Daedalus offers individual selections and collections at approximately 25% off regular retail prices.

Unlike music clubs, you can buy individual pieces without being required to purchase anything else later on.

Music Clubs

Columbia House (812-460-7000, www.columbiahouse.com) frequently changes its membership offers. It attracts customers with deals like "12 CDs for $1.99" and then requires you to buy more CDs at its "regular prices" to get the amazing offer.

BMG Music Service (www.bmgmusicservice.com), like Columbia House, has a large selection, and like Columbia House, features substantial discounts from list prices.

These kind of music clubs can be a good deal if they offer a large selection of music you want to buy (most selections are at least a year old).

Fill in shadows by using natural reflectors. Move the person close to a neutral-colored building or wall, which will reflect light more evenly.

Problem: *When people are not in the center of the photo, they look out of focus.* Most point-and-shoot cameras automatically focus the lens on the center of the frame unless you override it.

What to do: Point the focusing indicator in the viewfinder onto your subject. Push the shutter release button halfway down to lock the focus. While holding it halfway down, recompose your picture. Finish by pressing the release down.

Problem: *Subjects' eyes have red dots in their pupils.* There are steps you can take even if your point-and-shoot camera lacks an automatic red-eye reduction feature:

- Increase the light indoors by turning on lamps and raising window shades.
- Have your subject look directly at a light source for a moment just before you shoot the picture.

In both cases, shrinking their pupils will eliminate or minimize red-eye.

Bob Shell, award-winning photographer who often works with a point-and-shoot camera. He is author of 17 books on photography and editor of *Shutterbug*, 5211 S. Washington Ave., Titusville, FL 32780.

Welcome to the World of Digital Imaging

Digital imaging now offers a practical, affordable complement to film photography. With a digital camera you can take a picture, view it immediately, share it on the Web—or make a print. A scanner lets you convert favorite photos into image files that you can retouch and restore on your computer and distribute on-line...or as prints.

Most photo centers can now upload pictures captured on film to the Internet, as well.

While film still offers the most economical solution for quality prints, digital imaging's advantage and appeal is as an extension of your computer system for visual communications.

How It Works

A digital image begins as a file of information. That file is the digital equivalent of a negative, but you can work with it in ways never practical with film—revise it, enhance it, archive it to disk or transmit it over the Internet. Some basics:

Resolution The quality of a digital image is defined by its *resolution*, expressed in pixels—the more pixels the better.

Most digital cameras offer several resolution modes, from standard to superfine. Typically, the higher the resolution, the higher the quality of the image. Resolution determines the size of the image file.

Image Capture This is accomplished with a CCD (Charged Coupled Device) or CMOS (Complementary Metal Oxide Semiconductor) image chip. A CMOS is better for dim lighting situations, but a CCD is said to deliver cleaner images generally.

Pictures are stored in microchips or PC cards as a kind of "digital film." These are removable memory cards, such as CompactFlash, MiniatureCard or SmartMedia. With removable storage cards you can take unlimited pictures by just replacing them.

Printing Producing a quality print from a digital image at home requires buying inks and paper. Even then, the results may not be what you would expect from film. However, you can also have them printed at a photo lab, as well as share them on-line.

What You'll Need

Imaging System The computer is the core of any digital-imaging system. Know your system specifications when you shop for a camera. Suppliers publish the minimum requirements in computer RAM, processor speed and hard drive needed to support their cameras or scanners.

Cameras Digital cameras start in the $200 range and climb to more than $1,000. Available from traditional suppliers of photographic, computer and electronics equipment, they are best purchased in stores specializing in these products where experts are available to advise you.

If you merely want to share photos on-line, an entry-level camera will prove adequate. These are the digital equivalents of a point-and-shoot 35mm camera and offer basic features.

To print your images at home, you'll need a digital camera that offers at least a million pixels. The latest models go up to 4 million pixels. They cost $500 and up. Features include a zoom lens, larger LCD screens and several flash and shooting modes.

Scanners A scanner offers a less-expensive entry into digital imaging. Basic flatbed scanners, adequate for home users, sell for $100 or less. These "read" your photos, reflective art or text documents and convert them into a digital file within seconds.

Many people find the scanner the ideal way to copy treasured family photos, preserve them on disk and share them with family and friends. With the right paper, some photo realistic printers can give the images from your digital camera or your scanner the look and feel of prints from regular 35mm film.

Save Money: Watch the Rehearsals

Organizations such as the **New York Philharmonic** have free rehearsals of specific performances throughout the year. All you have to do is show up (and keep quiet). Most performers expect you to stay through the entire rehearsal. Check with the orchestra, ballet or other performance groups in your area and find out what you can see for free.

Sometimes open rehearsals are restricted to contributors, but if you give $50 (which is tax deductible) and see three or four rehearsals, you're ahead of the game.

117

University-Sponsored Movie Nights

Many universities and colleges offer low-cost or no-cost movies to the general public. These movies are usually current or recent releases, or movies that have not yet reached the video store.

Check Student Information Centers, bulletin boards or Web sites of your local college.

Digital Services Want to experiment with digital imaging without buying new equipment? Inquire at local photofinishing centers about what digital services they offer. Most now "digitize" film as part of their basic services.

Along with prints, you can copy photos to CD-ROM or upload to the Internet to a photo-sharing site such as www.clubphoto.com or www.picturetrail.com—where they can be shared by family and friends.

You'll also find more of these centers equipped with digital minilabs and self-serve kiosks. These minilabs combine traditional print and digital services, regardless of what camera you use. With the kiosks, you step up, insert your digital "film," place your order and it's ready in minutes.

Taking Images On-Line

There are two ways to share images on-line:

E-Mail Compose a message, attach an image file and send. All the recipient needs to do is click on the message and view the image. Or, you can upload images to your Web page or a commercial Internet site for viewing.

Upload to the Internet You can also have your photofinisher digitize and upload your pictures to the Internet. Once there, the images are assigned a URL, which you and others can use to view the pictures.

Help on the Web

For product reviews and information, check out these sites:

- www.camerareview.com
- www.cnet.com
- www.consumersearch.com
- www.consumereview.com
- www.dpreview.com
- www.epinions.com
- www.megapixel.net
- www.zdnet.com

Bill Schiffner, editor in chief of the imaging industry publication *Photographic Processing* and a contributor to *Digital Photographer* magazine and *JetPrint Photo.com*. Mr. Schiffner has been covering the photo industry for more than 15 years.

Bargain Movie Prices

Find out what hidden discounts are available at theaters near you. With some persistence, you can find deals even on first run films.

Bargain Matinees

Most movie matinees are less expensive than evening shows. The best way to save a couple dollars on your movie ticket is to go to an afternoon or twilight show. Matinee shows can be as inexpensive as $4 a ticket.

Large theater chains like Loews Theaters, Sony Theaters and Cineplex Odeons all have bargain ticket times. Bargain matinees are usually considered all shows that start before 6 pm. But this varies according to area and theater chain.

Discount days: Some theaters charge lower prices on a certain day of the week, often Monday or Tuesday. Check with individual theaters to see what they offer, and then plan to make that night your weekly movie event.

Senior and Child Discounts

If you are a senior citizen or have small children, be sure to ask about senior and child discounts. Don't expect a discount to be offered to you. Most theaters sell senior and children's movie tickets for a couple dollars less than the price of an adult ticket.

Discount Theater Chains and Lesser-Known Theaters

There are many discount chain theaters and small-town theaters across the country that show movies for a fraction of the price of regular chain tickets. Frequently the movies shown at these movie houses are no longer playing in regular theaters, or have been on the market for a month or more already.

Discount Chains Theater chains like O'Neil and Rio Entertainment, located in the South, have extraordinarily low ticket prices (sometimes as low as $1.50 a ticket for all shows or shows before 6 pm). Some of these chain theaters sell adult tickets for $3 and frequently offer matinee bargains and senior, student and child discounts as well.

Small-Town Theaters If you know of a theater that specializes in discount ticket rates, it may be worth your while to travel a short distance to pay less, especially for a large group.

Often small theaters have special rates for their ticket prices as well. Sometimes these theaters are located in small, less populated towns. Call the theaters in advance and compare ticket prices instead of automatically choosing the closest theater.

Finding Affordable Theater

Going to the theater does not have to mean spending a fortune. You can find low-cost theater options all over the country. From your local community theater to a neighboring city's theater hall, finding inexpensive ticket prices depends on knowing where to look.

Broadway's Best Bargains

Even the most popular Broadway shows can be seen at bargain prices.

Two organizations in New York City, **TDF** (212-221-0013) and the **Hit Show Club** (212-581-4211), offer ways to pay less for the best shows around.

TDF, through their **TKTS ticket booths**, sells tickets for Broadway and Off-Broadway theater shows at 25% to 50% below box office prices. There is a $2.50 service charge per ticket when you purchase your tickets at one of these booths. There is a TKTS ticket booth in Manhattan at Broadway and 47th Street. You can buy tickets on the day of performances only, for evening shows and Wednesday, Saturday and Sunday matinees. You need to pay for the tickets in cash.

With a Hit Show Club coupon, you can save 40% on Friday evening tickets or 2 pm Wednesday matinees of hit shows. Sometimes there are other special performance times when the coupons are also valid. You cannot request specific coupons from the Hit Show Club. You must leave your name and address on their machine and coupons will be sent to you in the mail.

Dining Card Alert

The listing of a dining card's participating restaurants may be out of date. Be especially cautious if the restaurant has opened in the past year. New restaurants sometimes use discount cards to promote themselves. Often, after restaurants have established a client base, they no longer accept the discount cards. Make sure the restaurant still accepts your dining card before you sit down.

Community Theater

Most areas have a community theater. If you enjoy seeing plays, dance recitals and shows, but don't want to spend a fortune, this may be your best theater bargain. Check with your local community center to find out about plays or shows scheduled throughout the year. Request a calendar of events.

School-Run Theater

Another option for inexpensive theater is to look into the performance schedules or calendar of events at your local high school or college. Most schools charge less than $10 per ticket.

Many secondary schools and colleges hold plays, shows, dance and music recitals during the entire academic year. You can save money and support the developing talent at your local high school or college.

Religious Organization Performances

Also, many religious organizations sponsor low-cost entertainment and theater performances. So, if you don't have a community theater, check with your local church or synagogue to see if they have performances and to request a calendar of events.

Matinees May Save You Money

Matinees usually cost less than evening theater performances. If you want to save money, but still want to enjoy a play or dance performance, consider going to a matinee.

Many theater organizations and performance centers offer discounted rates for matinees. All you have to do is ask.

Membership Discounts

By becoming a member of a theater or performance organization you can sometimes receive a discount of 20% to 50% on all ticket prices.

In most cases, you can become a member by donating a certain amount to the organization. Donation amounts depend upon the organization and area, but usually you don't have to spend more than $50 a year.

If you enjoy the theater in your area, ask about its membership options and other ways to save.

Seasonal and Subscriber Packages

If you know you'll want to see at least two performances offered by a particular theater company or auditorium this year, look into buying a seasonal or subscriber package. You will save at least 20% on individual ticket prices. Most companies and performance centers offer packages that have a range of performances and prices. Next time you go to a theater, be sure to get information on its ticket packages.

Discounts with Dining Cards

Discount dining cards offer savings of up to 30% on your bill at participating restaurants. That can amount to savings of approximately $1,560 a year if you dine out twice a week and spend about $50 a night.

To find cards in your area: Scan the local newspapers for ads placed by regional dining card companies. Frequent travelers should consider plans that offer good deals at your travel destination.

Which card is best for you? Call the different dining card companies and ask for a list of restaurants that accept the card. If you don't frequent the restaurants on a cards list, don't pay for the card. Even if a card covers restaurants you patronize, read the fine print. For example, iDine sets a $600 monthly limit in charges per month per restaurant. Some of the restaurants they list are starred, and discount only the first visit each month.

In Good Taste (IGT) The IGT card offers a 25% discount at participating restaurants for an annual fee of $25. Tips and taxes are not discounted. The IGT card is currently honored at approximately 3,500 establishments in metropolitan areas such as New York, New Jersey, Connecticut, Philadelphia, Atlanta, Chicago, Miami, Los Angeles, San Francisco and Washington, DC. For more information contact IGT at 800-444-8872 or www.igtcard.com.

Le Card Le Card is a perk offered to members of the Diners' Club. It grants a 20% discount of the entire bill, including tax and tip, at more than 1,700 restaurants nationwide. Membership in the Diners' Club costs $80 annually. For more information, contact the Diners' Club at 800-234-6377 or www.dinersclubus.com.

iDine Prime iDine Prime is the 800-pound gorilla of the discount dining card industry. Cards from Transmedia and Dining a la Card are now iDine Prime cards, and many prominent private label cards (for example, NY Times Card) are really handled by iDine. It offers discounts at approximately 7,000 participating restaurants nationwide. *Special plus to avoid possible embarrassment:* Register your regular credit card with iDine and pay for the meal with no other identification. Your meal will be discounted on the credit card bill. Membership is $49 annually and gives you a discount of 20% off the total bill, including food, drink, tax and tip…restaurant reviews…locations…and sample menus. Call 800-422-5090 or www.idineprime.com.

Vermont Restaurant Card The Vermont Restaurant Card offers two-for-one dining at each of more than 100 restaurants plus a bonus of four-for-three dining on all return visits to each restaurant with no dollar limits on your free entrée. It provides a 64-page

Restaurant Reviewer's Dining-Out Secrets

- Never order fish on Monday—odds are, it was fresh on *Saturday.*

- The best time to make a dinner reservation at a popular restaurant is about six hours before you want to eat. That is when cancellations start coming in.

- Avoid dining out on holidays. Restaurants are so overbooked that they often charge double for the same meals they serve every day. *Better:* Have your special meal the day before or after the holiday.

- Become a regular. The best restaurant is the one at which you are known.

- Go out for lunch. Restaurants that are always full for dinner are often desperate for midday business and may charge half as much then for the same menu items.

- Avoid new restaurants for at least three months—while they work out the kinks.

- Be nice. It's the surest way to get good service.

   Steven Shaw, a New York–based food critic for *Commentary* magazine and others. His Web site is www.fat-guy.com.

Eat Out for Less

If you love going out to eat but want to save money, consider these alternatives to going out for a full dinner.

Lunch: Meeting friends for lunch instead of dinner will save you 20% or more on your total bill. This is a great way to try out popular new restaurants, since it's much easier to get a reservation for lunch than dinner, the food costs less, the service may be better and the food will taste the same.

Dessert and coffee: Going out for dessert and coffee costs about 80% less than going out for an entire meal.

Appetizers and salads: Appetizers and salads are priced far lower than entrées, and portions are often more than large enough for an entire meal.

Buffets: Many restaurants offer all-you-can-eat lunch or dinner buffets that cost less than individual items on the menu.

Prix fixe: If you like to order several courses, try to find restaurants that offer prix-fixe (fixed-price) dinners, which usually include a limited selection of soups, appetizers, entrées and desserts for a reduced price.

Early and late: Eating at off-peak hours (before 6 pm or after 9 pm) will usually save you about 10% on your meal. In retirement communities, discounts are often even higher.

Bar food: Restaurants with bars usually have a limited number of appetizers, sandwiches and entrées you can order in that area. Since food on the bar menu is meant to be a complement to your drinks, it often costs less than it does in the dining room.

Birthday freebie: Some restaurants give customers a free dinner on their birthday. Ask at your favorite restaurants when you visit.

dining guide with the $35 per year membership. *For more information:* 802-658-3744 or www.vermontrestaurants.com.

Shrewd Way Into a "Booked" Hotel or Restaurant

Anyone can get a last-minute reservation at a popular restaurant or a room in a hotel that is booked solid—*if* you know what to say and how to tip.

Restaurants

You call at the last minute and are told no tables are available. What to do:

- Ask to speak with the maître d'. Get his/her name before your call is transferred.
- When the maître d' picks up, address him by his first name, and give your own full name. That creates the impression that you have been to the restaurant before and know him.
- After you give your name, say with empathy, "I know how busy you are tonight. But if you could find a way to have a table for me at 8 pm, I would be happy to take care of you the right way." This language may feel uncomfortable or cagey, but it is the language that service professionals recognize.

Helpful: Never mention a dollar figure—it is offensive and demeans his craft. Be precise in what you want. Otherwise you could end up eating at 5 pm or midnight.

- If the answer is still no, take one last shot. Say, "I don't mind waiting in the bar for a bit if it would help you out." Your flexibility lets him know that you are experienced and not unreasonable.
- If you get a table, tip the maître d' discreetly. Give him the folded bill(s) in your handshake.

The tip amount depends on the caliber of the restaurant, how badly you want to get in and how hard the maître d' had to work to get you the table—$10 is fine for a good restaurant on a typical night…$20 to $50 for more extreme circumstances, such as conventions, holidays, etc.

Valet Parking: Keeping Your Car Up Front

When your waiter hands you your check, hand him your valet ticket stub, and ask him to give it to the valet, so that your car is waiting up front by the time you pay the bill and leave the restaurant.

Hotels

You are told no rooms are available. What to do:

- Don't waste your time asking a clerk for special service. Ask to speak to the reservations or general manager. Be sure to get the manager's name before your call is transferred.
- Address the manager by Mr. or Ms. Unlike restaurants, better hotels are quite formal.
- Give your name (using Mr. or Ms.) and say with empathy, "Mr. or Ms. _____, I know how busy you are, but I'm in a bit of a spot. I'm meeting with an important client. If you could find a way to reserve a room for me, I can promise that you won't be disappointed."

Change the explanation, if appropriate, but keep it brief. Again, don't mention a specific dollar amount.

- If the answer is still no, don't give up. Try again by saying, "I can imagine how many calls you get like this, but I do a tremendous amount of business in the city. If you could help me out, I would really make it worth your while."

If this doesn't work, add, "If it would make life easier for you, I would be willing to arrive after 6 pm when you might have more cancellations." Be polite—there is a big difference between being persistent and being insistent, which is obnoxious.

- When you get your room, a tip of $20 is probably fine, but go as high as $50 if, say, the city is booked solid for a convention.

Mark Brenner, author of Tipping for Success: Secrets for How to Get In and Get Great Service *(Brenmark House) and founder of Brenmark House, a marketing solutions think tank for companies that require branding, marketing, sales and advertising strategies, Sherman Oaks, CA. www.brenmarkhouse.com.*

Breakfast at a Racetrack

You can often get a very inexpensive cup of coffee, and sometimes a full breakfast, during the horses' exercise hours at a racetrack. You don't have to pay an admission fee and you may even get a free barn tour. Contact a racing group, such as the **New York Racing Association**, to find out what you can do for free at stables like those at Saratoga Springs.

And you may want to consider staying for the day because general admission at racetracks is usually very inexpensive, especially if you can resist making bets and simply enjoy the thrill of the races instead.

Adult Membership Associations Cut Recreation Costs

Adult membership associations can really cut your recreation costs. If you are a member of AARP, AAA or a senior community center, you may be missing out on discounted recreation deals without even knowing it.

AARP (800-424-3410) AARP offers anyone 50 and older the opportunity to receive a variety of membership discounts. For just $10 a year, you can join AARP and receive discounts on airfare, auto rentals, flowers, travel accommodations and sightseeing tours and facilities.

Big-City Entertainment Treasures

The Learning Annex offers inexpensive classes and workshops to residents of the New York (212-371-0280) and San Francisco areas (415-788-5500). You can take writing and publishing classes, business classes, real estate classes, computer classes, health and spirituality workshops or a seminar on how to be your own boss.

Annual VIP membership entitles you to reduced prices on seminars, discount coupons, home delivery of the Learning Annex catalog and a waiver of the $10 per month registration fee for all classes for one full year. See www.learningannex.com for information on Los Angeles, San Diego and Toronto.

Also, as an AARP member you receive a copy of *Modern Maturity* magazine, a publication that focuses on the life, recreation options and welfare of adults over 50. You also receive a monthly AARP bulletin as well as a discount on America Online (an Internet access company).

Call AARP customer service toll free to become a member. You can call the regional office to get a listing of local services, activities, programs and services that AARP provides.

American Automotive Association (AAA) AAA is a nationwide organization that offers more than travel and automotive-related services. For approximately $50 a year ($20 for each additional driver), AAA offers roadside assistance, travel guides, maps and planning tips, and 10% to 30% discounts at restaurants and amusement areas around the country.

Once you join, be sure to ask for a listing of participants so you can take full advantage of the discounts AAA offers.

Senior Community Centers Many senior community centers issue membership cards that get you discounts at local establishments. Each center is individual, so you must ask about what it provides.

Also, many senior centers offer inexpensive recreational activities and programs. You can take a poetry course, join a nature club or go to a spring dance. Just because you're over a certain age doesn't mean you have to stop learning or having fun.

Look in your local *Yellow Pages* under "Senior Services" for a center near you.

Great Deals on Your Favorite Sports

I t's not hard to find good deals on playing (or watching) your favorite sport. If you like tennis, swimming or baseball, here's how to enjoy them for less:

Playing a Sport for Less

Most towns and communities have sporting programs and facilities with very low usage fees. Also, you may want to consider checking out the policies at your local high school's or college's swimming facilities—sometimes you can swim for free or at the discounted student cost.

Golf Courses Town or county golf courses usually charge residents of the area much lower greens fees than nonresidents. And residents usually get priority on booking tee times. Many times you can also rent golf equipment, saving you money on expensive clubs and golf bags. Sometimes there are additional fees for renting

a cart or having a caddie carry your bags. Call your state's department of recreation to locate municipal and public courses in your area and ask about pricing.

Tennis Courts Frequently, you can play tennis at a municipal, high school or college campus tennis court for free or at a low cost. You will most likely need to sign up for a court ahead of time. You usually need to have your own tennis racket and balls. Locate the recreation departments of your town or local school, and ask about the policies of playing tennis at their courts.

Recreational Leagues for Children and Adults Many towns and cities have recreational softball, basketball, tennis, football and soccer leagues for children and adults. Some of these leagues charge a higher fees than others, but most of the time you pay less than $50 for a season.

Contact your town or city's recreation department to find out if there are any local recreational sporting leagues.

Sporting Associations That Cater to 50-Plus Adults

All around the nation, there are a variety of sporting associations and clubs that cater to members age 50 and up.

Aerobic and Fitness Association of America Aerobic training instruction is a program associated with this organization that trains senior fitness instructors to conduct and develop exercise programs for the 50-plus participant. (818-905-0040, www.afaa.com)

International Swimming Hall of Fame The International Swimming Hall of Fame sponsors and promotes swimming activities including diving, water polo and water aerobics to encourage swimming as a physical activity to help older Americans keep fit. It supports numerous over-55 swimming competitions and events each year. (954-462-6536, www.ishof.org)

National Recreation and Parks Association The National Recreation and Parks Association represents more than 4,000 parks and recreation facilities that offer programs in recreation and physical activity. It has a special leisure and aging division catering to the interests of older adults. (703-858-0784, www.nrpa.org)

North American Senior Circuit Softball This group sponsors a fall tournament for senior softball players. There are 16 regional tournaments where older adults compete in five-year age divisions. The event is endorsed by the American Softball Association. (586-792-2110 or 586-791-2632)

Road Runner's Club of America The Road Runner's Club is a not-for-profit running club dedicated to promoting long-distance running as both a competitive sport and recreational exercise, and 35% of their members of are over age 50. It has more than 600 clubs throughout the US, and hold an annual convention. (703-836-0558, www.rrca.org)

Alumni Discounts

If you're a member of an alumni association, you may be able to get discounts on hotels, car rentals, theater and sporting events. For example, being an alumni association member of a state university may get you discounts to the school's football games or the state's symphony orchestra.

If you're an alumni member, call the alumni department of your school and ask about what discounts you may be missing out on. Or if you're not a member of your school's alumni association, call and ask how you can become one and if there are any member benefits.

Senior Golf Vacations

John Jacobs' Golf Schools offer instruction nationwide at premier golf courses and deluxe resorts. Options include half-day, two-day and three-day sessions, and a full-week golf school that covers all aspects of the game.

Persons age 62 and older receive a 10% discount from July through December. Juniors age 17 and younger receive a 20% discount year-round—making it an attractive intergenerational activity. *Details:* 800-472-5007 ...www.jacobsgolf.com.

Bargain Sports Events

Finding a bargain at a sporting event may be just a matter of rooting for the second-best team. If you love sports and don't need to watch top players, there are tons of ways to see an event for less than $20.

Major League Ticket Pricing Professional sports admissions tickets can range from very expensive (and impossible to get) to relatively reasonable ($15 or so). Be warned, however—less expensive tickets may mean that your seat is far, far away from the playing field.

Minor League Teams You can be a spectator at a minor league game for approximately $14 for the best seats. If you are willing to sit further from the action, you can purchase a ticket for around $5 to $7 a game.

Call the local stadiums that hold sporting events and ask for a calendar of events and ticket pricing list. Or call your state's second-tier teams for a schedule of their home games, and watch sports up close at a price you can handle.

College and High School Sporting Events Another alternative to expensive professional sporting events is being a spectator at college or high school games. Some schools offer free admission to their games. Contact a school and ask for an event schedule and pricing policy sheet.

Keep in mind that, like top professional teams, top college teams may be sold out for most games as soon as the season begins. For great bargains in sports it is important to think ahead and make your plans before the start of the season. Also, some schools may give priority ticketing to their students and alumni, so if you know someone who goes (or went) to the school, you may want to consider asking them to get you tickets for a game or a season ticket package.

Spring Games and Preseason Training

A great way to save money on sporting events is to watch preseason training workouts and games. Since training times are not as intense as the regular season, you may even get a chance to meet (or shake hands with) your favorite players. Call the stadium where your favorite team plays and ask where you can get information on practice sessions and preseason games.

For about half the price of a regular season ticket, you can be a spectator at most spring training baseball camps. Call your favorite team and ask for its between-season schedule. Also ask how and where you can watch the players train, or when you can purchase tickets for preseason games.

For baseball spring training camps and session information in Florida, call the Florida Sports Foundation (850-488-8347, www. flasports.com) to receive a guide of spring training information

and contact numbers. Tickets are usually less than $15 for box seats and approximately $8 for general admission seats. The highly ranked teams may charge higher fees, even for spring training games.

Guide to Getting Started in Golf

Three million Americans take up golf each year...and an equal number give it up. If you're eager to start, it's best to begin simply in order to avoid frustration.

Equipment

The basics—an inexpensive starter set of four clubs, including a single wood, middle iron, short iron and putter—cost approximately $20 to $50 per club.

This is all you need for at least the first few months. Any knowledgeable salesperson can help pick the right-sized clubs. Buying used clubs at driving ranges, pro shops or used sporting-goods stores makes starting even less expensive. Having fewer clubs minimizes confusion. Beginners can concentrate on the fundamentals of the swing, not on minuscule differences among the 14 clubs in a full set.

Attire

Most players use gloves and golf shoes, but neither are required. *Clothing:* Basic slacks, Bermuda shorts or khakis...collared shirts ...a hat. No cutoffs, tank tops or T-shirts.

You will need a bag for clubs, balls, tees and a bottle of water.

Logistics

Golf is a walking game, but these days, many players rent carts. If your golf bag is too heavy, try a pull cart with wheels.

Costs to play: From $10 for nine holes at a municipal course to $350 per round at the prestigious Pebble Beach resort in Carmel, CA. Figure $50 to $60 on average, plus about $10 to $20 per person for a cart.

Learning the Game

Bookstores and magazine stands overflow with golf-instruction tools.

Some favorites: *Ben Hogan's Five Lessons* (Simon & Schuster)... *Learn Golf in a Weekend* by Peter Ballingall (Knopf).

But books and tapes are no substitute for direct feedback. Without an instructor's trained eye, it's impossible to know whether your grip, stance, alignment or swing changes are effective.

Two Money-Saving Tips for Golfers

Pay *per round* if you play only occasionally and live near a club that allows non-members on the course. This saves annual dues, which average $4,000, and initiation fees, which can cost $20,000 or more.

If the club near you does not allow pay-per-round, ask about a *scaled-down membership*, perhaps weekday-only or other restricted play, for greatly reduced initiation fees and monthly dues.

Forbes, 60 Fifth Ave., New York 10011.

Book an off-season discount golf tour. **Leisure Link International** offers tours to areas with multiple courses. Prices include discounted lodging and off-season greens fees. *Information:* 888-801-8808...www.eleisurelink.com.

Discount Mail-Order Golf Supplies

With **Ralph Maltby's GolfWorks** catalog (800-848-8358, www.golfworks. com) you can get golf supplies for less. From clubs to balls to bags, shopping through this catalog may save you enough money to pay the extra caddie fees. Save 50% by purchasing unassembled golf clubs (they're easy to put together). You'll also find informative golf booklets which may help you improve your game at 15% lower prices than retail.

Best way to start: Private lessons several times a month. As you improve, once a month. After a year or so, get an occasional tune-up.

Lessons are offered at private and public golf courses and most driving ranges. *Best:* A certified PGA teaching professional.

Cost: $20 per hour to more than $500 per hour for a "big name" instructor.

Golf schools and camps are popular, but it's difficult to assimilate the torrent of information provided in a typical three- to five-day course.

Cost: Depending on the school's amenities and the celebrity quotient of the instructors, fees can range from $40 for a short clinic to $3,000 per week at a posh resort.

Golf school is best for players who have some experience, although almost any resort has teaching facilities, a driving range and at least one course that won't be too taxing.

Practice Efficiently

For all players, but especially beginners, short-game practice is essential. Most shots in golf come from within 100 yards.

A great new book on how to practice at the driving range is *Range Rats* by Roger Maltbie (Woodford).

Maintain contact with someone who knows your game and swing…and who can catch and correct bad habits before they become ingrained.

It's best to play with someone a bit better than yourself, preferably someone with patience. But lots of people fall in love with the game just playing on their own.

Joel Zuckerman, golf writer and single-digit handicapper, based in Savannah.

Buying a Tennis Racquet

Buying a tennis racquet is more complicated than you may believe. However, if you know what to look for, you'll get the best deal for your money. Factors that determine your choice when buying a tennis racquet include your level of expertise and your type of play.

Racquets come in varying weights, head sizes, lengths, shapes, stiffness and grip sizes. Heavy racquets (11 ounces or more) add power. Mid-weight racquets (9.8–10.9 ounces) fit most players. Light (9–9.4 ounces) offer excellent shot control and are easier for smaller players to use.

Racquet Heads (measuring the strung area) vary from 125 square inches down to under 100 square inches. The heads offer increasingly better control as they decrease in size. Heads come in oval or teardrop shapes. The oval provides better feel of the racquet. The teardrop has a larger area for the sweet spot.

Lengths (from top of head to bottom of grip) run from traditional (27.5–28 inches) to long (up to 29 inches). The longer racquets enable you to cover more of the court and hit with more power. The shorter racquets are more comfortable for smaller players and offer more control.

A too-small grip will lead to tennis elbow. To choose the best grip, measure your tennis hand from the bottom horizontal crease in your palm to the tip of your ring finger. This is your ideal grip size.

- **Beginners:** Look for an oversized (107–125 square inches) pre-strung racquet. It offers a large sweet spot and is the most versatile.
- **Intermediate:** (Play once a week.) Power players should look for a lighter, smaller racquet giving better swing control. If you're a finesse player, choose a larger racquet to provide extra power.
- **Advanced:** (Play in a league and more than once a week.) Look for the latest composite racquets that provide power with lighter weight.

If you're a recreational player, pre-strung racquets are perfectly acceptable. Unstrung racquets enable the advanced player to customize the string and tension to fit his/her playing style.

For more information: Frog Trader (866-444-FROG, www.frog trader.com).

Buying a Bike

Bicycles aren't toys. They are an investment in transportation, exercise, pleasure and a sense of well-being. How to get the best value for your dollar is an important consideration.

Wise move: Buy from a reputable bicycle store where proper fitting and adjustments, as well as knowledgeable advice, comes with the purchase.

What you plan to do with the bike determines the type you should look at:

- **Bicycles come in various flavors**—mountain bikes (rugged for off-road use)…road bikes (designed for pavement riding and speed)…hybrid bikes (cross between mountain and road bikes and great for commuting)…cruisers (made for the casual rider)…comfort bikes (hybrids with more upright riding position, softer saddle and lower gearing)…niche bikes (recumbents/tandems/electric assist).
- **Wheel size and frame size vary**—choose the appropriate combination for your size. The length of your inseam determines the correct frame size. (*Note:* Toy stores rarely have a choice of frame sizes.) Generally, 2" of clearance between crotch and the

Best Bowling Balls

- **Beginning bowlers:** Buy a conventional ball with a plastic outer layer (about $60). Or consider one of the new clear balls with a colorful design inside, including Mickey Mouse and other Disney figures ($100 to $125). *Top brands:* Columbia White Dot… Ebonite Maxim.
- **Skilled players:** Try a ball covered with reactive resin ($100 to $300). It grips the lane better, hooks more and drives through pins with more force. *Top brands:* Brunswick… Columbia…Ebonite.
- **Professional-level players:** High-tech balls have a reactive-resin cover embedded with tiny spikes for more grabbing power on the lanes ($100 to $300). *Top brands:* Brunswick…Columbia.

Pro shops or bowling centers will custom-drill finger holes. Holes drilled in discount stores are unlikely to fit properly.

You don't have to buy the most expensive ball for the best performance. Midpriced lines can be just as good. Ask your pro-shop operator for a recommendation.

Denny Torgerson, PBA Champion who bowls in 30 to 40 tournaments a year. He is a consultant to top bowlers and pro-shop operators, Maquoketa, IA.

Best Time to Buy Skis

Skis are a bargain in the spring. Dealers start marking down prices in February, but big discounts—up to 50%—come in May and June. Boots, poles and winter clothing are discounted, too.

Best buys: Models whose manufacturers plan to change graphics or colors next season.

Pat McDonald, general manager, Fiorini Sports, Seattle, quoted in *SmartMoney*, 1755 Broadway, New York 10019.

crossbar is sufficient for road bikes and trail bikes. Mountain bikes should allow for 3" to 6" of crossbar clearance. A competent bike shop should be able to guide you based on your physical measurements and the type of riding you'll do.

- **Test ride the bike before you buy.** Be aware of seat comfort, leg extension, arm reach to the handle bars, hand position on the grips, pressure on hands, arms, shoulders and neck.
- **Get a written receipt with the bike's serial number.**
- **Understand the warranty.**

Good sources of information: www.bikesrnottoys.com, National Bike Dealers Association (www.nbda.com).

Choosing Snorkeling Equipment

You don't have to be a scuba diver to visit the intriguing and colorful world under the sea. Snorkeling is an easier and more economical way.

To snorkel, you need very little equipment—just a mask, snorkel and fins. A disposable underwater camera and fish identification card can enhance the fun.

Before You Go

Color plays a big part in water safety. Make yourself visible with a brightly colored snorkel, mask, fins and bathing suit. Hot pink, lime green and yellow are more noticeable than dark colors.

Mask A fitted mask is the key element of a good snorkeling experience. *Cost:* $30 to $50. You can also find masks at discount stores for as little as $10.

Test for an airtight seal by putting a mask over your face—be sure all your hair is brushed away from your skin. Inhale through your nose, and hold your breath. If the mask stays on your face, you have an airtight seal.

Before you use a new mask, treat it to prevent fogging. Scrub the inside of the lens with toothpaste or Soft Scrub cleanser. Thereafter, before you go into the water, wipe a defog solution (available in dive shops)—or your own saliva—on the inside of the mask lens. Then rise with water (sea or fresh).

If nearsighted: Wear contact lenses with a regular mask—or buy or rent a corrective mask. *Cost:* $100 to $150 to buy…about $3 to $5 per day to rent.

Fins Water booties are your best bet and should be worn with an open-heel fin. For bare feet, choose shoe fins. You want to protect your feet if snorkeling near reefs, lava or rocks. *Cost:* $30 to $130.

Snorkel Choose a snorkel with a comfortable silicone mouthpiece and a self-draining purge valve. It is also good to have a brightly colored tube—it will be the only thing sticking out of the water.

Extra Equipment A flotation device—inner tube, boogie board, kick board or snorkeler's vest—can greatly enhance the experience for novice snorkelers. These items are also available in dive shops to rent or purchase. *Price:* $60 to buy a boogie board...about $2 to $10 per day to rent.

Casey and Astrid Mahaney, Reno, NV-based authors of *Diving & Snorkeling Hawaii* (Lonely Planet) and five marine-life identification books. Their dive travel Web site is www.bluekirio.com.

If You Spend More Than An Hour in a Casino... Collect Freebies

If you gamble at a casino, you're probably eligible for free or discounted meals, rooms, show tickets and, in some cases, cash or merchandise.

Before You Go

Several Web sites offer free information about casino "comps" that are available. My favorites:

- **Casino Central** (www.casinocentral.com). Room, meal, beverage and other US casino promotions...coupons that can be downloaded and printed...and comps sent to your E-mail address.
- **Las Vegas Online Entertainment Guide** (www.lvol.com). Internet links to individual hotels that list comps and other promotions.
- **About.com** (www.about.com). The Casino Gambling portion of its Web site has loads of information about comps as well as gambling articles. Click on "Comps" and then choose the "Funbook Coupons" link.

Once You Arrive

Join Your Hotel/Casino's Slot Club Membership is free or for a low fee. Once you join, you receive a plastic card that earns points each time you play a slot or video-poker machine. Points can then be used toward discounts on food, drinks and merchandise.

Smart play: Earn points twice as fast by requesting two member cards for the same account. On your first visit, request one for yourself...on a later visit, ask for one for your spouse. Benefits:

- You earn points on the same account.
- You will receive twice as many offers in the mail for free rooms.

Best Bargains for Senior Skiers

The **Over-the-Hill Gang** has more than 6,500 members across the US, all skiers ages 50 and up. The annual membership fee is $40 per person or $65 per couple ($285 to $485 for a lifetime membership), and members participate in highly discounted group ski trips (both downhill and cross-country) to ski resorts in this country and overseas. Members also receive lodging and transportation discounts when they ski on their own.

The Gang takes advantage of group, seasonal and age-related discounts to bring you high-quality skiing at the lowest possible prices. Packages include lodging, lift tickets and social activities, plus airfare on overseas trips. And, no doubt, you'll meet some of the country's top mature bargain hunters on your trip.

More information: Over the Hill Gang, 1820 W. Colorado Ave., Colorado Springs 80904, 719-389-0022, www.othgi.com.

Have Fun at The Casino

- **Set a gaming budget**—the amount that you can afford to lose—and stay within it.

- **Play slowly.** Join tables or games with several other players. You'll meet more people and the slower play will make your budget last longer. Even slot machines are more fun when played slowly.

- **Join the casino's "slot club."** Nearly every casino has a club that provides members comps, such as free meals, discounted rooms and tickets to shows.

- **Enjoy the chance of winning**— but don't count on it. Never believe anybody's claim to have a system to beat the casino.

Anthony Curtis, publisher, Las Vegas Advisor, *3687 Procyon Ave., Las Vegas 89103.*

- You'll be able to book back-to-back reservations for longer discounted stays.

Ask the Pit Boss to Rate or Monitor Your Play for Comps When you join a table game such as blackjack, the pit boss will track your play to determine the value of comps you are due. The quality of your comps depends on the table's minimum bet...how many hands you play...and for how long.

Examples: Four hours spent playing at the $25 blackjack table usually entitles you to a free meal at the casino's buffet restaurant. Eight hours of play often results in a free room or a complimentary round of golf.

Top Las Vegas Comps

Tickets to Shows Play the $75/hand blackjack table for three hours and receive a free $100 ticket. Most hotels also "bill back" free show tickets. This means if you play for three hours at one hotel/casino, you can request a ticket to a show at another hotel/casino.

Important: Let the pit boss know which show you would like to see as soon as you sit down at the table.

Pick Up a Boarding Pass Club Card This free, frequent-player program is offered at the four Station casinos in Las Vegas—Boulder Station, Palace Station, Sunset Station and Texas Station. Each time you play the slot machines or gaming tables, you earn points for free rooms, food and movie tickets.

Top Atlantic City Comps

The following casinos are the most generous with all comps—cash back, rooms, food, show tickets and special promotional items. They each return at least 25% of revenue in comps:

- **Caesars**—voted "best" blackjack tables in Atlantic City.
- **Hilton** offers great funbooks filled with discount coupons. Room and package discounts are often available.
- **Trump Plaza**—two-for-one cards can be used.

Other favorites:

- **Harrah's.** Total Gold Card is good at all 19 of Harrah's US properties. Comps include preferred restaurant seating...airline and other travel benefits...show tickets.
- **Showboat.** Voted best casino for quarter players. Cash-back incentives for all...room discounts for higher-level players.

Gayle Mitchell, president, Casino Players Workshop & Seminars, 4001 E. Bell Rd., #114-270, Phoenix 85032. Her book is All Slots Made Easier *(Casino Players Workshop & Seminars).*

Never Be Lonely Again

Living alone can be peaceful, but it can also be isolating. If you're feeling a bit cut off, the following resources can help you reconnect with others and stay actively involved in life:

Adopt a Pet

Purina Pets for People Program (www.purina.com) enables you to adopt an older homeless animal at minimal cost—with Purina covering adoption fees, vaccinations, spaying or neutering, initial veterinary costs and a starter kit that includes a pet-care booklet and videotape and a coupon for Purina pet foods.

Host Visitors from Around the World

US Servas is an international cooperative of hosts and travelers that is open to persons of all ages. Participants make their own arrangements for a two-day minimum visit. Those who can't host overnight visitors can become day hosts. *Cost:* $65/annual membership.

US Servas, Inc., 11 John St., Rm. 505, New York 10038, 212-267-0252, www.usservas.org.

American Field Service (AFS) enables you to host a high school student from another country. Placements are made on a combination of interests, temperaments and lifestyles. A local AFS liaison provides orientation and counseling. Students attend the local high school during their stay.

Host families are not paid, but can take a $50 tax deduction for every month they house a student. If a teenager sounds too challenging, you may host a teacher.

American Field Service, 71 W. 23rd St., 17th Floor, New York 10010, 800-237-4636, www.afs.org.

Volunteer in Your Community

Retired Senior Volunteer Program (RSVP) offers assignments to retirees age 55 and older. There are no income or educational requirements. Assignments may involve social service in schools, courts, libraries, day care centers, hospitals or community centers.

Transportation to and from the site is reimbursed, depending on location.

Retired Senior Volunteer Program, 929 L St. NW, Washington, DC 20001, 202-289-1510, www.familyandchildservices.org.

Service Corps of Retired Executives (SCORE) gives retired business owners, executives, accountants, attorneys and military officers a chance to provide free advice to companies starting, growing, developing or exiting a business. Volunteers receive no salary, but expenses are covered by SCORE.

No Cost Ways to Beat Boredom

Break out of boredom by changing your habits...

- Revisit old fantasies and make time for something you always wanted to do. Write the book you tell everyone you are going to write.

- Start building a new network of friends—check out a local bookstore, community gathering place, even on-line chat rooms.

- When you know you'll have a long wait somewhere, take something to do with you.

- In the next week, do 10 things you never thought of doing.

Ernie J. Zelinski, creativity consultant, Edmonton, Alberta, Canada. He is author of The Joy of Not Working: A Book for the Retired, Unemployed and Overworked *(Ten Speed).*

When You Travel With Grandkids

- Give the parents a complete itinerary with phone numbers.

- Talk to parents about the kids' routines and health and safety needs.

- Take along healthful snacks. Don't forget moist towelettes for cleanup.

- Discuss behavior expected during the trip—including how much money kids can spend, and on what.

- Have alternative plans in case of bad weather or other problems. Include quiet time in your planning.

Adele Malott, syndicated weekly columnist, writing in *The Mature Traveler*, Box 1543, Wildomar, CA 92595.

Service Corps of Retired Executives, 409 Third St. SW, Sixth Fl., Washington, DC 20024, 202-205-6762, www.score.org.

Strengthen Bonds With Grandchildren

Grandtravel is a special vacation program that encourages grandparents and grandchildren to travel together. One- to two-week vacations are offered every summer throughout the US and abroad. Accommodations are deluxe. *Cost:* $4,565 per person (seven nights in Washington, DC) to $8,950 per person (two weeks in Australia).

Grandtravel, 6900 Wisconsin Ave., Ste. 706, Chevy Chase, Maryland 20815, 800-247-7651, www.grandtravel.com.

Ellen Lederman, an occupational therapist based in Alpharetta, GA, and author of *Making Life More Livable: A Practical Guide to Over 1,000 Products and Resources for Living Well in the Mature Years* (Fireside).

8

Stay Healthy for Less

Savvy Ways to Cut Your Medical Bills

You can cut the cost of your medical bills without sacrificing top-quality care. All it takes is a few extra minutes to plan ahead.

Avoid Office Visits

You can save a lot of money by avoiding unnecessary visits to the doctor's office. Consider calling your doctor's office for answers to questions about medications, reactions to treatment or recurring problems—instead of paying for a full visit.

Ask if there are particular times of the day or week which are better for phone consultations, and make sure to ask if there is a charge for such calls.

Avoid the Emergency Room

Prepare yourself for minor illnesses and injuries with a home first aid kit.

Keep your first aid supplies in a sturdy container with a lid, such as a tool box. Place a piece of masking tape on the outside of the box, with your local emergency phone number and the number of the poison control center.

Keep the kit in a dry area (not the bathroom), and out of the reach of small children. All household members (except small children) and your baby-sitters should know the location of the kit.

Supplies for Your First Aid Kit

❑ Ace bandage (3" width)

❑ Adhesive bandages (various sizes)

❑ Antibiotic ointment

❑ Antiseptic washes

❑ Bar of plain, non-scented soap

❑ Calamine lotion

❑ Cotton-tipped swabs and cotton balls or absorbent cotton pads

❑ First aid manual

❑ Flashlight with extra batteries

❑ Hydrogen peroxide

❑ Individually packaged, sterile gauze pads

❑ Large safety pins

❑ Large triangular bandages

❑ Oral or rectal thermometers

❑ Petroleum jelly

❑ Roll of adhesive tape (1" width)

❑ Rolls of gauze bandages (2" and 4" widths)

❑ Safety matches

❑ Scissors

❑ Small bottles of aspirin and acetaminophen

❑ Tissues

❑ Tweezers and sewing needles

Stay Away From the Emergency Room

Emergency rooms are extremely expensive for nonemergency care. You may pay up to 10 times more than you would for the same treatment at your doctor's office. Many insurance plans, such as HMOs, are refusing to pay bills for visits to the emergency room that aren't life threatening.

If you're concerned about a child's earache or sore throat, call your doctor to find out how serious the problem is, and if it can be treated at home.

Or you may want to consider using an ambulatory care center for basic medical problems, such as cuts, sprains, broken bones and sore throats. Most centers cost considerably less than hospital emergency rooms, and many are open 24 hours a day.

Buy a 90-day Supply of Drugs

If you buy drugs with a co-payment, ask your doctor or pharmacist for a 90-day supply instead of three 30-day supplies. This way you will only have to pay one co-payment instead of three. *Warning:* Many plans cover only a 30-day supply at a time.

Helpful Hints to Lower Your Hospital Bills

To lower your medical costs, make sure every procedure, test or hospital stay is absolutely necessary.

Outpatient Procedures

Many procedures that used to require an overnight hospital stay can now be done on an outpatient basis, which can cost 50% less than a regular hospital procedure. Ask your doctor about new, minimally invasive surgical techniques, which may be less expensive and less traumatic than their predecessors.

A Second Opinion

Before admitting yourself to a hospital for surgery, you should always get a second opinion. Unnecessary surgery is a physical and economic risk most people can't afford to take.

Discuss Your Hospital Options

Don't allow a hospital to be chosen for you. Most doctors are affiliated with more than one hospital, so you should discuss your options. Many community hospitals may be 25% cheaper than for-profit hospitals, which may order more tests and have bigger markups on procedures and services. Be sure, however, that the reputation of a less expensive hospital is just as good as a more expensive private facility.

Question Testing

Ask your doctor why each hospital test must be done. And consider insisting that the hospital get your advance approval for all tests and procedures.

Don't Pay Hotel Prices

Hospitals have check-in and check-out times, just like hotels. If you arrive early or leave late you will be charged for an extra day. Consider calling ahead to find out the check-in time. When you're ready to leave, check out promptly.

Also, you may want to avoid weekend admissions if possible. In many cases, specialized medical care won't be available and you may be charged premium rates for basic care.

Make sure you check to see what the hospital charges for various services, like filling out forms for you, health and beauty aids and the cost of medication you may need when you leave. Instead of paying $50 to $100 for these incidentals, ask to fill out your own paperwork, bring your own toiletries and consider filling new prescriptions at a pharmacy outside the hospital.

Inspect and Dissect Your Hospital Bills

Unfortunately, hospital bills are frequently inaccurate. Consider checking with your surgeon after surgery to find out if all the equipment that you were billed for was used. Make sure that there wasn't any medication on your bill that you did not receive. And if you do find discrepancies, call the hospital billing department and ask that your bill be reduced.

Savings Are in The Details

You can avoid being overcharged on your hospital bills by requesting a fully itemized bill and reviewing it carefully.

Since billing mistakes are common, you may want to document all of your medications, procedures, tests and services throughout your stay. You can compare your log to the hospital's bill.

Here's what to look for when reviewing your bill:

- Duplicate billings (often for tests or X rays).
- Unauthorized tests (especially if you have asked for advance approval).
- Phantom charges (often for medications that have never been administered to you).
- Bulk charges (if there is a broad heading, such as Pharmacy, you can't know if the total is accurate. So ask for a more detailed breakdown of the charges incurred).

What Hospitals Don't Want You to Know

Hospitals are fighting for their survival. Cutbacks from the federal government and from managed-care plans have reduced their revenue streams. Throughout the US, hospitals are closing, merging or implementing draconian cost-cutting measures.

But it's not just hospitals that are at risk. Cutting corners also threatens the well-being of patients. Here's what hospitals don't want to tell you—and what you can do about it:

They're Discharging Patients "Quicker and Sicker" To save money, hospitals are routinely discharging patients much earlier than they used to. If they plan to send you home, be sure you'll have the support services you may need, such as visiting nurses and physical therapists, and that family members will be able to perform

About Hospital Consent Forms

Hospital consent forms may contain provisions you don't like. Sign a form only if you fully agree with—and understand—what is in it.

Clauses to watch out for: Permission to videotape or photograph your operation or have spectators watch. If you do not want this, cross out the provision or write your wishes on the document. *And:* Any statement that a procedure will be performed "under the direction of" your doctor or by others "selected by him/her." This could mean a medical resident will do your surgery.

Charles Inlander, president, People's Medical Society, Allentown, PA. He is coauthor of This Won't Hurt: And Other Lies My Doctor Tells Me *(People's Medical Society).*

any duties expected of them. If you don't feel your condition or home circumstances make discharge safe, alert your doctor. If necessary, file an appeal with your insurer.

They've Cut Their Nursing Staffs Even though doctors get most of the glory, it's the nurses who run hospitals. They monitor your condition, administer medications and make sure medical equipment functions properly. But maintaining a skilled nursing staff is expensive, so hospitals have found it cheaper to substitute "aides," many of whom have little bedside training.

You have the right to inquire about the qualifications of anyone who treats you. Ideally, your main nurse will be a registered nurse (RN). Each nurse working on a typical medical or surgical ward should be caring for no more than five patients or no more than two in an intensive-care unit.

If the nurse-to-patient ratio is much higher than that, consider having family members stay with you at all times while you're hospitalized or, if you can afford it, hire a private-duty nurse.

They Reuse Disposable Medical Equipment Some equipment, such as dialysis catheters, intended for single-use only are routinely cleaned and reused, raising some concerns about infection and product failure. While reusing equipment is not illegal, I recommend requesting that only new equipment be used.

They Don't Report Lousy Doctors Although the law mandates that incompetence or misconduct among physicians must be reported to the federal government, 60% of hospitals have never filed even a single disciplinary report in the last decade. Part of the reason is that doctors are hospitals' "cash cows." They have the power to direct their patients to competing hospitals, so there's an incentive to not make waves.

Your best bet: Avoid potentially dangerous doctors by learning as much as you can about your condition and medications. The more you know, the better your ability to spot a bad apple.

They Overwork Residents and Interns Despite regulations that prohibit most doctors-in-training from working more than 80 hours a week, these limits are routinely violated. If you are admitted to a teaching hospital, ask your resident or intern how many consecutive hours he/she has been working. Thirty-six-hour shifts are still routine. If you're concerned, it's your right to refuse care from anyone who looks too exhausted to provide it.

If you believe a hospital is doing anything that imperils patients, I recommend reporting it to your state's regulatory authority or contacting the not-for-profit Joint Commission on Accreditation of Healthcare Organizations (JCAHO) at 800-994-6610 or by E-mail at complaint@jcaho.org.

Timothy McCall, MD, a Boston internist and author of Examining Your Doctor: A Patient's Guide to Avoiding Harmful Medical Care *(Citadel) and a commentator for the National Public Radio program "Marketplace."*

Get the Respect You Deserve in the Hospital

A hospital stay should be a time of healing. But all too often the experience erodes a patient's personal dignity. Here's how to ensure that your needs are met and your dignity stays intact during hospitalization:

Ask About *Everything* Let your doctors and nurses know that you plan to play a major role in your care. Inquire about your treatments and prognosis.

Don't worry that your doctor will think you lack confidence in him/her. Or that asking questions will cause resentment among the hospital staff, producing worse care.

Hospital patients who ask questions receive better and more respectful treatment, studies have shown. Questions encourage the medical staff to pay more attention to you.

If medical personnel use jargon, ask them to explain it.

Always inquire about the medication you are given. If you receive a new drug, ask: "Why is this different from what I was getting before? Who ordered it?"

Asking questions also helps prevent medical mistakes. Nearly 100,000 hospital patients die every year from medical errors, such as wrong medications and botched surgery.

Know Who Is Treating You Hospital staffing levels have been drastically reduced. A person in a white uniform is not necessarily a doctor or nurse. In fact, it may be someone with almost no training, such as an orderly.

If someone comes into your room to perform a procedure—and you don't know who that person is—ask: "Who are you? What do you do here? Are you a licensed practical nurse (LPN) or registered nurse (RN)?"

If you are concerned that the person is not fully trained in the procedure, refuse it. You'll be surprised at how quickly you receive treatment from a nurse.

Don't Be Shy About Seeking Help If no one responds to your call button within a few minutes, pick up the phone. Call the hospital operator and ask to be connected to the nursing station on your floor.

When the phone is answered, say you need help in your room—immediately.

Important: If you have a complaint, you have the right to a response in a reasonable period of time. If you're not getting one, ask to see the hospital's "patient representative" or "ombudsman," who mediates between staff and patients. See what the representative can do to resolve your situation.

Hospital Self-Defense

As soon as you are admitted to the hospital, ask your doctor to prescribe all the pain medication he/she thinks you may need. That way, nurses won't have to get the doctor's clearance when you need the medication

Also: Ask for a phlebotomist to draw blood. It will be less painful than when taken by most nurses. Requesting a small-gauge needle also helps.

Charles Inlander, president, People's Medical Society, 462 Walnut St., Allentown, PA 18102.

Doctor Checkup

Don't be afraid to ask a doctor if he/she has ever been sued.

You owe it to yourself to find out about the competence of people your life may depend on. If the doctor was sued, ask why and how the case was decided.

Other sources:

❏ County court records of lawsuits, although most malpractice settlements are secret.

❏ State medical licensing boards.

❏ *Questionable Doctors*, a multi-volume set published by the **Public Citizen Health Research Group**, available in many libraries, lists disciplinary actions taken against physicians. However, many actions do not reflect on professional competence.

Note: The *National Practitioner Data Bank*, the most authoritative compilation of information, is not available to the general public.

Charles Inlander, president, The People's Medical Society, 462 Walnut St., Allentown, PA 18102.

If there is no patient representative or the representative isn't helpful, ask to see the medical director or the hospital administrator.

Have Someone With You at All Times If you are seriously ill or undergoing surgery, you probably won't have the energy or mobility to protect your rights. So have someone with you 24 hours a day.

Enlist family and friends, and work out a schedule. As long as your "advocate" is not interfering with the delivery of care, he has a right to be there.

Talk to the Staff About a Schedule That Fits Your Needs A shift change may be the only reason a nurse is taking your blood pressure at midnight. If that's the case, tell your doctor or the head nurse that you'd prefer not to be awakened at night.

Make Sure the Food Is Appetizing Notify the hospital dietitian if fresh fruits and vegetables aren't served...the food doesn't arrive hot... the meals are served at unusual times for the convenience of the staff...or you lack sufficient time to eat.

Better: Have visitors bring food to supplement hospital meals. Make sure they are aware of any special dietary restrictions you have. Tell the doctor or nurse that this is what you intend to do.

Know Your Rights You have a right to say no to any medical procedure. You have the right to see your medical records. You have the right to check yourself out at any time, even against the advice of hospital personnel. You have the right to fire your doctor. You have the right not to be treated by a medical student, if you so choose.

How to Find the Best Doctor

When choosing a doctor, most people rely on the recommendation of a friend, family member or another doctor. Few of us seek enough specific information from the prospective doctors themselves to predict the quality of care we will receive.

If you don't feel comfortable speaking directly to a doctor about his/her qualifications, ask to talk to the office manager when you call to make an appointment. This person should be knowledgeable about the doctor's background.

The renowned American Medical Association (312-464-5000, www.ama-assn.org) also provides biographical information about physicians—but the AMA does not judge quality.

To ensure that you have enough information about a doctor, ask him these questions:

- **Are you board certified?** Whether you're choosing a primary-care physician or a specialist, board certification is the best indicator of competence and training.

  Every medical specialty, including family practice and internal medicine, has a governing board that sets and enforces professional standards. Board certification means the doctor has completed an approved residency program and passed the board's rigorous examination.

  The American Board of Medical Specialties (866-275-2267, www.abms.org) can tell you if a doctor is board certified.

- **Where did you complete your residency?** Look for a physician with at least three years of postgraduate specialty training in a residency program at a major hospital. This ensures that the doctor has gained experience in treating patients under the supervision of leading specialists.

  It's fine to ask where a doctor attended medical school, but don't place too much emphasis on it. All accredited medical schools meet high standards, requiring graduates to pass standardized tests and compete for prestigious residencies.

  Graduates from foreign medical schools must pass the same exam as US medical school graduates—and complete the same residency requirements—to receive board certification from the appropriate governing board in the US.

- **How long have you been in practice?** If you put a premium on a doctor's clinical experience, you're likely to prefer an older doctor who has been in practice for a number of years.

  However, many people prefer doctors who completed their residency within the past five years, assuming they will be more familiar with the latest treatments.

  Regardless of whether the doctor is old or young, he should have a lot of experience with your particular condition.

- **With which hospital are you affiliated?** Most doctors have admitting privileges at one or more hospitals. This allows them to admit patients to the hospital and care for them there.

  Choose a doctor who has privileges at a major medical center with a good reputation. The best doctors typically practice at the best hospitals.

  Helpful: Each year, *US News and World Report* ranks the best US hospitals. You can find details at www.usnews.com.

Choosing a Specialist

For serious medical problems, including those that require surgery, your primary-care physician will often refer you to a specialist. Request more than one recommendation so that you'll have a choice.

To Get a Quick Appointment With A Specialist

To get an appointment with a specialist sooner, tell the nurse at the specialist's office that you are anxious about your condition. If this does not work, emphasize that your primary-care physician wants you to be seen by the specialist quickly. If this still does not work, ask your primary doctor to make the appointment for you. If your own doctor cannot get a prompt appointment, call the specialist and ask for a referral to someone who is more readily available. This will often work, since doctors do not want to lose patients.

Susan A. Albrecht, PhD, RN, associate professor, University of Pittsburgh School of Nursing.

Psychotherapy Fast…Easy… And On-Line

Consulting a psychotherapist on-line—rather than in person—is quick, easy and inexpensive compared with an office visit. Key, of course, is being able to communicate in writing, since it takes place via E-mail.

When to Use E-Therapy
Relationship problems, marital strife, fear, anxiety, grief, career problems and issues associated with life transitions all respond well to E-therapy.

Important: If you have a personal crisis or a serious mental illness, such as schizophrenia or manic depressive disorder, on-line therapy is not appropriate.

Choosing a Counselor
Look for a therapist who:
• Has "seen" at least six on-line clients.
• Has been on-line for at least a year.
• Guarantees responses to your E-mails within 48 hours.

Important qualifications: License to practice from a state board or a national licensing organization, such as the National Board for Certified Counselors. *Also:* A professional degree in counseling or psychology, such as a PhD, PsyD or LCSW.

Best sites for E-therapists: www.helphorizons.com…www.metanoia.org.

John Grohol, PsyD, Boston-based psychologist and author of *The Insider's Guide to Mental Health Resources Online* (Guilford). He is chief operating officer of www.helphorizons.com, a directory of more than 500 credentialed E-therapists.

Ask these questions to confirm a specialist's qualifications:

• **Are you board certified in the appropriate subspecialty?** A doctor who is board certified in a subspecialty has completed additional fellowship training in that particular area.

Example: A hand surgeon may be an orthopedist or a plastic surgeon who completed fellowship training in hand surgery.

• **How often have you performed this procedure?** Look for a doctor who has performed a procedure, such as laparoscopic surgery or open-heart surgery, as often as every day or every week for several years.

For rare procedures, such as removal of certain types of brain tumors or liver malignancies, the frequency would be less. The more experience a doctor has performing a procedure, the greater the odds of success.

Caution: Every year, hundreds of physicians are disciplined or put on probation by their state medical authorities for improper behavior, substance abuse, fraud and other problems.

To avoid these doctors, call your state's medical licensing authority (check the state government listings in your phone book) or visit the Association of State Medical Board Directors Web site at www.docboard.org.

In addition to asking the right questions, patients can receive recommendations from area support groups and branches of national organizations, such as the American Diabetes Association.

Use the triangulation method: If three people whose opinion you respect recommend the same doctor, he is likely to be a good choice.

John J. Connolly, EdD, former president of New York Medical College in Valhalla. He copublishes *America's Top Doctors* (Castle Connolly Medical Ltd.), an annual guide that lists top specialists in a variety of fields, based on each doctor's credentials, experience and assessments by his/her peers.

Get Your Money's Worth From a Medical Checkup

The managed-care revolution has drastically reduced the amount of time doctors spend with patients. During the typical office visit, your doctor barely has time to investigate troublesome symptoms and check your weight…pulse…heartbeat…blood pressure, etc. That's not enough.

A thorough exam should also address your overall physical and emotional well-being…diet…lifestyle…and any "silent" symptoms that can increase your risk for health problems.

Most doctors take a medical history, listing current health issues…prescribed medications…allergies, etc. This information is critical.

Helpful: When writing down your concerns, give your doctor additional information that he/she may fail to include in the medical history:

- How's your diet?
- Are you taking any herbal or dietary supplements?
- Do you get enough sleep?
- Are you physically active?
- Are you experiencing sexual problems?

Also mention if you smoke, how much alcohol you drink and whether you're having difficulty in your personal relationships. Try to keep the list to one page.

The Physical

To save time, doctors often take shortcuts during the physical. This can affect not only your current diagnosis and treatment—but also your future health. Here are the steps most commonly omitted…

Blood Pressure This vital sign is typically checked in one arm while the patient is sitting. For a more accurate reading, blood pressure should be tested in *both* arms, preferably while you're lying down.

If blood pressure differs by 15% or more between arms, there may be blockages in the large blood vessels.

Important: If you're taking blood pressure medication—or if you get dizzy when you change positions—your doctor should check your blood pressure immediately after you stand up. If the pressure drops by more than 10%, a change in dosage of blood pressure medication may be needed.

Eyes Most of us go to an ophthalmologist or optometrist. But if you don't see an eye specialist regularly and you're age 40 or older, your internist or family practitioner should measure the pressure on your eyeballs to test for glaucoma and look for lack of lens clarity—an early sign of cataracts.

Bonus: A careful eye exam can also reveal blood vessel narrowing or small hemorrhages on the retina—indicators of vascular conditions that increase your heart disease risk.

Hamstrings Few doctors test these muscles at the back of the thighs to identify potential back problems. To do so, the doctor should ask you to lie on your back and lift each leg to a 90° angle.

If you can't perform the lift, you may need a stretching program to relax the hamstrings.

Lymph Nodes The lymph nodes in your neck are typically checked, but doctors should also check those in the groin and under arms. Swollen lymph nodes may signal infection. Lumps could indicate cancer.

Fend Off Diseases Naturally

You can save money by fending off disease with natural substances. Consider adding garlic, ginger and green tea to your diet. A number of important and interrelated benefits are associated with these three foods:

Garlic has been shown to lower blood pressure and cholesterol levels, and reduce the risk of clogged arteries. It also appears to boost the immune system and stimulate your body's natural defenses against cancer. One to two cloves a day is ideal. If eating them raw or sliced in food doesn't appeal to you, add fresh garlic to food you're cooking a few minutes before the dish is ready.

Ginger can be a great help for upset stomachs. Ginger works by interrupting the nausea signals sent from the stomach to the brain, perhaps by absorbing stomach acid.

For motion sickness, ginger is even more effective than Dramamine. Two 500-mg ginger capsules (available at drug and health-food stores) every few hours can help upset stomachs, stomach discomfort caused from traveling, and pregnant women dealing with morning sickness.

Ginger can be consumed raw, cooked or pickled (which is how it is served at Japanese restaurants).

Green tea contains substances called catechins, which lower cholesterol, improve lipid metabolism and reduce cancer risk. Experts recommend one to two cups of decaffeinated green tea a day.

How to Evaluate On-Line Medical Advice

To evaluate on-line medical advice, check the source. Educational sites, which end in *.edu*...organizational sites, which end in *.org*...and government sites, which end in *.gov*, tend to be more reliable than *.com* sites.

Look for sites with an editorial or medical advisory board that checks content. Check the date on which information was posted. Discuss the information with a health-care professional before taking action.

Tom Ferguson, MD, adjunct associate professor of health informatics, University of Texas Health Science Center, Houston, TX. www.fergusonreport.com

Pulse Points Your doctor probably checks the pulse in your neck and/or groin—but may skip your feet. If pulse strength differs in these three areas, it can be a sign of peripheral arterial disease.

Skin Many doctors ignore the skin altogether, assuming that it should be examined by a dermatologist. Not true. The skin should also be checked during a general medical checkup.

To examine your skin, your doctor should ask you to disrobe so he can look for moles on all parts of your body, even your scalp and the bottoms of your feet.

If you have moles larger than one-half inch—or if your moles have gotten larger, darkened or changed their shape—you should get a referral to a dermatologist for a melanoma screening.

Thyroid This butterfly-shaped gland at the base of the neck is often missed during the lymph node exam. By palpating the thyroid, your doctor can screen for thyroid cancer.

For Women Only

Breast and Reproductive Organs Most doctors check the breasts for suspicious lumps, but few doctors show women how to perform monthly exams at home.

Helpful: When performing a self-exam, move all eight fingers, minus the thumbs, up and down instead of in a circle. That way, you'll cover the entire breast.

If you don't see your gynecologist regularly, your doctor should also perform rectal and vaginal exams. These exams should be performed simultaneously—it makes it easier to identify suspicious masses.

For Men Only

Testicles and Rectum When examining men age 40 or older, most doctors perform a digital rectal exam to screen for prostate cancer. However, they often fail to perform a testicular exam to check for testicular cancer. Your doctor should also teach you how to do a testicular self-exam.

Beginning at age 50—earlier if there's a family history of prostate cancer—every man should have a prostate-specific antigen (PSA) blood test performed every three years...or more often if abnormalities are found.

Laboratory Tests

Routine blood tests include cholesterol levels...liver and kidney function...blood glucose levels...and a white blood cell count. But we now know that other blood tests can be important if a patient shows signs of certain conditions. These tests include:

- **C-reactive protein.** Elevated levels of this inflammation marker can indicate heart disease risk.

- **Homocysteine.** Elevated levels of this amino acid are linked to heart disease and stroke.

  Helpful: The B vitamin folate, taken at 200 mcg to 400 mcg daily, reduces homocysteine levels.

- **Iron.** Elevated levels of this mineral cause iron overload (hemo-chromatosis).

- **Lipoprotein (a).** Elevated levels of this blood protein increase the risk for blood clots.

- **Magnesium.** Low levels of this mineral can cause fatigue, generalized pain and/or muscle spasms.

- **Zinc.** A deficiency of this immune-strengthening mineral can lead to frequent infection.

  Leo Galland, MD, director of the Foundation for Integrated Medicine in New York. Dr. Galland is author of *Power Healing* (Random House).

How to Choose the Right Surgeon

Besides the severity of your medical condition, probably the biggest factor in determining the success of any operation is the surgeon. Obviously, good ones have better technical skills. But they are also more likely to be affiliated with the hospitals and other professionals—such as topflight registered nurses and anesthesiologists—who will increase your odds of a positive outcome. Even so, many people simply use whatever surgeon they are assigned by the hospital, their primary-care provider or HMO.

It's not necessary to find the absolute *best* surgeon—usually, that isn't even possible. Your job is to make a reasonable choice in the time available and—most important—to avoid a bad surgeon. Here's what I suggest:

Get a Few Names to Begin Your Search If you have a primary-care doctor you know and trust, ask which surgeon he/she would choose for a loved one—and why. Also ask which surgeons are held in particularly high esteem by their colleagues. The answers may differ.

Remember, doctors sometimes make referrals based on friendship, reciprocal business relationships (you refer to me, I'll refer to you) or institutional affiliations, so it's wise to cast a wider net. If you have friends who work in local hospitals or clinics or who are otherwise in the know, ask them for the scuttlebutt on top surgeons.

Check Credentials If the surgeon is on the faculty of a local medical school or on staff at a respected hospital—both good signs—chances are, he is board certified. This means the doctor has

Don't Waste Money on Rashes

If your child comes down with a rash, do some investigative work on your own before you spend money on hefty doctor's fees.

Ask yourself: Did you just change laundry detergents? Was last night the first time your child ever ate shellfish? Many rashes are simple reactions to a new food, lotion or sunscreen with PABA.

If you answer "no" to the above questions, or your child's rash is accompanied by a sore throat or joint pain, it's time to call your doctor.

Pay Attention to The Codes

When a doctor's office gives you an insurance form filled with codes, ask for the meaning of each code. Incorrect codes are a major reason insurers reject bills, which then become the patient's responsibility.

completed a residency at an accredited hospital and passed a rigorous certifying exam. To find out if a doctor is board certified, consult the American Board of Medical Specialties Web site at www.abms.org or call 866-275-2267. Also check the fields in which the doctor is certified. For example, a doctor who performs liposuction should be certified in plastic surgery, not just in general surgery or family practice.

Ask About Surgical Experience How many times has the doctor performed the operation in question? How many of those procedures were done, say, this year? There's no magic cutoff, but the more a doctor has performed, the better. For heart surgery, I'd want a surgeon who does at least 100 a year.

Experience is particularly important for complicated operations, such as heart or brain surgery, and for newer procedures, including some "minimally invasive" laparoscopic operations, with which most doctors may have only limited experience. Ask the doctor what specific training he has had in the proposed procedure.

Ask About the Surgeon's Track Record You want to find out not only how many operations a doctor has done, but also how his patients have fared. Did they experience wound infections or need to have the procedure repeated? Which complications have been most common? If a surgeon you're considering bristles at these questions or declines to answer, look elsewhere.

Ask Where the Operation Will Be Performed For heart surgery, you want to be at an institution that does at least 200 a year, according to recent studies. Community hospitals may be fine for routine procedures, such as hernia repair or gallbladder removal. But for complex or rare procedures, you are generally better off at a major teaching hospital.

Be Suspicious of Surgeons Who Are Too "Gung Ho" Surgeons who always want to operate make me nervous. That's because surgery may *not* be the best option. One of the best orthopedic surgeons I've ever met routinely tries to talk patients out of having any operation he isn't convinced will help them. When he recommends surgery, you know you need it.

Timothy McCall, MD, a Boston internist, is author of *Examining Your Doctor: A Patient's Guide to Avoiding Harmful Medical Care* (Citadel) and a commentator for the National Public Radio program "Marketplace."

Finding Reliable Medical Information on the Web

The Internet has become one of the best ways to research medical conditions. More than 98 million Americans regularly do just that. But two fundamental problems confront Web surfers. Where do you find the best information? And who is trustworthy?

Although some Web sites dispense sound medical advice, many spread misinformation—some of it potentially dangerous.

Luckily, you can maximize your chance of locating the facts you need while minimizing the risk of getting bad information. Here's what I suggest:

Look for Sites Run by Reputable Medical Organizations and Federal Agencies Typically, experts review the articles for accuracy, and the sites list the dates on which the articles were posted or updated.

As a starting point for general medical research, try the federally sponsored site Health Finder, www.healthfinder.gov, which links to dozens of other government agency sites. CBS HealthWatch, www.cbs.healthwatch.com, is an excellent commercial health site. For specific medical topics, try these sites:

- **Alternative medicine.** National Center for Complementary and Alternative Medicine, http://nccam.nih.gov.
- **Alzheimer's.** Alzheimer's Association, www.alz.org.
- **Arthritis.** Arthritis Foundation, www.arthritis.org.
- **Cancer.** The University of Pennsylvania's Oncolink, http://onco link.upenn.edu.
- **Diabetes.** American Diabetes Association, www.diabetes.org.
- **Heart disease.** American Heart Association, www.american heart.org.

Learn How to Perform Medical Searches To answer a specific medical question, consider using a search engine such as Yahoo!, www.yahoo.com, or AltaVista, www.altavista.com.

There are also search engines, including Achoo, www.achoo. com, and Health A to Z, www.healthatoz.com, which are specially designed for people seeking health information. To search the top medical journals, use Medline, www.nlm.nih.gov.

Critically Evaluate Any Web Site You Visit *Ask yourself:* Who's running this site? What's their motivation in providing the information? Are they trying to sell something? Do their claims sound too good to be true?

Don't Be Overly Influenced by a Web Page's Appearance A questionable site may have slick graphics while a reliable site may be plain-Jane.

Guard Your Privacy Any personal data you volunteer could be sold to marketers, compiled in databases or intercepted and traced back to you. Since details about your health could affect your job or your ability to get insurance, it's a good idea to provide as little information as possible.

Read the privacy policies of Web sites you visit. If you still have doubts about what might be done with any information the site requests, don't hesitate to use a pseudonym, a phony address, age or other information.

Get the Best Deal From Your Dentist

- Always ask about cost, and how and when you are expected to pay. Does the dentist participate in your health plan? Make sure that you understand the fees and the method and schedule of payment before you agree to any treatment.
- Call around your community to compare factors like location, office hours, fees and emergency arrangements. If you're comparing fees, ask for estimates on full-mouth X rays and preventative dental visits that include an oral exam and tooth cleaning.
- Ask about your treatment options. Which treatments are absolutely necessary and which are elective?
- If you don't understand any part of what your dentist recommends, don't be afraid to ask for more information.

Dental Discounts

You can get quality dental care at low cost from dental school clinics or centers. *Costs are almost always lower than private services:* An average checkup runs about $35 to $135. And some schools, such as **New York University Kriser Dental Center**, offer fee discounts of 10%–20% to patients over 65. If you live near a university with a dental school program, consider calling to find out about their clinic hours, procedures and costs.

Most dental schools have an experienced dentist on hand to assist the students with all procedures.

Here are some examples of dental schools that have outpatient facilities:

- **NYU Kriser Dental Center**
  New York City, 212-998-9800,
  www.nyu.edu/dental
- **Indiana University School of Dentistry**
  Indianapolis, 317-274-7957,
  www.iusd.iupui.edu
- **Oregon Health Sciences University**
  Portland, 503-494-8867,
  www.ohsu.edu
- **University of Florida College of Dentistry**
  Gainesville, 352-392-8014,
  www.dental.ufl.edu
- **University of North Carolina Dental School**
  Chapel Hill, 919-966-1161

Check With Your Doctor Before Acting If you find potentially useful data or anything that addresses your treatment, print it out and take it to your next appointment—or mail it to him/her ahead of time. Be reasonable, though. You can't expect a busy doctor to wade through a 50-page printout.

Timothy McCall, MD, a Boston internist, is author of *Examining Your Doctor: A Patient's Guide to Avoiding Harmful Medical Care* (Citadel) and a commentator for the National Public Radio program "Marketplace."

What Doctors Use on Their Own Children

Parents will be happy to know that there are some low-cost home remedies to treat your child's colds, fevers and sunburns. You can also try these home-style treatments on yourself and other adults.

The Common Cold

Decaffeinated Spice Tea Add lemon and honey, and wait until it cools slightly. The tea is soothing and hot, which will combat stuffiness and open up the nasal passages. The honey in the tea can help soothe a sore throat as well. The lemon soothes and coats your throat with vitamin C.

Old-Fashioned Chicken Soup Or use low-sodium canned soup. Not only will it make your child feel better, but making the soup keeps you too busy to worry.

Fun Fluids Make colorful Jell-O water by doubling the amount of water in the Jell-O recipe, offer enticing flavored ices or serve watered-down Gatorade. The more fluids a sick child can drink, the better. The fluids help clean out the child's system.

Fever

Fever is not usually as dangerous as most parents believe it to be. It is a sign that the body is fighting infection. If you're concerned, take your child's temperature and make sure to tell the doctor how and when you obtained it.

If a high fever is not responding to the fever reducer prescribed by your doctor, try a warm bath, which will dissipate body heat. There is no reason for the water to be cold. Besides being unpleasant for the child, a cold bath can be dangerous and cause the child's body to go into shock or seizure. Alcohol rubs should be avoided for the same reason.

Sunburn

For sunburn relief, try tea bags. Let the bags steep in boiled water for five minutes. After they cool, remove them from the water and apply the wet bags to burnt skin.

Slash Dental Costs

The best way to save money on your dental care is to prevent a problem before it occurs. Experts believe that how well you take care of your teeth will determine how much money you will need to spend on them.

Dental Home-Care

Did you know that many dentists advise brushing your teeth twice a day for at least two minutes? Many people don't brush for a long enough time to kill all of the germs and odor. Other people brush too vigorously, which can lead to gum recession and expensive dental repair.

How to Brush Dentists say that if you brush for two minutes (at a 45º angle) with soft, rounded, polished bristles, you will clean your teeth the best and save your mouth from gum disease.

Remember to clean the inside teeth surface where plaque deposits are heavy, and to clean the back teeth and tongue.

Dentists also advise replacing your toothbrush once every three or four months, or as soon as the bristles become worn, splayed or frayed. Replacing your toothbrush is important because a hard, brittle brush can injure your gums. Children's brushes may need to be replaced more often, because they wear out more quickly.

Flossing Flossing your teeth thoroughly once a day can be as important as brushing your teeth, since you are defending your teeth against plaque buildup that your toothbrush can't reach.

Sealants Sealing your teeth, to protect the enamel from plaque and acids, will cut the costs of your dentist bills. Toothbrush bristles cannot reach all the way into the depressions and grooves to extract food and plaque. Sealants protect vulnerable areas by sealing out plaque and food. Sealants cost about $25 a tooth, not much compared to the cost of filling and refilling cavities.

Fluoride Toothpaste Fluoride toothpaste can also add to prevention of dental disease. If you use a fluoride toothpaste or mouthwash, you are helping to inhibit the growth of bacteria in your mouth and keep plaque from sticking to your teeth.

How to Find a Quality Dentist

The American Dental Association suggests these simple ways to find a good dentist near you:

Generic Medicines: The Good and the Downright Dangerous

You can save anywhere from 30% to 70% off the costs of a brand-name medicine by buying the generic version. These become available as patents expire. The FDA requires thorough testing to assure that the generic version contains the same active ingredients in the same strengths and is as effective as the brand it replaces.

Are There Any Problems?
Generics may use different colorings, fillers and flavorings. In some rare cases, the user may have allergic reactions or experience other subtle differences.

Danger: Recent concern has focused on a class of drugs called *narrow therapeutic index (NTI)* drugs. These work in a narrowly defined level in the body and any variation can be dangerous. Generics may have slight differences in the manufacturing process that may cause different levels of the drug in the body. One study found that patients taking the NTI antiepileptic drug phenytoin, the generic form of Dilantin, had lower levels of the drug in their bloodstream.

Sticking with One Pharmacy Can Help You Stay Healthy

Pharmacists keep a record of their customers' medications so that they can warn you when a new prescription may interact dangerously with one that you are currently taking.

If you use one pharmacy, you can also create a relationship with your pharmacist that will enable you to ask questions that may help you save money.

You can ask a pharmacist about a new drug that your doctor has prescribed for you, how the drug will help you, how you should take it and what the possible side effects may be.

Also, you can ask your pharmacist for advice about nonprescription medications such as cold and stomachache remedies. Most pharmacists will be able to recommend over-the-counter treatments that will save you money in doctor's bills.

- Ask family, friends, neighbors or coworkers for recommendations, or ask your family physician or local pharmacist.
- Call or write to your local or state dental society which is listed in the *Yellow Pages* under "Dentists" or "Associations."
- Ask your current dentist to make a recommendation if you're moving to a new area.
- Call or visit more than one dentist before making a decision.

Pharmacy Savings

Don't hesitate to call several pharmacies to find which one has the prices that will save you the most. Some pharmacies will charge as much as they can for medications, while others sell below cost to get customers into their stores.

Alternatives

On-line pharmacies offer bargains and convenience—but there are many unscrupulous scam artists on the Internet as well.

Key: Seek a reputable on-line pharmacy to meet your needs.

How: Look for a site that requires a doctor's prescription and is licensed in your state.

Useful: Look for a seal on the pharmacy Web site indicating it is a Verified Internet Pharmacy Practice Site, which assures these conditions are met.

For additional useful information about safely buying drugs on-line, visit the Web sites of the Food and Drug Administration, www.fda.gov/oc/buyonline, and the National Association of Boards of Pharmacy, www.nabp.net.

Simeon Margolis, MD, PhD, medical editor, *Health After 50, The Johns Hopkins Medical Letter*, 550 N. Broadway, Ste. 1100, Baltimore 21205.

Mail-Order Pharmacies

You may be able to order your prescription drugs through a mail-order pharmacy and get considerable savings, especially if you take long-term medication. Mail-order won't automatically be less expensive than your cheapest local pharmacy, but it's worth pricing along with your other options.

Some mail-order firms deal only with patients belonging to specific insurance plans, but others sell directly to the general public.

AARP (800-456-2277, www.aarp.org) also provides low-cost alternatives to retail pharmacy prices (almost 40% less). Even though the pharmacy exists in conjunction with AARP, the service is available to people of all ages. AARP members are eligible for additional discounts. Product orders are usually shipped within 48 hours.

Unexpected Side Effects From Common Drugs

About 40% of the people who take prescription drugs experience side effects...yet many don't make the connection between their symptoms and medications they are taking.

Subtle Symptoms

Antidepressants, such as Paxil and Prozac, cause diminished desire for sex. This symptom is often mistakenly blamed on stress, lack of sleep or relationship problems.

Zocor and Lipitor, which are taken to lower cholesterol, can produce symptoms that mimic the flu. Doctors can easily miss the connection, but muscle aches may signal tissue breakdown. That can lead to serious kidney damage.

Be suspicious of any changes in your behavior or in the way you feel after starting a new prescription, especially if the drug you are taking has only recently been approved by the Food and Drug Administration.

The Uncertainty Factor

Product information sheets list common side effects, but that information may not be the whole story:

Limited Data Initial side effects are based on the experiences of people who have taken the drug *before* it was approved for widespread use. Preapproval studies include a relatively small number of people over a limited period of time.

Many drug side effects, therefore, are discovered only after a drug is put on the market.

Additional consideration: The population studied is often not representative of the general public. People who are very ill or who must take several medications, for instance, are often not included in clinical studies. Women are also often underrepresented in drug studies.

Unexpected Side Effects These may be serious.

Example: The drug Rezulin, recently approved for use in treating diabetes, was found—before approval—to cause a small amount of liver irritation in some cases. After the drug was in widespread use, however, it caused at least 80 deaths and hundreds of cases of severe liver damage before it was taken off the market.

Unique Response Drug companies anticipate certain side effects based upon reactions of the sample population. But—every individual is a special case. So your experience may not be the same as that of another person.

About Medicinal Herbs

Learn which herbs work and which are mostly hype. Check out the **HerbClips** database created by the **American Botanical Council**. The information is distilled from scientific journals, government reports and the media. www.herbalgram.org.

Questions to Ask Before You Sample The Latest Drug

Drug companies spend millions to influence the prescribing habits of doctors. Typically, they try to get doctors to recommend brand-new drugs with high price tags (and profit margins). What you want, however, is the best drug for your condition.

Ask your doctor if there are any drugs that have been on the market longer and whether it would be acceptable to take those drugs instead. In general, older drugs have longer track records of safety and are usually less expensive than new ones.

Be careful if a doctor wants to give you free samples of drugs that he normally would not prescribe. Most patients love getting free samples. But drug companies give most of these samples for the newer drugs that they're trying to promote. These are often drugs with which doctors aren't too familiar yet.

Before accepting a sample, ask your doctor how good the new drug is and whether there is another drug that is more established and less expensive.

Dosage Dangers

As many as 80% of side effects are dose-related. If you begin taking a new drug, ask your doctor if it is possible to start with a small dose. You can always step up the dosage later if necessary. But for many people, a lower dose is just as effective as a higher dose... and with minimal side effects.

Jay Sylvan Cohen, MD, associate professor of family and preventive medicine, University of California, San Diego, School of Medicine. He is author of Make Your Medicine Safe: How to Prevent Side Effects from the Drugs You Take *(Morrow).*

Low-Cost Tips to Keep You Fit

Reduce your risk of premature illness. If you recognize how your mind and body interact to create health or become vulnerable to disease, you can build a lifestyle to help protect yourself from health crises.

Purify Your Drinking Water Consider purifying your drinking water. Drinking water is a major source of environmental toxins. Experts say that more than one million Americans drink water that contains significant levels of cancer-causing chemicals, such as arsenic, radon and chlorine by-products. Similarly, the US Centers for Disease Control and Prevention report that millions of Americans become sick from waterborne microorganisms every year.

Take Your Vitamins Think about taking daily vitamin supplements. Some experts believe that vitamins may improve healing and wound repair, decrease heart disease and reduce the body's ability to produce free radicals (negatively charged ions that cause tissue damage and promote cancer). Check with your doctor to be sure which supplements are appropriate for you.

Exercise Try to exercise at least five days a week. The key is to find a way to use your body that is sensible and not traumatic.

Any type of exercise that raises your heart rate is beneficial. You may wish to start with a brisk 10-minute walk, working your way up to 45 minutes.

But if you already have an exercise routine that gives you a workout, there's no need to change.

Sweat for Success Consider taking a weekly sauna or steam bath. In addition to its ability to cool the body, sweating is one of the most important self-healing mechanisms because it allows the body to rid itself of unwanted or excess minerals and toxins.

Sweat in dry heat (sauna) or wet heat (steam), or a combination of the two. If you don't belong to a gym, try steaming in an

enclosed shower for 15 to 20 minutes. Be sure to drink plenty of water before you enter the sauna or steam room, and drink enough afterward to replace lost fluids.

Eat Right Think about getting potentially unhealthy foods out of your refrigerator and pantry. Certain foods are suspected of inhibiting your body's ability to heal itself. They include polyunsaturated oils (safflower, corn, sunflower), artificially hardened fats (vegetable shortening, margarine), artificial sweeteners (aspartame, NutraSweet, saccharin) and artificial colorings.

Experts believe that polyunsaturated oils oxidize rapidly when exposed to air. Oxidized fats can damage DNA, promote cancer development, and speed aging and degenerative changes in body tissues. Use olive oil in moderation instead.

Consider adding fruits and vegetables to your diet, especially cruciferous vegetables (broccoli, cabbage), dark-colored fruits (red grapes, blueberries) and cooked greens (Swiss chard, kale, collards). In addition to their high fiber and vitamin/mineral content, cruciferous vegetables and dark-colored fruits have been shown to have significant anticancer properties.

Try to eat more whole grains and soy products. Data show that a diet rich in fiber can enhance digestion, reduce the risk of colon cancer, help lower cholesterol and slow the absorption of sugar into the bloodstream. Whole-wheat bread, brown rice and buckwheat are particularly beneficial.

The addition of soy products not only increases your overall fiber intake, but also provides a form of protein that is lower in saturated fat than animal products.

The Art of Breathing

Focusing attention on your breathing can enhance your ability to relax and promote your body's good health and self-healing. Breathing exercises may help make your visit to the doctor's office something to smile about.

Here are some breathing exercises that experts suggest:

Inhalation Breath Observation Sit in a comfortable position with your back straight and eyes closed. Focus attention on your breathing, noting the point where you inhale. Do this for five minutes each morning.

Exhalation Breath Observation Sit in a comfortable position with your back straight and eyes closed. Focus on your breathing, but concentrate on when you exhale instead of when you inhale.

Relaxing Breath Sit in a comfortable position with your back straight and eyes closed. Touch the tip of your tongue to the inner surface of your front teeth and then slide it upward slightly to rest on the ridge between the teeth and the roof of your mouth.

Double the Strength of Your Pills and Save

You can save money on prescription medicine by asking your doctor to prescribe double-strength pills and then cutting them in half with a pill cutter. Half doses of larger-dosage pills are usually cheaper than full doses of smaller-dosage pills. (Don't try to divide capsules or time-release preparations.) You can buy a pill cutter for about $5.

Economy Size May Cost More

Buying the large economy size of an over-the-counter drug isn't a good deal if its expiration date arrives before you use it up. Consider buying only the amount of medicine that you'll use in one year. And check the expiration date on an over-the-counter drug before you make a purchase. You don't want to buy something that will only be good for one more month.

Keeping it there, inhale through your nose for four seconds. Hold your breath for seven seconds. Exhale through your mouth. Repeat four times. This can be done in the morning or evening.

Stimulating Breath Sit in a comfortable position with your back straight and eyes closed. Touch the tip of your tongue to the inner surface of your front teeth and then slide it upward slightly to rest on the ridge between your teeth and the roof of your mouth.

Breathe in and out rapidly through your nose, keeping your mouth closed slightly. Your breathing should be audible. Try this exercise for 15 seconds, and then increase the time by 10 seconds each time until you can do it for up to one minute. This exercise is best practiced in the morning.

Start Walking for Your Exercise—It's Free!

Walking is a great way to exercise for free. While a leisurely stroll has only minimal health benefits, studies show that moderate to brisk walking at a three- to five-miles-per-hour pace can significantly improve your fitness level.

Stretch Before and After You Walk

To avoid any injuries that would increase your medical expenses, it's important to stretch before and after you walk.

At the start and finish of your workout, spend two minutes stretching your calf muscles, the hamstrings in the back of your thighs, the quadriceps in the front of the thighs, the inner thigh muscles and the lower back.

Be careful not to overstretch, particularly when muscles are not warmed up. Stretch only to the point of gentle tension in the muscles.

Mall Walking Is Weather-Friendly Walking

You can walk in a mall for free and be protected from unpredictable weather. Many shopping centers open early so people can walk there in the mornings. Also, you don't have to worry about potholes or oncoming traffic. Mall walking is a great activity for beginners who want to walk at a relaxed, moderate pace.

Fitness Guidance For Seniors

You are never too old to become physically fit, and with medical bills as high as they are for seniors, staying healthy and out of the hospital can help you avoid paying high doctors' bills.

You may be surprised to find out that becoming and staying physically fit can be accomplished for very little money.

Before You Begin

Before beginning a fitness regimen, it is essential to see your doctor to make sure that you don't have a condition that would make exercise a harmful activity.

Next, it's important to give your muscles a good warm-up before strenuous exercise. Begin with a slow walk, or do some simple stretches.

After you exercise, it is also important to cool down before you collapse onto a chair. Stopping abruptly after a vigorous workout may give your heart an unwelcome shock. Try to move around for at least five minutes after you work out. Consider taking a slow walk as your cool-down option.

You may also want to take a warm shower or bath after exercise. This can help prevent your muscles from stiffening.

Workout Options

Aerobic exercise may provide the maximum health benefits. Keeping your heart rate up for approximately 20 to 30 minutes, three or four days a week, can keep your heart healthy. Aerobic exercise is also good for weight loss.

Speed walking is a great alternative to paying for an aerobics or exercise class. You can speed walk around your neighborhood for free. You can also take advantage of shopping malls that open early, and walk in a weather-protected environment for free.

Lifting weights is a great way to keep aging bones strong. If you don't want to spend the money on two- or five-pound weights, you can lift 12- or 28-ounce cans instead.

Health-Club Money Savers

To save money when joining a health club, don't join an expensive club that offers more equipment or activity options than you will ever use. For example, if you want to lift weights or take an exercise class, a health club with a sauna or pool may be an unnecessary additional cost.

Cut the Cost of Prescription Drugs

Be willing to take medication several times a day—doctors often prescribe more expensive one-dose-per-day drugs, assuming patients prefer them.

Use medication as prescribed. When a patient fails to follow instructions—often because of unpleasant side effects—a drug may not work. Your doctor may then prescribe a more expensive substitute when it may be possible to adjust the inexpensive prescription you're already taking.

Important: Ask your doctor to help. Doctors often don't worry about drug costs, assuming insurance covers them.

Harvard Health Letter, 10 Shattuck St., Boston 02115.

Free-Medicine Programs

Free prescription drugs are available to patients with financial difficulties. Most drug manufacturers' giveaway programs target the poor, but people with incomes around $50,000 sometimes qualify.

Example: A person with high medical costs and no insurance coverage for prescriptions...or someone who has reached his/her prescription coverage limit.

Most free-medicine programs require patients to apply to drug companies through doctors.

If you think you might qualify: Get a free brochure and application from The Medicine Program, 573-996-7300...www.themedicineprogram.com.

Also, before you join, ask about new member perks, such as a free session with a personal trainer.

And, if you may need to take a long-term break for travel or other reasons, find out if the club can freeze your membership and start it up again on your return. Then you won't have to pay for the time you're not using it.

Judging Whether a Club Is Worth Your Money

One of the best ways to choose a quality health club that's worth your money is to thoroughly inspect its facilities. Good health clubs will be equipped with certain features, such as:

- Trainers and instructors who are certified by agencies like the American College of Sports Medicine (317-637-9200, www. acsm.org) or the Aerobics and Fitness Association of America (800-445-5950, www.afaa.com).
- Orientation sessions for new members.
- Staff members who monitor the exercise areas.
- Classes at several levels of skill.
- Clean and updated equipment and locker rooms.
- Safety and club rules clearly posted.

If you are still unsure whether to join after you thoroughly inspect a club's facilities, you may want to check with your state or local consumer protection agency or the Better Business Bureau to find out if any negative reports have been filed against the club, and what they were about.

Before You Commit

Before making a commitment to an annual membership, consider whether you're investing your money in the right place. Here are some tips on how to safeguard your money:

- Consider trying out a club before you join.
- Visit the club on the day that you would want to work out. Notice if the club is too crowded, and if the equipment or class you want is accessible.
- Think about joining a health club that offers several free visits or a short, low-cost trial membership.
- Try to arrange paying for your membership on a monthly basis, or join a club that offers a 90-day trial membership.
- Try to negotiate your membership fees. You may be able to join the club at a price that is lower than the initial offer.
- Always check out the club's refund policy before you sign up. You don't want to find out after you join that your satisfaction is not guaranteed for more than one or two weeks.

Health Clubs to Check Out

Many health clubs are individually run and owned, but there are a few chains that have facilities nationwide.

Here are some nationwide chain facilities you may want to check out:

- **Gold's Gym** (800-457-5375, www.goldsgym.com)
- **World Gym** (310-827-7705, www.worldgym.com)
- **Bally Total Fitness** (800-348-6377, www.ballyfitness.com)

Some chains, such as Bally Total Fitness, offer a two-week guest pass, and others have newsletters with free health and fitness information. Your best option may be to join a club that offers the perks that suit your own interests and fitness goals.

How to Find Them To find health clubs near you, look in your *Yellow Pages* under "Fitness Clubs" or "Health Clubs." Once you find some that are conveniently located, you can then do some inspecting and make some cost comparisons.

Consider the YMCA/YMHA Many YMCA/YMHAs across the country offer low-cost, quality health and fitness programs.

If you are interested in swimming, running or walking around a track, or joining a low-key exercise class, you may want to opt for joining a YMCA/YMHA program. Joining a Y will give you the opportunity to make a small investment for a fitness program before you invest a lot more money in a private health club. Some are at least as good as private clubs. And many Ys have senior health programs that enable people over 50 to work out with their peers.

How to Decipher Confusing Drug Labels

- **Take on an empty stomach:** Take two hours or more after eating a full meal.
- **Take with food:** Eat with a meal or something small (crackers, etc.)
- **Avoid excessive sunlight:** Wear protective clothing and sunblock (at least SPF 15) when you go outside.
- **Take with plenty of water:** A full eight ounces.
- **Take at the same time every day:** Take within two hours of the same time.

Susan Proulx, PharmD, president, Med-ERRS, Institute for Safe Medication Practices, 1800 Byberry Rd., Ste. 810, Huntington Valley, PA 19006.

Low-Cost Help for Embarrassing Medical Problems

If you suffer from a backache or dizziness, it's easy to tell your doctor. But what about those nagging symptoms you are too embarrassed to discuss?

Unfortunately, many patients deprive themselves of effective treatment and, in some cases, endanger their long-term health by failing to disclose certain medical problems. How to get help:

Bad Breath

Saliva production diminishes during sleep, allowing food debris to stagnate in the mouth. Bacteria break down these residues, producing an unpleasant smell. That's why almost everyone has bad breath (halitosis) upon waking. It usually disappears after you brush your teeth.

To determine if you have bad breath: Lick the inside of your wrist, wait four seconds, then smell.

Work Out at Home

To boost motivation and sense of purpose, consider trying health-club techniques at home:

- Sign in whenever you exercise.
- Install a mirror so you can check form.
- Use a floor mat for stretches and strength training such as abdominal crunches and side-lying leg lifts.
- Buy a rubber mat to place under your equipment in order to cut noise and vibration and protect the floor.
- Wear appropriate exercise clothing, such as breathable, lightweight sportswear.

Persistent halitosis is typically caused by gum disease (gingivitis). If your gums bleed when you brush your teeth, you probably have gum disease and, as a result, bad breath. What to do:

- See your dentist for a checkup and thorough cleaning.
- Brush your teeth at least twice daily. *Best method:* Clean teeth two at a time for six seconds, moving the brush in a small circular motion while angling it toward the gum. Or consider buying a battery-powered toothbrush, which often controls gum disease better than manual brushing. *Cost:* $20 to $120.
- Clean the back of your tongue, where bacteria accumulate. Use your toothbrush or a tongue scraper.
- Use an antibacterial mouthwash, such as Biotene Antibacterial, Cepacol Antiseptic or Listerine Antiseptic.
- Floss nightly—especially the molars.

If halitosis persists: See your doctor.

Excessive Perspiration

Perspiration itself isn't smelly, but it is a breeding ground for bacteria that quickly break down into malodorous fatty acids.

Excessive perspiration (hyperhidrosis) can affect armpits, feet or palms. What to do:

Armpits Women and men should shave their armpits to reduce bacterial buildup.

Also switch to an antiperspirant with an active ingredient different from what you're currently using.

Feet Wear clean, loose-fitting socks made of wool or cotton and at least 30% man-made fiber, such as nylon or polyester. Wash socks in hot water to kill bacteria.

Avoid shoes made from synthetic materials. They trap moisture, which allows bacteria to multiply. This is also true for sneakers, so don't wear them for more than four hours a day.

Bathe your feet daily in warm water that contains about 10 drops of tea-tree oil per pint of water. It has antibacterial properties. Use a pumice stone to remove hardened, dead skin from your heels and soles.

Palms Rub palms every few hours with an astringent oil, such as cypress or geranium. These essential oils, available at health food stores, can be added to almond oil or a lotion.

If self-treatment doesn't help: Discuss the problem with your doctor. He/she may prescribe a 20% *aluminum chloride* solution or an anticholinergic drug, such as *propantheline* (Pro-Banthine), to reduce the perspiration.

Botulinum toxin (Botox) injections are also a new treatment option for severe hyperhidrosis.

As a last resort, surgical division of the sympathetic nerves that cause sweating is almost 100% effective for feet and palms and about 40% effective for armpits.

Feminine Itching

Itching of the vulva (vulval pruritis) is usually caused by a vaginal yeast infection. What to do:

- Try an over-the-counter cream, such as *butoconazole* (Gyne-Lotrimin) or *miconazole* (Monistat 3). If this doesn't help within a few days, your doctor may recommend a prescription medication, such as *fluconazole* (Diflucan).

 Other possible causes include eczema, psoriasis or an allergy.

 To relieve the itch: Soak in warm water that contains two handfuls of Epsom salts or ordinary kitchen salt...or dip a washcloth into a salt water solution and apply to the affected area.

- Wash only with unscented cleansers, such as Dove Unscented Beauty Bar or Neutrogena Transparent Dry Skin Formula Fragrance Free. When shampooing your hair, don't let the foam touch your vulva.
- Don't use feminine deodorants or apply deodorant or perfume to sanitary pads...wash underwear with an enzyme-free, perfume-free detergent for sensitive skin...don't use fabric softener ...and avoid swimming in chlorinated water.

Flatulence

It's normal to have some gas. Air swallowed during eating typically collects in the stomach and is passed via belching.

Bacteria also cause certain foods, especially beans, to break down into hydrogen, methane and carbon dioxide.

Most people experience gas (flatulence) more than 10 times a day. What to do:

- Avoid eating large quantities of gas-causing foods at one time. These include beans, peas, broccoli, cauliflower, artichokes, cabbage, raisins, prunes and apples. They contain hard-to-digest carbohydrates that ferment in the bowels.

 Foods that don't cause flatulence: Potatoes, rice, corn and wheat.

- Avoid carbonated beverages and hot drinks.
- Take your time while eating. Don't rush when you eat...put your fork down between bites...and be sure to chew food thoroughly.
- Don't chew gum.

 Over-the-counter antiflatulence aids—such as Beano, charcoal tablets, Gas-X or Phazyme—can also relieve flatulence.

Fifty-Plus Fitness Association

The **Fifty-Plus Fitness Association** (650-323-6160, www.50plus.org) is an organization that provides a combination of information about aging, exercise and a variety of fitness activities.

For $50 per year, you can become a member of Fifty-Plus and enjoy social gatherings such as talks, seminars, walks, bicycle rides, runs, swims and other exciting adventure events. You'll be notified of health improvement programs, athletic and health-club incentives (such as a free week's use of a selected club), seminars and an annual fitness weekend (including sporting events and a health fair).

If there isn't a Fifty-Plus group in your hometown, you can become an ambassador and help to hold events and develop a local membership. By becoming a member, you can learn how to bring the Fifty-Plus program to where you live.

Health-Club Savvy

Save on a health-club membership by joining during the summer—which is off-season for gyms.

Be sure to get a cancellation clause in any long-term contract in case you move, the club changes its hours or policies or illness makes it hard for you to exercise. Strike any clauses you dislike from the contract before signing.

Caution: Never join a club that is still under construction. Its opening could be delayed for months or even years.

Nancy Lloyd, personal-finance commentator on national radio and television, Washington, DC, and author of *Simple Money Solutions* (Times Business).

Discounts on fitness-club membership are offered by many health insurance plans. Plans typically have negotiated discounts of 10% to 40%. For details, check the insurer's Web site or call your customer service representative.

Walter Cherniak, public relations manager, Aetna, US Healthcare, Health Insurance, Washington, DC.

Jock Itch

Jock itch (tinea cruris) causes an itchy, red rash in the groin area. The rash is triggered by the same fungus that causes athlete's foot. In fact, it's often "caught" from your own feet. What to do:

- Try an over-the-counter antifungal cream, such as *tolnaftate* (Tinactin). If this doesn't help, consult your doctor.
- Wear loose-fitting, 100% cotton underpants.
- Wash with unscented soap, and dry your groin area carefully after bathing.
- Wash underwear with an enzyme-free, perfume-free detergent.

Margaret Stearn, MD, a physician who practices general medicine in Oxford, England, with a special interest in diabetes and urologic medicine. Dr. Stearn is a Fellow of the Royal College of Physicians and the author of *Embarrassing Medical Problems: Everything You Always Wanted to Know But Were Afraid to Ask Your Doctor* (Hatherleigh Press).

Deep, Restorative Sleep Without High-Cost Medicines

For tens of millions of Americans, getting a good night's sleep is an elusive dream. But there is good news: Via self-hypnosis, it's usually possible to overcome sleeplessness—even if you've struggled with the sandman for decades.

First Things First

Sleep remains mysterious, even to longtime sleep researchers. But falling asleep clearly involves slowing the mind and body. People suffering from insomnia find that all but impossible.

If you haven't already, take these basic steps to curb mental and physical arousal before bedtime:

Avoid Caffeine It takes at least three hours for blood levels of this stimulant to drop. Think twice before having that late-afternoon cola...or that after-supper coffee or tea.

People who are especially sensitive to caffeine should avoid it after *early* afternoon—even the small amounts in chocolate, coffee yogurt or any dessert made from coffee beans.

Even the tiny amounts of caffeine in decaffeinated coffee can cause problems for some people.

Many cold remedies, diet pills and headache medications also contain caffeine.

Avoid Alcoholic Beverages For at Least Four Hours Before Bedtime Alcohol causes drowsiness right away, but it leaves you wakeful in the middle of the night.

Make Sure Your Bedroom Is Quiet and Completely Dark Even dim light —a distant streetlamp shining through half-closed blinds, for example—can make for restless nights.

Avoid Mental Stimulation For at Least One Hour Before Bedtime That goes for thriller novels...demanding mental work...loud, stimulating music...action TV shows...etc. A less involving book or calming music should be okay.

Have a Light Snack Before Bed If You Are Hungry Good choices include a small cup of soup or a glass of warm nonfat milk. Avoid sugary foods.

The Power of Suggestion

People troubled by insomnia often become convinced that sleep is simply impossible.

The power of positive suggestion enables you to bypass the doubts and worries of the conscious mind...and communicate directly with the subconscious mind. That part of the mind doesn't say, "I can't."

For most people, the process takes a few weeks.

Relax and Visualize

During the day, practice calming your body. Teach yourself to use the power of visualization.

Sit in a quiet, comfortable place. Focus your attention on something in front of you—a plant, the back of a chair or even a spot on the wall. Take three slow, deep breaths. Relax as you release the third breath, letting built-up tension drain out of your body.

Imagine the numeral 25. Slowly count backward, visualizing each numeral in turn.

When you reach one, pause for a few seconds. Then count forward to three. Open your eyes. You should feel relaxed and refreshed.

Practice this exercise twice a day for seven days. You're learning not only to relax, but also to enter a hypnotic trance that makes you responsive to positive suggestions.

Continue to practice relaxation during the day, and add a session at bedtime.

Autosuggestion

As you lie on your back in bed, rest your hands gently on your chest. Choose a positive suggestion to give yourself—something short and direct.

Example: "Tonight I will sleep deeply and peacefully...and I'll wake up tomorrow morning feeling great."

Repeat the suggestion 10 times slowly in your mind—or out loud, if doing so won't disturb a bedmate.

Meditation Is a Free Way to Relax

A great way to reduce stress, pain, anger and anxiety (for free) is to turn inward and meditate.

There are many ways to meditate and many thoughts on how to do it. But most experts agree that, no matter what your reason or method, spending 10 to 20 minutes (twice a day, every day) relaxing your mind may help you lead a healthier and happier life. Try this simple technique:

• Choose a word, sound, prayer or phrase on which to focus.

• Sit in a quiet, comfortable place.

• Close your eyes and begin to breathe slowly and deeply while relaxing your muscles.

• Repeat your focus word, prayer or phrase silently to yourself as you exhale.

• As your mind starts drifting, acknowledge it—and return to your repetition.

161

Where to Get The Best Deals On Vitamins And Supplements

Don't focus on price. Buy from well-known suppliers with reliable products and rapid turnover, so products are fresh.

- **Large specialty chains**, such as GNC, have good prices and sales.

- **Discount chains** like Wal-Mart have competitive prices but a limited range of products.

- **Web sites** of drugstore chains—such as www.cvs.com—or purely Internet stores, such as www.drugstore.com—also offer competitive prices.

Beware: Operators that promise low prices...then use bait-and-switch tactics or supply inferior or old products. When information matters more, try:

- **Nondiscount drugstores**. Pharmacists are available for advice.

- **Health food stores**—with a wide range of products and helpful staff.

Charles Inlander, president, The People's Medical Society, 462 Walnut St., Allentown, PA 18102.

Each time you repeat the suggestion, gently press your fingers into your chest. This helps "anchor" the suggestion in your body. Keep your eyes closed at all times.

After a week, it's time for:

Putting It All Together

On an index card, jot down your autosuggestion. Carry it with you. From time to time throughout the day, find a quiet place to sit and relax. Focus your gaze in front of you. Then hold up the card and focus on your suggestion.

Breathe deeply as you imagine yourself doing what you've written. Feel and see the result you desire.

As you exhale, let the card slip from your fingers. Inhale and exhale deeply again. The third time, let yourself enter a state of deep relaxation.

Instead of counting down from 25, let the suggestion on your card repeat itself over and over. In your mind's eye, see yourself sleeping peacefully...then awakening refreshed and fully rested.

Do this twice a day for three weeks. Give yourself the same suggestion at night, and soon you'll be sleeping better than ever before.

Secrets of Success

The message you give yourself must be *believable*. If you've had insomnia for years, it's unrealistic to suggest that you will sleep for 10 hours at a stretch. Your mind will reject the idea. Pick something less extreme.

Examples: "Every night it's easier for me to fall asleep quickly" ..."I'm learning to sleep peacefully through the night"..."The power of my subconscious mind will help me sleep peacefully."

Some people find it helpful to *tape-record* their autosuggestion and play the tape at odd times during the day and at bedtime.

This auditory reinforcement can be especially helpful for people who are unable to visualize vividly.

To make the recording: Write down three positive suggestions about sleep. Practice saying them aloud until you feel comfortable repeating them. Strive for a steady rhythm. Don't worry, you're recording this for your ears only—to send a message of relaxation.

Record slow-tempo instrumental music in the background. *Mozart's Piano Concerto No. 21* or another calming, classical selection is good. As the music plays softly, tape yourself repeating each suggestion several times. Pause between each one. Return to the first suggestion and again repeat it several times.

Let the tape end with the music gently fading away.

Alex Lukeman, PhD, a psychotherapist and certified clinical hypnotherapist in private practice in Fort Collins, CO. He is author of *Sleep Well, Sleep Deep* and *Nightmares: How to Make Sense of Your Darkest Dreams* (both published by M. Evans & Co.).

Natural Remedies For Allergies

With this type of treatment, your goal is to strengthen the immune system and soothe symptoms with nonsuppressive medications. Here's my approach to fighting allergies...

Take Vitamin C and Bioflavonoids I typically recommend 2,000 mg of vitamin C and 500 mg each of the bioflavonoids *quercetin* and *hesperidin*, taken twice daily with food. These supplements reduce inflammation and lower histamine levels in the blood. Do not expect them to act as quickly as Benadryl. You need to take them for at least two weeks before the anti-allergy effect kicks in.

   Caution: High doses of vitamin C may cause diarrhea. If this occurs, reduce the dose.

Curb Stress Studies show that allergy symptoms are much worse when a person is highly stressed. Stress aggravates the immune system, making it more likely to overreact to irritants, such as pollen. To prevent this, meditate for 15 minutes each day, do aerobic exercise early in the morning when the pollen count is low, take vacations regularly and talk out your emotional conflicts with a counselor if necessary.

Irrigate Your Nose To reduce your exposure to pollen, rinse the nasal passages twice daily. You can buy a nasal saline spray in drugstores or health-food stores. Or you can make your own by mixing one-quarter teaspoon of sea salt with one cup of warm water. Fill your cupped palm with the warm salt water, close one nostril with your finger and gently inhale the water into the other nostril. Perform the same process on the other side. Tip your head back for 10 seconds, then gently blow your nose. Repeat on each nostril.

Use Herbs Stinging nettle (*Urtica dioica*) and eyebright (*Euphrasia officinalis*) reduce acute allergy symptoms, such as burning eyes, runny nose and congestion. I typically recommend taking these herbs in tincture form because it works quickly.

   Typical dose: 30 drops of tincture of each herb in four ounces of water four times daily. Take 15 minutes before eating.

   Jamison Starbuck, NC, a naturopathic physician in family practice and a lecturer at the University of Montana, both in Missoula. She is past president of the American Association of Naturopathic Physicians and a contributing editor to *The Alternative Advisor: The Complete Guide to Natural Therapies and Alternative Treatments* (Time Life).

Health Hotlines

You can get a free copy of *Health Hotlines*, a directory of the addresses and toll-free numbers of 250 helpful organizations that deal with asthma, Parkinson's disease, migraines and more. Write to Hotlines, National Library of Medicine Information Office, 8600 Rockville Pike, Bethesda, MD 20894, for your free copy. www.nlm.nih.gov.

9
Smarter Money Management

How to Start Making
Smart Financial Decisions

Analyze the way you use money. One way to be smart is to reduce the amount you're paying to banks and credit card companies.

Add up what you're paying your bank for using your own money, and then shop for a bank with lower fees on the services you use. For example, if you use the ATM, look for a bank that doesn't impose a charge for withdrawals. If you write only a few checks each month, look for a basic account. Compare the costs of small local banks to better known large ones that have branches in your community. Find out whether there's a way to get a better deal by consolidating your banking business in one place.

Figure out what using your credit cards is costing you. If you're paying an annual fee, look for a card that doesn't charge one. Compare the interest rates various cards charge, especially if you occasionally have to spread out your payments. Find out what it

costs to take a cash advance instead of using an ATM that debits your checking account.

Does Having a Budget Matter?

If you're always out of cash at the end of the month, you have to make changes in the way you're spending. The first step is to know how much is coming in and where it's going. Not everybody has the personality to track every penny. But you do have to have a clear sense of what your fixed costs are and how much you can spend on discretionary items. Creating a budget can help you discipline—and reward—yourself. It can also keep you from slipping into debt.

The Five Biggest Financial Mistakes People Make

- Not paying your credit card bills in full every month, which means you pay huge amounts of interest.
- Not putting as much as you can into a 401(k), IRA or other retirement plan.
- Withholding too much for income tax, thinking that the money you get back is a "gift." It's *your* money that's been sitting in Uncle Sam's account.
- Sticking with an investment that's producing a poor return just because you're not sure what else to do with your money.
- Letting yourself be persuaded that you can make lots of money risk-free.

The Five Smartest Investment Decisions that You Can Make

- Create a long-term investment plan and stick to it.
- Invest at least 10% of your gross income every year.
- Do your own research before you pay for investment advice.
- Be sure that you thoroughly understand an investment before you put money into it.
- Make sure you don't put all of your eggs into one basket.

Insider Tips for Cutting the Costs of Managing Your Money

Financial services are products, the same way clothes or cars are. To get the best deals, you have to know what you're looking for. The key to making your money work hardest for you is becoming an educated consumer.

Virginia B. Morris, PhD, the author of several books on money management, and the editor of the *Wall Street Journal Guide to Understanding Personal Finance.*

Down With Debt

A good credit rating can help you get the right job, the right apartment and the right interest rates on your credit cards, loans and mortgages. Here are some tips to help you keep your debt in check:

❏ Keep track of every penny you spend during the next month. Categorize your spending into the narrowest categories possible: Movies, dinners out and concerts instead of a broad category like entertainment. Once you see where the money is going, it is easier to budget a realistic spending amount for the future—and to identify areas where you would be comfortable cutting back.

❏ Cancel overdraft protection for your checking account—it makes it too easy to write checks for more money than you have.

❏ To get out of credit card debt quickly, pay at least double the minimum payment every month.

❏ Don't be fooled by the illusion of security if you have some savings in the bank but almost as much credit card debt. The 15% to 20% you're paying in interest on your card purchases far outweighs the scanty earnings on your savings or money market account. Get ahead now by using your savings to pay off those high-interest credit card bills.

❏ Plan to purchase cars or durable goods with cash. Make a plan for everything your family wants to buy—and prioritize.

For Seniors and Retirees

There are plenty of free and inexpensive resources, government perks and discounts available to help make your retirement years as happy, healthy and comfortable as possible.

Free or Almost Free Consumer Credit Counseling

Having trouble managing your debts? Confidential counseling is available to you from a trained budget-management counselor, for free or at minimal cost, depending on your financial situation. Under this plan, most creditors will work with you and your counselor to make realistic repayment arrangements. This not-for-profit program is supported mainly with donations. Call the **National Foundation for Consumer Credit** (800-388-2227, www.nfcc.org) for the office nearest you.

Tax Tips Just for You

Did you know that you might be able to deduct all of your home mortgage interest? Or you might qualify for the dependent care credit if you pay for a spouse's care to enable you to work.

These and other important filing questions are answered in the free newsletter *Protecting Older Americans Against Overpayment of Income Taxes*, published by the United States Senate Special Committee on Aging. Updated every January, this straightforward publication will keep you abreast of the latest changes to the tax laws that affect you, and will let you know in plain English which deductions, exemptions and credits you qualify for. For your free copy, contact the Special Committee on Aging, 631 Dirksen Senate Office Building, Washington, DC 20510, 202-224-5364, www.senate.gov/~aging.

Free Tax Counseling

Need help preparing your return? The IRS sponsors a number of programs offering free, individual tax assistance. Volunteers for Tax Counseling for the Elderly (TCE) have been specially trained by the IRS to assist individuals 60 and older with their tax returns. They visit nursing homes and community centers, and will even make a house call if necessary. VITA (Volunteer Income Tax Assistance) is another government program offering individual tax advice to elderly, disabled, low-income and non-English-speaking individuals.

To find out about the VITA or TCE program nearest you, call the IRS Information Line at 800-829-1040, www.irs.gov.

Legal Services for Seniors

A number of different organizations across the country cater to the specific legal concerns of senior citizens. Some give advice and referrals. Others will handle your case directly. Some work pro bono. Others offer services on a sliding-fee scale based on age and income. Whatever your concerns, these organizations are designed to help you through all aspects of the legal process:

National Offices

National Senior Citizens Law Center
1101 14th St., NW, Suite 400, Washington, DC 20005, 202-289-6976
or 3435 Wilshire Blvd., Suite 2860, Los Angeles 90010
213-639-0930, www.nsclc.org

National Academy of Elder Law Attorneys
1604 N. Country Club Rd.
Tucson, AZ 85716
520-881-4005, www.naela.org

California

Senior Legal Hotline, Legal Services of Northern California
515 12th St., Sacramento, CA 95814
520-623-5137, 800-231-5441, www.aoa.gov/legal/hotline.html

District of Columbia
Legal Council for the Elderly
601 E St. NW, Bldg. A, Fourth Floor, Washington, DC 20049
202-434-2120

Florida
Legal Hotline for Older Floridians
3000 Biscayne Blvd., Fifth Floor, Miami 33137
305-576-0080, www.myflorida.com/doea/healthfamily/
publications/elderservices/doeaofh.html

Pennsylvania
Legal Council for the Elderly
800-262-5297

Texas
Legal Hotline for Older Texans, State Bar of Texas
815 Brazos, Suite 1100, Austin, TX 78701
800-622-2520 or 512-477-3950, www.tlsc.org/hotline.html

Elder Law Resources on the Internet
Visit www.seniorlaw.com to find links to many useful elder law and legal resources on the Internet.

Social Security Lessons: What Everyone Should Know

More than one in six Americans—almost 46 million individuals—receive a Social Security check each month. But more people could qualify for benefits if they knew the ins and outs of Social Security regulations. This is important if you or someone in your family is disabled or you are a surviving spouse and are caring for children generally until age 18 or 19 who are still in high school. Misconceptions about benefits also keep people working who would prefer to retire early.

Here's what you need to know in order to receive all the Social Security benefits to which you are entitled:

Qualifying for Disability
If you meet the tests for disability, you, your spouse and your children can qualify for benefits regardless of your age. This has major implications for younger people, who stand a greater chance of becoming disabled than they do of dying. As of December 2001, Social Security was paying disability benefits to 5.2 million workers and to 1.7 million of their spouses and children.

Free Financial Advice

The **Federal Reserve System** publishes free newsletters on a host of topics relating to money and monetary instruments, banking, investments, international economics and consumer protection. To receive your free copies, contact the Board of Governors of the Federal Reserve System, Publications Service, MS-127, Federal Reserve Board, Washington, DC 20551, 800-688-9889. Find consumer information on money topics at www.consumer.gov.

The **Finance Center** (www.financenter.com), a financial Web site, features dozens of articles and free useful tools, including calculators, which will help you calculate everything from a basic monthly budget to how long it will take you to become a millionaire. Get answers to this and hundreds of other financial questions—for free!

Financial Planning— For Free

Planning a realistic budget (one that takes into account your day-to-day priorities, yet enables you to meet your long-term financial goals) is the single most important thing you can do to ensure your financial well-being. If you're having a problem putting together—or sticking to—a budget, or you're trying to make sense of your financial options, free advice may be available. Many **County Cooperative Extension** offices offer free pamphlets and even free classes to help you make the right decisions.

To find out what kind of help is available in your area, look in your local blue pages for the nearest County Cooperative Extension office, or contact the national office at Cooperative State Research Education and Extension Service, US Department of Agriculture, Room 3328, Washington, DC 20250, 202-720-8482, www.usda.gov.

Social Security has a strict definition of disability. To qualify, you must be unable—or expected to be unable—to do almost any sort of work for at least one year, starting with your "disability onset." This is usually the date you are no longer able to work. Actual payments begin about six months after onset.

This is different from corporate disability policies, which normally pay benefits after a much shorter period...and from private insurance, which generally will cover you if you can't perform your normal and customary job. Because of its tough definition of disability, Social Security approves only about 50% of the claims filed. But those who qualify receive an average monthly benefit in 2002 of $874. And they receive an additional 50% for a spouse who cares for their minor children. The 2002 average monthly benefit for a disabled worker, spouse and one or more children is $1,360.

To coordinate Social Security with any coverage you get through work and any private insurance you may have, assume that you'll receive the average amount after six months of disability.

Use your group coverage at work *and* a private policy to fill in the gap before Social Security kicks in.

Those who have received Social Security disability payments for at least two years qualify for *government-subsidized health insurance*. That's when they automatically qualify for Medicare.

Disabled Child

Your disabled child may qualify for lifetime Social Security benefits on the basis of *your* earnings record.

This can be enormously helpful to parents caring for physically or developmentally disabled children and facing continuing childcare costs, even after the parents are retired.

To qualify, the child must meet the same definition of disability as an ordinary worker and the disability must have started before the child reaches age 22. Once a parent retires, the disabled child receives 50% of his/her parent's full retirement benefit and 75% of that benefit after the parent dies.

Divorced

You may be entitled to receive benefits even if your former spouse has remarried and is still working.

It used to be that divorced spouses were subject to the same rule as current spouses—the "ex" could not draw benefits until the former spouse retired. But some former spouses held grudges and vowed they would never retire, thus preventing their ex-partners from ever receiving benefits.

The law was changed, but you must meet three important tests to qualify:

- You must have been married to the person for at least 10 years.
- You must be at least age 62.
- You must be unmarried.

If you have worked yourself (either before or during the marriage or after the divorce), Social Security will automatically check to see if you can draw more on your own earnings record than your former spouse's and will pay you the higher of the two amounts.

Fraud and Errors

Contact Social Security immediately if you suspect someone is fraudulently using your Social Security number. While it's very rare for someone to deliberately appropriate and misuse your Social Security number, it does happen occasionally. Usually such fraud occurs with nonexistent numbers or with the numbers of deceased individuals.

Trouble more often arises when there is a mistake in the payroll process and a Social Security number is entered incorrectly. But the Social Security Administration says it has a 99.1% accuracy rate for individual earnings' records.

If an error does occur, the best way to catch it is to take the time to carefully read your Social Security earnings history. The government now automatically mails these records annually to every worker over age 25 (about three months before your birthday). Eyeball the numbers to make sure they agree with your recent annual earnings. If they don't, call the toll-free number on the statement to make corrections.

A more common problem is when you are confused with someone who has a similar name. Often, you first learn of this when that person applies for a loan or mortgage...and you are notified by a bank or credit union that you are being denied credit because of the other person's credit problems.

Immediately notify the major credit-reporting services in writing that you are not the person in question and demand that your credit history be corrected.

The Bottom Line on Banks

All banks were not created equal. Big commercial banks offer more financial services, but at the price of steep fees and often poor customer care.

While local banks and credit unions usually offer better rates and a more service-oriented environment, the trade-off can be convenience. Smaller banks keep shorter business hours and offer fewer services, sometimes even limiting access to your cash.

The bank and type of account you choose can save you—or cost you—hundreds of dollars a year, so it pays to choose wisely. Also make sure you understand the terms of your account, since many accounts have minimum balance requirements. If your balance dips below the monthly minimum, you may be fined.

When to Take Social Security Benefits

Congress has repealed the reduction in Social Security benefits that used to be imposed on persons who worked after age 65. Now, many people who still work after 65 may be tempted to delay taking benefits.

For every year that the start of benefits is delayed, the amount of benefits increases by about 6%. So persons who don't need benefits right away may put off taking them to get larger benefits later.

Problem: Most people do better by taking benefits at age 65 rather than later—even if they don't need them. That's because taking more years of smaller benefits starting at 65 is very likely to exceed fewer years of larger benefits taken later.

Key: The increase in benefits that results from delaying the start of benefits is actuarially balanced—calculated so that over your life expectancy it will just offset the loss of the benefits you chose not to take up front. That means you have to survive beyond your life expectancy to profit by waiting to take the larger benefits.

The best decision will depend on the facts of each case. In general, unless your health is such that you are confident of living a longer-than-average life, you'll do better by taking benefits at age 65 rather than later.

Craig Hoogstra, manager of financial products for AARP, 601 E St. NW, Washington, DC 20049. www.aarp.org.

Social Security Help by Phone

Call the **Social Security Hotline** if you have any questions about your benefits. A copy of your **Personal Earnings and Benefits** statement, which reflects the income your benefits are based on, is mailed automatically about three months before your birthday. Call the Social Security Hotline at 800-772-1213 or visit www.ssa.gov.

Good News About Credit Unions

There are more than 6,000 federal credit unions in the nation catering to more than 44 million consumers. While most credit unions provide services for the middle class, many are now also targeting moderate- and low-income neighborhoods, where commercial banks are scarce or their overpriced services are unaffordable for low-income consumers. Not only can you feel good about banking with a credit union, but, because they are not-for-profit, credit unions return surplus funds to their customers in the form of lower rates.

Size Matters Credit unions aren't always a bargain. The smaller organizations are often too small to offer competitive rates. The best deals can be found at the larger credit unions.

Give and Take While credit unions have fewer branch offices and many do not yet have ATMs, these inconveniences are offset by lower and fewer fees and a commitment to customer service.

Keeping Prices Down Credit unions offer comparative bargains on car loans, credit cards and mortgages. Their ATM fees (when they have them) are usually lower and the basic requirements for qualifying for a loan are also generally more relaxed. *One thing to watch out for:* Most—but not all—credit unions are insured by the FDIC. Make sure yours is.

Call the Credit Union National Association at 800-358-5710 (www.cuna.org) to find out about credit unions in your area.

Checking Accounts: Getting More and Paying Less

Free checking accounts are becoming harder and harder to find. Banks know that they provide necessary services and most are going to make you pay for them—and pay well. According to the Federal Reserve Board, less than one-tenth of all commercial banks offer free checking. And even if you can find a free checking account, many banks will find ways of slipping in hidden charges, making your account less free than you think. There are ways, however, to beat the banks and lower your checking costs:

- If you're age 50 or older, you might be eligible for a low-fee or free checking account for senior citizens.
- Having your canceled checks returned costs the bank—and you —money. If you waive this privilege, you might save on fees.
- Ask your employer if you can have your paycheck deposited directly into your account. You save time, hassle and you might also save money, since the bank may pass the savings in processing costs on to you in the form of lower fees.
- Some banks offer package accounts, allowing you to combine several accounts such as CDs, savings, checking and even your mortgage balance to qualify for free checking and reduced fees on loans and credit cards.

ATM Traps

- Nearly half of all banks now charge you for using ATM machines that are not owned by your bank—often as much as $2 per transaction. If you use ATMs frequently, such charges can quickly erode your balance.
- Reduce electronic banking fees by choosing a bank that doesn't charge for using its ATM (there are still a few out there!) or allows you a reasonable number of free ATM withdrawals per month.
- Avoid ATMs belonging to other banks.
- Withdraw larger amounts that will last you longer.
- Consider banking the old fashioned way—by visiting a teller during bank business hours. Not only will you avoid the hidden costs of electronic banking, but your bank staff will get to know you personally—an important advantage when it comes time to apply for a loan or settle a charge dispute on your monthly statement. But watch out for sneaky teller fees! Some banks now charge you for talking to a teller.

CDs: High Interest, Low Risk

Certificates of Deposit (CDs) offer security, flexibility and a pretty good yield—if you know where to look. Smaller banks that are aggressively seeking cash to make loans or investments offer the most competitive rates. These can vary considerably from bank to bank—by as much as 2%, depending on the term of the CD. Smart investors shop via phone, mail and the Internet to get the best rates. Use CDs as places to park emergency savings and rainy-day funds rather than as long-term investments. Any CD purchased from an FDIC-affiliated institution is insured for up to $100,000.

To find the CD with the best yield, consult the business pages of your nearest big-city newspaper or your favorite personal finance magazine. *The Wall Street Journal* and the business pages of the Sunday *New York Times* list the best rates across the country.

The ultimate resource for finding the best rates, however, is the Internet. Hundreds of banks offer CDs and money market accounts on-line—often at rates one percentage point or more above what banks offer at branch offices. Get daily updates from the Bank Rate Monitor's Internet Banking Deals Web site (www.bankrate.com) or at BanxQuote (www.banx.com).

Other Banking Alternatives

Asset Management Accounts Some discount brokerage houses are now offering asset-management accounts—investment accounts that offer the flexibility of a checking account without the hidden expenses. TD Waterhouse (800-934-4448, www.tdwaterhouse.com) offers a no-fee Investor Money Management account, with no check minimums and free ATM withdrawals. Although the account

Beware of New Social Security Scam

Don't be fooled into providing personal information if you receive a flyer promising additional Social Security payments.

More than 25,000 people were recently duped by two anonymous flyers that falsely promised them money from the government if they mailed their name, address, phone number, date of birth and Social Security number to a post office box.

One flyer promised higher Social Security benefits to "notch babies" born between 1917 and 1926. The other promised a $5,000 payment under the fictitious *Slave Reparations Act*.

If you suspect fraud: Call the Social Security Administration fraud hotline at 800-269-0271, www.ssa.gov.

James G. Huse, Jr., Inspector General of the Social Security Administration, Baltimore.

Protecting Your Social Security Benefits

Your Social Security benefits are exempt from your creditors if you're in financial trouble. This means that department stores, credit card issuers and collection agencies can't go after your retirement checks.

requires a $1,000 minimum balance, the money is invested in securities rather than sitting in a low- or no-interest checking account.

Internet Banking If you're already on-line, you might consider switching to an Internet bank. Although you won't get personal service, you also won't be saddled with teller fees. Several virtual banks are offering no-fee checking accounts with unlimited ATM use and free electronic bill payment. Bank Rate Monitor at www.bankrate.com will alert you to many of the latest on-line banking deals.

Guaranteed Checks for a Lot Less Money

Postal money orders are a versatile and inexpensive alternative to bank checks, certified checks and even wire transfers and money-grams. US postal money orders cost between 90¢ and $1.25, plus the face value of the check up to $1,000 per money order—making them the cheapest guaranteed check available. At any one time, you can purchase money orders worth up to $3,500.

International money orders are similar bargains, with rates ranging from $3 to $8.50, depending on the country of issue. They can be converted to cash immediately and are fully refundable if lost or stolen, provided you hang on to your receipt.

Check Fraud Self-Defense

Recently a close friend bounced a pile of checks—not because of faulty bookkeeping, but because checks written by someone else were charged to his account. It took months to resolve the problem.

Check fraud is increasing. What can we do to protect ourselves? I put that question to Frank Abagnale, world-famous expert on white-collar crime. Frank really knows—as a young man, he cashed more than $2.5 million in fraudulent checks. He was released from prison only after agreeing to help the government fight white-collar crime.

"Most people know the basics," says Frank, "but think it won't happen to them. It does—to thousands every day. Don't leave a blank space when writing dollar amounts...avoid abbreviations—'IRS' can be made into 'MRS'...don't leave checks in your mailbox." More steps:

Order Checks From Your Bank This is more costly than buying from a mail-order firm, but the checks are harder to alter.

Protect Deposit Slips *Common scam:* Con artists deposit worthless checks into your account—and get back some of the deposit as cash.

Review All Canceled Checks Be sure they are still made out to—and endorsed by—the intended party. If you notice any irregularities, notify the bank within 30 days.

Warning: Not reviewing could be costly. New laws assign responsibility to whoever was in the best position to prevent or identify the fraud.

For business owners:

- Keep signatures of authorized check signers out of the public eye. Use a fake signature for your company's direct-mail solicitations.
- Establish a separate account for incoming wire transfers.

Check fraud could happen to you—more than 1.3 million worthless checks are written every day. Don't risk the aggravation and expense.

Marjory Abrams, editor of Bottom Line Personal, *Stamford, CT 06901.*

Credit Card Traps

Because of intense competition, credit card issuers are trying to lure you with the flashiest and most irresistible introductory teaser APRs, consumer perks and rebates. There are some tremendous deals to be found out there, but don't be taken in the process.

Credit cards can be damaging to your budget if you forget that carrying a balance is the same as borrowing money—at an unusually high rate of interest.

Different Cards for Different Customers

Shop around for the credit card terms that best suit your budget and repayment style. For instance, if you routinely pay your bills in full each month, focus on the amount of the annual fee and other charges.

If you will be paying your credit card debt off slowly, however, shop for a low APR and consider how your issuer calculates finance charges. In either case, your costs will be affected by whether or not the company offers a grace period.

Here are some key issues to consider:

- Annual Percentage Rate (APR)
- Annual fee
- Grace period
- Cash advance fees
- Late payment charges
- Over-the-limit fees

Elite Cards Elite cards, such as the Visa Signature card and the WorldMasterCard, are giving American Express a run for its money. These cards, aimed at the roughly 3% of American households with annual incomes above $100,000, offer enticing perks, such as guaranteed airport parking, air miles reward programs that

Social Security Traps for Citizens Abroad

Social Security beneficiaries who live outside the US for 30 consecutive days or more must notify the Social Security Administration of their address, even if benefits are directly deposited in a bank.

US citizens usually will continue to receive all benefits, but restrictions may apply to noncitizens, particularly those who receive dependent or survivor benefits. Other rules:

- If you receive benefits while working outside the US, are under the full retirement age (age 65 in 2002) and your wages are not subject to US Social Security taxes—working more than 45 hours per month will cause your benefits to be withheld.
- Many foreign countries tax US Social Security benefits. Check the rules with the country's US embassy before going abroad.
- Medicare generally does not cover health services received outside the US. So if you plan to be away from the US for a substantial period, you *may* not want to continue Medicare Part B, due to the premium cost. However, if you return and wish to enroll in Part B, you are subject to the general enrollment period, which is January through March with entitlement effective the following July. There is a premium surcharge of 10% for each full year of nonenrollment.

J. Robert Treanor, principal, William M. Mercer Inc., 462 S. Fourth Ave., Ste. 1500, Louisville, KY 40202.

Best Time of Year To Retire

Best time to retire is early July. A full-time worker will have accumulated the 1,000 hours required during a calendar year for full benefits.

Summer retirement lowers stress—major lifestyle changes are easier to handle when days are warm, there is plenty to do outdoors and many people are away from work as well.

Caution: Retirement in summer can eliminate a year-end bonus, and can have Social Security implications. Consult your financial adviser.

Lee Rosenberg, certified financial planner, Valley Stream, NY.

can be applied to all airlines, special services at luxury hotels and VIP access to symphony orchestras and sporting events.

While not quite as comprehensive as the advantages offered to American Express Platinum card holders, Visa and MasterCard issues are also considerably less expensive—with annual fees as much as 80% lower than American Express, depending on the issuer. Visa Signature cards and WorldMasterCards also have no preset spending limits and sometimes low APRs. Terms and fees vary from issuer to issuer.

Rebate Cards A lot of credit card issuers are scaling down or eliminating costly rebate programs. Still, there are some excellent programs out there that provide a way to accumulate air miles or give you a rebate on your next car purchase. But beware of the high APRs more and more frequently associated with rebate cards. These cards can be a great value only if you pay your balance off promptly. A large balance carried month to month can easily cancel out any benefits of the rebate.

Mall VIP Visa Offered at more than 400 malls across the nation, the latest incarnation of the rebate card offers cardholders a 2% rebate on card purchases at participating mall outlets such as J.C. Penney and Sears, and a 1% rebate everywhere else. The rebate comes as a coupon redeemable at any of the malls' shops. No annual fee and an introductory interest rate of 6.9% make this card an especially attractive offer for shoppers.

Ask at your local mall about this or similar offers.

Debt Consolidation If you have a lot of credit card debt spread over different cards, consider consolidating it on one low-rate card. Card issuers supply courtesy- or convenience-checks, or balance-transfer forms to pay off your other cards (although sometimes with hefty transfer fees). Make sure that the low interest rate on your new card lasts long enough to pay off your debt. Switching your debt from card to card looks bad on your credit rating.

Plastic Not-So-Fantastic

Hard to believe, perhaps, but many card issuers are actually looking for ways to trip you up. Interest rates are swelling and grace periods shrinking. Make one or two late payments and you might be socked with a higher interest rate, not to mention a late charge of $25 or more. Some issuers are levying penalties if a payment is even a day or two late. Also, annual fees associated with cards have started to jump, reaching as high as $35 in some cases.

Even if you pay off your balance within the grace period, banks will sometimes find ways to sneak in extra charges. If you pay your balance off like clockwork, look out for clauses concerning "inactivity" or "account closing fees" in your cardholder agreement. If you keep a zero balance and have a history of good credit, your card issuer may even find ways of penalizing you for

your good behavior. Remember, card issuers like customers who keep high balances on their credit cards. This is how they make money. Indeed they may even deny you rewards, cancel your account or deny your application if your credit rating is too high.

Whatever you do, don't forget to read the fine print on credit card applications, cardholder agreements and correspondence from your credit card company. Big traps lie hidden in tiny type.

Best Ways to Borrow

When people need to borrow, most head to the local bank. But there are better ways to borrow for every major need:

Auto Loans

Best bet: *Manufacturer financing.* The slowing economy has resulted in bloated car inventories and manufacturers' annual percentage rates (APRs) are at historic lows.

Important: Don't forget to negotiate a good price for your vehicle. Avoid extra charges, such as credit life and disability insurance.

Home Mortgages

Best bet: *Web shopping.* Do an Internet search using the words "mortgage search." Through some Web sites, you can reach 30 potential lenders—banks, credit unions and savings and loans—with a single application.

A rate that is even a single percentage point below what you would have paid at your local bank translates into savings of some $50,000 over the 30-year term of a $200,000 mortgage loan.

Most lenders are willing to write mortgages of shorter length—and usually at slightly lower rates. Get quotes on 15-, 20- and 25-year mortgages in addition to the standard 30-year mortgage.

A 25-year mortgage isn't that much more per month, yet you save five years of monthly interest payments.

Also consider paying half your monthly mortgage twice a month, on the 15th and 30th, rather than the typical once a month. Unless your mortgage specifically bars this—and most don't—it will save you thousands of dollars over a 30-year term because of the cumulative interest saved. It is convenient, too—since most people receive their paychecks twice a month.

Education Loans

Best bet: *Government-sponsored loan programs,* which offer need-based loans.

Perkins loans have a maximum annual interest rate of only 5% and can total as much as $20,000 for an undergraduate education. Subsidized Stafford loans have a maximum rate of 8.25% and can total as much as $23,000 for a dependent undergraduate student.

War Widows' Benefits

The ***Veterans Benefits Act of 1998*** stipulates that the spouses of deceased veterans who lost VA survivor benefits when they remarried may be eligible for **Dependency and Indemnity Compensation (DIC)** benefits if they are no longer married. This applies to World War II and Korean War widows.

Important: Benefits are not restored automatically—you must reapply and give proof of the termination of a subsequent marriage. The amount you receive is dependent upon the veteran's date of death.

The restoration is *retroactive* to October 1998.

For further information: Call the Department of Veterans Affairs, 800-827-1000, www.va.gov.

Ken McKinnon, public relations spokesperson, Department of Public Affairs, 810 Vermont Ave., Washington, DC 20420.

Pension Warning

Pension danger for people rehired after quitting or retiring: Even a company that gives credit for the years of service before you left may give it in a way that significantly reduces your pension. Calculations can be very complex.

Self-defense: If you are planning to return to a firm where you worked previously, use your own financial adviser to analyze what will happen to your pension and help you negotiate a better deal.

Allen C. Engerman, president, The National Center for Retirement Benefits, Inc., 666 Dundee Rd., Suite 1200, Northbrook, IL 60062.

What You Should Know About Your Pension Rights is a free booklet published by the Pension and Welfare Benefits Administration. Request this and other publications by calling 800-998-7542 (www.dol.gov/dol/pwba).

Interest charges won't kick in—and loans typically don't have to be paid back—until after graduation.

Next best: Unsubsidized Stafford loans are available to students regardless of need, but interest charges start as soon as the loan is taken.

Parents can get Plus loans, with interest rates of up to 9%.

Contact the school's financial aid office—you may qualify for other grants and monies as well, which traditional financial institutions won't tell you about.

Personal Loans

Best bet: *Borrowing against a cash-value insurance policy or investment account.* This is usually at much lower rates than a bank loan.

If you borrow from a bank: Insist on a simple-interest loan. The standard installment loan charges interest on the full amount of the loan over the entire term. A simple-interest loan calculates interest on the declining balance. If a lender refuses simple interest, go elsewhere.

Example: On a $10,000 48-month loan, simple interest will save $400, versus a traditional front-end-loaded installment note.

Next best: Private lenders are not just for entrepreneurs and high rollers. Borrowers who have been rejected by banks might find private lenders more flexible. Ask local accountants and tax attorneys for a referral. While this is common for small business loans, it is a worthy route even for a mortgage. Collateral requirements, terms and rates are competitive with those offered by banks. Additional costs, such as closing points, are often waived.

Important: Show the loan documents to an attorney before signing. Don't have the attorney close the loan—just pay for an hour or so of his/her time.

Loans to Avoid

Too expensive: Revolving credit card debt…department store/appliance store credit arrangements.

Too risky: Home-equity credit lines require borrowers to risk their homes to pay off small sums. Even when you can deduct the interest portion from your taxes, setup costs often trump potential tax savings.

Edward F. Mrkvicka, Jr., former chairman of a national bank and currently president of the financial consulting firm Reliance Enterprises Inc., 22115 O'Connell Rd., Marengo, IL 60152. He is author of *Your Bank Is Ripping You Off* (St. Martin's Griffin) and *J.K. Lasser's Pick Winning Stocks* (Wiley).

Ways to Save at Tax Time

Tax legislation in recent years has brought with it a dizzying 1,000+ changes to the Tax Code. Some of these changes are staged in over several years and may save you a good deal of money now.

Making the Most of the Tax Law Changes

While the reforms are advantageous to most taxpayers, making sense out of them can be a confusing and time-consuming process. Here are some of the big changes that could benefit you:

Estate Taxes The law makes it possible to leave more money to your heirs tax free. This figure will increase from $1 million in 2002 to $3.5 million in 2009. There is no estate tax in 2010 and when the estate tax kicks back in in 2011, the exemption is again $1 million.

Child Tax Credit You can claim a $600 yearly tax credit for each child under 17 years of age. The credit is refundable to the extent of 10% of your income in excess of $10,000.

Tax-Free Profit on Home Sales You are eligible for $250,000 of tax-free profit on the sale of your home if you file an individual return, and $500,000 if you file jointly. To qualify for the break, you must own and live in the house for two of the five years prior to the sale. This tax break can be used again and again, although only once in any two-year period.

Tax-Free Gifts Make the most of the annual federal gift tax exclusion, which is indexed for inflation starting after 1998. In 2002, you can give tax-free gifts of up to $11,000 per person per year. These gifts aren't taxable to the person who receives them, either.

The Roth IRA Just because the Roth IRA doesn't offer tax deductions for deposits doesn't mean it's not a bargain. These back-loaded IRAs, which let you take tax-free withdrawals after age 59½, are ideal for higher-income taxpayers who aren't eligible for deductible IRAs.

There are other perks to the Roth IRA. You're still allowed to contribute to one even if you're covered by a retirement plan at work or through your self-employment. And there's no mandatory withdrawal age: Tax-free inheritance can compound for your beneficiaries.

Roth eligibility begins to be phased out at modified adjusted gross income (MAGI) of $150,000 on joint returns and $95,000 on individual returns. The income cutoffs are $160,000 and $110,000 respectively.

If you have a traditional IRA, consider converting it to a Roth IRA. You'll owe tax on the value of your account at the time of conversion, but all future earnings can be tax free. *Eligibility for conversion:* MAGI up to $100,000.

Home Office Deductions You can deduct expenses for a home office that you use exclusively and regularly to perform administrative and managerial duties, even if it isn't your primary workplace.

Banking Cost Cutters

- Analyze your statement to make sure that your bank isn't nibbling away at your balance with sneaky fees and penalties. If you feel that your bank has not been straightforward about charges that are levied on your account, don't hesitate to complain to the manager. If the dispute isn't settled to your satisfaction, contact your **State Banking Commissioner** to help you resolve the problem.

- Pay bills right after a deposit has cleared to reduce the chance of bouncing a check.

- Keep only the minimum required for low fees in your checking account. Put other savings in a higher-interest money market fund or invest them in a short-term CD. Letting your savings languish in low- or no-interest accounts can cost you literally hundreds of dollars a year.

What Banks Don't Tell You

Big commercial banks are currently charging about $15 for 200 basic single checks and up to $32 for designer versions. To save half—even two-thirds—on these steep prices, you are entitled by law to order your checks from a third-party supplier.

Here are some companies offering the best deals in mail-order checks, with prices as low as $7.50 for 200 basic single checks to $15 for special editions. And there are often even better deals for first-time customers.

Order ahead: Mail-order suppliers have a two- to three-week processing period from the time they receive your order until you receive your new checks.

- **Checks in the Mail** (877-397-1541, www.citm.com)
- **Checkstore** (800-424-3257)
- **Checks Unlimited** (800-533-3973, www.checksunlimited.com)

Tax-Wise Investing

Smart investing isn't only about getting the best return with the least risk, but also about protecting your assets at tax time. Here are a few simple steps you can take to keep more of your money compounding:

- Maximize your retirement account contributions to 401(k)s, 403(b)s and IRAs that allow you to deduct your contribution as well as benefit from tax-deferred compounding on your investment returns. Contribution limits for 2002 have increased.
- Contribute to a nondeductible IRA or Roth IRA if you have maxed out on your 401(k) contributions.
- Consider other investments offering tax-deferred compounding, such as cash-value insurance policies, annuities and Series EE and I savings bonds.
- Favor appreciating assets, such as growth stocks and growth mutual funds that let you make the most of the 20% maximum capital gains tax rate.
- Choose tax-exempt income investments. Municipal bonds issued in your state are exempt from local and state as well as federal taxes. US Treasury bills are free from local and state taxes.

Shrewder Contributions

Make sure your charitable dollars work harder for your favorite cause—and you.

It can be difficult to keep track of small charitable donations made haphazardly throughout the year. Better to plan at the beginning of the year what you're able to give and allot it to just a few of your favorite organizations.

Not only will you have a better idea of what you can deduct come tax time, but small donations of $10 or so are often not cost-effective for nonprofit organizations to process. Giving larger gifts to fewer organizations will ensure that more of your dollars are working for the causes you care about, and fewer are paying for administrative overhead. If you can't afford to give much, consider pooling it with donations from friends, relatives or coworkers.

Tips for Charitable Givers

- Check to see if your employer offers matching contributions as part of its benefits package.
- Check the tax status of the organization you're considering giving to. Contributions to tax-exempt groups aren't necessarily tax deductible. Ask if a charity is designated by the IRS as a 501(c)(3) organization.
- Hang on to receipts for expenses that you have incurred doing charitable work. For example, you may be able to deduct taxi fares, driving costs (including tolls and parking), uniforms, transportation and lodging costs if you travel for charity.

- Protect your charitable deduction by obtaining an acknowledgment letter for any single gift of $250 or more.

Benefit Your Favorite Charities—And Yourself Come Tax Time

Donate Stocks Instead of Cash Appreciated securities that you have held for longer than a year are deductible at their current market value. Thus, if you purchased shares of stock for $1,500 five years ago and they are now worth twice that price, you are entitled to a tax deduction of $3,000, free of capital gains tax, if you make a charitable gift of them.

Donate Your Used Goods If you donate used clothing, furniture, appliances, vehicles or other items, you can deduct their fair market value.

Donate Your Old Car If you're in the market for a new car, consider donating your old one to your favorite charity, or selling it yourself and donating the proceeds. You can value it for a tax deduction using the *National Automobile Dealer's Association Blue Book*, available in your community library. The Heritage for the Blind (800-2-DONATE, www.cardonation.com) accepts boats, trucks, RVs and more—running or not—and will pay for immediate towing.

Social Security Tax-Saving Strategy

Social Security recipients lose a significant portion of benefits to taxes if their income exceeds certain limits. More specifically, when Modified Adjusted Gross Income (MAGI)—which is Adjusted Gross Income increased by tax-free interest on municipal bonds, certain exclusions and a portion of Social Security benefits—exceeds:

- $32,000 on a joint return or $25,000 on a single return, up to 50% of Social Security benefits are included in taxable income.
- $44,000 on a joint return, $34,000 on a single return or zero if married filing separately, up to 85% of Social Security benefits are included in taxable income.

Tax-Saving Strategy

Reduce tax on your Social Security benefits by reducing your MAGI. How:

Defer Income Invest for growth rather than income. Postpone realizing gains on investments and taking discretionary distributions from IRAs and other retirement plans.

Finding the Best Credit Card Deals

Free Weekly E-mail Newsletter
If you're not yet among the Web-savvy, *CardTrak*, the country's only consumer credit card newsletter, gives you the latest news on the best credit card deals across the country. The newsletter (updated monthly) costs $5 per issue. Call 301-631-9100, or send $5 to CardTrak, P.O. Box 1700, Frederick, MD 21702, www.cardtrak.com.

Federal Reserve System Reports
The **Federal Reserve System** (202-452-3819, www.federalreserve.gov) publishes a biannual report on the terms and conditions that apply on credit card plans offered by financial institutions. Consumers are advised to contact the credit card issuer for current rates and to find out about the latest offers.

How to Get Your Money's Worth From Your Credit Cards

Get your credit card bills under control by changing to a card that best suits your needs.

❏ **Balance below $2,000.** Look for a card with a very low interest rate and no annual fee.

❏ **Balance of $4,000 or more.** Look for a gold card with low rates but expect a higher annual fee.

❏ **Charge a lot—pay your balance in full each month.** Select a credit card that has rebates or rewards for services you use.

❏ **High credit limit.** Consider platinum cards. Expect interest rates in the mid-teens and credit limits of $25,000 to $100,000.

❏ **Debt transfer.** Look for credit cards with reasonable rates and high credit limits for consolidating your debts.

Robert McKinley, president of CardWeb, Inc., which tracks nationwide credit card rates, Gettysburg, PA.

Make Tax-Free Investments Roth IRA payouts of earnings are tax free if certain conditions are met, so fund a Roth IRA rather than a regular IRA.

Interest from tax-free municipal bonds is included in MAGI for purposes of determining tax on Social Security benefits—but municipals pay a lower interest rate than taxable bonds.

Shift Income Make estate-tax-reducing gifts of property to younger family members by shifting income-producing property.

Deduct Losses At year-end, take "paper" investment losses to off-set income from gains and up to $3,000 of ordinary income. You can repurchase the loss investment after 31 days, or a similar but not identical one immediately.

Barbara Weltman, an attorney practicing in Millwood, NY. She is author of *Bottom Line's Shrewd Money Book* (Boardroom Books).

You Have a Very Special Friend at the IRS

When you have a problem with the IRS, the last place you would expect to find help is within the bureaucracy. But that's where you and your adviser should turn.

The *Taxpayer Advocate*, the representative of taxpayers within the IRS, has received additional authority and resources since 1998 —increasing its ability to act on behalf of taxpayers facing unfair collection actions or "impossible to solve" problems:

- There is now a Taxpayer Advocate in every IRS District and in each of the 10 Service Centers throughout the country.
- They are receiving increasing staffing and resources. Most other departments of the IRS are being cut back.
- They have been made completely independent of other local IRS officials and now report directly to the National Taxpayer Advocate.

Who Is Eligible?

Seek immediate help from the Taxpayer Advocate if you face an imminent adverse action on the part of the IRS—such as a lien, levy or property seizure—that you believe is improper or unfair and that will be costly or damaging to you.

First step: File IRS Form 911, *Application for Taxpayer Assistance Order.* Your case will receive immediate review.

Example: Jane gets a wage levy notice. If it takes effect, she won't be able to pay rent and will be evicted. The Taxpayer Advocate can stop the levy immediately on grounds of hardship.

When you have a nonemergency problem with the IRS bureaucracy—such as a misapplied payment or missing refund—you must first try to resolve the problem through normal channels, such as letters and calls to the IRS branch that contacted you.

Keep copies of all correspondence and records of conversations with the IRS. If you fail to resolve a specific problem in at least two attempts—or the IRS fails to resolve the problem by a promised date—you can go to the Taxpayer Advocate.

Note: The Taxpayer Advocate tackles administrative problems only. It will not intervene in legal disputes.

How to Get Help

Call toll-free 877-777-4778 to obtain the phone number of your local Taxpayer Advocate...or visit the Taxpayer Advocate's Web page on the IRS Web site, www.irs.gov. Click on "Tax Information for You."

Other useful materials on the Taxpayer Advocate's Web page:

- Annual reports of the National Taxpayer Advocate, which describe its programs, objectives and priorities.
- Free tax counseling for small businesses, tax-assistance programs for the elderly and much more.
- IRS Form 2848, *Power of Attorney and Declaration of Representative*, which you can file to authorize another person (or your professional adviser) to represent you in dealings with the Taxpayer Advocate or the IRS.

Frederick W. Daily, Esq., tax attorney, 595 Market St., San Francisco 94105. He is author of *Stand Up to the IRS* and *Tax Savvy for Small Business* (Nolo.com).

How to Get Your Credit Card Rate Reduced

Use the secret word, "Please." It's a smart move in this *very* competitive environment.

- If your account is in good standing, call and ask for a rate reduction. The credit card company may agree to a reduction of a point. Even a fraction of a point is worthwhile over time if you carry a balance.

- If you pay an annual fee, ask that it be cancelled. Customer service people know that you can easily switch to a competitor's free card.

- If you mistakenly make a late payment, ask that the penalty and the interest be cancelled. Most companies extend this courtesy one time.

How to Lower Property Taxes

Don't just grumble and accept a property tax bill you feel is too high. You have the right to appeal an assessment. But before you do, make sure you have a fact-based case. Steps to take:

- Find out where to file an appeal and when the deadline is. The deadline is usually statutory and can't be extended.
- Call the assessor's office—or pay a visit—to find out exactly how your tax figure was determined.
- Look for mathematical errors in the calculation of your tax.
- Look for factual errors in the description of property that overestimates its value—a basement erroneously listed as finished ...a one-car garage listed as a two-car...incorrect lot size, etc.
- Compare your assessment with your neighbors'. To see if there is "discrimination," check the assessments of your block and

Courtesy Checks Warning

Does your monthly credit card statement arrive with free courtesy checks along with a reminder encouraging you to use them to consolidate your debt or make purchases?

Before you start using them, make sure you understand the hidden costs sometimes associated with these checks. Often they are treated as cash advances by your credit card company and carry very high finance charges.

compare them to value to determine a ratio. If your figure is correct but theirs are underestimated, find out the practice in your area. The answer may be that they will raise your neighbors' taxes and not lower yours.

- Compare the assigned market value with recent sales prices of comparable houses in the neighborhood.
- Make sure you have any tax breaks for which you qualify—senior citizen...disabled...veteran...low income.

If you feel you need professional advice, look for an attorney who specializes in this work or a licensed appraiser with the qualifications MAI (Member of the Appraisal Institute) or SRA (Senior Residential Appraiser). *Note:* In most cases, their services are on a contingency fee basis.

Once your research is done, file your appeal and attach copies of any relevant backup materials to support your case.

David Schechner, Esq., real estate attorney, Schechner & Targan, West Orange, NJ.

Turn Old Clothes… Appliances…Furniture And More…Into Cash

What do you do with those old clothes you don't wear and the household items you no longer use? Turn these items into cash by giving them to charity and taking an itemized deduction on your tax return.

Be sure to follow a few simple—but important—rules:

Get a Dated, Signed Receipt from the Charity It should list exactly what items you've given rather than something vague like "three bags of clothing" or "two boxes of small appliances."

Assign Fair Market Value to Each Item The IRS allows you to claim a tax deduction for the amount that the items would likely sell for in a thrift or consignment shop. One way to determine these amounts is to check prices at a thrift shop. However, few people will visit a thrift shop to do this.

The book *Cash for Your Used Clothing* details the fair market value for more than 800 different items. Examples:

Man's dress shirt: $14	Iron: $6
Woman's dress: $40	Microwave: $60–$80
Boy's denim jeans: $12	10-speed bike: $40–$80
Girl's sweater: $14	Sofa: $120–$210
Electric blender: $8	Table/chairs: $120–$200

Someone paying 34% combined state and federal taxes would save $13.60 in taxes from a single woman's dress.

Condition does matter: Items must be in good shape and not ludicrously out of style.

If the Total Deduction Exceeds $500, file Form 8283, *Noncash Charitable Contributions*. You must itemize instead of taking the standard deduction.

Understand How the IRS Views These Matters Someone with an Adjusted Gross Income (AGI) of $75,000 to $100,000 typically can report an average of $2,500 in noncash donations without raising eyebrows at the IRS.

Someone reporting $20,000 in income who takes a $2,500 deduction for noncash donations should be ready to have his/her return questioned. Your total donation cannot exceed 50% of your AGI for the year. If it does, the remainder can be carried over for up to five years.

Vital: Receipts to prove the donations and proof you assigned fair market value in a reasonable way.

William R. Lewis, CPA, president of Client Valuation Services, Box 22031, Lincoln, NE 68542. He is author of *Cash for Your Used Clothing—Tax Year 2001*, available through his company. 800-875-5927.

Internet-Based Credit Cards

Internet-based credit cards that claim "risk-free" on-line shopping are not much safer than ordinary cards.

Under federal law, a cardholder's liability for unauthorized card use is limited to $50. Internet-based cards—which promise you will never pay a penny for unauthorized use—are simply letting you off the hook for the $50 liability. But—many conventional cards will waive the $50 liability if you ask.

Gerri Detweiler, education adviser, Debt Counselors of America, Gaithersburg, MD.

Cut Your Investment Costs

Your success as an investor is more important to you than to anyone else. Nobody knows more—or cares more—about your long-term financial needs than you do. Much of the overhead associated with investing comes from paying someone else to make financial decisions for you—someone who may be more interested in selling you products than making you money. Why pay someone to do what you can do yourself? Not only do the following strategies save you money, but they put you in charge of your own financial future.

Golden Rules for Smart Investors
No matter what the market is doing, there a few simple steps you can take to protect your nest egg:

- You're already ahead of the game if you keep your investment costs as low as possible. The better informed you are, the less money you'll have to pay out to investment professionals.
- Choose your investments for the long term. Market timing is a dangerous game, especially for the amateur investor. Studies consistently show that the people who make money in the market are people who invest for the long haul. Don't be alarmed by short-term market fluctuations.

Paying With Savings vs. Credit Cards

If you pay a $500 bill with a credit card that carries 17.99% interest and send in $20 a month, you will pay a total of $715 and it will take 59 months to pay off the bill. But if you simply put $20 a month into a savings account earning 2.1% interest, you will build up $500 in 24 months and can then pay cash for what you want.

Bottom line: Saving is a cheaper and faster way to pay for what you want without debt.

Steve Rhode, president, Myvesta.org, nonprofit financial-solutions organization, Rockville, MD.

- Protect your investments from heavy taxation. That means keeping trading to an absolute minimum, whether you're investing independently or with a mutual fund. Choose mutual funds with low portfolio turnovers. And invest for growth, not income.
- Diversifying your portfolio will give you peace of mind. Diversify your investments between stocks and bonds, and between domestic and foreign funds.

The Virtues of Virtual

Why pay exorbitant brokers' fees when on-line financial sites provide all the facts (for free) necessary to make informed investment decisions? At last count there were more than 250 investment-oriented sites on-line, and this number is quickly growing. The services and information offered vary from site to site, providing everything from real-time stock quotes and SEC filings such as annual and quarterly reports, to state-of-the-art graphing tools that let you compare the past and present performance—and the future outlook—of your favorite companies.

These sites are giving professional brokers and investment counselors a serious run for their money and offer comprehensive company information. But just because you have Web access doesn't necessarily mean it's time to send your broker packing. The array of information on the Web can be dizzying to the newcomer, and it's important to learn how to evaluate the quality of your sources and information before sinking all your retirement savings into an E-mail stock tip. Start out by choosing a few high-quality sites that offer a diversity of services.

Don't Go Broke With Your Broker

Brokerage houses come in three flavors—full-service, discount and deep-discount. Full-service brokers help clients set investment goals and give advice—in exchange for a 3% commission or more on every purchase or sale.

Many discount brokers are now offering services comparable to their pricier counterparts, such as research and monthly statements—but can save you more than 50% on commissions.

The experienced investor may want to choose among the deep-discount brokerage firms, which cut commissions by as much as 90% but provide no services—and certainly no handholding.

The cheapest way to trade is on-line. All of these leading discount brokerage houses also offer on-line trading services:

- **Fidelity Broker Services** (800-544-7272, www.fidelity.com)
- **Quick and Reilly** (800-793-8050, www.quickandreilly.com)
- **T. Rowe Price Discount Brokerage** (800-225-5132, www.troweprice.com)
- **Charles Schwab** (877-476-2370, www.schwab.com)
- **TD Waterhouse** (800-934-4448, www.tdwaterhouse.com)

On-Line Brokers

On-line trading is revolutionizing Wall Street, and everyone is jumping on the bandwagon. For the knowledgeable investor, trading on-line keeps overhead to an absolute minimum. Charles Schwab (www.schwab.com), for instance, offers Web trading to its customers for a low $29.95 commission for up to 1,000 shares (and 3¢ for each additional share).

No-Load Mutual Funds

No-loads, mutual funds that don't charge commissions when investors open or close accounts or reinvest their dividends, have been outperforming load funds by a full percentage point for the past three years. Here are some tips on how to keep more of your money compounding:

- Even no-load funds sometimes charge 12b-1 fees, which are passed along to investors, to cover advertising and marketing costs. High 12b-1 fees can leave a serious dent in your earnings. Check your prospectus to see whether your mutual fund is assessing 12b-1 fees, and what percentage of your assets they amount to.
- Look for funds that have lower than average expense-to-asset ratios. Management fees can range from as low as 0.25% to as high as almost 2% of your initial investment.
- Portfolio turnovers (frequency of buying and selling stocks—which means extra fees and sometimes taxes for fund owners) are posted in mutual funds' semiannual and annual reports. Make sure your fund—or prospective fund—is keeping tax-costly trading down to a minimum.
- Depending on the fund you choose, your investment may also be subject to exit fees (if you leave the fund), redemption fees (if you withdraw some of your investment before a certain period of time has elapsed) or deferred sales charges. Some low-cost funds don't charge these fees. Others waive them after a specified minimum investment period, usually five years.

Mutual Fund Networks

Mutual fund networks make it easier—and cheaper—than ever to diversify your investments among different fund families. This lets you take advantage of strongly performing funds in different families—a growth fund in one and a GMNA fund in another, for example. These top fund networks give access to hundreds of funds in dozens of fund families:

- **Fidelity's Funds Network** (800-544-6666, www.fidelity.com)
- **Charles Schwab's Mutual Fund Marketplace and One-Source** (800-435-4000, www.schwab.com)
- **TD Waterhouse** (800-934-4448, www.tdwaterhouse.com)

Pay Your Bills On-Line

If you have a home computer and a modem, you may want to see if your credit card and utility companies offer on-line payment services. Many companies offer discounts or savings plans to customers who pay on-line because it saves them the cost of mailing paperwork. **AT&T** (800-222-0300, www.att.com) and **MCI** (800-444-3333 for Long-Distance Customer Service; 877-777-6271 for Local Customer Service, www.mci.com) are among the companies offering substantial discounts to customers who pay on-line. Other companies have services in the offing.

Bills It's Okay To Pay Late

Sometimes it is tough to pay all your bills on time.

Utility payments can usually be paid late—and without bad entries on your credit report. Call telephone, gas, electric and cable companies to make deferred-payment arrangements.

Other options:

- Renters can ask landlords about paying later. There is little chance it would be reported to credit bureaus.

- Those with good credit may be able to transfer credit card balances to a new card with a lower interest rate—and gain 30 more days to make a payment.

- Stores will often let customers negotiate missed payments on their credit cards without penalty. Get a promise—in writing—that a missed payment will not be reported to credit bureaus.

Important to pay on time: Mortgage, auto loans and leases, American Express bills.

David Masten, consumer finance and credit consultant, Jersey City, and author of The Fix Your Credit Workbook *(St. Martin's).*

Free Investment Advice

How and where you decide to invest is a personal decision, and no investment recipe will be to the taste of every investor. It's important to know where to find reliable data so you can make the right choice.

- **The Securities and Exchange Commission (SEC)** can provide general information about laws governing securities, including stocks and bonds, as well as tell you whether a particular brokerage house is being investigated. You can also request any of their free publications, including *Invest Wisely: An Introduction to Mutual Funds* and *Get the Facts on Saving & Investing* (SEC, Office of Investor Education and Assistance, 450 5th St. NW, Washington, DC 20549, 202-942-8088, www.sec.gov/investor.shtml).

- Want more facts and less hype? Call a company's investor relations department and ask for a free copy of Form 10-K. It contains no-nonsense information you won't find in annual reports, and can help you make sound investment decisions.

- Weekly top-10 lists of stocks and mutual funds in major newspapers can be excellent information sources if you follow them on a regular basis. A stock or fund new to the list may be a buying opportunity—especially if it is in a sector like technology or drug-company stocks in an under-performing period.

- **Morningstar**, a Chicago-based firm which tracks the performance of more than 8,000 stocks and mutual funds, is your ultimate resource for finding the best deals and helping you build the portfolio that's right for you.

  Morningstar's Web site provides up-to-date information and lets you generate spreadsheets comparing the performance of funds according to category, risk, volatility and return. The company also publishes two newsletters, *The Morningstar Stock Investor* and *Morningstar Mutual Funds*. Their newsletters may also be available at your local library. Call 800-735-0700 to order the newsletters or check out their free Web site at www.morningstar.com.

- **Quicken** (www.quicken.com) provides comprehensive information for selecting, evaluating and tracking investments. Includes links to mutual funds' prospectuses.

Keeping In the Green—In More Ways Than One

There are at least 25 mutual funds that cater to socially and environmentally conscious investors who want some control over who and what their money finances.

Depending on your concerns, you can select funds that refuse to buy stock in companies that sell tobacco, produce weapons, exploit economically disadvantaged workers or engage in discriminatory practices. Although the performance of some of these funds to date is uneven, there are a few standouts. One such fund is Dreyfus Premier Third Century (800-782-6620, www.dreyfus.com), the oldest and one of the best of the socially responsible funds.

Undervalued Stock

Don't be seduced by what some experts call glamour stocks—high-priced growth stocks that often promise more than they deliver. Not only do these stocks carry inflated price tags, but they tend to need a quick turnaround to pay off, so are not well-suited to the average investor. Instead, look for undervalued stocks—those whose prices are temporarily beaten down in relation to their earnings outlook.

Undervalued stock presents a golden opportunity for investors with money to invest in the market. Even better, the risk of buying undervalued stock is much less than that of buying stocks that are hitting new highs. Identifying undervalued stock is an investment strategy that can work for you regardless of the economic climate, and their bargain prices will provide insulation from market ups and downs in the years ahead.

Be a Contrarian Consider buying stock in companies that no one else wants to touch. These companies may have delivered recent bad news about earnings or future growth, or they may have suffered adverse legal decisions or damaging litigation—which has sent their stock prices down.

Look for companies that are in the midst of corporate change. They might be selling off some of their assets, spinning off divisions or subsidiaries or undergoing top management changes. These stocks can be a steal because they tend to be inefficiently priced, particularly when such developments first become public.

Identifying Undervalued Stock Look for stocks that are currently hitting new lows and are selling at a 40% to 50% discount to the companies' values. To determine a company's value, look at its current and projected cash flows, its assets and how these compare to the competition.

Compared with cheap stocks, bargain stocks tend to have relatively high price-to-earnings ratios (P/Es), although lower than the average P/E of the S&P 500. P/Es reflect past earnings and are used to project future expectations. If the market believes that a stock has a bright outlook despite poor recent performance, the price will be high in relation to its recent earnings. A stock's P/E can be found in the stock tables of many newspapers.

Cheaper Alternatives to Bank Loans

Why owe money to a bank when you can borrow from yourself? You might end up paying a lot less interest. Here are some close-to-home sources for quick cash.

Your IRA
If you only need the money for a short time, consider borrowing from your IRA. There is a 60-day grace period for replacing withdrawn amounts. What you do with the money in the interim is your business. Of course, if you are even a day late paying it back, you'll be slapped with a penalty on the total withdrawal plus a 10% penalty if you're under age 59½.

Your Whole Life Insurance Policy
You can usually borrow the equivalent of the cash value of your whole life insurance policy, and the rates are competitive. Remember, of course, that whatever is taken out and not paid back will leave less for your heirs.

Your 401(k)
In some cases, you are allowed to borrow up to 50% of your invested account, up to $50,000. Rates are competitive—often the prime rate plus 1%. And you generally have up to five years to pay the money back with regular payroll deductions.

Your Brokerage Account
Interest rates when you borrow against your investments are usually lower than the rate your bank would offer.

Avoiding Trading Traps On the Internet Isn't Hard

Every day, more than a million trades are performed on-line. But despite its popularity, on-line trading has risks, especially during extreme volatility—as we have had recently.

401(k) Plan Trap

If you borrow funds from your 401(k) retirement account and leave your employer before repaying the loan, the entire outstanding balance will be taxable income to you. If you are under age 59½, it will be subject to an early distribution penalty as well.

Self-defense: If you plan to retire or leave your employer and have 401(k) loans outstanding, repay them before you leave.

Whenever you take out a 401(k) loan, be aware of the tax risk should you leave your employer unexpectedly.

Terry Savage, author, The Savage Truth on Money *(John Wiley & Sons) and a syndicated* Chicago Sun-Times *financial columnist.*

System Overload During periods of high-volume trading, on-line brokerages' Web sites can crash. Some firms may institute controls —such as the suspension of trading—to restore order.

Self-defense: Make sure you can place a call to execute a trade during busy times. And—research articles on how your brokerage fared during high-volume days.

Use *Limit Orders* A limit order is an instruction to buy or sell a security at a specific price. Unlike a market order, which is executed at the prevailing price, a limit order guarantees you will not pay more than a certain amount for a purchase or receive less than a specific amount for a sale.

During a volatile market, a stock price on the computer screen may not reflect the actual price of the stock at the time the order is executed (the price could have increased or decreased substantially). This is another good reason to place a limit order instead of a market order.

Monitor the Status of Your Orders Buy and sell orders are not placed instantaneously. Don't assume your order has been lost and place another one. You could end up owning twice as many shares as you wanted or selling stock you don't own.

Self-defense: Ask how you can check an order's status—especially during fast markets—before placing it again.

Carefully Track Your Trading Keep a diary in case you have a problem with a brokerage firm. Keep copies of transaction statements and confirmations.

If you have a problem: Try to work it out with the brokerage branch manager or supervisor. If this does not work, contact the firm's legal department. If you still have not received a satisfactory response, file an arbitration claim with NASD Dispute Resolution. *General information:* 202-728-8958 or 646-835-5700, www.nasdadr.com.

Mary L. Schapiro, president, NASD Regulation, self-regulatory organization of the securities industry and NASDAQ Stock Market, Washington, DC.

Dollar Cost Averaging With Mutual Funds

Most mutual funds will automatically deduct a nominal amount from your checking or money market fund account every month—as low as $25—to buy additional shares, regardless of whether the price of the shares is falling or rising. Not only does this system take some of the hassle out of investing, but studies show that average investors get better returns if they invest regularly regardless of intermittent highs and lows.

Dollar Cost Averaging

	APRIL	MAY	JUNE	JULY
Amount invested	$100	$100	$100	$100
Average share price per month	$22	$17	$14	$18
Number of shares bought	4.55	5.88	7.14	5.56

AVERAGE SHARE PRICE

$$\frac{\text{Average price per month}}{\text{Number of months}} = \text{Average share price}$$

$$\frac{\$22 + 17 + 14 + 18}{4} = \$17.75$$

AVERAGE SHARE COST

$$\frac{\text{Total amount invested}}{\text{Total shares purchased}} = \text{Average share cost}$$

$$\frac{\$400}{4.55 + 5.88 + 7.14 + 556} = \$17.29$$

Free Credit Reports—For Some of Us

Although most credit bureaus won't advertise it, by law they must furnish at least one free credit report annually to residents of Colorado, Georgia, Maryland, Massachusetts, New Jersey and Vermont if requested. Elsewhere, you are entitled to a free copy if you are unemployed, on public assistance or if you think your credit file contains inaccurate information about you because of fraud. You can also request a free copy if you were denied credit, employment, insurance or housing.

Begin by calling each bureau to request your report—after you've been notified of a credit rejection. Here are the phone numbers of the three national credit bureaus.

- **Equifax**
  800-685-1111, www.equifax.com
- **Experian**
  888-397-3742, www.experian.com
- **Trans Union**
  800-888-4213, www.transunion.com

Inexpensive Legal Help

Believe it or not, you needn't pay exorbitant attorneys' fees to answer your legal questions or even settle a dispute. The government will answer many of your questions for free, whether you want to clarify tax issues regarding your retirement and pension plans, create a living will or file a charge of discrimination. Even if operators can't answer your questions, they can refer you to someone who can.

IRS Legal Hotline If you have tax questions relating to your pension or retirement plan, the IRS operates a legal hotline just for you. Get advice from lawyers specializing in retirement and pension plan issues. The service is offered Monday through Friday, from 8:00 am to 6:30 pm EST at 877-829-5500, www.irs.gov, Employee

Saving for The Inevitable

Prepaid funerals are *not* a good idea. Despite widespread problems—shady companies stealing from prepaid trust funds and contracts loaded with restrictions that don't cover the costs—prepaid funerals and burials now account for 20% of funeral business.

They spare families the anxiety of planning a funeral at an emotional time and allow them to lock in a price, but families will spend less if they plan the traditional way. The average funeral today costs about $7,500, including burial expenses.

Consider: A certificate of deposit or a life insurance policy earmarked for funeral costs.

Ric Edelman, founder and chairman, Edelman Financial Services, Inc., Fairfax, VA, and author of Ordinary People, Extraordinary Wealth *(Harper). www.ricedelman.com.*

Plans Technical and Actuarial Division, Internal Revenue Service, US Department of the Treasury, 1111 Constitution Ave. NW, Washington, DC 20224.

Legal Services Corporation The government operates not-for-profit law offices across the country to provide legal services of all kinds to low-income individuals. Staffed by lawyers and paralegals, these offices handle cases directly and for free. Certain financial criteria apply to determine eligibility. To find out about the program nearest you, look in your local blue pages or contact the Legal Services Corporation, 750 First St. NE, 10th Floor, Washington, DC 20002, 202-336-8800, www.lsc.gov.

Law School Legal Clinics If your case doesn't qualify for the Legal Services Corporation, don't despair. The law school of your local college or university may offer a not-for-profit legal clinic. These on-campus clinics are supervised by legal professors and usually staffed by conscientious law students eager to get practical experience in the field. Contact the law school of your nearest college or university for information.

10
Shrewd Home Buying and Selling

New Times...New Rules
For Real Estate

The residential real estate market is changing dramatically. Buying a home can still be a solid investment, but don't count on a windfall if you're selling your home. The old rules no longer apply:

Old Rule Buy your home—renting is throwing away money.

New Rule Buy only if you plan to stay at least five years. It will take at least that long to build up enough equity in a house to earn back real estate taxes, homeowner's insurance, upkeep and lost investment opportunities from tying up your down payment.

Old Rule Buy a starter house as soon as you can afford it, then trade up as your income increases.

New Rule Buy your "second home" first. Starter homes used to be quick paths to the good life because values rose so quickly.

Costco Real Estate Service

Costco, the company that operates Costco and Price Club warehouse stores, is starting a real estate service that will rebate home buyers and sellers thousands of dollars in broker commissions and mortgage fees.

Buyers and sellers must be executive members of Costco, which currently costs $100.

Once a member, you can work with a Costco-referred real estate agent to buy or sell your home. At closing, members receive a rebate based on the negotiated sales price. Find program details on-line at www.costco.com (800-774-2678).

If you use the Costco mortgage broker service to find a loan, you will also receive a rebate of nearly 1% of the mortgage amount.

At best, expect a 12% annual pretax appreciation over the next 10 years. That's solid, but many people with small homes could get stuck for years, waiting out drops in the real estate market.

Key question: Can you handle the mortgage payments?

While many banks allow a buyer's monthly mortgage payments to be as high as 38% of net income, I advise my clients not to exceed 30%. For a primer on "how much" house you can afford and how different factors affect your potential mortgage costs, go to www.smartmoney.com/home/buying.

Old Rule Opt for a 30-year fixed mortgage when you buy a house.

New Rule Ask your mortgage broker or banker about a shorter, balloon-like, adjustable-rate mortgage (ARM), unless you can get a very low 15-year (6%) or 30-year (6.5%) fixed rate with no prepayment penalty.

A balloon-like ARM runs five years at a low fixed rate, but the principal is amortized as if it were over a 30-year term. When the shorter term expires, the balance of the principal comes due or it automatically becomes a one-year ARM. Few borrowers ever have to make this balloon payment. It can be refinanced with another short-term ARM, often with the same lender.

Example: Based on a $200,000 loan, the monthly payment for a five-year balloon-like ARM at 6% is $1,199, versus $1,264 for a 30-year, fixed-rate mortgage at 6.5%. That's a difference of $3,900 over five years.

Mortgage-rate-spike self-defense: Choose a lender that offers a reasonable ceiling on the interest rate if you renew—no more than five percentage points above the beginning rate.

Old Rule Vacation homes are only for the affluent.

New Rule They are excellent long-term investments for almost anyone because of demographic trends—an aging population with leisure time and disposable income. And with the new fear of flying, drivable destinations are attractive.

Vacation homes needn't be a financial drain. Redirect money you would spend on vacation travel toward the home. Or consider renting out the home during peak summer or winter seasons. Depending on the market, a few weeks of income a year may cover taxes, maintenance, utilities and a portion of your mortgage payments.

Follow these guidelines to maximize your potential profit:

- Select an accessible area near water, woods or a ski resort.
- Make sure future development in the area is limited. Check with the local chamber of commerce.
- Avoid places where prices have risen 20% or more in recent years. Prices that rise so dramatically can also crash.

- The community should have a variety of leisure activities (golfing, gambling, etc.) and some industry beyond tourism. The local government should aggressively promote the area.
- Look for a local mortgage lender. They generally offer the best rates.
- Ask local insurance agents and lenders about flood insurance. This is available through the Federal Emergency Management Agency's National Flood Insurance Program, 888-FLOOD29, www.fema.gov/nfip.

If you plan to rent out your vacation home:

- Get a rider to your homeowner's liability insurance policy for property damage and/or injury to a part-time tenant and the tenant's guests.
- Be vigilant about IRS regulations. Rules for part-time landlords are complex. Consult a tax professional.

General rule: If you lease your vacation home for two weeks or less a year, you don't have to report the income.

Old Rule Buying distressed property with no money down can make you a fortune.

New Rule Fixer-uppers aren't priced as attractively as they were 10 years ago, when foreclosures were rampant. Few banks are willing to extend loans for the necessary repairs. And refurbishing a place for big profits is *not* a part-time job.

Better: Become a landlord. The demographics are promising. Children of baby boomers are renting apartments, and aging baby boomers themselves are selling their homes to move into rentals. Strategies:

- Look for rental properties in college towns where students stay after graduation. *Examples:* Austin, Texas...Amherst, Massachusetts...Coral Gables, Florida.
- Focus on buildings with easy access to parking, highways and public transportation.
- Consider buying a small apartment building or condominium of up to six units, rather than a larger dwelling that requires a lot of upkeep.
- Research local real estate laws—some areas strictly regulate rental property.
- Look for unoccupied properties or those that have tenants with short-term leases. Tenants with long-term leases often pay below-market rents. Discount your expected income from the property by at least 25%. You can't always count on full occupancy.
- Be prepared to make a 25% down payment to buy rental property and pay at least one-half point above the rate on a primary residence.

The Scoop on Schools

SchoolMatch (800-724-6651, www.schoolmatch.com) is a service that provides current, objective information on all US public schools and accredited private schools. You can order varying levels of information by phone or on the Internet.

SchoolMatch's **Snapshot** is a brief summary of key school district statistics ($19 by phone or fax, $10 on the Internet). The **Report Card** is more detailed, taking into account 22 different factors ($49 by phone or fax, $34 on the Internet).

House Hunting On the Internet

Shopping for a home on the Internet is becoming increasingly popular. It saves time and helps buyers become familiar with the real estate market. An excellent site for real estate resources is **RealtyGuide** (www.xmission.com/~realtor1), which offers a resource library and newsroom, links to real estate brokers and lenders and even a chat room.

To look at homes on the Web, begin with the **International Real Estate Digest** (www.ired.com). This Web site contains links to sites that list homes in a wide variety of areas. Most of the linked sites are local real estate agencies that showcase the homes they are selling.

Other good sources for homes are the national Web sites that offer selected homes from multiple-listing services. While most cover many areas of the country, there is no one complete listing, so you still have to search around. Web sites you may want to visit include:

- **The National Association of Realtors** (www.realtor.com) Probably the largest source of listings.
- **Cyber Homes** (www.cyberhomes.com)
- **Homes.com** (www.homes.com)
- **HomeScout, HomeGain** (www.homescout.com)

- Retain a real estate attorney who specializes in landlord-tenant law. To be successful, landlords must be vigilant about screening tenants, collecting rent and starting legal eviction proceedings against problem renters.

There are complex tax breaks for landlords. Ask a tax adviser about:

- Deducting mortgage interest and real estate taxes as you do on your principal residence.
- Deducting operating expenses (insurance, homeowner-association fees, repairs and maintenance, yard care, etc.).
- Depreciating the cost of residential buildings over a 27½-year period.

Stephen M. Pollan, Esq., financial expert, real estate attorney and partner at the law firm of Warshaw Burstein, 555 Fifth Ave., New York 10017. He is co-author of The Die Broke Complete Book of Money *(HarperBusiness).*

Shrewd Alternatives to Buying a Home

Before you decide to put down your money on a new home, consider the pros and cons of renting versus leasing it with either an option-to-buy or lease-purchase arrangement.

There are subtle differences between the terms "rent" and "lease." Renting implies that you intend to occupy a residence for a comparatively short time, perhaps less than a year. Leasing means that you plan to hold on to the residence for far longer. A lease is a contract to pay rent for a fixed period of time. A lease with option to buy arrangement gives the tenant the right, but not the obligation, to buy the residence at an agreed-upon price during the leasing term. A lease-purchase arrangement obligates the tenant to purchase the property at the end of the lease. Most lease-option or lease-purchase arrangements run from one to two years. Both lock in the selling price.

Advantages of Renting

- You don't have to tie up large sums, and the monthly cash outflow will probably be less compared to buying an apartment or house.
- You'll be able move out whenever you wish, without worrying about getting out of a long-term financial commitment.
- You have no investment to lose if there's a slump in housing values.
- As a renter, you have no worries about maintenance.

Advantages of a Lease-Option Purchase
Compared With Simply Buying the Property

- A smaller up-front cash payment is required (covering the first month's rent plus a nonrefundable option consideration—sort of a security deposit—that is applied to the final price of the property).
- A negotiable percentage of the monthly rent is applied to your eventual purchase.
- You'll be able to "test-drive" the property before buying it. If there are problems you haven't anticipated, you haven't committed large sums of cash in a residence that might be tough to resell.
- If you must move, you can elect not to exercise your option to buy. (You do forfeit the option consideration.)
- You'll lock in the purchase price at today's market.
- You'll be building equity in the property.
- If the value appreciates during the term of the lease, you'll be able to sell and clear a profit while investing very little.
- If the value of the house falls, you don't need to exercise your option.
- The longer the term of the lease, the greater your chances are to realize appreciation over time.

Clever investment strategy: Start advertising the property a few months before your lease expires. If you can get a good price, exercise your option to buy the property and sell it immediately.

For more information: RealEstateInvesting.Com (www.realestate investing.com)...Southcast Properties, Inc. (www.housedeal.net) ...Lease2Purchase.Com (www.lease2purchase.com).

Buying Foreclosures

Foreclosures are pieces of real estate being sold to repay a debt. They can be tremendous bargains for a buyer. There are many ways to buy a foreclosure property. You can buy directly from a distressed owner before foreclosure, at the foreclosure auction or through government agencies and lenders who have taken over foreclosed properties.

Finding opportunities takes a bit of effort. You can ask a real estate agent to track down any foreclosures on the Multiple Listing Service or contact lenders and government agencies. Another, perhaps easier, way is to use a service that gathers information from a variety of sources and makes it available in one place, such as **Foreclosures Online** (www.4close.com).

Before You Buy a New Home

A home is the largest purchase most people will ever make. This decision will affect your life for many years, so you want to make sure that you get the best deal you can.

Once you have made the decision to buy a home, it's tempting to run out, grab a real estate agent and start shopping right away. But in order to find the right house and get the best deal on it, there are several things you need to do before the search begins.

Know What You're Looking For

Your first task is to decide exactly what you want in a new home: A two-bedroom condominium, an older house in an historic neighborhood or perhaps a recently built home in a newly developed area.

Choosing a Home Inspector

Ask your agent, lender, lawyer or friends for referrals to home inspectors. Most states don't require home inspectors to be licensed, so keep these tips in mind when searching:

- Ask if the inspector belongs to the **American Society of Home Inspectors (ASHI)** (www.ashi.com) or the **National Association of Home Inspectors (NAHI)** (www.nahi.org).

- Find out how long the inspector has been in the home-inspection business.

- Ask about the inspector's qualifications. Retired county and city building inspectors often make excellent choices.

- Get the names of several past clients. Call these people to see if they were satisfied. If they've been in their home at least six months, they will have had enough time to see if something unexpected came up that wasn't discovered by the inspector.

- Look for an inspector who has errors and omissions (E and O) liability insurance, which will protect you if it can be proven that the inspector was negligent.

The more thought you've given to what kind of home, neighborhood and amenities you're interested in, the easier it will be to weed through all the homes that are available. You may want to make a list to rank details in the order of their importance to you.

Know What You Can Afford

The most important thing you need to figure out is how much money you can afford to spend on a house. For most people, this means how much money a lender will let you have in the form of a mortgage. Keep in mind that no matter how much a lender approves you for, only you know how much money you spend each month and what your lifestyle is. Don't overstretch your limits, or you could wind up in financial trouble before you realize what's happening.

Prequalification

Prequalification is the easiest and least time-consuming way to determine your price range. To prequalify, visit a lender and honestly answer questions about your income, debts, savings and credit. The lender will perform some quick calculations and tell you about how much money you could get on various loans. This whole process only takes 10 or 15 minutes, after which you'll have an idea of what the maximum is you can spend on a new home. There may be a fee, though, so ask first.

Preapproval

Lenders aren't required to give you a loan just because they say you're prequalified for it. They are obligated to give you loans you're preapproved for, however, and pre-approval makes you more attractive to sellers who won't have to wonder if your loan will come through.

So when you're seriously ready to buy, consider applying for preapproval for a specific loan. Do your homework and interview a few lenders. Some lenders will preapprove you for free, while others may charge you a fee. (Paying for a credit report is fairly standard.) Then bring all the information the lender requests to complete the application. Approval can take from a few days to several weeks.

If you find a good rate, you can lock it in, which means you get that rate even if rates in general go up. Be sure to ask what happens if the rates drop even further before you buy your home. Usually you can negotiate to get the lower rate. Some lenders require a deposit (which will be returned to you at closing) to lock in a rate. But remember that you'll lose your deposit if you don't close on the loan.

When to Buy

There are a couple of factors you should consider before deciding when to purchase your new home.

Time of Year Believe it or not, the month of the year you buy your home in can affect the deal you get. The best time to buy is close to the holidays in December. Statistics show that there are fewer home sales between Thanksgiving and New Year's than any other time of year. Most buyers are busy with the holidays and put off shopping for a home until after the new year. Sellers realize this and many take their homes off the market. The ones who keep their homes for sale during this time are usually desperate to sell. This is a big advantage for the buyer in negotiations.

If you choose to buy a home in spring, however, sellers have the advantage. The majority of buyers are shopping then, generally because families with children prefer to move at the end of the school year. More buyers mean more competition for you and less chance of a low bid being accepted.

Real Estate Climate Is it a buyer's or seller's market? Take the time to learn about the market you are entering. It will help you determine your negotiating strategy and give you a better idea of what to expect when you begin looking at homes. You will also learn how the market will affect the value of the home you buy.

In a buyer's market, you may be able to get a lower price or better terms from the seller. However, what's known as a buyer's market is actually a declining market. If you buy in a declining market, you may find a few years later that you can't sell for what you paid.

In a seller's market, there will be fewer homes for sale and more buyers competing for them. Chances are that you will pay close to asking price for your home and have less negotiating room on the terms. In very hot markets, you may even have to pay more than the asking price.

A seller's market is a rising market. Your new home will be a better investment if you buy in the initial stages of a rising market. But don't make the mistake of buying a home at the top of a rising market. When prices are at all-time highs, the market usually peaks and begins its decline. Remember, real estate markets run in cycles and no one market lasts forever.

Tag Along With the Home Inspector

One of the best ways to get to know the home you're buying is to accompany the inspector on the house tour. Listen carefully to all comments and don't be afraid to ask questions. You'll learn a lot of useful information that probably wouldn't be included in the report. You may even get suggestions on how to repair minor problems that the seller will not be responsible for.

Finding the Best Agent

Choosing the right agent is an important task for home-buyers. Look for someone who is active and very familiar with the area where you want to buy. Look for agents who have a number of properties listed and can demonstrate they've made a number of sales in the past few months.

Be sure to ask about particular neighborhoods to see how much the agent knows. A good agent should be able to tell you about the school system, the price range of homes and how many are for sale in a particular neighborhood.

Negotiating a Lower Mortgage Rate

You don't have to take an off-the-rack mortgage. Now you can have your mortgage custom tailored to your financial needs—it's referred to as a customized loan.

The best place to go is to your local bank's real estate department and sit down with a mortgage officer and talk over your financial situation.

How it works: He/she will go on-line and check out your credit history and with that in mind, negotiate with you to find the mix of options that will give you the lowest rate possible.

Feeling comfortable with your agent is equally important. You want one who will listen to you, inquire about your needs and wants, offer suggestions and pleasantly answer all of your questions.

Who's Who

Real Estate Agent A real estate agent is paid by the seller, but spends most of the time with the buyer. Agents show you several different homes and help you begin negotiations on the ones you're interested in.

Buyer's Agent Buyer's agents usually show you a larger selection of homes, provide more information about the sellers and fight more for concessions in your favor. They are paid through the listing agent, but you may have to pay them an up-front retainer based on the purchase price of your new home.

How to find a buyer's agent: There are two associations that can give you referrals to buyer's agents in your area:

- **Real Estate Buyer's Agent Council** (800-648-6224) maintains a list of its members. Look for an agent who holds an Accredited Buyer's Representative (ABR) designation. The Council awards this designation to agents who have passed a two-day training program, a written exam and have been buyer's representatives in at least five closed sales. You can search for agents in your area on the Internet at www.rebac.net.
- **The National Association of Real Estate Buyer Brokers** (650-655-2500, 800-874-6500, www.realtor.org) will also help you find a buyer's agent in your area.

Realtor A Realtor is an active member of a local board of Realtors affiliated with the National Association of Realtors.

Broker Brokers are people who have a real estate broker's license, who cannot only make real estate transactions for others in exchange for a fee, but can also operate a real estate business, and employ salespeople and other brokers.

Multiple Listings Multiple listings are proprietary database services run by local or regional boards of Realtors. Member real estate offices use these computerized networks to share listings and sales information.

House Hunting

When you begin house hunting, take the time to find out as much as you can about the areas you are interested in. Nearly every city has neighborhoods on the upward swing that promise increased home values in the near future. Here are some signs of a growing neighborhood:

- An increasing number of homes are being sold to people from other areas of the city or from out of town.
- New and existing homeowners in the neighborhood are investing in home remodeling and renovations.
- The majority of homes are owner-occupied, not rented. The neighborhood has an active community association.
- Transportation projects (new roads, bridges, mass transit) are under way to improve access to the area.

Schools

Even if you don't have children, it's wise to buy a home in a strong school district. It will be much easier to resell and will appreciate more quickly. Try to find out what local test scores are, where the high school graduates go to college and whether the district has a good reputation statewide.

Crime

For concrete information on crime, call the local police precinct. Ask for crime statistics for both the city and the particular neighborhood you are considering. The police should be able to give you the current figures as well as comparisons with previous years—listed by type of crime as well as by neighborhood.

Commute

Don't rely solely on the commute times given by neighbors you talk to on the street or the owners of a particular home you are looking at. Make the actual commute from the neighborhood to your place of work (and back again) during rush hour to find out how long it's really going to take.

Homeowners' Associations

The neighborhood you are interested in may have a homeowners' association. It usually charges dues and comes with a set of rules that all homeowners must follow. Ask for a copy of the rules before buying and make sure you can live with them.

Zoning and Developments

It's a good idea to check whether any zoning restrictions apply to the area you are considering. For example, building and home additions are tightly restricted in coastal zones and historic districts.

You should also examine the area with an eye to what *could* be. If you see undeveloped areas, such as empty lots, woodland or farmed fields, check with the local zoning board or planning department to see if development is pending which might lower home values.

Mortgage Brokers

Mortgage brokers deal with many different lenders and will do the work of shopping around for the best deal for you. They can be particularly helpful in matching the right type of loan to your needs. This service is not free, however. You will pay the broker anywhere from 1% to 2.5% of the mortgage amount. Often the lender will pick up the tab for the broker, but be sure to find out in advance.

When choosing a broker, consider the following information:

- How long the firm has been in business.
- What the firm's reputation is for violations and consumer complaints.
- If the broker is a member of the **National Association of Mortgage Brokers**.
- How many lenders the mortgage broker represents (keeping in mind that more is better).
- What previous customers have to say about a broker's services and professionalism.

Internet Mortgages

Technology has made it possible to shop and apply for a loan without ever leaving your home. Obtaining a loan over the Internet can benefit you by saving time, especially if you live in a rural area and would have to drive long distances to see a lender. It can also save you money by cutting mortgage costs.

Even if you don't want to go through the mortgage application process over the Internet, there are many Web sites that offer a wealth of easy-to-understand information about shopping for mortgages. You can also compare rates and calculate what size mortgage you qualify for.

One interesting site is **CASA** (Characteristics and Sales Analysis), run by the consulting firm **Case Shiller Weiss** (www.cswv.com). It provides analyses of prices and market trends in major areas around the country.

Here are some other Web sites to check out:

- **Countrywide**
  (www.countrywide.com)
- **Homebuyer's Fair, Homestore.com**
  (www.homefair.com)
- **Irwin Mortgage**
  (www.irwinmortgage.com)
- **HSH Associates**
  (www.hsh.com)
- **HomeShark**
  (www.homeshark.com)
- **Bank Rate**
  (www.bankrate.com)

Making an Offer On a Home

You've found the home you want to buy. Now it's time to make an offer (in the form of a sales or purchase agreement). If you submit a sales agreement and it is accepted and signed by the seller, it is a legally binding contract. So make sure that your initial offer leaves nothing out.

All agreements should set a time limit (no longer than 48 hours) within which the seller must respond in writing or the offer will be void.

Decide What Price to Offer

Making a bid on a home requires an educated negotiating strategy. Ask your agent to give you as much information as possible about the selling prices of comparable homes in the area. Try to determine the average percentage the selling price was below the asking price.

Lowball offers are tempting to make. If the seller agrees to it for whatever reason, then you will have gotten a terrific deal. Be careful, though. Sellers tend to be emotionally attached to their homes and an overly low offer may insult them. You should try to keep your offer within reasonable limits that will encourage the sellers to respond with a counteroffer.

Elements of a Good Sales Agreement

You will probably want to include these terms in your offer:

Earnest Money Deposit Protection The sales agreement should specify who is to hold your deposit, such as the real estate agent, a title company, an escrow service or an attorney acting as an escrow agent. Never hand your deposit over to the sellers. No matter how honest they seem, you are opening yourself up for problems. Be sure to spell out how the deposit will be returned to you if the sale does not go through.

Settlement and Possession Dates Your sales agreement should specify the date of settlement and when you are to take possession of the house. It's a good idea for the agreement to state that the sellers are to be out of the house one day before closing, or actual signing, of the sale documents. This will help eliminate any problems getting the sellers to move.

If the sellers are not sure they will be able to move by that time, you may agree to rent the home to them for a certain number of days. Make sure that the sales agreement includes the amount of daily rent and acceptable length of time for the sellers to stay.

Personal Property List all items you would like to have included with the home, such as appliances, carpeting, light fixtures, fireplace screens, sheds and fences.

Physical Inspection Include in the sales agreement your right to a final inspection. The wording should specify the time of inspection as "one to three days prior to closing." If a specific date is written in and escrow takes longer than expected, your inspection could be worthless.

Remember, the final inspection is not the time to find problems with the home. This is simply to ensure that everything is in working order, no recent damage has been done and the sellers have removed all of their belongings. This is also a good time to check that all personal property written into the contract has been left there as agreed.

Financing Contingency clauses make the entire sales agreement subject to a certain action. Making the purchase contingent on your getting satisfactory mortgage financing is a popular clause. If you have been preapproved, there is no need for this contingency.

It's possible to negotiate for the seller to pay all or part of the expenses involved with financing, such as discount points and appraisal fees. You may also ask the seller to finance a portion of the purchase price. Be sure that all information and terms are outlined in the agreement.

Home Inspection You should definitely include a contingency clause making the purchase subject to your approval of a home inspection. Your approval is an important point. You can refuse to approve the inspection until the sellers come to terms with you on repairs.

Termite Inspection Require a termite inspection along with language that allows you to void the agreement or negotiate with the seller for extermination and repairs.

Environmental Hazards You may want to include environmental inspections as a contingency of sale. Hazards to test for include asbestos, lead paint, radon and buried oil tanks. You can negotiate who pays for these inspections and what will be done if any hazards are found.

Property Boundary Disputes

Property disputes are among the most common claims against homeowners. Most title policies do not insure against them unless a formal geographical survey has been made.

Self-defense: Consider having a formal survey made before you buy a home.

Max Bazerman, PhD, professor of dispute resolution and organizations, Kellogg Graduate School of Management, Northwestern University, Evanston, IL, and author of *Smart Money Decisions* (John Wiley & Sons).

The Scoop on Mortgages

There are so many different varieties of mortgages that there is sure to be one that suits your needs. The trick is to find it. You can read mortgage and real estate books, explore options on the Internet and talk to different lenders to find out what mortgage is right for you. Another option is to hire a mortgage broker.

How to Hire a Selling Agent

Hiring a selling agent is like choosing a work partner—you want someone who will do the absolute best for you. To begin your search, look to see what names appear most frequently on "For Sale" signs in your neighborhood. Then, call several real estate brokers active in your area, and ask who their award winners or top performers are. Invite at least three who work regularly in your neighborhood to come by separately and give a listing presentation.

Here are a few things to do when you meet each agent for the first time:

- Ask how many properties the agent has listed in the past six months. Then ask how many have been sold.

- Ask for a list of clients whose homes the agent has sold recently. Contact them to see if they were satisfied with the agent's performance.

- Find out how long the agent has been in the real estate business— the longer, the better.

- Inquire about professional organizations the agent belongs to. Look for membership in the local real estate board, a multiple-listing service and the State and National Association of Realtors.

- Ask what kind of marketing plan the agent proposes for your home. A good agent will be able to give you an immediate, direct and comprehensive plan of action.

- Find out how knowledgeable the agent is about your neighborhood. You'll want to know about recent selling prices, competing properties, market value in your area and anything else that will affect the selling price.

Comparing Loans

You have to learn a whole new vocabulary when you shop for a mortgage.

The two most popular loan types are fixed-rate mortgages and adjustable-rate mortgages (ARMs). With a fixed-rate mortgage, your interest rate stays the same throughout the life of the loan (and so do your payments). An adjustable rate fluctuates according to the terms of the loan, and usually means your payment changes from time to time. Make sure when you look at rates that you are comparing apples to apples. To compare the benefits of one loan to another you may need the help of a lender or mortgage broker.

When comparing rates from different lenders, people commonly look at interest rates and points. Interest rates are fairly easy to understand, but points are a bit more confusing. Basically, a point is an up-front payment of interest that lowers the interest rate. Each point equals 1% of the loan and lowers your interest rate a certain amount, usually 0.25%. The best deal is a combination of the lowest interest rate and the least number of points.

The annual percentage rate (APR) is the most accurate device for comparing loans. The APR is the cost of your loan expressed as a yearly rate.

Penalty Clauses

There are two penalty clauses to watch for in loan agreements: Refinancing and prepayment penalties. Make sure that your agreement doesn't charge for either. You will always want the option of refinancing at a lower rate in the future. Prepayment penalties will prevent you from paying extra money toward your loan that could save you a substantial amount of money in interest.

Low Down Payments

If you are short of cash for a down payment, you have several options. You can look into government-backed loans and learn more about the special programs offered by Fannie Mae, Freddie Mac or individual states. You might also buy private mortgage insurance (PMI). With PMI, you receive a regular loan but insure it against your default. The cost of private mortgage insurance can be added to your loan amount and will increase your cost of buying. Once the amount of equity in your home exceeds 20%, you will no longer need insurance. Make sure that your lender eliminates PMI when enough equity is built up.

Special Loan Programs

FHA and VA mortgages are government-insured loans. FHA loans are guaranteed by the Federal Housing Administration and VA loans by the Veterans Administration. To qualify for a VA mortgage, you must have been on the active list of the armed forces

during certain periods of time. Check with the Veterans Administration for the specific requirements.

FHA and VA loans require low down payments and may have lower rates. There are limits on the amount of money you can borrow, however, which vary by region. FHA and VA loans are also assumable, provided the buyer who wants to take over the loan is qualified for the mortgage and meets all requirements.

If you belong to a union, check to see if it participates in the Union Privilege loan program offered by the AFL-CIO. Union Privilege loans require as little as 3% down and usually have interest rates at or below national averages.

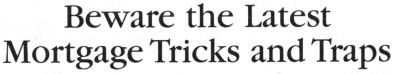

Lead Alert

If your home was built before 1978, you must give buyers a brochure explaining lead paint hazards. Get brochures and information from the **National Lead Information Center** (800-424-5323, www.nsc.org/chc/lead.htm).

Beware the Latest Mortgage Tricks and Traps

Before you rush to buy a house—or refinance your existing mortgage—beware of these potential rip-offs. Offers that sound great often need close scrutiny.

Unbelievably Low Rates

Even seemingly reputable lenders have been known to use deceptive marketing practices. An advertised rate or one quoted over the phone that sounds especially low probably does not include closing costs. And the rate usually changes daily.

Self-defense: Always request a good-faith estimate from any lender. This should include all fees, taxes and other closing costs, such as private mortgage insurance (PMI), if applicable. If you see something you do not understand, ask about it. Remember—costs such as post-closing and document-preparation fees are often negotiable.

Point Pushers

Many banks claim that you can save big by paying *points*—equal to 1% of the mortgage amount—in exchange for a lower interest rate. To make this worthwhile, make sure you receive at least a 0.25% (25-basis-point) reduction for every point you pay. But pay points only if you plan to stay in your home for more than four years.

Example: If your bank is offering a 7% mortgage rate, paying two points should reduce the rate to 6.5% or lower.

Caution: Many banks offer less of a reduction after the first point. Do the math, and negotiate before you agree to pay more points.

Special Mortgages

Banks offer a variety of esoteric mortgages, which only *appear* to offer real savings over typical mortgages. Two loans that are rarely worthwhile:

Tax Savings When You Sell

You owe no tax on profits of up to $250,000 ($500,000 if you're married and filing a joint return on the sale of your house) when you sell your home.

You must have owned and lived full-time in the home for at least two out of the five years leading to the sale, and can't take advantage of the savings more than once every two years. For more information, request the publication *Selling Your Home* from the IRS Forms Line (800-829-3676) or read it on-line at www.irs.gov.

Reverse Mortgages Designed for seniors—borrowers must be at least 62 years old to qualify—who may be house rich but cash poor, these loans are made against the equity in your house.

As the name implies, they act like the opposite of regular mortgages. Instead of borrowing a lump sum from a lender and then repaying the loan with interest, you receive money from the lender in a lump sum...as a monthly payment...or as a credit line. The amount is determined by your life expectancy, the value of your home and current interest rates. The loan, plus the accrued interest, must be repaid when the last surviving borrower dies or sells the home.

Regardless of how much you receive, you can never owe more than the value of your home at the time of repayment.

Reverse mortgages cost more than regular ones and have higher interest rates, closing costs and origination fees. They are offered through state and local governments and private lenders. The Home Equity Conversion Mortgage (HECM) programs are least expensive.

Shared Appreciation Mortgages (SAMs) SAMs can make buying a home and managing debt easier. In exchange for a below-market-interest-rate loan (typically two percentage points below conventional mortgage rates), you agree to share a portion—from 30% to 60% (the higher the percentage, the lower the mortgage rate)—of your home's future appreciation.

SAMs are touted as an opportunity to borrow more money because of the lower rates. As with most "special" mortgages, however, expenses, such as appraisal and operating costs and points, can be thousands of dollars more than with conventional mortgages.

If you make any home improvements, such as renovating the kitchen or adding a bathroom, you pay the full renovation cost—but you must share the resulting appreciation in the value of your home.

Bottom line: Reverse mortgages and SAMs are appropriate only for those who have tried all other loan options.

Gary Schatsky, Esq., president, Independent Financial Counselors, a fee-only financial advisory firm, 250 W. 57 St., New York 10019. He is past chairman of the National Association of Personal Financial Advisors.

Reduce Your Closing Costs

Your lender is required under the Real Estate Settlement Procedures Act (RESPA) to give you a good-faith estimate of what your costs for the loan will be within three days of when you make a formal application. While costs for a loan are not your only closing costs, they make up the largest percentage. There are some areas where you can cut these costs.

The time to negotiate is right after receiving the good-faith estimate, not on the day of closing. If some costs seem unreasonable and the lender refuses to negotiate, you can shop for a new lender. If many people are buying homes, creating a high demand for mortgages, you may not be able to negotiate the fees down very much. But when there are fewer buyers, you may have more leverage.

Following are closing costs for a loan that you may be able to negotiate:

Document Preparation Fee You shouldn't pay more than $50 for your lender to prepare documents. You can refuse to pay at all, but your lender can also refuse to loan you money if you don't.

Loan Fee A high loan fee is ridiculous if you are paying points and a document fee. Try to find a lender who either doesn't charge a loan fee or charges only a minimal amount.

Account Setup Fee This is another fee you should negotiate lower.

Impound Account and Setup/Service Fee Some lenders require that you set up an impound account to hold and pay tax and insurance on your home. Negotiate to lower the charge.

Attorney Fee This fee is for the lender's attorney. Since most lenders have an attorney on staff, this fee should also be negotiated.

Getting Your Home Ready to Sell

If you want to sell your home quickly and for the most money, you've got to make it a hot commodity by making a few preparations. There are four areas to concentrate on: Repairs, curb appeal, indoor appeal and home information.

Repairs
Look at your home objectively. Make notes of all repairs, major and minor, that need to be done. Then you can determine which repairs to make and which ones not to make. You want to do the minimal amount of fix-up work required to get the maximum price for your home. However, any repairs that aren't made could be potential bargaining points for buyers. So carefully weigh the cost of repairs you make yourself against the discounts buyers may want for them.

Curb Appeal
The goal is to make your home appealing to buyers on first sight. To pique their interest immediately, keep the grass cut and landscaping neat. You may want to paint the front door, even if it

Hire a Sitter for Your Vacant Home

If you move into a new home before you sell your old one, you are at a disadvantage. An empty home is much harder to sell and you are probably paying two mortgages, which means you want to sell quickly. Consider finding a friend to stay in your house or hiring a house sitter.

Caretakers of America/America's Home Tenders (303-832-2313, 316-682-1104, www.caretakers-of-america.com), currently available in 14 states, provides a prescreened house sitter to live in your home at no cost to you. The house sitter pays all utility costs and is responsible for trash removal, minor repairs and keeping the home in ready-to-show condition. Caretakers provide furniture for a model-home look. Caretakers' sitters not only maintain your home and help it sell faster and for a better price, but they are prepared to move out within 10 days on written notice.

Hiring a Mover

When hiring a mover, ask for a *fixed bid*. This will put a ceiling on your moving costs. If you ask only for an estimate, the final bill could be much higher than you expect.

The bid will not include insurance unless you ask for it explicitly. Purchase *full replacement value insurance* from the mover. Find out which items are not covered under the mover's insurance, and buy a floater policy—also from the mover—to cover them.

Examples: Antiques...artwork. Have the mover pack fragile items—they will not be covered by insurance if you pack them yourself. Buy boxes from a moving supply company. Movers' boxes are typically more expensive.

Caution: Free used boxes—from grocery and liquor stores—are often infested with mites.

Marge Fisher, management and relocation consultant, Riverside, CT.

doesn't really need it, and place pots of colorful flowers on either side. Keep the lights burning, so your home looks inviting to people who happen to drive by at night.

Indoor Appeal

Cleaning house is one of the most important ways to prepare your home. Everything should be spotless and should stay that way. If someone wants to view your home, you will only have a few minutes to straighten up and make things look perfect. Nothing will turn off buyers quicker than an untidy or cluttered home.

Here are some tips for making the inside of your home as appealing as possible to buyers:

- Rearrange or store some of your furniture to make the house seem larger. Also, clear out closets and remove some of the clothes to make them appear more spacious.
- Try hanging a mirror in a small foyer or hallway to make it seem larger.
- Clean all light fixtures and install the maximum wattage in them.
- Remove heavy curtains and open windows if weather permits. Light, sheer curtains will emphasize the spacious, airy feeling you are trying to create.
- Make the house smell good and fresh. Try boiling cinnamon sticks on the stove, placing fresh flowers throughout the house or lighting candles.
- Buy new shower curtains and throw rugs for the bathrooms.
- Create counter space in the kitchen by removing all unnecessary items.
- Keep in mind that when it comes time to actually show your home, you should store all valuables in a safe place that cannot be accessed by potential buyers.

Home Information

Make a binder of neatly organized information available for interested home buyers to view. Include:

Property Tax Statements Even if property taxes are reassessed in your state upon sale, this will give buyers an idea of what to expect.

Utility Bills Include copies of the past year's bills for gas, electric, water, sewage, garbage collection and any other utilities. If you don't save your bills, contact the utility company and ask for a printout of the past year's invoices.

Maintenance Records This shows the care you have taken with your home. Of special interest to buyers will be records of roof repair, appliance repair, plumbing service and electrical work.

Warranties Include all warranties still in effect on any part of your home.

Pricing Your Home

Choosing a listing price for your home is extremely important. You don't want to charge too much or too little. If you ask more than the market value of your home, it will take longer to sell—and you will probably have to lower your price in order to sell at all. If you ask less, you won't get the best deal.

Look at Comparables

The selling price of comparable homes is the key to pricing your home. Your agent should be able to supply you with a list of comparables. If you are selling your home on your own, you can still get this information from agents. Simply call several and ask for it. Inform the agents that you are selling by yourself, but will keep them in mind. Most will be happy to oblige you in the hopes that if you eventually decide to use an agent, they will get the listing.

If you are having trouble finding comparable sales to help you set your asking price, try Home Price Check at www.domania.com. Here you'll find the largest free on-line archive of United States home sales. Want to know what your neighbor sold his house for? You can search the database by specific street address and find out.

Do Some Legwork

Don't trust that the homes on the list you receive are truly comparable. Check them yourself. If a home has a different number of bedrooms or bathrooms or other amenities, you can rule it out. Next, look at only the most recent sales. Lastly, drive by the homes that seem truly comparable to see how yours stacks up.

Evaluate the Numbers

Once you have a list of accurate comparables, look at their prices. If one price is substantially higher or lower than the others, discard it. Special circumstances were probably involved. Now you should have a range of prices to base your asking price on. It's generally safe to go with the average list price, hoping that a buyer will offer the average selling price.

"For Sale by Owner"

Selling your home by yourself and saving the substantial amount of money normally paid to agents in commission is a tempting prospect. However, it requires a good deal of work, preparation and real estate know-how—and a concrete plan of action.

Manufactured Homes

Manufactured homes, upscale versions of mobile homes, are becoming increasingly popular. The houses are built in factories, moved on trailers to the site and installed.

Financing a manufactured home is more expensive, however, because manufactured home buyers usually must get a personal property loan instead of a conventional mortgage. The exception to this is if the home sits on a permanent foundation and you own the land beneath it.

Another expense to factor in is the cost to buy a piece of land or rent a lot. Many dealers operate manufactured housing sites. If you lease a site, be sure to sign a binding rental agreement to prevent tenancy conflicts.

One problem with manufactured homes can be shoddy installation. If your home is not attached to the ground properly, it will be very vulnerable to storms such as tornadoes and hurricanes.

The Modular Alternative

For better quality and durability than with manufactured homes, look into modular homes. They are more expensive than manufactured homes, but are made to meet the highest state building codes. All the parts are transported to the building site by truck and then put together by a contractor. Once constructed, the finished homes are difficult to distinguish from regular homes. Modular homes are financed with conventional mortgages.

Modular homes and manufactured homes that are designed like conventional houses and situated on owned land will appreciate in value the same as site-built homes. Even manufactured homes on leased lots can appreciate if the land rents are stable and the location is desirable.

Before you make the decision, do a little research. Use all the resources you can find, including books with worksheets and sample documents as well as the Internet.

Learn About Loans

Agents often help buyers arrange financing. To make buyers feel comfortable buying without an agent, you should learn a bit about the different types of mortgages. It's also a good idea to contact several lenders in the area. They can provide you with information and prequalification forms to give potential buyers.

Protect Yourself

When selling on your own, you can protect yourself by hiring a real estate lawyer to look over and prepare documents. Be sure to negotiate the fee in advance. Another option is to pay an agent a set price to handle the paperwork.

A real estate lawyer can also inform you of the laws in your state concerning disclosures of problems with your home.

Consider Partial Commissions

Most buyers go to agents when they begin looking at homes. This makes it very difficult for people selling their own homes to attract buyers' attention. Offering a partial commission to buyers' agents is one way to reach all of those buyers. Here are several different ways you can make this offer:

Hire a Discount Broker Some agents offer limited services for a small commission (1% to 2%). Others provide certain services, such as listing your home on the multiple listing service, for a flat fee. The listing usually requires you to pay a 3% commission to the agent bringing the buyer.

Sign a Temporary Listing Contract This is an agreement with an agent who has an interested buyer for a reduced commission, usually half the going rate (2% to 3%). The agreement should specify the name of the prospective buyer, the time limit for the agent to bring you a purchase offer and the asking price for this transaction. You may decide to raise the price a bit to help cover the cost of the commission.

Advertise an Open Listing To do this, specify in your ads that you will pay a reduced commission, usually 3%, to any agent who brings you a buyer. You will sign an agreement with each agent who comes by. It's not necessary to specify a particular buyer, but you should write in an expiration date in case you later decide to sign an exclusive listing with one agent.

Offers and Counteroffers

When you receive an offer for your home, you have three choices: You can either accept the offer as is, reject it completely or make a counteroffer. If the offer is close to what you want in price, terms and other areas, by all means accept it. It's usually best not to reject an offer completely. You stand to lose nothing by making a counteroffer that doesn't give much away on your part. If the buyers are serious, they will accept or make their own counteroffer.

While any part of the sales agreement is negotiable, there are four areas that most people counter on: Price, terms, occupancy and contingencies.

Price

How far is the offer from your list price? Is it near the average selling price on your list of comparables? If it is lower than you hope to get, counter with something lower than your list price but more in line with what you expect. Never reveal the rock-bottom price you will sell for.

Terms

You can use terms that favor the buyer to get a price offer that's closer to what you're asking. For example, if the buyers want seller financing, you might consider it. But, in turn, negotiate for a shorter mortgage or higher interest rate than a lender might offer.

Occupancy

The key to occupancy disputes is to be flexible. You don't want a good deal to fall apart over when you move out and the buyers move in. Be creative and try to come up with a compromise that will suit everyone.

Contingencies

You will likely run into several contingencies. These are useful to buyers because they provide an out. Consider whether each contingency is reasonable or not. If it's not, you can counter by crossing it out as unacceptable. However, an easy way to deal with contingencies is to set a time limit and keep it as short as is reasonable.

Condos and Co-ops

Many people choose to buy condominiums and cooperative housing. These options are especially popular for first home purchases and retirement homes because they usually cost less than single-family homes and require little maintenance.

Mortgage for Fixer-Uppers

Fannie Mae's (800-7-FANNIE, www.fanniemae.com) new **Homestyle Mortgage** lets buyers borrow based on the appraised value of their house after renovations. The renovation portion of the loan is held in an escrow account (similar to a deposit) from which their lender pays contractors directly. Adjustable rate and 15- and 30-year fixed-rate mortgages are available, and interest rates should be on par with the national average.

For homeowners who have already purchased, Fannie Mae also has a home equity line of credit, which lets you borrow as much as $50,000 (or 90% of the value of your home after repairs). *But beware:* You could be stuck with a mortgage that is worth more than your house if renovations go awry.

Turn Your House into a Money Maker

Look for an existing house that can be converted into several units. There is tremendous appreciation through this type of renovation. An older one-family house is more valuable with several rents coming in. Look for a building in which each apartment will be about 800 square feet. A third-floor apartment can be as small as 500 square feet.

If you move into the house, you can renovate unit-by-unit and do all the work in your spare time. As you convert each apartment, you'll have more money coming in to help pay off the mortgage. And, because it's investment property, half the costs of renovating, improving and repairs can be applied as an income write-off. If you don't reside in the other half, it's all deductible.

A condo or co-op is a unit within a building or complex. In both housing types, you share the common areas of the building or development with other owners. With condos, you own your unit outright, but with co-ops, you purchase shares in the cooperative that entitle you to live in one of the units.

Market Values

Though condos and co-ops are often less-expensive alternatives to single-family homes, their values are more volatile. They are usually the first to feel the effects of a declining market and the last to gain the benefits of a rising market. This means that condos and co-ops are harder to sell and do not appreciate as well as single-family homes. Units located in major metropolitan areas, such as New York City, Boston and Chicago, or near perennially popular resorts, are exceptions.

When buying, beware of complexes that contain a large percentage of absentee owners who rent their units. The more renters there are, the lower your unit's value can slip.

Maintenance Fees and Regulations

In both condos and co-ops, the board of directors handles the maintenance and upkeep of all shared areas, inside buildings as well as outdoors. All condos and co-ops charge owners a monthly maintenance fee to pay for upkeep, taxes and management. Generally, the more amenities a complex has, such as a pool, playground or community center, the higher the maintenance fee will be. Owners of this type of housing are also subject to the rules set by the board of directors.

Financing the Purchase of Condos and Co-ops

Buying a condo or co-op is similar to buying a single-family home. When figuring the size mortgage you can afford, remember that a maintenance fee will be added to your monthly costs. In co-op purchases, you will receive shares and a certificate of occupancy instead of a deed to a unit.

Fixer Uppers

Homes that have been damaged—this can range from holes in the walls to property that has been flattened by a tornado—are often referred to as fixer uppers, handyman specials or damaged properties.

People buy fixer uppers for a variety of reasons, most commonly because they can be potential bargains (since the property has been damaged, the price is reduced). Other people who love the creative process of renovation work with real estate agents who show them only distressed properties. And some people

aren't looking for a fixer upper at all, but happen to fall in love with an older home that needs a lot of work.

For whatever reason you buy a fixer upper, it can be a good financial deal and a rewarding experience if you go into it with your eyes open and have a plan for repairing the damage.

Sometimes It's Just Not Worth It

Renovation is a good investment—per square foot, you can't build for the price you can restore. The problem is that many families spend the bulk of their available cash to buy a fixer-upper, and are left with nothing to pay for fixing it up.

What to Watch Out For

Avoid houses with damaged roofs, water in the basement, termite damage, off-level foundations and sagging floors that can't be easily straightened (no matter what the bargain price is) unless you're sure you can handle the repairs. Keep in mind that if the building doesn't qualify for a certificate of occupancy, you'll have to get a building loan, which costs more than a mortgage.

If the house's price and contractors' bids are too high, and it doesn't add up to a financially sound investment, wait for something better to come along. There are a lot of opportunities out there.

If This Is Your First House

If you're buying your first house, it is usually wise not to take on a major renovating job. Get experience, get to know prices and learn a little about plumbing, heating and electricity before making your first renovation. If the price is right, however, you might want to take a chance.

Before Buying a Fixer Upper

Picking out the right home is tricky. Picking out the right home that needs work is doubly difficult because old houses almost always come with surprises. *The first rule of renovation:* It always takes longer and costs more than you expect. Before you buy, take a good long look at the following:

Yourself

- How much of the work are you prepared to do?
- What tasks do you have the skills, time and desire to do?
- Are you flexible enough to own a house that will be full of surprises?

Checking Out the School District

Ask a school official whether any significant redistricting is being considered.

To find a school official and information: Call the local Board of Education...go to National School Reports (www.homefair.com)...or ask your agent for a printout of the schools' contact information, accreditation, news clips and academic performance.

Karen Eastman Bigos, real estate broker, Burgdorff ERA Realtors, Short Hills, NJ.

- If you are going to live in the house while it is being renovated, can you live in a dusty, dirty environment?
- Do you want to live in the home, and if so, for how long? Or will you resell as soon as possible for profit?

The House

There are basically three categories of fixer uppers: Those needing a face-lift, those requiring cosmetic surgery and those destined for major surgery. The last category requires new plumbing, heating, electrical systems, footings and siding. Have an engineer (or someone familiar with old houses) look over the structure with you. *Pay particular attention to the basics:* Foundation, plumbing, wiring and roof. Try to inspect the home just after a rainstorm. Keep in mind that it is harder to renovate a building that already has been poorly remodeled. If others tried and it didn't work, don't burden yourself with their problems.

Your Finances

You don't have to repair your home all at once. However, be sure that you will have a way to finance your repairs once you've closed on your home. Get quotes from several contractors who work on old homes. Be prepared to spend twice the highest amount because of inevitable surprises.

The Neighborhood

Financially, the location may be more important than the home itself. Is the area on the upswing? Is the house in an historic district where you will need to comply with certain regulations? Is it zoned for single-family dwellings or can you subdivide? The potential gain—as well as the risk—is more if you buy in a fringe area that hasn't been gentrified yet, as opposed to buying in a more established area.

Fixing It Up

Once you buy, put together a plan of action before anyone lifts a hammer. It is important that you think through the big picture before beginning work on any individual projects.

The Plan

Structure a plan of attack for your new home, regardless of whether it needs extensive rehabilitation or just some cosmetic work. The most important factors in the plan are establishing what work needs to be done and realistically determining what you can (and will) do yourself—and what you should hire someone else to do.

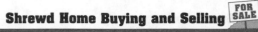

Creative Visualization

Walk around the building and figure out how the space can be used more efficiently. What rooms can be opened up? Where can extra storage be created? Can some of the rooms be better utilized?

Beware of Over-Renovation

Over-renovation is any improvement to a structure that costs more than the value it adds. If you are going to live in the house, an expensive project could be worth it if it brings enough pleasure into your life to justify the cost. But don't price your property beyond its value and the value of the other properties in the neighborhood. Once you've reached the level of adjoining properties, stop.

What an Architect Can Do for You

If your fixer upper requires more than cosmetic work, a professionally drawn set of comprehensive plans and specifications prepared by an architect will save you money and frustration in the long run. Here's what an architect can do:

Make Structural and Aesthetic Decisions Even if you know how you want your home to be renovated (where the walls and windows will go), an architect can make sure that everything fits (from your plumbing pipes to the refrigerator), comment on your design, give you advice on the latest materials available and let you know if the building will be structurally sound. Architects know building codes, and can subcontract an engineer if needed.

Put Your Vision on Paper The architect's clear and scaled-to-size drawings will be invaluable for you. Contractors will have something to bid on, and, as work progresses, you can return to the drawings again and again to answer your questions.

Eliminate Any Potential Bureaucratic Hassles In most municipalities, any time you are going to make any structural changes, the local building department must be notified. And you must get a building permit before work can begin. Even if not absolutely required, the architect's signature on an application for a building permit will often smooth the approval process.

Owning Your Own Home As You Get Older

Despite ever-rising costs and more space than is needed, most seniors continue living in their own homes. There are options to make this more affordable.

Helpful Resources For Seniors

- **The Consumer's Directory of Continuity Care Retirement Communities** is a 600-page book listing retirement communities in all 50 states. *Cost:* $35 plus $3.50 shipping. Call 800-508-9442 to order.

- For help in locating an assisted-living facility, call **The Assisted Living Federation of America** at 703-691-8100 or visit www.alfa.org.

- For help in finding an attorney who specializes in elder law, contact the **National Academy of Elder Law Attorneys** at 520-881-4005. You can search a directory of elder law attorneys at www.naela.org.

- For a free copy of **Your Home, Your Choice (Living Choices for Older Americans)**, call the Federal Trade Commission at 202-326-2222, www.ftc.gov.

Save Treasures For Reuse

As you demolish, don't forget to save removable pieces such as doors, windows, doorknobs, porch balustrades, mantels and moldings to reuse. Once stripped, shined or repainted, they can add character and remain part of your home's history. When the time comes to put your house back together, you'll have a hard time buying these treasures at any price.

Rent Out Rooms

Many senior organizations are beginning to establish programs to match older people who need good affordable housing with other retirees who have extra space in their homes. Ask your local senior center for more information. But be sure local zoning laws permit renters.

Move to a Less Expensive House

If you move to a significantly smaller, less costly house or condominium, you can invest remaining profits from the sale of your original house and use the income it produces for living expenses.

Try a Reverse Mortgage

If you are living in a home that is paid for, you can turn it into a reliable source of income through a reverse mortgage. Instead of paying a monthly check to the bank, the bank pays you. But remember, it's a loan and will eventually have to be repaid. How much money you can draw out is based on the amount of equity in your home, an annual percentage rate applied against that equity and your life expectancy.

For more information, call The National Center for Home Equity Conversion (651-222-6775, www.reverse.org/nchec.htm) for a free copy of their reverse mortgage locator. Or contact AARP (800-424-3410) for their free guidebook, *Home-Made Money: Consumer's Guide to Home Equity Conversion.*

How Seniors Can Save On Housing Costs

As you get older, your income tends to be less than it used to be. So if you want to continue living in your home, you may have to find alternate ways to finance it.

Tax-Postponement Programs

Many states have adopted over-65 property-tax-postponement programs. These allow older people to put off paying property taxes on their residences until after death. At that point, the taxes are paid before heirs take their inheritance. For information, call your local property-tax assessor's office.

The Home Energy Assistance Program

You can save on expenses through this program which helps low-income homeowners and renters cut their energy costs. Some states limit assistance to heating expenses, and others help with lighting and cooking costs as well. File an application with your local department of social services early in the year.

Supportive Housing for the Elderly

If you meet certain income guidelines, your rent will be no higher than 10% to 30% of your adjusted income. Plus, many of these buildings offer coordinators to help with senior needs. Call your local public housing office for information.

HOME Repair/Modifications Program
For Elderly Homeowners

Low-interest loans are available to low-income seniors for home repairs. To locate the closest program and application information, contact Community Connections at 800-998-9999.

Housing Voucher Program

Low-income senior tenants may be eligible for coupons worth the difference between 30% of their income and the market value of the apartment. Check with your local housing authority for more information.

Other Senior Housing Options

Continuing-care retirement communities or assisted-living facilities might offer you the security, help and companionship you need. In general, those sponsored by religious organizations, fraternal groups and other nonprofit agencies tend to be more reasonably priced.

Always Inspect

In older homes, inspectors look for wear and tear on high-cost items, such as roofs and heating systems, that may need replacement. In new homes, inspectors focus on whether building codes have been met...quality materials have been used...and the interior and exterior have been finished properly.

Caution: Flaws in new homes are often not visible to a buyer. *Cost:* $250 or more, depending on the region.

Stephen Elder, home inspector and home repair specialist, Pittsboro, NC.

Find the Right Retirement Community

While you are strong and healthy, energetic and living comfortably in a community where you have good support services, friends and family, you probably give little thought to the prospect of moving to a full-service retirement community.

But—this is precisely the time to investigate possible future living arrangements. You don't want to delay the search until you are sick, injured or have lost a helpful spouse.

Look for a retirement living community (RLC) leisurely and carefully. The search can be very enjoyable.

Start With a Paper Search Think of it as gathering information for a vacation spot. Ask friends...and the children of people you know who have moved to such communities...and senior citizen groups in your community what places they know of *both good and bad*. Send for literature on RLCs located in areas you might find attractive.

For Home-Based Businesses

In many localities, laws enacted before the rise in popularity of telecommuting and home-based businesses make it *illegal* to conduct a business in one's home. Although originally intended to bar retail or industrial businesses, the rules may equally apply to home-based service businesses.

Some localities simply want revenues from permits for home-based businesses. Check local laws at town hall or with a local lawyer before starting to work from home.

Barbara Weltman, attorney, Millwood, NY, and author of The Complete Idiot's Guide to Starting a Home-Based Business *(Alpha).*

Be open about location. Don't think only about how convenient a place is to your children or other family members. *You* will be there 100% of the time and that's what counts most.

Review Your Finances This will be your first opportunity to analyze the financial implications of a move to an RLC. You will have to make a substantial advance payment—in many cases more than $100,000—to qualify for most RLCs.

Be realistic about what you can afford. Above all, ask lots of questions and compare the costs of your prospective RLC with your current expenses.

Check Them Out

Visit as many RLCs as you can. Arrange short excursions or vacation travel so that you can spend some time at a prospective RLC. Call ahead in plenty of time to arrange a stay—at least one night, but preferably longer—in a guest house or guest room in the community. Check out:

- **The food and ambience of the communal dining facilities.** Meals tend to be a focal point of your life at any such facility. *Opportunity:* The dining room is the best place to meet and talk with the residents to get an idea of whether they are people you would like to spend time with.

- **Nursing and custodial services and facilities.** *Preferable:* A special wing for residents with Alzheimer's or other forms of dementia. Such people need special care and may disrupt other residents who require health care. *Extras:* Be sure to get a clear—preferably written—explanation of what extra costs might be involved if one spouse needs special nursing care while the other is well enough to live independently in the RLC with minimal care.

- **Transportation.** Even if the RLC has its own golf course, swimming pool and other sports and community facilities, you will probably want the ability to travel easily to nearby shopping malls, theaters, concert halls and houses of worship. Make sure there is regular, convenient and economical van or bus service. Use it during your visit, even if you have your own car.

What It Costs

Once you narrow down your prospects, talk seriously about finances with staff members of the RLC.

Don't be pushed into a premature discussion of a contract and finances by overeager staffers during your visit. The most desirable RLCs have waiting lists. In fact, beware of those with an occupancy rate under 85%—*and* hard-sell tactics. Ask about:

- **Advance payments.** What is refundable, partially refundable or nonrefundable.

- **Monthly charges.** And what they cover—specifically. Ask what the guarantee is that the charges will not increase—or how such increases will be determined.
- **Added charges.** Charges that might be added if you need more intensive nursing or medical services…or if you have to be moved to an affiliated hospital, rehabilitation facility or medical center.
- **All special fees.**
- **Special benevolent funds.** Should you or your spouse live well beyond any reasonable life expectancy, you could run out of money and you may need to rely on these special funds.

Once a particular RLC begins to seem like an attractive possibility, ask for a complete package of its financial statements. The RLC must make them available to you.

Be sure the statements are recent and audited by a reputable professional. Even if you feel comfortable making sense of balance sheets and profit-and-loss statements, have a CPA evaluate them. You don't want to make a substantial advance payment and then find yourself in a community that begins to skimp on services because of financial problems.

If you decide to sign a contract and get on the waiting list, you can be confident that you've done all that you can to assure yourself the best care.

Deborah Freundlich, copublisher of *Briefing*, a restaurant marketing newsletter from American Express, and author of *Retirement Living Communities* (Macmillan).

Temperature Check for Seniors

Don't lower thermostats too far. Too-low temperatures can increase the risk of hypothermia in people age 60 and older.

At greatest risk: People with arthritis or thyroid deficiency and those who take tranquilizers, sleeping pills or antidepressants.

Self-defense: Set the thermostat no lower than 68° F. Dress warmly in layers or stay under an electric blanket.

Richard Havlik, MD, MPH, chief, laboratory of epidemiology, demography and biometry, National Institute on Aging, Bethesda, MD.

11

The Savvy Car Owner

Never Get Taken Again: How to Buy a Car

An educated buyer can save as much as $5,000 more than an uneducated buyer on an average-priced new car. To be an educated buyer, avoid the following traps:

Trap *Showing too much enthusiasm.* If you act too excited, the salesperson will know that he/she has something you want...and that you'll pay top dollar. Keep your enthusiasm in check until you've completed the transaction.

Trap *Buying in haste.* Take your time to comparison shop. Use Internet car-buying sites to help you decide how much to pay for a car. Do not feel that you must buy on your first visit to the dealership. If you take your time and are willing to walk away from an unacceptable bid, the price will fall.

Trap *Giving a deposit before the dealer approves your offer.* A deposit at this point in negotiations is simply a way to keep you around while trying to convince you to pay more.

Trap *Being pressured into a lease when you want to purchase.* Dealerships make much more profit leasing a vehicle than selling it. So they try to turn buyers into lessees.

Perhaps leasing is what you would prefer—it may be cheaper for you if you are shopping for a business car. But don't decide to lease without mulling over the financial implications.

Trap *Financing through the dealership before considering all your options.* Take a copy of the dealer's filled-in contract to your bank or credit union to compare costs. If the dealer won't give you a copy of the financing agreement, odds are it's *not* the cheapest.

Help for Used-Car Buyers

The same strategies for buying a new car apply to buying a used car—but there's even more to think about. To avoid rip-offs:

- **Have a mechanic check the car before you buy it.** Use a diagnostic center or an independent service shop. A complete checkup should cost about $125.
- **Make sure that necessary repairs are included in the purchase price.** Negotiate with the seller to include the cost of any repairs your mechanic deems necessary.
  Example: If a seller wants $8,000, but the vehicle needs $1,000 in repairs, pay no more than $7,000.

- **Forget about the asking price.** Bargain *up* from the loan value—not *down* from the asking price. Loan value is what a bank or credit union will lend you on the vehicle. If the loan value is $6,000, but the seller is asking $8,000, negotiate up from $6,000.
- **Don't talk warranty until *after* settling on a selling price.** You want at least a 30-day, 100% drivetrain warranty. Never accept a 50-50 warranty where the dealer pays only half of warranty-covered expenses. The warranty should pay 100% of covered expenses. Keep in mind that the price of an extended service contract agreement is negotiable.
- **Shop around for financing.** Rates are usually much higher for financing used cars than for new vehicles. If a new car can be financed at 8% a year, a two-year-old car might have a 15% financing rate at the dealership.

Just as with a new car, get a copy of the proposed finance contract and see what your bank or credit union will offer you.

Using the Internet

It's *possible* to buy a car on the Internet, but it's hard to negotiate a good price. For many people, dealerships remain the cheapest place to buy. Still, the Internet is the best place to find out how much you should pay for a car. Helpful Web sites:

Edmunds.com (www.edmunds.com) is the best place to get pricing information for a new car.

Car-Buying Trap

A dealer who concedes a low price on a new car may more than make it back by giving a low price on the car buyer's trade-in vehicle.

What to do: Decide on the trade-in price you want for your old car before buying a new one. The best way to learn the local market value of your old car is to look at newspaper classified ads for similar vehicles (remembering that you will receive somewhat less than that retail price).

Alternative: Look up the value of your car in *Kelley Blue Book* (or visit www.kbb.com) or another trade publication—but keep in mind that prices quoted in consumer editions of such guides are somewhat below wholesale.

Art Spinella, vice president, CNW, auto industry market research firm, quoted in SmartMoney, 250 W. 55 St., New York 10019.

Kelley Blue Book (www.kbb.com) lists how much a used car is worth—the blue book cost.

Cars.com (www.cars.com) gives dealer invoice price and "target price"—the price you should aim for in negotiations with the dealer.

CarFax (www.carfax.com) lets you run a "lemon check" to see if the car you want to buy has a history of problems.

National Highway Traffic Safety Administration (www.nhtsa.gov) shows the results of government safety tests.

AutoByTel.com (www.autobytel.com) is a car-buying site that directs you to the dealership that has the car you're looking for.

CarsDirect.com (www.carsdirect.com)—another on-line buying site—acts as a broker for you rather than directing you to a dealer.

Microsoft Car Point (www.carpoint.com) has information on new and used cars, including consumer articles offering buying tips.

ConsumerGuide.com (www.consumerguide.com) is the best overall guide to used cars on the Web—pricing information as well as recall and repair records.

Consumer Reports (www.consumerreports.com) offers unbiased information about cars and pricing. Its inexpensive new-car price service includes current rebate figures, dealer incentives and dealer invoice prices, as well as the manufacturer's suggested retail price (MSRP).

Remar Sutton, president and cofounder, Consumer Task Force for Automotive Issues, Inc., in Atlanta, and author of Don't Get Taken Every Time (Penguin).

Manufacturers' Promotions Explained

What is a manufacturer's promotion?

Auto manufacturers sometimes need to help dealerships sell their cars, and to do this they sponsor promotions or incentive programs. Promotions sometimes contain rebates, discounts, free equipment and special low-interest financing. In my experience, promotions sell more cars for automakers, and that's why they're out there.

When is the best time of year to buy a new car?

Promotions may run any time of year, but they heat up during certain times. Keep an eye out for advertised rebates and specials during major holidays. The end of the month or business quarter can be a good time to buy as well, because many dealerships get a bonus for selling a certain number of cars within a specific time

period. If they're near their quota, they may unload the last few cars for cheap—and you might get a manufacturer's rebate as well.

What kind of special rebates and discounts are available?
Recent college grads often qualify for a lower rate loan and a $500 rebate.

Many automakers will give a $1,500 to $2,000 rebate to drivers with physical disabilities, and may even pay for the outfitting of special driving equipment.

Most auto-makers offer rebates to members of special organizations such as the Farm Bureau and the Board of Realtors.

Are there any certain cars you're more likely to get a deal on?
Sometimes companies want to have the top-selling car for marketing purposes, and they will spend a fortune at the end of the year trying to sell enough cars to take that number-one car spot.

Premium brands like Mercedes and Toyota come at premium prices. Carmakers like Nissan and Hyundai have more to prove. Nissan is a good company that's not on a lot of people's shopping lists. So to sell their cars, they have to offer big discounts. Hyundai doesn't have a good reputation, but has made big improvements. You'll be able to get a better deal from these automakers, but your resale value will suffer because their products are less desirable in the general marketplace.

Are there promotions for leased cars?
It's not uncommon for a manufacturer to give a $5,000 lease subsidy. That means the lease will be based on a car price that's $5,000 lower than the sticker price—and that's a huge savings. Chances are, if a special lease is being run, you won't be able to find a better deal.

Sometimes, if you're already leasing a car, certain automakers give you a bonus at the end of the term, called a loyalty bonus. If you sign a new lease with them, they'll waive one monthly payment or the security deposit. They might even waive your termination fee and maintenance fee when you return the car at the end of the lease.

Ron Pinelli is the president of Autodata Corporation in Woodcliff Lake, NJ, a company that helps auto companies keep competitive by analyzing prices. His pricing experience has made him an expert on automobile manufacturers' promotions.

Grab the Leftovers
Late in the model year, dealers offer great deals on leftover cars. But as soon as you drive it off the lot, a leftover will automatically lose one year's value. That means that after you've owned the car for only one year, it will have two-years' worth of depreciation. Still, if the price is right and you're planning to keep the car for a long time, leftovers can be great bargains.

Money-Saving Strategies

Once you've narrowed your search, look up the invoice price or the dealer's price in a book like *Edmund's New Car Price Guide* (St. Martin's Press). The invoice price is not the Manufacturer's Suggested Retail Price (MSRP) or sticker

Look Into Twins

American car manufacturers some-times produce two of the exact same car, but alter their appearances slightly. The **Ford Taurus** and **Mercury Sable** are common examples of these twins. The only real difference between the two cars is their price tags.

Twins also occur when Japanese car manufacturers assemble a second version of one of their cars in the US and give it an American name. For example, the **Chevy Nova** is essentially the same car as the **Toyota Corolla**. For a bargain, shop for both cars and find out which one will cost you less.

price. The MSRP includes profit for the dealer, while the invoice price does not (and is therefore lower). Start your bargaining at the invoice price and bargain up from there. A good deal is 2% to 5% more than the invoice price.

Look at cars that have MSRPs 15% to 20% above your budget, which should put you in the right price range. Remember, if you tell a salesperson that you can afford a $20,000 car, they will show you a car with a $20,000 MSRP and you won't get a bargain. But if you ask to see a $23,000 car, you can probably bargain the dealer down to $20,000.

But be realistic. Dealers need to make a profit, and no dealer is going to sell you a car for $50 over the invoice price.

Supplemental Paks

Many times, dealers post a supplemental pak next to a car's MSRP. The pak includes the price of extras such as paint sealers, rust protection and car alarms. These supplements are hugely over-priced, and sometimes downright undesirable. For example, many automakers warn against using dealership rustproofing because it can damage electrical equipment. In some cases, it will even can-cel out your factory corrosion warranty. Dealer-installed car alarms, another common extra, are often overpriced by up to 1,000%.

These extras are not automatically included with the car, but dealers do their best to get you to think you need them. If a dealer adds a pak you didn't want to your car, refuse to pay for the sup-plements or demand to get the same car—without the pak—fresh from the factory.

Options

Options are a way for dealers to increase their profits once they've got you hooked on a specific car. An option can be power steer-ing, power windows or a sunroof. Don't buy any options that you don't need. If you want a few options, however, ask if the dealer-ship offers an options package. Packages can significantly reduce the price of a group of options, though any package is apt to have some extras you don't want.

Trade In or Sell?

Never talk trade-in until you've agreed on a firm price with the dealer. Otherwise, the dealer might give you the full value of your used car while at the same time adding some of that cost to the final price of the car you're purchasing.

Better move: If the dealer tries to give you less than you deserve for your old car, sell it yourself. Selling your old car on your own almost always gets you the most money.

Yes…You Can Get That Hard-to-Get Car Without a Long Wait

The hottest new cars are sometimes in short supply. If you want one of these models—or others that are in short supply—there are ways to speed up the process:

Put Yourself on Waiting Lists in Several Geographic Areas

This requires a little creative work because manufacturers don't reveal the number of cars they supply to each dealer.

Best approach: E-mail dealers with your request. Web sites that help you find E-mail addresses for dealers:

DealerNet (www.dealernet.com).

National Automobile Dealers Association (www.nada.com).

Links on Sites of Big Auto-Makers *Examples:* www.audi.com… www.mbusa.com (Mercedes-Benz)…www.bmwusa.com…and www.honda.com.

Once you have the dealer E-mail addresses, key questions to ask:

- How many orders do you have?
- How many cars are you getting?
- In what colors…and what options will they have?
- Do you expect a delay in the delivery date?

If a dealer indicates the model you want will be delayed, ask to sign up on the waiting list—even if it is long.

Reason: Many customers back out when they realize they'll have to wait an additional six months to get the car they want.

And—you might also move up the waiting list by accepting the more unpopular colors or the more expensive options.

Least-popular colors for hard-to-get cars: White in cold-weather states…mineral green and translucent black in hot-weather states.

Plan to spend an additional $1,000 to $2,000 to ship an out-of-state car to where you live and register it.

Deal Directly with the Fleet Managers At Local Dealerships

Stop in to see the fleet manager at the dealership. The idea is to sell him/her on selling you the car. To let him know you are serious:

Offer to Put Down a Deposit Many dealers don't ask for one, so leaving a deposit of $500 to $1,000 will make an impression. Put

Keep Salespeople Out of Your Wallet

Dealership salespeople use a variety of sneaky techniques to figure how much money you have to spend. For example, they may ask you for your driver's license, Social Security or credit card number.

Do not give them any of these. While you're waiting, they may secretly do a thorough credit check on you and even fill out loan applications on your behalf. This allows them to get an upper hand in bargaining because they'll know exactly how much you can spend. If you are pressed by the salespeople for any of these items, show them your license —but don't let them take it. If they pressure you further, walk out.

What if You Have a Lemon?

A lemon is a car still under warranty that has a problem or defect that damages its value, hinders its use or threatens your safety. For instance, a car with a brake light that continues to malfunction after a few repairs is not a lemon. But a car whose faulty electrical wiring system often bursts into flames, even after a few repairs, certainly is.

If you think you have a lemon, contact the **National Highway Traffic Safety Administration (NHTSA**, 800-424-9393, www.nhtsa.dot.gov) or the **Center for Auto Safety** (202-328-7700, www.autosafety.org).

The NHTSA is a government organization where you can make a complaint. There you can find out if your vehicle was recalled and, if so, where to take it. The Center for Auto Safety is a private, nonprofit, consumer organization with similar information that tends to be more up-to-date. The Center can also recommend a lawyer who specializes in lemon laws. And, if you have a lemon, that's probably what you need. You can try working through the manufacturer, but you may have difficulties. Often a lawyer and the threat of a lawsuit are the only way to get a refund or a replacement vehicle.

the deposit on a credit card, and make sure you get a written agreement that makes it fully refundable in the event you take yourself off the waiting list or the dealer doesn't come through.

Agree to Accept Much Less for Your Trade-In Local dealers will give you preferential treatment if they know they can make a big profit on your used car. If your car is less than three years old, accept its wholesale value or less. If the car is more than three years old, accept half the wholesale value.

Best Web sites to determine the value of your used car: www.car prices.com...or www.edmunds.com.

Offer to Pay More Than the Manufacturer's Suggested Retail Price (MSRP) Many dealers won't accept amounts higher than this price because they want to maintain goodwill with automakers, which frown on the practice.

But it's completely legal to *offer* more, and it may be worth a shot.

Also, if the buyer on the top of the waiting list withdraws, the car may go to the highest bidder, not the next person on the waiting list.

Some dealers still tack on an additional dealer markup (ADM). If you agree to pay this fee, it could also help move your name up on the waiting list.

Avoid the Dealership Completely

Services have emerged recently that help people who don't like haggling with auto dealers to buy hard-to-get new cars. The different types of services:

Car Brokers These are usually former car salespeople who maintain close relationships with fleet managers at car dealerships.

Because they bring in lots of business, they get sneak peeks at incoming inventories—and preferential treatment on waiting lists.

A car broker is paid by the dealer who sells you the car. A broker should never ask you for a fee or payment for his services.

How it works: I wanted a Lexus SC 300 (MSRP—$47,479). But all my local dealerships had nine-month waiting lists.

It took an auto broker just three weeks to find the car for $43,000. He also got the dealer to waive the $600 dealer prep fee and delivered the car right to my house. I never had to speak with the dealer, and the whole transaction took 30 minutes.

Most brokers' connections are limited to the small region in which they operate. Brokers also advertise only by word of mouth.

Best sources to find a car broker: People who have bought the type of car you want...and your auto mechanic.

Car-Buying Services They charge an up-front fee that ranges from $150 to $500 to locate a hard-to-find car.

Many car-buying services work with all makes and models and with dealerships throughout the US. They also work exclusively for you—not the dealership.

However, if a car-buying service finds a car for you, but you decide not to buy it, you still must pay its fee.

Examples of car-buying services: www.autoadvisor.com and www.carbargains.org.

Speculators These are private individuals who have purchased hard-to-get cars and then sell them within six months.

When buying from a speculator, expect to pay the list price for the car—even though it may have a few thousand miles on it. Examples of speculators:

- **www.autoweb.com.** Large database of new and used cars with a free referral service for new cars.
- **www.cars.com.** Lets you fill in the make/model/year of the car you want, as well as a search radius.
- **www.classifieds.yahoo.com.** Search ads by metropolitan area or state and type of seller—private party or dealer.

Check the Newspaper to See if Someone Is Selling the New Car as "Pre-Owned" In order to sell new cars at a premium, some people will buy new cars from dealers or private individuals. Then they will re-sell the cars immediately as *pre-owned* cars.

Catch: Slightly used cars go for as much as 30% more than the sticker price—because of limited availability.

Example: A dealership in Florida has a two-year waiting list for the Mercedes CLK430 Cabriolet. The list price is $47,900, plus options, taxes and fees. But you can buy one with 55 miles on it for $60,500 immediately from an individual.

Unofficial Web Sites

Type the model name of the car you want followed by the word "clubs" into any Internet search engine, such as www.altavista.com.

You'll get a list of enthusiast Web sites. These sites often include comments from dealers about cars that manufacturers haven't made public yet. They also post classified ads.

Example: www.geocities.com/motorcity/downs/9323/links.htm. It offers gossip and updates about Mercedes-Benz cars. It has a chat room as well as links to other Mercedes enthusiast sites.

Jeff Ostroff, president of ConsumerNet Inc., a company that offers free consumer information on dealer scams, 7706 NW 25 St., Margate, FL 33063. He is creator of the Web site www.carbuyingtips.com, which educates consumers about buying new cars.

Leasing On-Line

If you're still unsure of whether you should lease or buy, **LeaseSource** (www.leasesource.com) can help. You'll find explanations of new leasing laws and other up-to-date information. You can even take an interactive quiz that helps you decide whether to lease or buy.

If you want to calculate the cost of a lease on a particular model, the best places to go are the automakers' own Web sites. They'll have on-line leasing calculators and data on the specific leasing terms of their cars.

Tax Deductions

If you drive your car for business, leasing can mean a sizable tax deduction. Figure out the percentage of time you use your car for business, and deduct that percentage from your lease payments and your cost of gas, repairs and car insurance.

For instance, if you use your car for business 75% of the time, you can deduct 75% of the cost of the lease. This deduction is greater than what you would receive on a vehicle you own because there are dollar limits on depreciation.

How and Why to Lease a Car

More than 30% of new cars are leased, not bought. Despite the popularity of leasing, however, it's only really a bargain for a small group of people. Consider leasing only if you:

1. Don't plan on keeping the car for more than three or four years.
2. Can't afford a down payment of more than 20% of the total value of the car.
3. Are diligent about maintenance and car care.
4. Drive fewer than 15,000 miles a year.

If you fit these four categories, you're a good candidate for leasing.

Lease Basics

Leasing saves you money by allowing you to pay only for the time you use your car. You also pay sales tax on only a portion of the car's price. But even though you don't own the car, you are responsible for it. You need enough insurance so that if it is stolen or destroyed, you can pay back the car company.

Before shopping for a lease, make sure you understand these basic terms:

Capitalized Cost The price of the car that the lease is based on.

Money Factor The interest rate on the lease.

Up-Front Charge The down payment or amount of the capitalized cost you pay up front, plus other charges. These are usually the first and last months' lease payments, a bank fee and a security deposit.

Mileage Allowance The yearly amount of mileage you're allowed to put on a car. If you exceed your mileage allowance, you'll pay between 10¢ and 16¢ for each additional mile—and that adds up fast. But if you pay for a higher mileage allowance and come in at a lower rate, you can usually get the extra payment refunded.

End-of-Lease Fees What you have to pay at the end of the lease for any damage to the car beyond normal wear and tear.

Early Bailout The cost of terminating your lease early. These penalties are usually quite large, so make sure you can handle the lease throughout its term.

Shop Around

You don't have to get your lease from the dealership. A bank or credit union might offer you a better deal. If it does, choose the

car at the dealership but insist on using the financing company you want.

Figure Out the Total Cost

Because leases are complicated and their wording is often confusing, any help can be valuable. A group of consumers headed by Ralph Nader have compiled a *Reality Checklist* that makes it easier to understand and compare leases. Send $1.50 to the Consumer Task Force for Automobile Issues, Box 7648, Atlanta 30357.

You can also simplify the process of lease shopping by using Lease Wise (800-475-7283, www.checkbook.org/auto/leasew.cfm), a nonprofit, national shopping service. For $290, Lease Wise provides you with five competing lease quotes. This can save you time and money—and the hassle of trying to calculate what a lease should cost and whether you could get a better deal by buying.

Negotiate the Lease

Shop around. Leases may offer the biggest rebates and subsidies in the car market. Then negotiate the capitalized cost just like you would the price if you were buying the car—find out the invoice cost in a new-car price guide and negotiate up from that. But also make sure you get the mileage allowance you want. Some dealers will give you a lower capitalized cost but then lower your mileage allowance.

The money factor (interest) is also negotiable, even though the dealer doesn't have to tell you what it is. Talk only to dealers who will tell you the money factor.

Get It in Writing

When negotiating the lease, make sure you and the dealer discuss exactly what kind of damage exceeds normal wear and tear—and get it in writing. Then, before returning your vehicle, document all car damage and get a repair estimate from your own mechanic. If the dealer's charge for repairs seems too high, take the car to your own mechanic for repairs.

The Length of Your Lease

A two-year lease is a good idea because you'll be covered by the car warranty, and you'll probably have fewer wear-and-tear charges to pay off. But short-term leases are expensive because you're paying for the steepest depreciation on the car. A three-year lease is usually a better deal because there's much less depreciation from the second year to the third.

Buying Out

Leasing gives you the opportunity to test a vehicle's performance for a few years before you decide to buy it. This can be a great source of comfort, especially if you're buying a car model that's only been out for one or two years.

Subsidized Lease Bargains

Subsidized leases are nationally advertised, cut-rate leases and they offer incredible deals. For a listing of all the subsidized leases available in the US, visit **The Car Center** Web site at www.intellichoice.com.

Cars coming out of a subsidized lease may offer the greatest bargains for buyers interested in higher-end cars. In a subsidized lease, monthly payments are kept low by increasing the cost of buying the car when the lease ends. Because of this, most people don't buy their cars at the end of their lease, but neither will the dealer, who would rather unload it cheaply and quickly.

By shopping for used cars from subsidized leases, you might even find a used sports or luxury car for the same price you would normally pay for a used mid-range car.

It Pays to Be Flexible

The key to getting a really great deal on a used car is flexibility. Remember, every used car is unique because of the way it was driven and maintained. Dealers demand a higher price if they think you're set on one particular car. But if you consider a few cars that have the features you're looking for, you'll be able to get a much better bargain. For example, if you're looking for a family car that gets good mileage and has a good safety record, look at a variety of four-door sedans, station wagons and minivans. Don't just focus on that red Volvo sedan you saw at one used-car lot.

If you think you might buy the car at the end of the lease, negotiate with the dealer on a preestablished price for the buyout option. Otherwise, when the lease expires, the price will be what is called a "fair market price," but is often higher than buying a comparable car secondhand. And remember, everything is negotiable. Unless the car is in incredible demand, it will probably be a good deal for the dealer to cut some money off of the buyout price in order to unload the vehicle quickly.

Buying out can be costly to you, however. The cost of the lease combined with the buyout price will probably be higher than if you had chosen to buy the car new in the first place. It is often a better a deal to buy a new model of the car than to buy the one you're currently leasing.

Selling Out

If the dealer wants to let you out of your lease early in order to sell your car to someone else, make the most out of the situation. Consider buying the car at the end of the lease and selling it yourself to make the most cash. Or agree to get out of the lease only if the dealer will sign a new lease for another vehicle—on your terms, which may include waving the up-front charge and reducing your capitalized cost.

Proven Ways to Avoid Sneaky…and Illegal Car-Leasing Traps

There are many virtues to leasing a car, but dealers push leasing for one main reason—it is often more profitable for them than selling cars outright.

Despite major investigations and new disclosure requirements for lease contracts, it is easy to mislead consumers about the costs of leasing versus buying. Common traps:

Bogus Lease Rates

Leasing companies and dealers are not required to disclose the effective *Annual Percentage Rate (APR)* on a car loan, which is now 8% to 9%.

Instead, a dealer may disclose only the *lease factor*—also called the *lease rate* or *money factor*—which is a much lower number. It is used to calculate the interest portion of the monthly lease payment. Multiply the lease factor by 24 to figure out the real interest rate.

Example: A lease factor of five is 0.005. So the actual interest rate is 0.005 x 24, or 12%.

A salesperson might inflate quotes on monthly payments on a purchase to make a lease look better. Or he/she might draw up a lease using an inflated cap cost—the car price used to calculate the monthly payments. This is higher than the actual price you would pay to buy the car outright. A higher cap cost is sometimes explained away by saying that it includes finance charges—but in reality it doesn't.

Self-defense: Don't sign a contract on the spot. Take it home, and do the math with a knowledgeable friend.

Lease-to-Own Trap

If a dealer claims that leasing can save you money even if you ultimately want to own the car, check the residual value—the *option-to-purchase* price in the lease contract.

Dealers often greatly inflate residual value to lower monthly payments, but at the end of the lease, you usually end up paying more than what the car is actually worth.

When your lease is ending, check residual numbers in the *Automotive Lease Guide*. It is available in most libraries. Check used-car values in car-buying guides, such as National Auto Dealers Association price guides. Your residual value should be no higher than the wholesale or trade-in price. Useful resources:

www.carinfo.com (click on *Leasing Secrets Part II*) to learn how to calculate lease payments.

Expert Lease Pro from Chart Software (www.autoleasingsoftware. com) analyzes auto leases for you. *Cost:* $69.95.

The Callback Trap

A few weeks after leasing, a customer may get a call from the dealer, asking for more money or saying he needs to sign a new lease because of a mistake in the contract or an unacceptable credit rating. The customer is told to sign a corrected copy, which might cost "just a few dollars extra" per month.

What to do: You are under no legal obligation to accept a new contract. Respond that you will not sign or pay anything without consulting your attorney, and ask the dealer to put his request in writing. In most cases, a dealer cannot legally rescind the contract or repossess your vehicle as long as you make your payments on time.

Self-Defense

If your dealer engages in any of these deceptive and illegal sales practices, contact your state's board that licenses auto dealers. That is usually the Department of Motor Vehicles.

Dig Up the Dirt

Once you're close to deciding on a specific vehicle, consider checking it out with **Carfax** (www.carfax.com or 888-4-CARFAX). For $14.99 on the Internet or $30 over the phone, Carfax will help you determine if the car you're interested in was ever seriously damaged in a crash. Carfax can tell you if the title is authentic, if the vehicle has been in a flood and if the odometer reading is accurate. Finally, it will determine if the vehicle was ever returned as a lemon. All you need is the VIN (vehicle identification number) listed on the car, and the title.

Info4cars (www.info4cars.com) provides a similar service for $14.95.

Buying a Used Car On the Internet

The Internet is the newest source for used-car information. Some free sites like **Auto-by-Tel** (www.autobytel.com), **Auto Town** (www.autotown.com) and **Mr. Car** (www.mrcar.com) offer interactive used-car shopping. They'll find you the exact car you're looking for by searching a dealership database. After that, you negotiate with the dealership. Still, never buy a car before you've seen it and test-driven it. And don't be surprised if the car you want has already been sold. Many times these sites are not entirely up-to-date.

You can also send for the free booklet *Keys to Vehicle Leasing* from the Division of Consumer and Community Affairs, Mail Stop 800, Federal Reserve Board, Washington, DC 20551.

Mark Eskeldson, consumer advocate and auto expert based in Fair Oaks, CA. His Web site, www.CarInfo.com, provides useful information on a wide variety of automotive topics. He is author of Leasing Lessons for Smart Shoppers and What Car Dealers Don't Want You to Know (Technews Publishing).

New Ideas on Used Cars

Buying a used car can be a great investment. New cars lose much of their value during the first two years of ownership. For example a $20,000 car will probably be worth about $14,000 after two years—a 30% decrease in value. If you buy this car used, however, you'll save $6,000 you would have lost buying it new and you'll still get a young vehicle with lots of miles left.

The competition to sell used cars is fierce, so there are deals to be had. There are more newer, high-quality, low-mileage cars available than ever before because of the growing popularity of leasing. Finally, the low cost of a used car may be your opportunity to pay cash up front and avoid the extra costs and hassles of financing.

Car Dealers

Some of the best used cars are available through massive superstores like CarMax and Auto Nation. These chains feature no-haggle pricing, meaning that their prices are firmly set and there's no negotiating. They tend to have high-quality vehicles, a huge selection, excellent customer service and on-site financing.

But while you'll most likely get a fair price from a place like this, don't expect a bargain. Average used-car prices have increased $500 or so recently because of no-haggle pricing and these superstores' ability to limit competition. Dealerships located near a superstore might beat the superstore price, but not by much.

For a better deal, consider shopping at new- or used-car dealerships in an area that's out of the influence of superstores.

Certified Used Cars

Smaller car dealers are competing with automotive superstores by offering certified used cars. These are low-mileage, late-model vehicles that have newer safety features. They are often referred to as pre-owned cars. Certified cars have a special warranty from the manufacturer and are certified by manufacturers' standards.

If you're comfortable buying a used car and you know how to evaluate a used vehicle, consider shopping for an uncertified car. You might be able to save as much as a few thousand dollars on a higher-end car and as much as a few hundred on a standard or economy car.

Used-Car Dealers

Used-car dealerships can be great places to find cars and negotiate good deals. But be warned—these places don't have repair facilities. They sell most cars as-is, which means there is no warranty at all. And the cars that do have warranties are barely covered for repair costs.

Only shop at dealers that have been in business for at least five years. Be sure the car you're considering has a Buyer's Guide sticker with warranty information on it. And compare prices by shopping around and consulting used-car pricing guides. The American Automobile Association (800-709-7222, www.aaa.com) offers a used-car pricing service for a small fee.

Used-car prices on the Internet: There are lots of listings for used-car prices. Four well-known ones are *Kelley Blue Book* (www.kbb.com), Edmunds (www.edmunds.com), *NADA Official Used Car Guide* (www.nada.com) and MSN Carpoint (www.carpoint.msn.com).

Finally, just because a car is sold as is doesn't mean it won't be safe or reliable. It's illegal for a dealer to sell you a car with faulty safety equipment such as a cracked windshield or broken taillight. Check vehicle reliability records in consumer advocacy publications, such as *Consumer Reports*, evaluate the car you're looking at thoroughly and make sure all the parts are in good working order. If any safety equipment is broken, demand that the dealer repair it before you purchase the car. If the dealer refuses, shop somewhere else.

Other Places to Buy a Used Car

- **Service stations.** Although selection is limited, buying a car from a service station can be a good bet. This is especially true if it's the service station where your auto technician works. The station might have worked on the car previously and know its service record.

- **Rental companies.** Rental companies usually carry a wide selection of used cars. But often they have high mileage and have not been driven with care, so be cautious.

- **Auto auctions.** Only buy a car at an auction if you're very knowledgeable about automobiles. You're not allowed to drive the vehicles and have only a limited amount of time to look at them. The cars are sold as is, and there's no telling how they were driven.

How to Size Up A Used Car

You'll get the best prices on used cars from friends, co-workers and private owners. That's because they won't be adding operating costs such as rent and advertising to the car's price. And a friend or coworker might cut you an extra good deal.

Don't Get Lazy

When you buy this way, however, you have to be especially careful. Do the same homework you would do if you were buying from a dealership, and thoroughly examine the car. Also insist on seeing the warranty booklet and all of the car's service records. These records will tell you about the car's repair history. And a car that has all of its records in order has usually been well maintained.

Odometer Fraud

Some dishonest sellers will try to roll back the odometer in a car to make you think it has less mileage. Protect yourself by doing the following:

- Check the odometer and its housing for scratches, nicks and other signs of tampering.

- Compare the odometer reading with any oil-change stickers on the windshield, in doorjambs or under the hood.

- Examine the title. Previous ownership by a wholesaler or auction company, a post-office box as an address, a title from another state or a duplicate title can be a sign of odometer tampering. Ask the seller for identification to confirm that the same name is listed on the title.

- Examine odometer readings on sales and service records, and make sure they increase progressively and consistently. For instance, an odometer that increases 5,000 miles for one six-month period and 500 for the next could mean something fishy is going on. Be polite and tactful, but ask the seller about such inconsistencies.

- Seats, pedals and floor mats that are extremely worn when the mileage is not very high are a sign of tampering. So are brand-new replacement seats, pedals and floor mats.

Read Between the Classifieds

You can learn a lot about who is selling a car from the way they write their classified ads. You can also spot potential bargains before even talking to the sellers. The best ads to pursue are usually vague, saying something like "Dodge Minivan, 1994, new tires." This seller probably doesn't know a lot about the car and doesn't want to find out. The seller probably just wants to get rid of the car as quickly and cheaply as possible. Also, "new tires" are not an essential part of a car, indicating that the seller probably isn't a good judge of value and could give you a great bargain.

A heavily abbreviated ad such as "Ford F150, MT/PS/PB/4WD/AC" usually comes from a knowledgeable seller and hard bargainer. If it's the type of car you're looking for, consider calling up the owner—just don't expect a super deal.

Beware of classified ads that seem like they're posted by private owners but advertise more than one car. This is a sure sign of used-car dealers who are trying to get you down to their lots by posing as private owners. The Cartalk Web site (www.cartalk.com) periodically weeds out such phonies from their free classifieds.

Evaluating a Seller Over the Phone

When talking to a private seller over the phone, ask these questions before you decide whether a trip to see the car is worth your time and money:

- **How much does the car cost?** This question can rule out a car pretty quickly.
- **Are you the original owner?** More than one owner is often a sign of poor upkeep.
- **How many miles has the car been driven?** On the highway or city streets? City miles are much harder on the engine than highway miles. They also strain the brakes and transmission.
- **What major repairs have been done?** Many repairs can be signs of a lemon or older car.
- **May I see the service records?** If not, forget about it.
- **Who's your mechanic?** A good mechanic will usually mean the car's in good shape.
- **Why are you selling the car?** An answer like, "My kid went to college" or "I'm buying a new car" is a good sign. An accident is a bad one. Always ask this question in the middle of the conversation to get a more spontaneous (and more honest) answer.
- **Is the car currently registered and insured?** If it's not, it probably hasn't been driven in a while. Besides, it's illegal to test-drive or have a mechanic work on such a car, so don't bother with it.
- **Was it ever vandalized or stolen?** These are two sure signs of damage and abuse.
- **Do you park it in the garage or on the street?** Garaged vehicles have much less weather strain and damage.

- **May I have my mechanic inspect the car?** If the answer is no, don't go.
- **Was the car ever recalled?** You can double-check this by calling the National Highway Traffic Safety Administration (800-424-9393, www.nhtsa.dot.gov) with the car's make and model.
- **Are you the primary driver?** The primary driver always knows the car best.

If you're satisfied with the answers to these questions, go take a look at the car.

Evaluating a Vehicle on Your Own

If a car still looks good after you've done the following inspections, it's worth hiring a mechanic to check it out.

Tires Place a penny in the tread with the top of Lincoln's head facing down. Move it along the entire tread. If the top of the head is ever visible, the tires are worn out and you'll need new ones.

Irregular or uneven wear can be a sign of an alignment problem, which can mean a repair job plus the price of new tires. It can also mean the car has been in an accident, something you'll probably want to avoid in a used car.

Steering With your foot on the brake, put the car in gear and turn the steering wheel back and forth. Everything should move smoothly. Listen for strange noises such as screeches and howls. While you're turning the wheel, there should be no more than a couple of inches of give before the tires start to move. If there's more, you could have a serious steering problem on your hands.

Brakes If the brakes vibrate, pulsate or screech, the car probably needs brake repair—which could run you a few hundred dollars.

Body The body panels should align properly, fitting together evenly and smoothly. If they don't, it's probably a sign of an accident or previous damage. Also check the entire body for leaks.

Look for rust everywhere, but especially under doors, in the trunk and in the wheel wells. Rust in those places is usually a sign of major body deterioration.

Air Filter Remove the top of the air filter. If there's oil around the bottom and sides, the engine will probably need $300 to $400 worth of repairs.

Controls and Accessories Check that all the car's controls and accessories are in working condition.

Exhaust Look at the color of the exhaust before and after your test-drive. If it's blue, the car could be burning oil.

Alignment Take the car out on a variety of roads, just as you would a new car. While driving it, check the alignment—on a level road, the car should stay relatively straight, not pulling very much in either direction.

Show 'Em The Money

Some brave buyers will offer to pay cash in exchange for a considerable discount on a used car. Some sellers would rather have cash in hand than deal with the anxiety and hassles involved with accepting a personal check or credit card.

Preventing Auto Theft

❏ Always lock the door. With an unlocked door it takes less than 30 seconds for a thief to start and steal your car.

❏ Buy a removable stereo system, and take it with you when you park the car.

❏ Buy an alarm system that disables the ignition when there's a break-in. Many car companies are now installing these kill switches.

❏ Don't leave valuables in plain view.

❏ Don't park where you have to leave your keys with an attendant. Try to find park-it-yourself parking garages.

❏ Install a metal steering wheel collar and use The Club.

❏ Never leave your keys in the car.

❏ Park in busy, well-lit areas.

Transmission   Make sure that the automatic transmission goes into gear smoothly with no lag time. If the car has a manual transmission, the clutch should always engage. If not, the car could have a major transmission problem.

Buying a Used Car? Lemon Self-Defense

Thinking about buying a used car? About 10% of new vehicles sold in the US are lemons. The percentage of used-car lemons is much worse, since car owners are more likely to dump problem vehicles back on the market—and some used cars have been in accidents or caught in floods.

Fortunately, there are ways to avoid problems:

Make the Right Moves

Ask the Right Questions   If you're buying from a car lot, start by asking who owned the vehicle previously. If the dealer says he/she can't share such information, just walk away.

If he swears it was purchased from "a little old lady who used it only to drive to church," ask to see the bill of sale. If he won't produce it, head elsewhere.

If you are buying from an individual, it still pays to ask to see the original bill of sale, so you can confirm he was the original owner.

Important: Ask if the seller has had any troubles with the vehicle. If it is a dealership, ask the salesman if he knows of any mechanical problems. Some people don't ask these questions, assuming that they won't get straight answers. You might not—but if you are sold a lemon, the fact that you were lied to can help you in court.

Watch for Lemon Tip-Offs When You Inspect the Car   There are a number of red flags that you or your mechanic can spot:

- **Check the trunk for water damage.** If the trunk doesn't seal properly, it might mean the car has been in an accident or simply is poorly constructed.
- **Check the floor for water damage.** This might be a sign that the vehicle has been in a flood.
- **Remove the wheels, and check for warped rotors.** Also make sure the antilock brake system (ABS) is connected. When the ABS goes bad, it can be extremely expensive to fix, so some unscrupulous sellers simply disconnect it and hope the buyer won't notice. If this is beyond your mechanical abilities, be sure your mechanic takes a look.

Consult the Right Experts It pays to go to the pros:

- **An independent garage inspection.** For about $50, the car's basic components can be checked for signs of major problems.
- **Government vehicle history records.** For $14.99, companies such as CarFax (www.carfax.com) will run any vehicle made since 1981 through state and federal databases to make sure it has never been labeled a lemon, a salvage vehicle or an obvious odometer-rollback vehicle in another state.

Since state laws regarding lemons vary, unscrupulous sellers can buy lemons cheaply in one state, then ship them to another state where they don't have to tag them as problem cars. This is known as *title laundering.*

You'll need the vehicle identification number (VIN), which can be found on the dashboard. This search is important everywhere, but particularly in states with notably lax lemon laws, such as Texas and many states in the Southeast, where title laundering is particularly prevalent.

You can get a good idea of a vehicle's history by accessing the federal government's service bulletins, recalls and consumer-complaint database at the National Highway Traffic and Safety Administration (NHTSA) Web site, www.nhtsa.dot.gov.

- **Dealership search.** Take the VIN to the dealership in your area that sells cars of that make, and ask if they would be willing to run it through their system for a record of complaints, service history, recalls or warranty items. All dealerships can do this, but you might have to wait for a slow moment at the dealership and offer $10 or $20 to get it done.

If You Are Stuck With a Lemon

Believe it or not, you do have some recourse if you get stuck with a lemon—even if your sales contract says you bought the car in "as is" condition. If the seller lied or intentionally concealed major problems when making the sale, you have recourse.

Precise definitions vary from state to state, but generally if your vehicle has a problem that *can't* be corrected with three trips to the garage, you have a lemon. Here's what to do:

- **Document the problem.** Keep all receipts…ask for mechanics' reports in writing…and get the opinion of an independent garage if you've been using the dealer that sold you the car to correct problems.
- **Send a registered letter to the seller detailing the problem and requesting compensation.** Include a copy of the independent garage's assessment.
- **Take the seller to small-claims court.** In my experience, lemon buyers have at least a 50-50 chance at satisfaction if it comes to this.

How to Drain The Radiator

1. Make sure the engine is cold and the ignition is off. Remove the radiator cap.
2. Open the valve at the bottom of the radiator (called the pet cock). Drain coolant into a bucket. (Make sure you put the bucket under the radiator before you open the valve.)
3. Close the pet cock. Fill the radiator with water.
4. Start the engine. Turn the heat up to full. Add cooling-system cleaner, and then idle the engine for 30 minutes.
5. Stop the engine and let it cool for five minutes. Open the pet cock and drain the system.
6. Close the pet cock. Fill the radiator with water and idle for five minutes. Stop the engine and cool for five minutes. Drain the radiator.
7. Close the pet cock. Install a 50-50 mixture of water and antifreeze.

Don't Change The Oil Yourself

Your best bet for an oil change is probably your local quick-lube or service station. Although it costs around $10 to $15 less to change your oil yourself, you need to have your own tools and you also have to dispose of the engine oil. Since it's an environmentally hazardous material, you must take old oil to a service station or municipal hazard waste station. That can be a hassle. Besides, many quick-lubes will check all of your fluids, test your tire pressure and clean your windows and floor mats while changing your oil. Just be sure that they don't try to charge you for any services you don't want.

Another good way to get a deal on an oil change is to have your mechanic handle it when you're dropping off your car for a tune-up. Since you're paying for a bigger repair, the mechanic will likely throw in the oil change for free.

Leverage: Most dealerships, especially large, established ones, are anxious to avoid court since the publicity could be bad for business. They also know that they might face double or triple damages in open court.

Phil Edmonston, Fort Lauderdale–based author of *Lemon Aid Used Cars 2000* (Stoddart). He is a former member of the board of Consumers Union.

Taking Care of Your Car

Good car care extends the life of your vehicle. And no matter how many money-saving tips you follow, the best way to save is by taking care of the vehicle you drive now.

Motor Oil

Clean motor oil is the key to keeping your car running smoothly. If your engine is properly lubricated, no moving part should ever come into contact with any other moving part. Oil also cools the engine. But once the oil is older, dirt and sludge build up on engine parts and can cause harmful friction. Since friction will wear your engine down, changing the oil is extremely important.

The 3,000 Mile Myth Experts used to say you should change your oil every three months or 3,000 miles. Today, studies show that changing the oil according to manufacturers' recommendations (about every 7,500 miles) is just as effective. So start changing your oil every 7,500 miles, and you'll spend less than half as much a year on oil and oil changes. Even if you drive your car under extreme conditions—in lots of stop-and-go traffic or extreme temperatures—you only need to change your oil about every 6,000 miles. And remember to always change the oil filter when changing the oil.

Check Your Own Oil To check the oil, turn off the car and wait a few minutes so the oil moving through the engine can return to the pan. If you don't wait, your oil level will read lower and you'll end up adding too much oil. A car with too much oil doesn't run efficiently.

Oil Grades and Additives Oil grade is much more important than brand. Most cars run on 5W-30, but always consult your owner's manual to confirm the best grade of oil for your car. Oil brands are fairly similar, so save some cash by buying a less expensive variety. And never use motor oil additives. They won't improve your car's performance, and can sometimes hurt it.

Radiator and Coolant

The radiator is responsible for keeping your engine cool while driving. The coolant or antifreeze also helps cool the engine, pro-

tects it from freezing in the winter and prevents rust and corrosion. Always keep an eye on your coolant level if you want your car to last.

Checking the Coolant   Check the radiator overflow area (a plastic container resembling the washer-fluid reservoir and connected to the radiator by a plastic pipe or hose). If it's more than halfway below the full line, open the radiator cap and fill it with a mixture of half water/half antifreeze. If you're driving in extremely cold weather, consider using about 65% antifreeze and 35% water.

Never go higher than 65%. Too much antifreeze will actually cause the engine to run hotter. Also, never open the radiator cap when the engine is hot. You can seriously burn yourself.

Flushing Out the Radiator   Flush your radiator about once every year. Drain the radiator and wash out all of the particles with a high-powered hose. Then refill with your water/coolant mixture. Or ask your mechanic to do the procedure for you.

Checking the Coolant Hoses   It's also important to check the hoses that are connected to your radiator, heater and water pump. If they're damaged or brittle, replace them.

Transmission

Modern transmissions are extremely complicated, and all serious repairs should be handled by a trained mechanic. Still, you can keep your transmission running smoothly by making sure your transmission fluid is always full. Consult your owner's manual for instructions on checking the transmission fluid. And have the transmission fluid and filter changed every two years.

Tires

Keeping your tires filled is not only essential for safety, it also improves your gas mileage, saving you money at the pump. Invest in a high-quality tire gauge to test the pressure, and fill the tires up to the pressure indicated on the sticker inside of the glove compartment or on the door frame. Tires lose air faster in hot weather, so check them more frequently during the summer.

If your tires show signs of bulges or excessive wear, it's time to buy new ones.

Shopping for a Mechanic

Modern cars have become so complicated that it would be almost impossible to try to fix everything on your own. Besides, there are plenty of good mechanics out there whose expert work will extend the life of your car and save you money in the long run.

Rx for Your Car

❏ **Wiper blades.** Change your blades every six to 12 months to maintain maximum visibility in the rain.

❏ **Battery.** Check your battery every six months. On a regular battery, pry off the plastic covers and check the water level. If it's low, fill it with distilled water. If you have a low-maintenance battery, check the power gauge or eye. The color yellow means it's time for a new battery.

❏ **Outer surface.** Dirt, debris, salt and chemicals can break down your car's paint and rust protection. Wash your car once or twice a week with a high-powered hose to rinse away salt and dirt that collects under the car. Or take it to a professional car wash.

❏ **Brakes.** Have the brakes inspected by your mechanic once a year.

❏ **Spark plugs.** Replace your spark plugs every 100,000 miles.

❏ **Air-conditioning.** Try out your air-conditioning system right before summer. If it's running badly, your car will guzzle gas. And remember to run it once a month in the winter to preserve the seals.

The Diagnostamatic Database

Cartalk (www.cartalk.com) offers an interactive database to help you figure out what's wrong with your car. Just type in the symptoms you're experiencing and the Web site will provide you with a good guess at the cause. And if you have to take it to the mechanic anyway, at least you'll sound like you know what you're talking about.

Choosing a Mechanic

One of the most important decisions you will make as a car owner is choosing a mechanic. If you can, avoid using someone who works for the dealership. An independent auto-repair shop will do repairs more cheaply. In addition, you won't feel like your mechanic has the dealership's best interest in mind when it comes to large repairs and key decisions.

Shop Around

Just like when you're shopping for a car, the key to finding a good mechanic is to do your homework. Get references from friends and coworkers, and go on-line. Cartalk (www.cartalk.com) has a list of viewer-recommended mechanics called the Mechan-X-Files. The American Auto Association (www.aaa.com) has a list of AAA-approved mechanics. Your local Better Business Bureau also keeps a list of approved mechanics.

Once you've chosen someone in your area, bring your car in for an oil change to check the place out. Look around and find out if it's clean, has modern equipment, offers a decent waiting room and has good customer service. Membership in a professional organization, such as the Automotive Service Association or Better Business Bureau, is always a good sign. And avoid the big chains, which usually rate the lowest in service and satisfaction.

Once You've Made Your Choice...

Have your new mechanic give your car a thorough tune-up. Then bring your car in for service according to the factory instructions. Don't follow dealer instructions—they often recommend overly frequent service. But it is important to follow your factory service schedule religiously. Failing to maintain your vehicle to factory standards could cause you to lose your warranty entirely. And then you won't receive free service or parts, and you won't be able to do anything about it if your car turns out to be a lemon. Also, make sure to keep a thorough record of all repairs.

Estimates

Every time you bring your car to the mechanic, make sure you get a written estimate for repair work. An estimate is a list of the repairs that your mechanic plans to do and an educated guess at how much they will cost. It is illegal for a mechanic to charge any more than the estimate without your OK.

If Your Mechanic Screws Up

If you bring in your car for a repair and the problem isn't fixed, don't immediately go shopping for a new mechanic. Modern cars are complicated to repair, and even the best mechanics will have problems with some jobs. Plus, sometimes a repair isn't done

properly because you might not have explained the problem clearly. If you stick with your mechanic after a first mistake, you'll probably get VIP treatment the next time.

If there are still problems after the second repair but the shop is willing to try again, give them one more chance. Otherwise look for a new mechanic and ask for a refund. If the repair shop gives you trouble, take all of your receipts and repair records, and make a complaint with a professional organization of which the mechanic is a member. If you can't get help this way either, file a complaint with the local Better Business Bureau and see a lawyer.

If you see another mechanic for repairs and you still have car trouble, you may have a lemon on your hands.

Breaking in a New Car

One of the best ways to get a longer life out of your new car is to break it in properly. For the first 1,000 miles, vary your speed as much as possible and never drive at full throttle. Also change the oil promptly after the first 1,500 miles. This will remove the bits of metal and grit found in every new engine.

Protect Yourself from Crooked Mechanics

Preventative Maintenance When you go in for an oil change, be wary of preventive maintenance checks. These are a list of seemingly important tasks that turn out to be nothing more complicated than topping off fluids and checking your tire pressure. But they can turn a $20 oil change into a $100 preventive maintenance check.

Shocks Some shops make easy money off of unnecessary shock absorber replacements. Only replace your shocks if your car sways back and forth, if the front end dips severely when braking or if you experience a very bouncy ride.

Battery If your battery is slow to charge, don't immediately take a mechanic's advice to replace it. First, clean the terminals and replace the cables. If this doesn't correct the problem, go ahead and get a new one.

Don't Be a Victim

Many times, crooked mechanics prey on travelers with out-of-state plates. That's why you should never leave your car unattended at a service station. Some mechanics will steal your gas cap, tamper with your battery or even make it look like your radiator is overheating. Then you end up paying a lot of money for unnecessary services.

Antilock Braking Systems

Antilock braking systems (ABSs) are superior to traditional brakes. If you use them properly, they'll give you greater control in cornering and on slick surfaces. But they must be used properly. Old braking techniques don't work. Never pump antilock brakes. This makes them ineffective. Apply steady pressure and don't let the pedal up. That grinding or pulsing sensation is perfectly normal.

Since many people are used to driving with non-ABS brakes, it's not a bad idea to practice braking in an empty parking lot. If you know how to use your brakes, your car will perform better and be much safer. But don't overestimate them. Antilock brakes are not anti-skid brakes.

Driving Your Car Forever (Or Almost)

One of the best ways to keep your car running longer (and with fewer trips to the repair shop) is to drive it properly. If you follow these tips, you'll put less strain on the engine and other parts, and take less money out of your pocket replacing them.

Warming Up

It may come as a surprise, but not only do cars require very little time to warm up, but letting them warm up for too long puts extra strain on the engine. Idling, or running the car in neutral, for more than 30 seconds is bad for your car. That doesn't mean you should just start your car in the morning and race off, however. Take it easy and drive slowly for the first few miles. Also, never rev the engine during warm up.

Even in the winter, it's not necessary to warm up your car for more than 30 seconds. Just drive cautiously. In cold weather, oil takes longer to reach the cylinders, and hard driving can cause parts to fail, resulting in premature damage to engine bearings. So take it easy and wait about three minutes before turning on the heat or any other power-hungry accessories.

Daily Driving

Avoid quick bursts of acceleration and sudden stops. These strain your engine, shocks, transmission and brakes. Quick acceleration eats up gas, too. Also, make sure you don't drive at high speeds for extended periods of time. Besides the fact that speeding is dangerous, cars get their best fuel mileage at 55 miles an hour.

Shift Properly

If you have a manual car, proper shifting can save your transmission and the thousand or so dollars that a replacement costs. Whatever gear you're in, keep the RPM (revolutions per minute) between 2,000 and 3,000. Avoid driving in a low gear at high speeds or in a high gear at low speeds.

Don't Use the Transmission as a Brake Consistently downshifting to slow the car puts a lot of stress on the transmission. And since a worn-out transmission is much more expensive to fix than worn-out brakes, it makes a lot more sense to use the brakes.

Only downshift to slow yourself on long declines. And, if you're making a three-point turn or parking, allow the car to come to a full stop before switching between first and reverse or vice versa.

Don't Ride the Clutch An overused clutch can wear out quickly. When waiting at traffic lights, put the car in neutral. And never use the clutch to hold yourself in place on a hill. That's why you have brakes.

Parking Brakes

Even if you own an automatic car and never park on a hill, you should use your parking brake once in a while. Not only does this keep the cable moving and free from corrosion, but it also works the self-adjusters on rear brakes, which helps your drum brakes continue working properly. Remember, if your brakes ever fail, your parking brake is your only backup.

Dangers of Worn Shocks or Struts

Worn shocks or struts are no bargain. They can lead to decreased braking effectiveness and poorer ride comfort and handling. See your mechanic if you notice that your car:

- Bounces three or more times when crossing an intersection or a dip in the road.
- Rocks back and forth several times when you stop quickly.
- Tends to drift left or right when you apply the brakes firmly at higher speeds.
- Rocks or sways from side to side when changing lanes quickly.
- Leans and sways on a tight curve, such as a freeway ramp.

241

12

Computer Smarts

Get a Good Deal
On a Computer

Computers have become a regular feature in many households. Whether you already have one in your home or are a first-time buyer, navigating the computer marketplace can be daunting and overwhelming. But, armed with the knowledge of what you need, good sources of information and a few good buying tips, you can get a great deal on the right computer.

Buying a New Computer

PC or Macintosh? For the most part, the decision to buy a PC or a Macintosh is based on personal preference. Here are a few factors to consider before choosing:

- PCs are cheaper than Macs. While the price for Macintosh computers has been dropping, PC prices are still lower.
- The PC market offers many choices and options. There are thousands of PC manufacturers available to choose from because the technology has been licensed for so long.

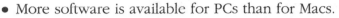

- More software is available for PCs than for Macs.
- Translation between the two systems has vastly improved over the years, but it is still easier to share files with a similar system.
- Know what you'll be using the computer for and whether you need to exchange files with other PCs or Macs.
- Macs handle graphic and video editing better than PCs.
- Macs are easier to set up and learn to use than PCs. The Windows operating system has helped make PCs user-friendly, but Macs are still more popular with beginners.
- Macs top the charts in user satisfaction and reliability.

What You Need To help you figure out what hardware you'll need, think about what you'll be doing with the computer. Are you using it for work, play, desktop publishing or as an educational tool for children? For example, if you want to have Internet access, you'll need a good modem. If you want to play games or use multimedia educational programs, your sound and video needs will increase.

A good way to get an idea of the computing power you'll need is to visit a computer store and read the minimum requirements on the sides of software boxes that interest you. *Good idea:* Read a few issues of magazines such as *PC Magazine* or *PC World.*

Computer Stores

There are two basic kinds of stores that sell computers: retail outlets that stock name-brand computers and custom stores that build no-name computers to your specifications. There are advantages to both.

Retail Stores Retail stores offer display models that can be tested, brand-name equipment, and a larger technical support staff. (Most stores also offer training.) But you are generally stuck with choosing from what's on the shelves and may get a system that's difficult to upgrade because it uses proprietary hardware. Sales help is often uninformed.

Custom Stores Do no-name computers really work...the answer is yes. Custom stores allow you to choose the components that you want to tailor your computer to your needs. They usually use brand-name internal components, but be sure to ask. The sales personnel are usually more knowledgeable than their counterparts at retail stores. The technical support and training available usually depends on the size of the store. There are large chain custom stores that offer all the support and training that retail outlets do, but small local custom shops may fall short in these areas. Keep in mind that custom computers are generally easier to upgrade and may cost less than brand-name computers.

Whichever store you decide to buy from, be sure to ask about warranties and return policies.

What to Ask The Salesperson

❏ Do you use name-brand internal components? (If talking to a custom builder.)

❏ When is your technical support available?

❏ What does the warranty cover? For how long?

❏ Do you offer training for customers? What does it cost?

❏ Can this computer be upgraded in the future? Will it require proprietary hardware?

❏ Is the equipment new? (Believe it or not, an increasing number of consumers are paying for new equipment but are being sent home with used or refurbished machines.)

Shopping for a Computer?

Watch out for any meaningless claims...

- Higher processor speeds do not speed up typical tasks, such as Web surfing, using E-mail and word processing.

- Lower-priced machines do not deliver the full megabytes of RAM they claim. Some of their memory is used to run video processors.

- Ignore the term Internet-ready. Few machines are more Internet-capable than others.

- Screen size matters less than actual viewing size, which is always smaller on traditional monitors.

Dana Blankenhorn, Internet consultant and writer, www.a-clue.com, Atlanta.

Buying through the Mail

Most people who buy computers by mail order do so over the Internet. But computer magazines are also chock-full of ads and buying advice. By shopping the ads carefully, you can get great bargains. Plus, established mail-order companies have a very high standard of customer service, good satisfaction guarantees and well-informed salespeople.

Beware: Buying by mail order is not for the timid. It can be a good choice if you are familiar with computers and have purchased computer equipment before. First-time buyers are better off buying from a store that can help them get their system up and running.

If you decide to buy a computer through the mail, here are some tips to keep in mind:

- Buy only from firms that sell equipment with full manufacturers' warranties.
- Buy only from firms that offer at least a one-month, complete satisfaction, 100% money-back guarantee.
- Check that a company has been advertising consistently for a year or more to ensure it is reliable.
- Pay by credit card. This will arm you better to deal with disputes.
- Ask about shipping and handling charges.
- Buy a well-known brand name unless you are familiar enough with computer equipment to be comfortable taking it apart and replacing internal components.
- Learn about any product before ordering so you can specify exactly what you want.

How to Get Started On the Internet

Ten years ago, few people had even heard of the Internet. Today, it is an integral part of the lives of millions, young and old, at home and at work.

Recent estimates put the number of Internet users worldwide at more than 200 million, and project nearly half a billion will be on-line within five years.

If you're not already among them, you're missing one of the most significant communications revolutions ever to shake the planet.

The Internet literally places all the information resources of the *world* at your fingertips. *Bonus:* You can use the Internet to find and communicate with people who share your interests.

Until you explore the Internet, you can't begin to comprehend the breadth or depth of all it offers. There's really not much required. All you need is a system, a connection...and curiosity.

The Basics

For most users, the *system* is synonymous with *computer*. Any new computer you buy today is Internet-ready. *Included in the computer package are...*

- Internet browser—such as *Netscape Navigator* or *Microsoft Internet Explorer.*
- Modem for connecting to the Internet over a phone line.
- E-mail program.

Expect to pay around $1,000 for a new Internet-ready computer. Minimum requirements in a Microsoft Windows system...

- 32MB RAM.
- CD-ROM drive.
- 56K modem.

All of Apple's iMac models are Internet-ready.

Alternative: If you have no real need for a computer but still want access to the Internet, look into WebTV/MSN TV. *Cost:* $49–$199 plus about $25 per month.

The system/service includes a box you connect to your TV, a remote and optional keyboard. It empowers your TV to bring the World Wide Web to your living room.

No-Risk Introduction

Most public, college and university libraries have one or more computers connected to the Internet. You can use these to sample how the Internet might benefit you before making any investment.

Before any system can connect with the Internet, it must first connect with a server, which is owned and maintained by an Internet provider.

Your Connection

Servers are your gateway to the Internet, and charge a monthly fee for the privilege. You have a couple of choices, but the basic package you get from any Internet service provider (ISP) is about the same. *You get...*

- User name and password.
- CD-ROM loaded with the required software tools for getting you on the Internet.
- E-mail account.
- Access to the Internet.

Most providers offer unlimited access, but some impose a surcharge after you've exceeded a set number of hours.

Average cost: Around $20 a month (depending on provider and services).

America Online (AOL) is the best known of the commercial on-line services. Others include Compu-Serve and the Microsoft Network.

Matching Prices

If you have purchased through mail order in the past and have a favorite company, consider applying the following strategy. Find the best price for the product you want in **PC World** or **Computer Shopper** and challenge your favorite mail order house to meet or beat the price. Many mail order houses advertise that they will make every attempt to match legitimate advertised prices.

Low-Cost Computers

Surplus Computers

Local colleges and universities sometimes have surplus computers which are offered at sales open to the public. Call the facilities or materials department to ask.

Employee Discounts

Find friends, family members or neighbors who work for computer companies, computer stores, colleges or universities. They can often get you an employee discount on computer equipment.

Well organized, they offer subscribers the company's unique content, events and services along with the Internet connection.

Internet Service Providers

If you only want access to the Internet and none of the many other options that services such as AOL provide, an Internet Service Provider may be a better bet than a commercial on-line server. As the name implies, its only service is connecting you with the Internet and providing technical help over the telephone when you have problems.

You're probably best served by a local ISP familiar with the local operating environment. Check the *Yellow Pages* under *Internet Service Providers.*

Other choices: WebTV or your local cable company, which may now be an Internet provider.

The cable modem access ISPs provide is considerably faster than basic telephone connections, but costs about twice as much.

The quality of service from ISPs can vary greatly, so carefully consider these points for comparison...

- Make sure you can connect by a local call.
- Find out how many hours of Internet access the monthly fees allow you.
- Ask if there are surcharges in addition to the monthly fee.
- Ask about the speed and types of connections the provider's system supports.
- Find out the number of users the ISP can handle at any given time.

Put these questions to the Internet service provider's customer/tech support line. Polite, informative answers are a good sign.

Caution: Be wary of any ISP whose tech support line is always busy or doesn't answer calls.

Get recommendations: Your best insight into the provider will come from other users. Ask around and find out how satisfied they are with the service, and what, if any, problems they may have had.

Joining the Revolution

Before you can connect to the Internet, you must create an account. The software supplied by your ISP reduces account creation to simply filling in the blanks with basic information about you and your system configuration.

You'll need to give a "user name," a password of your choice, the name and possibly a number address of your Internet provider and the addresses of its E-mail and news servers.

This takes only a couple of minutes to complete. If you have any trouble, the provider's tech support will guide you through the process.

Once your account is established, making the connection to the Internet is as simple as launching your Internet browser or E-mail program—just click on the provider's icon.

Once the Internet connection is established, your browser fills the screen with a "home page." You can change it later, but first time out it's usually the home page of your ISP or the supplier of your computer or browser.

Helpful: Every location, or site, you'll find on the World Wide Web has a name. If you know a Web site address you want to visit, just type it on the address bar of your browser and hit "enter" on your keyboard.

The best way to understand the way the Web works is simple —just start exploring.

Learn to use search engines. They can locate whatever you want on-line. (Try www.yahoo.com or, better still, www.google.com or www.altavista.com.)

Experiment with a few research projects. Track down information on a medical condition a relative is concerned about or a recipe that you have always wanted to try.

John R. Levine, coauthor of *The Internet for Dummies, Sixth Edition* (IDG Books WorldWide), and an Internet Web host, consultant and lecturer.

Buying a Used Computer

While used computers don't have all of the power or technology available in new computers, they are a much cheaper option. Many parents buy used computers for their children and they are also good for people with budding computer interests who aren't sure if they will actually use a computer once they've bought it.

Research carefully to be sure you get what you want. Be sure you stick to established used-computer businesses that offer refurbished equipment, warranties and technical support. Don't buy through swap meets or classified ads. The equipment may not operate properly, usually comes with no guarantees or warranties, and may be overpriced.

Basic Internet Terms

Browser A software application that allows you to move about and access information over the Internet's World Wide Web. The most popular browsers are *Netscape Navigator* and *Microsoft Internet Explorer*.

CD-ROM (Compact Disc-Read Only Memory) A compact disc that contains large amounts of information, including software applications. For this information to be accessed, a CD-ROM disc must be played on a CD-ROM drive or a DVD drive.

Modem A device that enables one computer to communicate with another, usually over phone lines. An internal modem is built into your computer, while an external modem must be connected to the computer.

Processor This refers to the central processing unit, the mind of the machine. May be described in terms of speed, like 350 Megahertz (MHz), as well as by a name, such as Pentium or Athalon.

RAM Random Access Memory, the built-in memory a computer uses to run software and perform tasks.

Server A computer that provides some service—such as access to information—to other computers, called clients, linked to it over a network.

Buying a Refurbished Computer

Buy a refurbished computer to save substantially and get a high-quality machine with a warranty.

The processor should be no less than a Power PC in a Macintosh or a Pentium MMX in a PC.

Cost of a good used computer: $300 and up. Refurbished machines with warranties typically cost $100 to $150 more.

For the best deals: Check on-line sites, such as www.icni.com...www.usedcomputer.com...www.getadeal.com.

Smart idea: Major manufacturers such as Dell, Gateway or Winbook offer factory refurbished computers with full warranties. (www.dell.com; www.gateway.com; www.winbook.com).

Alex Bassin, president, Creative Solutionz, computer sales and consulting firm, Los Angeles.

Web Site A specific location on the Internet that contains a set of information, including text and graphics. In order to reach a Web site, you must know its Web address (www.nameofsite.com).

John R. Levine, coauthor of The Internet for Dummies, Sixth Edition *(IDG Books WorldWide), and an Internet Web host, consultant and lecturer.*

How to Size Up an Internet Service Provider

Don't pay for more than you need. If you're looking for a new Internet Service Provider (ISP) or just want to check how good your present one is, think about how you plan to use, or are using, the Internet. Then ask these questions:

How Little Can I Pay? It depends on the answers to the questions below. Prices range from free (you'll probably have to put up with lots of ads; Juno.com is a popular free ISP) to about $9.95-$25/month for typical telephone connections. More if you want more. High speed access (cable, DSL, Wireless) start at about $40/month.

Do You Need Unlimited Hours of Access? If you plan to only use the Internet for email and an occasional search, you may be overpaying the ISP. Many ISPs offer several plans (including lowcost limited access plans that allow you fewer hours a month or provide metered service).

Do You Intend to Have Your Own Web Site? If no, why pay for it? Check with your ISP to find out if it has a plan that doesn't charge for a Web presence, or look for a lower-priced ISP who does.

Do You Need Instant Messenger? If you have no interest in "chatting" in real time with friends who may be online, why pay for it? Find a less expensive ISP who avoids this frill.

How Many E-mail Addresses Are Provided? Ask. You may wish to have more than one. Also check to see if the ISP provides spam filters (to eliminate junk mail).

Can You Go Online with the ISP Using a Local Call? There are a huge number of competing ISPs. Most communities are serviced by national, regional or local ISPs that provide access to local phone numbers (called points of presence). Verify with your phone company that the number really is a local call. Otherwise, you may pay a fortune in regional or long-distance charges. *Question to ask:* If you travel or have a vacation home, can you have access to a local phone number at the places you'll be visiting? (Most ISPs offer access through an 800 number if you can't access a local line, however, they usually charge .10/minute. You may find it

cheaper to place the call through a long distance discounter such as Qwest.)

Does the ISP Offer an Alternate Access Line in Your Area? You'll need this when the main line goes down or is busy.

Does the ISP's Local Phone Line Support Your Modem? If the ISP supports anything less than 56K (*note:* local conditions may not allow this speed–check) consider someone else.

Can You Contact Customer Service? Do they answer a your call with a machine or a person? Do they make a reasonable effort to help you get connected? Is it a 24/7 operation? Is the line usually busy or are you placed in a holding queue? (Call a prospective ISP at various hours and judge for your self.) Is tech service a toll call?

Is the Service Acceptable? Once you sign up you should be able to connect easily, and not be hampered by delays or by dropped connections. If you are currently experiencing these problems, consider moving to another ISP.

Is There an Objective Way to Check Performance of My ISP? For ratings of free ISPs go to www.internet4free.net. For cable connections go to www.cable-modem.net. For dial-up ISPs check out www.nwfusion.com or http://ratings.matrix.net.

Good sources for more information: www.computeruser.com; www.monitor.ca.

The Lowdown on Free PCs

There is no such thing as a *free* PC. Some companies say they will give you a PC if you sign up for a specific service—usually an Internet connection.

Typical deal: Get a $400 PC "free" by agreeing to pay about $20/month for three years of non-cancelable dial-up service. But the PC you get will be low-powered, with old and slow technology.

Internet access is changing rapidly, getting faster and less expensive. Committing to three years of dial-up service for $20/month is a bad deal. The service will likely be obsolete in less than three years as broadband connections, such as cable modem and DSL, become easier to get and less expensive.

Bottom line: Buy your own computer for as little as $400—and pick your own Web access.

Eric Grevstad, editor in chief, *Home Office Computing*, 156 W. 56 St., New York 10019.

Ways to Get More From the Web

The Internet is a wonderful research tool, but for new users, it can be difficult and frustrating. Here's how to find what you need without wasting time...

Selecting a Search Engine

There are dozens of search engines, and new ones pop up every month, each with a slightly different approach and purpose.

It's difficult to single out one search engine as best...and even if I could, the information might be out of date a month from now. Here's how to start...

- Consult a search-engine review site. *Search Engine Watch* (www.searchenginewatch.com) and *Search Engine Showdown* (www.notess.com/search) offer some insight on the ever-changing world of search engines.
- Find the search engine or directory site most appropriate for your search. Certain search engines and directories target a spe-

When to Upgrade/ When to Buy

Consider *upgrading* your computer—instead of buying a new one—if it is less than three years old. Do not spend more than $250—a good new computer can be bought for under $1,000.

Often worth upgrading: Random-Access Memory (RAM)—$50 to $225, depending on the size of the upgrade. Most people can add RAM on their own.

Other upgrades to consider: Improved video or sound card, $100 and up...larger hard drive, $120 and up—but you may have to pay about $80 for installation if you are afraid to do it yourself.

Robyn Bergeron, computer-industry analyst, Cahners In-Stat Group, Scottsdale, AZ.

cific range of topics, which can be a big help for avoiding off-the-mark information. Worth checking...

GPO Access for government documents and information. www.access.gpo.gov

HealthWeb for health information. http://healthweb.org

- Consider a directory indexed by a real person. Most search engines use a computer to index pages on the Internet. The terms you input are simply matched against what is located, regardless of context. A few, including Yahoo! (www.yahoo.com), are constructed by *humans*, so that users can move along topic branches to find what they need.

When other search engines turn up mostly unrelated items—say, you want to know about Ford Mustangs, and your search engine finds horse sites—these human-constructed directories can be particularly helpful.

- Try more than one search engine. Few people realize that search engines don't have full coverage. Even the largest search engines—including *Google* (www.google.com), *AltaVista* (www.altavista.com) and *Fast Search* (www.alltheweb.com)—each cover less than one-third of the Web. Smaller search engines might include even less than 10%.

You might be surprised by how many new choices a second search through a different search engine turns up.

Don't rely on "multiple search engines"—such as *C4* (www.c4.com)...*Dogpile* (www.dogpile.com)...and *MetaCrawler* (www.metacrawler.com). While these multiple search engines submit searches to a number of search engines in one swipe, they may fail to include the best one for your information needs...and they can be tricky to use.

Search Tricks

Consult each search engine's "help," "tips" or "info" section. Here are some tricks worth noting:

- With most search engines, putting a phrase in quotation marks ensures that the words you chose will appear exactly in the order you chose.
  Example: "ball point pens."

- Use the + symbol to make sure that the search engine looks for all the words you chose, but not in any order.
  Example: ball+point+pens. This will return all pages that list ball and point and pens, but may not be discussing ball point pens. It may be discussing a baseball game with bull pens and a point the umpire made.

- Use the − symbol to subtract a word.

Example: ball+point–pens. This tells the search engine to return all references to ball and point on a page but to ignore pens.

Additional Search Advice

Use Bookmarks Liberally—and downloads and printouts when appropriate. It's easy to jump from one site to another, ignoring other potential avenues. Using a browser's back arrow or saved history to return to promising sites can be helpful—but not if you've followed many click-throughs during your search.

Best: "Bookmark" the search results or promising sites you want to return to before proceeding with your search. Or use a site like www.backflip.com...www.blink.com...or www.clickmarks. com. These sites will organize your bookmarks into a Yahoo-style search engine.

Take Advantage of Prescreened Links and Guidance A number of libraries and library organizations offer links to sites that they have found particularly helpful. My favorites...

- The Internet Public Library (www.ipl.org).
- Librarians' Index to the Internet (http://sunsite.berkeley.edu/internetindex/).
- Saint Joseph County Public Library Hotlist (http://www.sjcpl. lib.in.us/homepage/reference/internetlinks.html).

A Search Engine May Be the Wrong Tool Chances are the information you need is on the Web, but that doesn't mean a search engine is the right way to find it. Digging up specific facts can be a time-consuming process on the Internet—perhaps even a waste of time. There are still plenty of times when other methods are faster and more reliable.

Helpful: Some encyclopedia publishers now make a large portion of their content available for free on the Web, including the well-regarded *Encyclopedia Britannica* (www.britannica.com). This site also includes a dictionary and links to related Web sites. Rather than using a search engine, consider heading there for certain specific information.

Additional source: *Infomine Scholarly Internet Resource Collections* gives links to almanacs, associations, etc. (http://brimstone.ucr. edu/reference).

Example: If you need to know the chief export of Azerbaijan, the quickest way likely is still to consult an encyclopedia or an almanac...or call your local library's reference desk.

Judith Pask, professor of library science at Purdue University, West Lafayette, IN. Pask teaches Information Strategies, a course on how to find and evaluate Internet information.

Proprietary Hardware Trap

To save manufacturing costs and produce smaller units, many computer makers create special components for their machines combining different elements in one piece. This is called proprietary hardware.

Upgrading proprietary hardware can be expensive at best or impossible at worst. For example, if you have proprietary hardware and want a faster modem, you may have to buy an entirely new motherboard. Plus, most proprietary hardware upgrades must be special ordered from the manufacturer.

Surge Suppressor Savvy

Get the right surge suppressor to protect your electronic equipment. Discount-store models may not do the job. Find a unit that guards power *and* phone lines...offers a warranty covering the value of your equipment...and can handle the large plug-in units found on many peripherals (Zip drives, external modems, printers, etc.). *Cost:* About $30.

Alternative: An Uninterruptible Power Supply (UPS) offers surge protection plus about 10 minutes of backup power—enough time for you to save open documents and shut down your system safely. *Cost:* $100 and up.

Mark J. Estren, PhD, technology columnist and consultant, McLean, VA.

Receive 10,000 Radio Stations

Internet radio can provide you with thousands of stations from around the world via your personal computer. This presents you with a number of valuable opportunities...

- Wherever you travel, you can listen to your hometown stations over your computer.
- You can listen to stations from around the world.
- You can find all kinds of music, sports, news, cultural and special events—and a great deal of unique "Internet only" programming, too.

Useful Web Sites

Yahoo! Events (http://broadcast.yahoo.com) A clearinghouse for all kinds of broadcast events.

Radio-Locator (www.radio-locator.com) A directory of more than 10,000 stations located from Antarctica to Yugoslavia, searchable by type of programming.

WindowsMedia.com (www.windowsmedia.com) Microsoft's Web portal for all sorts of media, including radio.

Policescanner.com (www.policescanner.com) An ever-popular site for listening to police and fire calls from around the US—and an example of unique Internet programming.

13

Great Low-Cost Vacations And Travel Deals

Get Paid to Take a Vacation

Cruise lines hire many retirees, semiretirees and students to work on their luxury cruise ships. And with many new ships entering service, hiring is increasing.

Trade-off: Cruise ship employees receive spartan accommodations compared with those provided to passengers, and are required to work to high standards. But they are paid for traveling the high seas and great rivers and lakes of the world, and for visiting exotic ports of call.

Jobs of all kinds are available on ships that often now resemble floating cities.

Examples: Purser, photographer, beautician, casino staff, counselor, host, clerk, doctor, nurse, youth counselor, sports trainer and many more. Persons with special skills may be hired as lecturers on subjects such as investing and the arts.

Pay range: From $1,700/month (bartender) to as much as $7,500/month (cruise director).

Vacation Loan Warning

Beware of the vacation loans made by some tour companies. For example, a cruise line might offer you a 24- or 48-month loan to cover the cost of your cruise at an annual interest rate of up to 27%. Some firms will even give you a loan for a second vacation while you're still paying off the first.

In the long run, you could end up paying an extra 50% or more for your vacation. For example, a four-year $5,000 loan at just 20% interest ends up costing about $7,300.

For more information:

- *How to Get a Job With a Cruise Line,* by Mary Miller (Ticket to Adventure Press), 800-929-7447, www.cruisechooser.com.
- **New World Cruise Ship Employment Agency.** Read the "Frequently Asked Questions" list at www.cruiseshipjob.com.
- **Cruise Lines Employment Guide,** www.cruiselinejob.com. Provides job descriptions, profiles cruise lines and offers a CD-ROM of contact numbers, employment contracts and other information for different cruise lines.
- **Small Ship Cruises,** www.smallshipcruises.com, provides a directory of small ships, windjammers and river barges that visit ports of call ocean liners never reach—for persons seeking special ventures.

When you find a cruise line that visits ports attractive to you, contact it directly or visit its Web site—many now post job openings on-line.

Herbert J. Teison, editor, *Travel Smart*, 40 Beechdale Rd., Dobbs Ferry, NY 10522.

Off the Beaten Path: Travel Destinations Around Our Country

Looking for great vacation spots that won't be overrun with crowds? We surveyed 24 authors from the *Off the Beaten Path* travel-book series for their favorite little-known spots throughout the country:

Southeast

Alabama Karl C. Harrison Museum of George Washington, Columbiana. Extensive collection of George and Martha Washington artifacts. Open Monday through Friday. *Admission:* Free. 205-669-8767.

Florida Ichetucknee Springs State Park, 35 miles north of Gainesville. Float down the scenic Ichetucknee River in an inner tube rented from one of many companies in the area—or bring your own. Open daily. *Admission:* $3.25/vehicle…river access is an additional $4.25/person. 386-497-4690, www.dep.state.fl.us/parks/district2/ichetuckneesprings/index.asp.

Louisiana Laura: A Creole Plantation, western side of the Mississippi near Vacherie. Plantation tour is chock-full of history and scenery. Open daily, except Creole and federal holidays. *Admission:* $10 adults, $5 children under 18. 888-799-7690, www.lauraplantation.com.

Mississippi Shack Up Inn, Clarksdale. Collection of old sharecroppers' shanties rounded up from the Mississippi delta. It now serves as a unique bed-and-breakfast. Mississippi Blues Alley, Delta Blues Museum and Muddy Waters' shack site are all nearby. Rooms start at only $50 a night. 662-624-8329, www.shackupinn.com.

Washington, DC Kenilworth Aquatic Garden. Twelve acres of wetlands, with birds and aquatic mammals. A unique spot that many Washingtonians don't even know about. Open daily. *Admission:* Free. 202-426-6905, www.nps.gov.

Northeast

Maine Maine Maritime Museum, Bath. An interesting taste of the state's shipbuilding and seafaring heritage. Located on the site of a 19th-century wooden shipbuilding yard. Open daily. *Admission:* $9.25 adults, $6.25 children under 17. 207-443-1316, www.bath maine.com.

Massachusetts Saugus Iron Works National Historic Site, Saugus. Reconstructed 17th-century ironworks. Peaceful location on the Saugus River, with a half-mile nature trail. Open daily. *Admission:* Free. 781-233-0050, www.nps.gov/sair.

New Hampshire Sculptured Rocks, located two miles west of Groton. This is the state's prettiest spot for picnics. A trail follows the river as it cascades through glacial potholes beneath the mossy rock walls of the gorge. Picnic tables overlook the waterfalls. It stays cool here—even on the hottest days of summer. *Admission:* Free. 800-386-4664, www.visitnh.gov.

New Jersey The A.J. Meerwald, based in Bivalve. Take a trip on this 75-year-old oyster schooner now used to conduct sailing tours of the Delaware Estuary. Daytime and sunset sails are offered. The ship sets sail from several different ports in New Jersey, Pennsylvania and Delaware. *Admission:* $25 adults, $12 children under 12. 800-485-3072, www.ajmeerwald.org.

New York African Burial Ground, Manhattan. In 1991, the oldest known African burial ground in the US was discovered at 290 Broadway. Open for tours Monday to Friday and one Saturday a month. Tours are free, but reservations are required. 212-669-7817, www.preserve.org/hdc/africanb.htm.

Northwest

Idaho Shoshone Falls, east of Twin Falls. The waterfall is 52 feet higher than Niagara Falls. Nearby Snake River Canyon has lots of hidden spots for boating, swimming or just exploring and picnicking. *Admission:* $3 per vehicle. 800-255-8946, www.visitid.org.

Montana Medicine Rocks State Park, near Ekalaka. Teddy Roosevelt called it "as fantastically beautiful a place as I have ever seen."

Autumn in The Caribbean

From September through early December, decreased demand triggers lower rates of 50% off or better at many **Caribbean** resorts. Airfare, cruise and restaurant prices are also reduced. Temperatures are just as pleasant as in winter, averaging between 82° and 86°. And there are fewer crowds and a more relaxed pace. Good autumn bargains include **Aruba**, the **Dominican Republic**, **Puerto Rico** and the **US Virgin Islands**.

Caution: If you go to the Caribbean, keep an eye on the weather. National Oceanic and Atmosphere Administration forecasters predict above normal hurricane activity for the next 20 years. Hurricane season runs from June 1–November 30, with September being the most active month.

Books on Volunteer Travel

Volunteer Vacations: Short-term Adventures that Will Benefit You and Others by Bill McMillon (Chicago Review Press, 800-888-4741). This 480-page book provides contact information and descriptions of more than 300 organizations around the world looking for volunteers. It includes prices, dates and application information for each program. Vacations range from day trips to several-month-long excursions.

Alternatives to the Peace Corps: A Directory of Third World and US Volunteer Opportunities, 9th edition, edited by Joan Powell (Food First Books).

Helping Out in the Outdoors: A Directory of Volunteer Work and Internships on American Public Land (American Hiking Association, AHS, Box 20160, Washington, DC 20041-2160). The American Hiking Association describes different ways you can combine service, travel and outdoor adventure.

Camping available in summer. *Admission:* Free. 406-232-0900, http://fwp.state.mt.us.

Oregon Shore Acres Garden and Sunset Bay, southwest of North Bend. Windswept bluffs overlook the Pacific Ocean. Six-acre garden is rimmed by pines. Perfect for picnics. Open daily. *Admission:* $3 per vehicle. 800-472-9176.

Washington Tennant Lake Natural History Interpretive Center and Hovander Homestead, House & Park, Ferndale. Gardens, wildlife and displays of old farm equipment. Open daily. *Admission:* Free. 360-384-3064.

Southwest

Arizona Hualapai River Runners, Peach Springs. A guide from the Hualapai Indian tribe leads rafting trips down a stretch of the Colorado River. One-day trips cost $250 per person. Make reservations at least one month in advance. 888-255-9550.

California Borrego Springs, near San Diego. This undiscovered desert retreat echoes Palm Springs before it became overdeveloped. Popular with movie stars. Stunning wildflowers in early spring and late winter. Free camping in the state park...or stay at hotels like the historic La Casa del Zorro for $75 a night and up. 760-767-4205, www.anzaborrego.statepark.org.

Nevada Cowboy Poetry Gathering, Elko. Cowboy poets, artists and singers come together for this annual event held at the Western Folklife Center. *Tickets:* $5 to $50. 775-738-7508.

New Mexico Spence Hot Springs, north of Jemez Springs. One of the more accessible of the hot springs in this region, which is under US Forest Service jurisdiction. *Admission:* $8 per vehicle. 505-842-3292, www.newmexico.org/scenicattractions/hidden_hot spgs.html.

Texas Neal's Vacation Lodges, Concan. Decidedly rustic cabins standing only feet from the lovely Frio River in central Texas hill country. Garner State Park, Devil's Sinkhole and Kickapoo Caverns are nearby. Cabins start at $60/night. 830-232-6118, www.neals lodges.com.

Central States

Colorado Trail Ridge Road, between Grand Lake and Estes Park. At an elevation of more than 12,000 feet, this is the highest paved through-highway in the country, offering spectacular views over its 50-mile length. Open Memorial Day through the first big snowfall —which is typically in mid-October. Traffic is possible on weekends at the height of summer. 970-586-1206, www.nps.gov/romo.

Kentucky Big Bone Lick State Park, Union. Incredible collection of locally discovered vertebrate fossils. *Admission:* Free. 859-384-3522, www.state.ky.us/agencies/parks/bigbone.htm.

Michigan Pictured Rocks Boat Cruise/Shipwreck Tours, Munising. Tour the scenic sandstone cliffs, or board a glass-bottomed boat for a look at some of Lake Superior's many 19th-century shipwrecks.

Example: A well-preserved wreck of the *Bermuda* is 10 feet below the surface.

Pictured Rocks Boat Cruises, 906-387-2379, www.picturedrocks. com; $24 adults, $10 children ages six to 12. Shipwreck Tours, 906-387-4477, www.shipwrecktours.com; $22 adults…$9 children 12 and under.

Ohio The Wilds, Cumberland. Conservation program offering tours of animals in a free-range setting, rather than a zoo. Open daily, May to October. *Admission:* $12 adults, $7 children 12 and under, $11 seniors. 866-444-9453, www.thewilds.org.

The 24 authors of the Globe Pequot Press's *Off the Beaten Path* travel series. The series includes guides for each of the 50 states, as well as many foreign countries.

Bed-and-Breakfast Club for Seniors

Bed-and-breakfast club for persons 50-plus has hosts in more than 1,500 cities in North America. You may stay in a private home, condo or farm for $25/day for two, breakfast included.

To be a member, you must be willing to be a host. There are more than 4,000 members and growing. Contact the Evergreen Bed & Breakfast Club, 800-962-2392, www.evergreenclub.com.

Dues: $75/year for two people, $60 for a single membership.

Volunteer Vacations

As a volunteer, you gain access to lesser-known areas that are rarely seen by the average tourist, and you have the chance to give something back to the community or environment. Best of all, service-oriented adventures are available at a fraction of the cost of most adventure trips, and the fees you pay are sometimes tax deductible. Most organizations require volunteers to be 18 or older, and many have trips for seniors.

American Hiking Society

The AHS sponsors two-week expeditions in all 50 states. Teams of 10 to 12 volunteers help build and restore hiking trails for the National Park Service. There are trips for both novice and veteran hikers. Volunteers provide their own camping gear and should be in good enough physical condition to hike five miles a day. The registration fee is $65, and the volunteer season runs from March through October.

More information: Send a self-addressed stamped envelope to AHS, 1422 Fenwick Lane, Silver Spring, MD 20910, 301-565-6704, www.americanhiking.org.

Volunteers for Peace

International volunteer excursions are sponsored by organizations in more than 60 host countries including Belgium, Guatemala, Spain and the Czech Republic. Groups of 10 to 20 volunteers live in work camps and assist in community development and international education. Programs cost $175 for two- to three-week sessions. Meals and lodging (but not airfare) are included.

Finding Hostels Around the World

- **At Home in Hostel Territory: A Guide to Friendly Lodgings from Seward to Santa Cruz** by Janet Thomas (Alaska Northwest Books).

- **The Berkeley Guides Series** (Fodor's Travel Publications).

- **Cheap Sleeps Series** (Chronicle Books).

- **Japan for the Impoverished: A Travel Guide** by Jim Richman and James Richman (Borgman Corp.).

- **Let's Go Series** (St. Martin's Press).

- **Lonely Planet Shoestring Guides Series** (Lonely Planet).

- **Moon Travel Handbooks Series** (Moon Publications).

More information: Volunteers for Peace, 1034 Tiffany Rd., Belmont, VT 05730, 802-259-2759, www.vfp.org.

Sierra Club Service Outings

The Sierra Club sponsors about 45 service-oriented trips around the US each year. Groups of 10 or so volunteers join Sierra Club cook and leader for week-long treks into the wilderness to maintain and repair trails and picnic areas, or work on documentation and conservation projects. Most trips alternate between work and recreation days. Most week-long outings cost around $325. Volunteers range in age from 20 and up.

More information: Sierra Club Outing Dept., 85 Second St., 2nd Floor, San Francisco, CA 94105, 415-977-5522, www.sierraclub.org/outings.

Alaska State Parks Volunteer Program

The program offers full-time volunteer positions for adults interested in assisting park rangers, giving natural history talks or working with trail crews. Lodging is included and most positions supply meals or pay an expense allowance of $100 to $300 a month. You must provide your own round-trip transportation.

More information: Volunteer Coordinator, Alaska State Parks, 550 W. 7th Ave., Suite 1380, Anchorage, AK 99501-3561, 907-269-8708, www.alaskastateparks.org.

Appalachian Mountain Club (AMC)

The AMC has 11 chapters throughout the northeastern US, each offering a variety of volunteer-vacation opportunities for ages 16 and up. For a program fee of $75 to $95 a week, you can join a Volunteer Crew responsible for maintaining and improving conditions along the trails.

You must have prior backpacking experience and your own camping equipment, but AMC will train you in hand tool techniques, safety procedures and trail construction and maintenance techniques. Crews usually consist of a leader and six to eight men and women of assorted ages. There are special Crew programs for teenagers, seniors and women-only. Most excursions include food and shelter, but specifics vary. AMC chapters also offer shorter trips, educational weekends and one-day events.

More information: Call your local chapter or contact AMC at 603-466-2721, ext. 192; www.outdoors.org.

Earthwatch Expeditions

Earthwatch volunteers assist in a wide range of scientific expeditions all over the world. Some trips cost less than $1,500. Fees cover food and lodging and support project research.

More information: Earthwatch Institute, 3 Clock Tower Place, Suite 100, Box 75, Maynard, MA 01754, 800-776-0188; www.earthwatch.org.

Amizade

Amizade offers alternative travel programs that are a mix of community service and recreation, providing volunteers with the unique opportunity to participate firsthand in the culture of the region where they are traveling. Programs are offered in the Brazilian Amazon, the Bolivian Andes, Australia, the Navajo Nation and the Greater Yellowstone Region.

Programs are open to ages 18 and older, although children ages 12 to 17 may attend the Yellowstone program with their parents. Amizade handles flights, accommodations, volunteering and recreation activities at reasonable, but not rock-bottom prices. For example, a two-week program in Brazil costs around $2,650. Part of the price pays for your travel and accommodations, and the rest keeps the program running. Amizade also runs programs in conjunction with Elderhostel (877-426-8056).

More information: Amizade Ltd., 367 S. Graham St., Pittsburgh, PA 15232, 888-973-4443; www.amizade.org.

Camping Without Gear

At various locations of **Kampgrounds of America (KOA)** you can show up in a car and stay at a so-called Kamping Kabin from about $35/night to about $47/night for two people. You supply linens or sleeping bags.

More information: Send $6 to *KOA Directory Road Atlas and Kampground Guide*, Box 30558, Billings, Montana 59114-0558.

Arthur Frommer's Budget Travel, 350 Fifth Ave., Ste. 2701, New York 10118.

Just for Seniors

There are several respected travel companies that specialize in vacations for seniors. Unlike most tour companies, these organizations prefer to work with individuals rather than travel agents. That means you'll have to contact them directly to receive information.

Elderhostel

You can choose from a fantastic selection of courses offered at hundreds of different schools around the world. You stay with other seniors in student accommodations or youth hostels, and eat in the school cafeteria or other group facility.

You'll receive around four and a half hours of instruction a day, depending on your field of study. The courses cover a wide array of liberal arts and health-related topics as well as local culture and geography.

Most courses offered in the US last one week, while overseas and foreign-language courses usually last for three weeks. *Tip:* Book early in the season for the best selections, although 95% of applicants get enrolled in their first-choice course. *Cost:* Price includes room, board and tuition. Overseas trip prices include airfare.

More information: Elderhostel, 11 Avenue de Lafayette, Boston 02111, 877-426-8056, www.elderhostel.org.

RV Vacations Look More Attractive Now

Travel by RV isn't just for retirees—celebrities like Tom Hanks do it, too.

There are more than nine million RVers on the road today (45% of whom are age 35 to 54), and more than 16,000 campgrounds for RVs across the US.

- **Low cost.** A family of four may save as much as 70% by taking an RV vacation compared with other forms of travel (such as by car or plane and staying in a hotel).

- **Convenience.** Your living quarters, kitchen, full wardrobe and personal effects are always with you, wherever you go.

- **Meets special needs.** Ramps, lifts and modified cabinets, sinks, etc., can be included in your RV setup.

- **Togetherness.** Families that travel together bond together.

You don't have to own an RV—you can rent one. And you don't have to drive from home to your destination—you can rent one there. RVs can be rented across the continental US and Hawaii, and in Canada, Great Britain, continental Europe, Australia, New Zealand and South Africa.

To find a dealer in the US or abroad, contact the **Recreation Vehicle Rental Association** at 703-591-7130, www.rvra.org.

Bernice Beard, a writer in Laguna Hills, CA, who specializes in RV travel. She is author of 301 Ways to Make RV Travel Safer, Easier, and More Fun (Arbor House).

Gadabout Tours

Gadabout specializes in tours in the US, but a few do go to overseas destinations. On special Unpack Once trips, you stay at one hotel for the duration and take a bus to and from different destinations each day. *Cost:* Prices average around $100 a day.

More information: Gadabout Tours, 700 East Tahquitz Canyon Way, Palm Springs, CA 92262, 800-952-5068 or 760-325-5556, www.gadabouttours.com.

Grand Circle Travel, Inc.

The company has three main divisions. Grand Circle Travel offers a wide variety of trips. Their live-abroad, extended-stay vacations include round-trip airfare to an overseas location plus accommodations in an efficiency or studio apartment, organized entertainment and some meals for around $100 a day. You can choose to stay anywhere from a week to several months. Overseas Adventure Travel offers light adventure trips for groups of seniors. Vermont Bicycle Tours offers bike tours in the US, Canada and Europe.

More information: Grand Circle Travel, 347 Congress St., Boston, MA 02210, 800-955-1034 or 617-350-7500, www.gct.com.

Saga International Holidays

A large British Company, it serves traveling seniors (ages 50 and up) from the United Kingdom, US and Canada. Saga deals mostly in bus tours, some of which combine tourists from all three countries. Besides the US, Canada and Europe, there are tours to Mexico, South America, Australia and the Far East, as well as cruises.

More information: Saga Holidays, 222 Berkeley St., Boston 02116, 800-343-0273.

Free Maps and State Travel Information

Most states have toll-free phone numbers you can call to order free tourism information. The type and amount of information you will receive varies from state to state, but items often include free maps, calendars of events, travel guides and brochures containing information about accommodations, campgrounds, restaurants and seasonal recreational activities.

Alabama Bureau of Tourism & Travel
800-ALABAMA or 334-242-4169
www.touralabama.org

Alaska Division of Tourism
907-929-2200; www.travelalaska.com

Arizona Office of Tourism
800-842-8257; www.arizonaguide.com

**Arkansas Department of
Parks & Tourism**
800-NATURAL or 501-682-7777
www.1800natural.com

California Division of Tourism
800-TO-CALIF or 916-322-2881
www.gocalif.ca.gov

Colorado Tourism Board
800-265-6723; www.colorado.com

**Connecticut Department of Economic
Development, Tourism Division**
800-CT-BOUND or 860-270-8081
www.visitconnecticut.com

Delaware Tourism Office
800-441-8846 or 302-739-4271
www.state.de.us

Florida Tourist Bureau, Inc.
888-735-2872 or 321-868-0091
www.flausa.com

**Georgia Department of
Industry, Trade & Tourism**
800-847-4842 or 404-656-3590
www.georgia.org

Hawaii Visitors & Convention Bureau
808-586-2423; www.gohawaii.com

Idaho Division of Tourism Development
800-635-7820 or 208-334-2470
www.visitid.org

Illinois Bureau of Tourism
800-226-6632; www.enjoyillinois.com

**Indiana Department of
Commerce/Tourism**
www.enjoyindiana.com

Iowa Division of Tourism
800-345-IOWA (tourism guides only)
800-528-5265 (events calendar)
www.traveliowa.com

Kansas Travel & Tourism Division
800-2KANSAS; www.kansas-travel.com

**Kentucky Department of
Travel Development**
800-225-TRIP or 502-564-4930
www.kentuckytourism.com

Louisiana Office of Tourism
800-33-GUMBO (tourism guides only),
800-261-9144 or 504-342-8119
www.louisianatravel.com

Maine Office of Tourism
800-533-9595 (tourism guides only)
800-932-3419 or 207-623-0363
www.visitmaine.com

**Maryland Office of
Tourism Development**
800-MDISFUN; www.mdisfun.org

**Massachusetts Office of
Travel & Tourism**
800-447-6277 or 800-227-6277
617-727-3201; www.massvacation.com

Michigan Travel Bureau
888-784-7328; www.state.mi.us

Minnesota Office of Tourism
800-657-3700
www.exploreminnesota.com

Mississippi Division of Tourism
800-WARMEST or 228-875-0705
www.visitmississippi.org

Missouri Division of Tourism
800-877-1234 or 573-751-4133
www.missouritourism.org

Montana Travel
800-VISIT-MT or 406-444-2654
www.visitmt.com

Nebraska Division of Travel & Tourism
800-228-4307 or 402-471-3796
www.visitnebraska.org

Nevada Commission on Tourism
800-NEVADA-8 or 702-687-4322
www.travelnevada.com

**New Hampshire Office of
Travel & Tourism Development**
800-386-4664 or 603-271-2666
www.visitnh.gov

**New Jersey Division of
Travel & Tourism**
800-JERSEY-7 or 609-292-2470
www.visitnj.org

New Mexico Department of Tourism
800-733-6396 (voicemail center,
tourism guides only)
800-545-2070 or 505-827-7400
www.newmexico.org

**New York State Division of Tourism,
State of Economic Development**
800-CALL-NYS or 518-474-4116
www.iloveny.com

**North Carolina Division of
Travel & Tourism**
800-VISIT-NC; www.visitnc.com

North Dakota Department of Tourism
800-435-5663 or 701-328-2525
www.ndtourism.com

Ohio Division of Travel & Tourism
800-BUCKEYE or 614-466-8844
www.ohiotourism.com

Oklahoma Tourism
800-652-6552; www.travelok.com

Oregon Tourism Commission
800-547-7842 or 503-986-0013
www.traveloregon.com

**Pennsylvania Office of
Travel Marketing**
800-VISIT-PA; www.experiencepa.com

Rhode Island Tourism Division
800-556-2484; www.visitrhodeisland.com

South Carolina Division of Tourism
800-346-3634 or 803-734-0122
www.travelsc.com

South Dakota Department of Tourism
800-732-5682; www.travelsd.com

**Tennessee Department of
Tourist Development**
800-462-8366 or 615-741-8299
www.tourism.state.tn.us

**Texas Department of Commerce
Tourism Division**
800-888-8839 or 512-462-9191
www.traveltex.com

Utah Travel Council
800-200-1160
800-233-8824 (southwest Utah only)
801-538-1030; www.utah.com

**Vermont Department of
Tourism & Marketing**
800-VERMONT; www.1-800-vermont.com

Very Special Museums...Off The Beaten Path

Lower East Side Tenement Museum (90 Orchard St., New York City, 212-431-0233, www.tenement.org)

Housed in a restored 1863 tenement. As many as 12 immigrants lived in one unit—a mere 325 square feet of living space and one window. The building is listed on the National Register of Historic Places. $9 adults; $7 students/seniors.

Historic Voodoo Museum (724 Dumaine St., New Orleans, 504-523-7685, www.voodoomuseum.com)

Elaborate altars, live snakes used in rituals, potions, spells and talismans are testament to the local practitioners of the voodoo religion in Louisiana.

Liberace Museum (1775 E. Tropicana Ave., Las Vegas, 702-798-5595, www. liberace.org/museum.html)

Outrageous collection of the late pianist includes a hand-painted Pleyel piano used by Chopin at Versailles...a glitzy Austrian rhinestone-covered piano and matching Mercedes. $8 adults; $5 seniors; 12 and under free.

Mutter Museum (College of Physicians of Philadelphia, 19 S. 22nd St., Philadelphia, 215-563-3737, www.collphy phil.org/muttpg1.shtml)

Showcase for antique medical instruments and rare anatomical and pathological specimens. $8 adults; $5 students/seniors; under 6 free.

Elvis Is Alive Museum (Wright City, MO, www.missourilife.com/muse010. shtml)

Recreation of Elvis's funeral...testimonies from friends and relatives...photos of Elvis "sightings"...and testimony that the King of Rock and Roll lives.

Sandra Gurvis, Gahanna, OH-based travel writer and author of *America's Strangest Museums* (Citadel) and *Careers for Nonconformists* (Marlowe).

Virginia Division of Tourism
800-VISIT-VA; www.virginia.com

Washington State Tourism Development Division
800-544-1800
www.experiencewashington.com

West Virginia Division of Tourism
800-225-5982; www.callwva.com

Wisconsin Department of Tourism
800-432-TRIP (out-of-state)
800-372-2737 (in-state)
608-266-2161; www.travelwisconsin.com

Wyoming Division of Tourism
800-225-5996; www.wyomingtourism.org

Low-Cost Fun at US National Parks and Forests

National Parks and Forests are federally protected historical, natural and recreational areas of national importance. They are located across the country.

Here are just a few favorites:

US National Parks

California Golden Gate National Recreation Area, located in San Francisco, Marin and San Mateo counties, is the largest urban national park in the world—it's more than twice the size of San Francisco. *Contact:* Western Information Center, 415-239-2366, www.nps.gov/muwo/index.htm.

Most of the park's recreation areas are accessible all year, but hours of operation vary according to facility. The park offers golf, picnicking, swimming, guided tours, scenic walks, hiking, biking and cultural programs and museums.

Fees: $2 entrance fee for Muir Woods and $1 daily use fee for Alcatraz (plus ferry to Alcatraz Island—$7.75 round-trip, $6 for seniors, $4.50 for children ages 5 to 11).

West Virginia Harpers Ferry National Historical Park covers 2,300 acres in the states of West Virginia, Maryland and Virginia (304-535-6298). Hours 8 am to 5 pm. The park offers hiking, fishing, camping, ranger-guided tours and Elderhostel programs.

Special events (304-535-6029, www.nps.gov/hafe/home.htm) are held throughout the year. For example, a Black History Month Program and Exhibit in February and a 19th century celebration of the fourth of July.

Fees: A three-day family pass is available for $5 per vehicle or $3 per person (cyclists and walk-ins). The Golden Age Passport is honored.

National Forests

The Inside Scoop The US Forest Service (202-205-1706) and the US Fish and Wildlife Service sponsor nature watches highlighting flora and wildlife abundant in the forests across the country.

Contact the service to find out what to look for when you go to a particular recreation area.

From April through August, you can call the Wildflower Hotline (800-354-4595), which features weekly updates on wildflower viewing sites and wildflower events across the country.

Missouri The Mark Twain National Forest, Roll (573-364-4621), lies mostly within the Ozark Plateau. The forest offers floating and canoeing, hiking, horseback riding, camping, hunting, fishing and in its less-developed areas, nature study.

Fees: A recreational fee of $2 is charged for daily parking. You can buy a seasonal pass for $20, which is good from May 1 to October 15.

Camping in designated campgrounds has an additional charge of approximately $8 for a single-family site and $16 for a double/multiple-family site. Generally it is free to camp outside of the designated camping areas. To reserve a picnic shelter equipped with concrete ground and electricity for family reunions and weddings costs $25. The Golden Age Passport is honored.

New Hampshire The White Mountain National Forest, Laconia (603-528-8721, www.ss.fed.us/online/white). The forest contains the highest mountains in the Northeast and is noted for its world-famous ski resorts. A guide providing detailed accessibility information for each campground is available from the District Ranger Office or the Forest Supervisor's Office.

Fees: A $5 recreation fee gives you a seven-day access pass to the forest area. A $20 annual pass is good from May 30 to April 30 of the following year. The Golden Age Passport is honored (50% discount).

Wisconsin The Chequamegon National Forest, Park Falls (715-762-2461). The forest contains 800 lakes and many campground and hiking possibilities. There are trails for mountain biking, skiing, snowmobiling and horseback riding, and some of the state's best hunting.

Fees: $3 per day is charged for parking at a hiking trail or picnic area. A $10 seasonal pass is good from April 1 to March 31 of the following year. The Golden Age Passport is honored.

Hunters must have a Wisconsin State Hunting License, but no additional fee is charged. There is an additional fee for camping, and the amount varies, depending upon the services provided and the site's proximity to the lakes.

RV Rental Savvy

Recreational vehicles should be reserved at least one month in advance —three months ahead if you will be renting during peak vacation periods. If planning RV travel in Alaska, reserve at least six months ahead.

Get a list of all furnishings included in the rental so you know what to bring. Ask your insurance agent for a binder to cover use of the RV—rental RV coverage generally is not included in personal auto insurance. Read instruction sheets and checklists before starting out. Be sure to ask how many free miles you get per day and what each mile above that will cost.

Shirley Slater and Harry Basch, Los Angeles-based authors of *Frommer's Exploring America by RV* (Hungry Minds).

George Washington Slept Here... Maybe

The National Trust Historic Hotels of America publishes a 224-page directory of member hotels located in 42 states. Each is at least 50 years old and is listed on, or is eligible for, the **National Register of Historic Places**.

Hotels range from small eight-room country inns to major downtown properties, and include all levels of accommodation and price ranges.

To order the directory, call 800-678-8946, write to Box 320, Washington, DC 20055-0320 or visit www.historic hotels.org. *Cost:* $3.50. Hotels also are listed on the Web site, and reservations can be made through the 800 number or Web site.

Herbert J. Teison, editor, *Travel Smart,* 40 Beechdale Rd., Dobbs Ferry, NY 10522.

Get the Most from Your Visit to the Zoo

With natural settings, modern zoos are more humane. But they make seeing the animals a challenge. To improve your chances:

Arrive Early Animals are more active in cooler temperatures. During the peak of the summer, morning is your best bet.

Strategy: Visit the outdoor animals first, then spend the warmest part of the day visiting birdhouses, aquariums, reptile displays and other indoor attractions.

If There Is a Crowd When You Arrive, Turn *Left* Many zoos feature a circuitous path, and virtually everyone turns right when they enter. If the zoo isn't laid out in a circle, start at the back.

Ask About Scheduled Keeper Talks and Feeding Times Most zoos offer presentations by the animal keepers in front of the animals' habitats. Animals often recognize their handlers' voices...and come close to investigate. And feeding time almost always brings them out.

Search the Shadows Outdoor enclosures are generally arranged so animals always stay within sight. If they're not readily visible, look in the shade. Many zoo visitors just move on if they don't see something at first glance.

Exception: To encourage breeding, habitats of endangered animals, such as the Columbus Zoo's Mexican wolves, might allow them to escape from view.

Don't Assume that Unpopular Animals Are Uninteresting The monkey house may be packed while the birdhouse is nearly empty.

Resource: American Zoo and Aquarium Association, www.aza. org, for links to accredited zoos nationwide.

Patty Peters, associate zoo director/marketing of the Columbus Zoo and Aquarium in Ohio, one of the nation's most popular zoos, with more than 1.3 million visitors per year. She is a 22-year veteran of the zoo business.

Museums Are for Everyone

Museums provide low-cost (or no-cost), high-quality entertainment for the whole family. They cover every area of interest from painting and crafts to methods of transportation and natural history and are found throughout the country.

Most state museums and public historical museums are free or ask you to make a small contribution/donation. At others, you will have to pay a fee, usually $10 per person, to enter the museum for the day. Some museums that charge admission may have a weekly "free" day, so it's a good idea to call before you schedule your visit.

Specialty Museums

Smithsonian Institution's National Air and Space Museum (NASM) (Washington, DC, 202-357-1400, www.nasm.si.edu/nasm).

The NASM is located on the National Mall in Washington, DC. It maintains the world's largest collection of historic aircraft and spacecraft, including the original Wright 1903 Flyer, the "Spirit of St. Louis," Apollo 11 command module and a Lunar rock sample that visitors may touch.

Hours: 9:30 am to 5:30 pm every day except December 25.

Fee: Free.

National Bottle Museum (Ballston Spa, NY, 518-454-5400, www. crisny.org). The museum highlights the history of the nation's first major industry—glass-bottle manufacturing—exhibits, researches and preserves historical bottles and related artifacts.

Fee: Suggested donation of $2 per person.

Virginia Quilt Museum (Harrisonburg, VA, 540-433-3818, www.vcq. org/museums.htm). The museum is the center for the study of the role of quilts and quilting in the cultural life of people around the world. It preserves quilts and related artifacts from all countries and cultures.

Fees: Adults—$4; Seniors and students—$3; Children 6 to 12—$2; Children under six—free.

Tour Historic Military Sites

Valor Tours, Ltd., hosts vacation travel with historic military themes. Most tours are to sites of World War II in Europe and the Pacific, but tours of important sites of other conflicts are offered as well.

Details: 800-842-4504 or www. valortours.com.

Halls of Fame Don't Cost a Fortune

A hall of fame is like a museum, but it focuses on famous and established people or topics. Located all around the country, they are most commonly dedicated to a sport and its heroes.

Halls of Fame Dedicated to Sports

National Baseball Hall of Fame & Museum (Cooperstown, NY, 607-547-7200, www.baseballhalloffame.org). Focuses on outstanding players, the historical development of baseball and its impact on our culture.

Legends of the Game Baseball Museum (Arlington, TX, 817-273-5099, http://texas.rangers.mlb.com/NASApp/mlb/tex/ballpark/tex_ ballpark_museum.jsp). The center features interactive exhibits about geography, science, math and history—all with a baseball spin.

International Tennis Hall of Fame (Newport, RI, 401-849-3990, www. tennisfame.org). You can view videos and see memorabilia from historic champions and today's superstars.

Members of AZA Go for Free

There is no zoo pass that allows visitors to attend *all* zoos at a discounted rate. If you become an annual member of the **American Zoo and Aquarium Association** (AZA, 301-562-0777, www.aza.org), however, you can attend many of their affiliated zoos and aquariums for free.

This association focuses on the conservation, education and research programs involved with the protection of endangered, threatened and rare wildlife. As a member, you'll receive a monthly newsletter as well as brochures designed to help support the association's goals.

Mississippi Sports Hall of Fame (Jackson, MS 601-982-8264). This large sports museum features the history of sports and all of Mississippi's sports heroes. There is interactive technology that lets you play championship golf courses or take kicks against a tough soccer goalie. You can even try your hand at being a sports announcer.

Green Bay Packers Hall of Fame (Green Bay, WI, 920-499-4281, www.packerhalloffame.com). Features the Packers' history highlighted by art exhibits, video theaters and multimedia shows. You can get in on the action with interactive football displays.

National Soccer Hall of Fame and National Soccer Museum (Oneonta, NY, 607-432-3351, www.soccerhall.org). Museum houses an extensive archive (covering approximately 20 years) of soccer memorabilia.

For a vast array of other sports museums and halls of fame, contact the International Association of Sports Museums and Halls of Fame, 312-551-0810, www.sportshalls.com. You'll learn about 134 places to visit including:

- **1932 and 1980 Lake Placid Hall of Fame** (Lake Placid, NY, 518-523-1655 ext. 226, www.orda.org).
- **Amateur Athletic Union** (Lake Buena Vista, FL, 407-934-7200, www.aausports.org).
- **ASA National Softball Hall of Fame and Museum** (Oklahoma City, 405-424-5266).
- **AWSEF Water Ski Hall of Fame** (Polk City, FL, 863-324-2472, http://usawaterski.com).
- **Babe Ruth Birthplace and Museum** (Baltimore, 410-727-1539, www.baberuthmuseum.com).
- **Harness Racing Museum and Hall of Fame** (Goshen, NY, 845-294-6330, www.harnessmuseum.com).
- **Indianapolis Motor Speedway Hall of Fame** (Indianapolis, 317-484-6784, www.brickyard.com).
- **International Afro-American Sports Hall of Fame** (Louisville, 502-895-4534).
- **International Boxing Hall of Fame** (Canastota, NY, 315-697-7095, www.ibhof.com).
- **International Jewish Sports Hall of Fame** (Potomac, MD, 301-299-3300, www.jewishsports.net).
- **International Snowmobile Racing Hall of Fame** (St. Germain, WI, 715-542-4488, www.snowmobilehalloffame.com).
- **International Wrestling Institute and Museum** (Newton, IA, 641-791-1517, www.wrestlingmuseum.org).
- **National High School Sports Hall of Fame** (Indianapolis, 317-972-6900, www.nfhs.org).
- **National Museum of Roller Skating** (Lincoln, NB, 402-483-7551, ext. 16, www.rollerskatingmuseum.com).

Halls of Other Kinds of Fame

The International Clown Hall of Fame (Milwaukee, WI, 414-319-0848, www.clownmuseum.org). This hall of fame celebrates the world of clowning and features weekend clown shows.

National Cowboy Hall of Fame and Western Heritage Museum (Oklahoma City, 405-478-2250, www.cowboyhalloffame.org). Features the history of Western life and the life of the cowboy. It holds special events that focus on everything from Native Americans to chuck-wagons to a chili cook-off.

National Inventors Hall of Fame (Akron, OH, 330-762-4463, www.invent.org). Wander through worlds of genius on five cantilevered tiers connected by fantastic flying staircases, create a percussion band using laser beams, send a stream of water shooting into space or spend hours of hands-on exploration, demonstrations and inventive fun.

Rock and Roll Hall of Fame (Cleveland, 216-781-ROCK, www.rockhall.com). Explore artifacts of the stars, listen to music, attend a concert, see videos, use interactive kiosks. The museum covers the spectrum of music from the blues, gospel and country of the 1900s to today's hip hop and pop sounds.

International Museum of Cartoon Art (Boca Raton, FL, 561-391-2200, www.cartoon.org/visit.htm). View a collection of more than 160,000 original drawings, enjoy films and tapes of animated cartoons and cartoon documentaries.

Beat the Disney World Peak-Season Crowds

If you're traveling to Disney World during the busy season, crowds and heat can easily spoil your fun—but they don't have to:

Stay on Disney Property Guests staying at Disney hotels can gain admission to the parks one hour *before* regular openings.

Use the "Fastpass" Rather than stand in line for 45 minutes, use this "VIP service" to make an appointment at some of the most popular attractions—Splash Mountain...Tower of Terror...Space Mountain. Simply stop at a Fastpass turnstile ahead of time.

Adjust Mealtimes When everyone else is standing in line waiting to eat, you can be enjoying attractions. Eat a late breakfast so you can have lunch after the crowds thin out. Or eat early—before 11 am for lunch and between 4 pm and 5 pm for dinner.

Even better: Bring a bag lunch (your hotel concierge can tell you where to buy food) to avoid the hectic and expensive restaurants.

Museum Memberships

It's hard to cover all the rooms and displays a large museum has to offer in just one visit. With membership, you save yourself from having to pay each time you enter the museum. Individual and family membership plans entitle you to free entrance for a year. Many times the membership also guarantees free admission to special museum events such as films or concerts, gallery openings and members-only lectures.

Some membership plans also include a monthly member's calendar that tells you about new exhibits and special programs.

You can visit several museums by buying a membership at just one. Most major art museums let members of affiliated museums visit their permanent collections—free. And members often get discounts of up to 20% at gift shops and restaurants.

Examples: A $175 patron of the Los Angeles County Museum of Art gets membership privileges at 21 museums, including the Art Institute of Chicago and Metropolitan Museum of Art in New York City...a $150 patron of the Museum of Fine Arts, Houston, gets reciprocity from 30 museums, including the Guggenheim Museum in New York City and the San Francisco Museum of Modern Art.

David and Linda Glickstein, editors, *The Discerning Traveler*, 504 W. Mermaid Ln., Philadelphia 19118.

Free Wine And Cheese

One of the best things about public gallery openings is the free wine and cheese you're provided with while you browse.

Gallery openings are generally held on Thursday or Friday evenings at 6 pm or on weekend afternoons.

An opening is the celebration of the beginning of a new display at a gallery. Openings are generally held to give buyers a sneak preview of the artist's work. But the free wine and cheese is for everyone who comes.

Bring Bottled Water Carrying water is especially important on super-hot days. Refill at a water fountain.

Dress Alike Wearing the same color T-shirt or baseball cap makes it easy to keep track of each other in crowds. Make it a bright color.

Wear Something With Big Pockets—for tickets, room keys, car keys, wallet, sunscreen and all the other necessities.

Women: A fanny pack or a backpack is better than a purse.

Carry a Change of Socks Clean socks will help soothe feet that start to ache midway through the day.

Women and Girls Wear a bathing suit top beneath your shirt. If you go on any water rides, you will get very wet.

Val Meyer, contributor to *Fodor's Walt Disney World, Universal Studios Escape and Orlando 2000 Spring/Summer Edition* (Fodor's Travel Publications).

America's Most Magnificent Rose Gardens

The average gardener can grow no more than a handful of the thousands of varieties of roses that are available. To see —and smell—more, a gardener must visit a public rose garden. Here are the most spectacular ones:

Boerner Botanical Gardens (Hales Corners, WI). The formal Rose Garden dates back to the late 1930s. The massive stone and wood arbor supports many stunning climbing roses. There are two fountains and one reflecting pool. The garden displays more than 5,000 roses of more than 550 varieties.

More information: 414-425-1130, www.countyparks.com.

Brooklyn Botanic Garden The lovely Cranford Rose Garden here is one of the country's finest, with more than 5,000 roses of nearly 1,200 varieties. Adults 16 & over, $3; children 16 & under, free; seniors & students with valid ID, $1.50.

More information: 718-623-7220. www.bbg.org.

Columbus Park of Roses (Whetstone Park, Columbus, OH). The rose garden of the former headquarters of the American Rose Society (ARS) is now the world's largest municipal rose garden, with more than 35,000 roses of more than 450 varieties.

More information: 614-645-3217 or 614-645-3337, www.columbus redpark.com.

Elizabeth Park (Hartford, CT). The oldest municipally operated rose garden in the US, this park is in the National Register of Historic Places. About 15,000 roses of about 800 varieties, including many historical varieties.

More information: 860-242-0017. www.elizabethpark.org.

Gardens of the American Rose Center (Shreveport, LA). Gardens created and maintained by the ARS. Founded in 1892, the ARS is a national organization dedicated to the enjoyment and enhancement of roses. The gardens have more than 20,000 rosebushes representing nearly 400 varieties of modern and old roses.
More information: 318-938 5402, www.ars.org.

International Rose Test Garden (Portland, OR). This is the oldest continuously operating test garden in the country, with 10,000 plants representing about 500 varieties. The roses here are carefully evaluated to determine how well they grow in the mild Pacific Northwest climate.
More information: 503-823-PLAY, www.parks.ci.portland.or.us/parks/introsetestgarden.htm.

New York Botanical Garden (Bronx). The Peggy Rockefeller Rose Garden has more than 2,700 plants of more than 260 varieties, including 84 old roses. The charming triangular garden was originally designed in 1916 by noted landscape architect Beatrix Jones Farrand.
More information: 718-817-8700, www.nybg.org.

Tyler Rose Garden (Tyler, Texas). The largest public collection of roses in America—30,000 bushes of more than 450 varieties, including many miniature and climbing roses. Tyler is the commercial rose capital of the country.
More information: 903-531-1213, http://dir.gardenweb.com/directory/trg.

Before you go: Call for hours and admission fees.
Best time to go: June, in most areas of the country, when most of the plants are in bloom.

Sheila Buff, author of many books, including *The Great Tomato Book* (Burford).

Fair-Weather Street Fairs Are Free

You can enjoy art for free at fair-weather street fairs. Many cities set up sidewalk art fairs during the spring and summer. Attending local street fairs is a great way to support your local artists and artisans. This is a great time to buy art at prices that are lower than at galleries or indoor exhibits, because you are dealing directly with the artist. You can find art that ranges from oil paintings and sculptures to woven baskets and jewelry.

But you don't have to buy anything. You can just enjoy the art as you would do in a museum. Check the entertainment section in your local papers for a listing of outdoor art events in your neighborhood.

Finding a Great Travel Agent

A good travel agent can save you a great deal of time and money, but a disreputable one can leave you stranded with no tickets and no money in your pocket. Since there are relatively few regulations governing travel agents, you need to take responsibility for finding a good one yourself. The search is worth the time you put in, since a good travel agent can save you 10% to 15% on the price of your trip.

Outdoor Dog Shows Are Free

Outdoor dog shows are totally free for spectators (you may have to pay a nominal fee for parking or a program). **Bucks County Kennel Club** (Pennsylvania), for example, holds an all-breed outdoor dog show (approximately 2,500 dogs) that has no spectator admission cost. You can also get free dog food samples from manufacturers that are promoting the show.

Check out other dog shows across the country that focus on things like beauty, how well a dog can track, herd or retrieve, and obedience. These events are usually free for spectators as well. Contact the **American Kennel Club** (919-233-9767) and ask for its geographical listing of the nation's dog clubs. Or check out their Web site at www.akc.org.

Where to Look

The secret to finding a good travel agent is to get references from friends, family members and business associates who like to travel the same way you do. Favor local agents who have been in the business for at least a few years and who use the most up-to-date computer systems. If the agent you like best is popular (and therefore hard to reach), ask the person who referred you to call the agent on your behalf to introduce you.

Background Check

When you find an agent you like, check to see if the agent is registered with one of the two main professional travel organizations—the American Society of Travel Agents (ASTA) or the Association of Retail Travel Agents (ARTA). Both require member agencies to post bond to protect their clients.

Also check with the Institute of Certified Travel Agents (ICTA, 781-237-0280, www.icta.com) to confirm that the agent is a Certified Travel Counselor (CTC). CTCs have at least five years' experience as travel agents and have completed ICTA's two-year, graduate-level program.

Refunds and Payments

Ask your agent up front about any extra service charges you should expect for faxes or long-distance calls. Also ask whether the agency will provide a refund (or partial refund) if a tour operator or airline goes out of business before your vacation. For added security, make sure you get commitments on cancellations and refunds in writing.

Find out how your travel agent is paid by the airlines. In the past, most agents received a 10% commission on the cost of each booking, which encouraged them to sell more expensive tickets. Recently, however, airlines have been cutting back agents' commissions to maximums of $20 per one-way flight, regardless of the ticket price. In response, some travel agents have started charging customers a service fee of around $35 for each booking. Find out in advance if your agent charges a fee.

Agent Expertise

Your agent should take the time to get to know you and your travel preferences, such as your favorite airlines, the hotels you like and your first choice for airplane seating. Good customer service means your agent should accept no calls and avoid interruptions while talking with you.

A good agent should be personally familiar with the trips and vacations you are considering, rather than just reading descriptions to you from a brochure or computer screen. You could find that information on your own. Agents in the know can give you suggestions about the best attractions, restaurants and shopping

areas. Plus, since the photographs and descriptions in travel brochures can make even the dingiest hotel look like an elegant resort, you need to be able to rely on your agent to make sure you get your money's worth.

Getting the Best Service

It pays to establish an ongoing relationship with your agent. When booking your first trip, let the agent know that you plan to come back for your next trip if everything works out well. The prospect of future business is the only real incentive a travel agent has to find you the cheapest fares, particularly if the agent gets a percentage of what you pay for your tickets.

It helps to be courteous as well. Try to give your agent at least four weeks' notice before you travel so the agent has the time to search for the best deals while there are still many options available. And if the trip goes smoothly, give your agent a call or write a short thank-you note.

Travel Agents' Secrets

Travel agents use computer systems created by airline companies. Although these systems search for all available flights, they may favor their mother airline by listing it first, updating its fares more quickly or making it more time-consuming for a travel agent to book with another airline.

Ask your travel agency which airline created their booking system and always question if a flight on that airline is really the least expensive option.

Airline incentive programs are another reason your travel agent may favor a particular airline. Using a concept similar to the frequent-flier miles programs, incentives reward agents for booking more tickets on the same airline.

The best agents use four or more Computer Reservation Systems (CRSs) to stay on top of last-minute price changes. CRSs can search for the best prices, fastest flights or particular airplane models.

Your travel agent should be able to suggest ways to save on your airfare, such as buying consolidator tickets, booking overnight flights or choosing weekend departures. Make sure your agent knows your top priority (whether it's saving the most money or avoiding layovers), because it may change your agent's search method dramatically.

You probably have multiple priorities, however. Many people would rather pay an extra $100 than have two four-hour layovers.

Finally, ask your agent to keep searching for cheaper flights even after you purchase your ticket. If she finds one at a significant discount, it may be worth the cancellation fee to rebook your flight. For example, most airlines charge a cancellation fee of $30 to $50 per ticket, but if the new flight saves you $200, it's certainly worth paying the fee to save $150 or more.

Great Gardens

While traveling around the US, take time to see:

- **Desert Botanical Garden**, Phoenix, 480-941-1225, www.dbg.org. Open all year.

- **Botanica**, the Wichita Gardens, Wichita, Kansas, 316-264-0448, www.botanica.org. Open all year.

- **Missouri Botanical Garden**, St. Louis, 800-642-8842, www.mobot.org. Open all year.

- **The New York Botanical Garden**, Bronx, New York, 718-817-8700, www.nybg.org. Open all year.

- **Dumbarton Oaks Gardens**, Washington, DC, 202-339-6401, www.doaks.org. Open March through October.

Sheila Buff, outdoor writer, 500 Milan Hill Rd., Milan, NY 12571, and author of *The Great Tomato Book* (Burford).

Save on Airfares

If you know what factors affect the price you pay for an airline ticket, you can get a good deal almost every time you fly. Here are some pointers:

Factor 1: How Flexible You Are

Take the time to do some research—call around and search the Web to get the best price but most of all be flexible about when you fly. Consider flying:

- On a different day.
- At a different time of day.
- During a different week of the month.
- At designated off-peak times.
- During special seasonal deals.
- On another airline.

Factor 2: When You Fly

You will probably get the best deal on flights shunned by business travelers. Consider:

- Late-night flights.
- Holiday flights.
- Round-trip flights that include a Saturday night stay-over,
- Weekend domestic flights,
- Weekday international flights,
- Off season—for example travel to the Bahamas or Hawaii in the summer and to Europe or Canada in the winter.

Factor 3: Where You Fly To and From

Consider flying in and out of small airports located within a one- or two-hour drive of larger hubs. *Examples:* Fly to Milwaukee instead of Chicago…Oakland instead of San Francisco. The smaller airport may even be closer to your destination, but even if it isn't, the money you save may well be worth an hour's car ride.

Warning: Make sure you've arranged for a car beforehand—you don't want to spend the money you've saved on a long taxi ride.

Factor 4: What Airline You Fly

Start-up airlines generally charge less than larger, established companies, but it's still wise to call around to get the best price.

Here are a few discount airlines and how to contact them:

Domestic Discount Airlines
- **Southwest Airlines** (800-435-9792, www.southwest.com).
- **Western Pacific** (011-683-6360).
- **JetBlue Airways** (800-JetBlue, www.jetblue.com).

International Discount Airlines
- **Air Jamaica** (800-523-5585, www.airjamaica.com).
- **Cathay Pacific** (852-2747-5563, www.cathaypacific.com).
- **Icelandair** (800-223-5500, www.icelandair.com).
- **Singapore Airlines** (800-724-3333, www.singaporeair.com).
- **Thai Airways** (800-426-5204, www.thaiair.com).
- **Virgin Atlantic** (800-862-8621, www.virgin-atlantic.com).

Factor 5: Who You Are

Status fares are cut-rate tickets for people who fit into certain groups. You can get up to 75% off your ticket price if you are a full-time student, a senior citizen, under 26 years old, an active-duty member of the military (or a dependent), a child traveling with an adult, part of a family flying together, a member of the clergy or a teacher.

Factor 6: How Resourceful You Are

You can find airline discount coupons in some unexpected places. Check out:

- Supermarket bulletin boards.
- Banks and credit unions (for members only).
- Packaging on computer supplies, film and other products.
- Credit card offers.
- Coupon books sold by charities and other groups as fund-raisers. They may feature friend-flies-free discounts, two domestic flights anywhere for say, $130, or 20% off any ticket. There will probably be a number of restrictions, but they still can save you a bundle.

Promotional Tickets

Some airlines offer Promotional Tickets (for standby travel) to travel agents as a bonus for booking a certain number of flights with them. Agents sometimes sell these tickets to customers looking for a really cheap flight. Ask your agent if this is an option.

Internet Fares

You can save a bundle on airfares by using the Internet. Several top airlines make certain low-cost, last-minute tickets for weekend trips available exclusively on-line. Destinations and costs become available each Wednesday for round-trip flights departing the following Saturday (occasionally Friday) and returning Monday or Tuesday. A wide variety of domestic and some European destinations are available each week. You can sign up on an airline's Web site to have these deals E-mailed to you once a week.

Web Sites for Cheap Tickets

Airlines of the Web (www.flyaow.com) offers general information on flying inexpensively, links to most airlines and on-line reservations.

About Passports

Obtain a Passport in a Hurry
The State Department's expedited passport service will provide a new passport to you in two weeks instead of the normal six weeks.

Cost: Service charge is $35 per application, plus a fee for overnight delivery. This is in addition to the $60 passport charge, $40 for renewal passports.

A passport can be obtained even more quickly by utilizing a private expediting service—usually for a fee of $150 or more.

Useful: The State Department's "Passport Services and Information" Web page provides all forms and information needed to get a passport...indicates which of the 4,500 public places nationwide that accept passport applications is nearest you. Visit www.travel.state.gov/passport_services.html.

Renew Your Passport by Mail
Plan ahead. Renewing your passport by mail is quick and cheaper than requesting a rush at the last minute. **The Passport Agency** has a new 888 telephone number, not free. For information, call 888-362-8668. (The 1-888 calls require a credit card for payment of a flat rate of $4.95 per call.)

Best Fares (www.bestfares.com), an electronic version of *Best Fares* magazine, features Internet-only deals, hidden travel deals, a currency exchange, ATM locator, ski resort information and travel articles. Some sections are free, but you have to be a *Best Fares* subscriber to access many parts of the site.

Cheaptickets.com (www.cheaptickets.com) claims an inventory of more than 1 million discount airfares. Deals are also available on cruises, hotels and rental cars. Registration on the site is required, but free. It offers a personal search profile and special E-mail discount fare alerts.

Expedia (www.expedia.com) searches multiple airlines to find the lowest fares. Their Fare Finders service will E-mail you the best current fares it finds to your chosen destination on a weekly basis. You can book flights, rental cars and hotels, check the weather around the world, read travel columnists' opinions and more.

FareChase (www.farechase.com) is an aggregator with a difference —they built their site as a *demonstration* of excellence of their proprietary search engine. But, it is a fully functional and effective way to gather, in one place, the real-time information from more than 80 global sites. They don't do bookings, but offer direct connections that allow you to book with any site offering you the best deal. Among their features is a FareAware service alerting you to new deals. All services are free.

Hotwire (www.hotwire.com) partners with eight domestic airlines and 23 international airlines and other vendors to offer unsold inventory, such as empty seats on flights, hotel rooms and car rentals. You must be prepared to be flexible about your travel plans to take advantage of their offerings.

Internet Travel Network (ITN) (www.itn.net) offers frequent-flier information, news on popular travel destinations, travel guide reviews, weather reports and the option to bid on or buy cruises, airfares and travel packages.

Orbitz (www.orbitz.com), owned by the nation's five largest airlines, scans more than 450 airlines for lowest airfares. You can then book your chosen fare through Orbitz (except for Southwest Airlines, where you must contact the airline directly). It also offers a free "care alert" advising you in advance of updates on gate and baggage claim assignments and warnings on weather that may affect your trip. *Note:* Orbitz does not offer unpublished discounted fares.

Qixo (www.qixo.com), unlike many other travel sites, is an aggregator whose free search engine compares fares from 25 major travel sites. The search includes most airlines as well as sites such as Orbitz, Travelocity, Lowestfare and 1800USAhotels. Once you locate a fare, you can be taken directly to the offering site to book.

Sidestep (www.sidestep.com) is an aggregator—a free Internet travel service that searches 90 travel sites and attempts to pull together the best travel deals in one place. You can then be connected directly to the airline, car rental and hotel brands you trust to book your reservation.

TRAVAC (www.travac.com) services more than 100 international destinations using 20 major airlines. Most flights are on major, scheduled carriers.

Travelbyus (www.travelbyus.com) directly owns travel packagers and boasts more than 900 supplier contracts. They offer exclusive cruise and vacation packages including discounts with major cruise lines. Booking can be done on-line through them or through your travel agent. A useful free service, called Travel Vault, allows you a place to record, on-line, such items as digitized images of your medical records, driver's licenses and other forms of identification.

Travelocity (www.travelocity.com) is powered by the SABRE reservations system used by travel agents. You can make last-minute plane, hotel, car rental or cruise reservations, check out their currency converter, vacation packages and get activity information by city.

Travelweb.com (www.travelweb.com) uses the travel agents' Pegasus computer system to let you find low airfares and make reservations on-line. You can also check out hotel rates and weekend getaways.

When Getting Bumped Is a Bargain

When a flight is overbooked—there are more people with confirmed tickets than there are available seats—the airline has to bump (remove) people from the passenger list. Airlines routinely sell more tickets than there are seats because they can predict the average number of ticket holders who will be no-shows.

How It Works

If your flight is overbooked, the airline representatives will ask for volunteers to take a later flight. As an incentive, they frequently offer volunteers a free voucher for a future round-trip domestic ticket on their airline. This can be a great deal, but make sure you know the details before you accept. Ask about any restrictions, such as blackout dates, expiration dates or required Saturday night stays that might make it difficult for you to use the ticket. Also ask how far in advance you can make a reservation.

To Protect Yourself from Vacation Disaster

Consider your need for two kinds of vacation insurance when booking an expensive trip.

Trip cancellation insurance covers nonrefundable fares and deposits if for some reason you can't make a planned trip. Cautions:

- Examine policy exclusions, such as for preexisting medical conditions that might prevent you from collecting.
- Buy insurance from a party other than the tour operator that books your trip—if it goes broke, you may lose the insurance, too.
- Use insurance only to protect significant expenditures. Airline tickets and hotel reservations usually can be "rebooked" for a small penalty fee, so they don't justify the expenditure for insurance.

Travel health insurance covers medical costs incurred outside the US. Medicare and most private insurance companies don't cover such costs—and even when they do, you probably wouldn't want to be stranded abroad waiting for reimbursement.

Best: Contact your current insurer to learn the extent of your coverage. For a trip, buy a rider or supplemental insurance that will pay for your emergency removal from abroad to the US, and for treatment incurred abroad.

Bob Carlson, editor, Bob Carlson's Retirement Watch, *3700 Annandale Rd., Annandale, VA 22003.*

Money-Saving Alternative to Flight-Accident Insurance

Flight-accident insurance is expensive —but the chances of dying in a plane crash are slim. It's a much better deal to make sure you have a standard life insurance policy with coverage enough to take care of your family no matter how you may die than to buy a one-time policy every time you board a plane.

Note: You may already be covered for no additional charge if you buy your ticket with certain credit cards. American Express, for example, provides free travel insurance (including travel to and from the airport). Check your favorite credit card's policies.

If not enough people accept the free ticket offer, the airline may begin offering cash payments in addition to the voucher, up to a couple hundred dollars. The price goes up once passengers are actually on board. If you volunteer to be bumped at the gate and then the airline later makes a better offer to someone on the plane, ask the airline to increase your deal to match the later offer. They may or may not agree, but it can't hurt to ask. There are no regulations on how much the airline has to offer volunteers, and payments may vary from one airline to another.

Get the Facts

There are a few things you should consider before you accept an airline's bumping offer. How long will the wait be until the next flight? Are you willing to wait that long? Ask if you will have a confirmed reservation for that flight or be flying standby, in which case you might not get on that flight either. If it's the last flight of the day, ask yourself if you are willing to spend the night in a hotel and whether you can get in touch with anyone who's supposed to meet you at your final destination.

Also ask the airline if they will pay for any meals, phone calls, hotel stays and other incidentals you may need while you wait. Otherwise, you may wind up spending any compensation you receive before you even get into the air.

Involuntary Bumping

On the off chance that the airline can't get enough volunteers and you are bumped against your will, you should know what to expect. Involuntary bumping is one of the few areas of air travel still controlled by the federal government, and the Department of Transportation requires airlines to give involuntarily bumped passengers a written statement describing their rights.

Basically, if an airline can find a way to get you to your destination within one hour of your scheduled arrival time, it is not required to reimburse you for your trouble. If, however, the airline can't get you there until between one and two hours of your scheduled arrival time (one and four hours on international flights), it must reimburse you on the spot the amount of your one-way fare, up to $200, for the inconvenience. This is known as denied boarding compensation. And if they can't get you there until more than two hours after you were supposed to arrive (more than four hours on international flights), they have to give you double the one-way fare, up to $400.

The airline is still responsible for getting you to your destination, even after paying you denied boarding compensation. If you'd rather find another way to get there, however, you can request an involuntary refund and try to make your own flight arrangements with another airline. This is a risky option unless you know you can get yourself there faster on your own.

Denied Boarding Compensation Limitations

Unfortunately, there are many circumstances under which the airline does not have to pay you denied boarding compensation:

1. You don't have a confirmed reservation (the status box on your ticket doesn't read "OK").
2. The flight you're confirmed on holds fewer than 60 passengers.
3. The flight originates outside the US (only the first half of a round-trip ticket to another country is covered).
4. You arrive at the gate after the check-in deadline.
5. The airline gets you to your destination within an hour of your scheduled arrival time.
6. You are bumped because the airline has to substitute a smaller plane for the original.
7. You are flying on a charter flight.

If the benefits of getting bumped appeal to you, find out from the airline ahead of time whether your flight is routinely overbooked. The flights most likely to bump passengers are those flying heavily-traveled routes at the most popular times of day. Get to the gate early, ask to put your name on the top of the volunteer list, don't check any bags and stay near the desk just before flight time.

The Newest Ways to Save With Charter Flights

When you book a charter flight, you're buying your ticket from a wholesale tour operator, not from an airline. Charter companies make deals with airlines to use their planes to fly specific routes at specific times. Then they sell tickets for these flights through travel agents or their own retail outlets.

Although charters used to be for tour groups only, individual travelers can now take advantage of charter fares without purchasing an entire vacation package. The savings are usually competitive with flights booked through a consolidator, and the best deals go to those who book the furthest in advance.

Like consolidator flights, charters are almost exclusively for international travel.

Who Can Fly on a Charter

You can usually save around $50 to $400 on a transatlantic coach flight by flying on a charter. The savings for first-class tickets can be even greater, with seats often costing less than half as much as comparable seats on a regular flight.

Get Cleaner Travel Facilities

If you are sensitive to smoke or just want a cleaner environment, ask for a smoke-free hotel room, transatlantic flight and car. The car-rental companies, notably **Budget** (www.budget.com), and the **American Lung Association** (www.lungusa.org) have cooperated to eliminate cigarette lighters in some vehicles. Ask your travel agent to enter this preference on your personal record, so it will be requested every time.

How to Find a Small Airport

To find lesser-known airports—and the less-expensive flights that usually go to them—visit www.priceline.com. Enter your location and destination. Before the name-your-own-price service tells you anything about money, it will give you a list of airports within two hours' driving distance from your destination. You can then search on Priceline or elsewhere for low-cost flights to specific airports.

Herbert J. Teison, editor, Travel Smart, 40 Beechdale Rd., Dobbs Ferry, NY 10522.

Charter companies are able to charge less than most airlines because they don't keep up regular schedules, flying only when there is enough demand to easily fill their flights. For example, a charter company might only have flights to Europe during the summer (when the most people are free to travel) or to the Caribbean during the winter (when the most people want to be at the beach). And even during peak vacation seasons, charters tend to fly less frequently than major airlines.

If you're planning far in advance to visit a popular vacation destination during tourist season, you should have no trouble finding a good deal on a nonstop charter flight. Your chances of finding a charter flight decrease significantly, however, if you're planning at the last minute to fly to an unusual destination for an odd time period or during the off-season. You will also be unable to find a charter flight if your destination country (like several in the Far East) has protectionist policies for its national airline.

Flying One-Way on Charters

While most people use charters for round-trips, it's sometimes possible to purchase one-way tickets (known as half round-trips) from a charter company for slightly more than half the round-trip ticket price.

It may even be possible to buy two half round-trip charter tickets arriving and departing from different cities. For example, you may be able to fly from New York to London on one charter flight, travel around Europe, and then fly from Paris back to New York on another charter flight. Ask your travel agent or the charter company if this could be a money-saving option for you.

Possible Drawbacks

There are several drawbacks to flying on a charter. Make sure the money you're saving is worth any extra hassles or worries you'll have.

Inflexibility Since they have fewer flights, charters give you less flexibility in your vacation schedule. If a charter makes only one round-trip flight weekly to your chosen destination, for example, you have to be prepared to arrive and depart only on those days.

Cancellations Charter companies make their money by booking each flight to capacity, so they might cancel your flight at the last minute if they don't receive enough reservations. Since other airlines are not obligated to honor your ticket, you may have to choose between being stranded until another charter flight is available or paying out-of-pocket for a ticket on a different airline.

Long Lines Charters are notorious for having understaffed check-in lines, and sometimes ask you to arrive three to four hours before your flight to be sure you get checked in.

Short on Comfort Charter flights aren't known for luxurious conditions or gourmet food. Expect a full cabin and a tight squeeze in your seat. This drawback is far more troublesome on a long flight to Southeast Asia than a short flight to the Bahamas.

Best choice: Wide-body Boeing 757s are the most comfortable charter aircraft to fly.

Worst choice: DC-10s and L-1011s that have been specially configured for charter flights are the least comfortable charter aircraft to fly, especially when filled to capacity.

Late Departures Operating on a tight budget, charter companies tend to have relatively small inventories of aircraft. Therefore, if your plane has a mechanical difficulty, you might have to wait hours, even days, until another plane is available. And you won't receive any compensation for your time unless you wait more than 48 hours.

The Mysteries of Air Courier Travel…Revealed

If a business needs to send a small package or document overseas quickly, it has two choices—send it as air cargo, which can be held over for a day by the foreign country's customs department, or use a courier company that gets someone—a courier—to fly on a passenger airline and check the package as personal luggage, which is not held over in customs. Businesses frequently choose the second option.

What You Get as a Courier

Almost anyone age 18 or older can get a flight as a courier, but you should know that fabulously inexpensive courier flights are mostly a thing of the past.

Still, low prices and even free tickets are not unheard of, especially if you're willing to fly to any of a variety of destinations on last-minute notice. The average courier ticket runs around one-quarter of the cost of a full-price economy-class ticket. *Caution:* A popular destination may not offer significant savings over charter flights and other bargain tickets. Be sure to check around to see if you are really saving money.

The Best Deals

The best deals for couriers are on last-minute deliveries. As deadlines approach, companies grow desperate and start dropping the price on what they expect you to pay. Costs tend to be lowest from January 1 to March 15; highest, during the summer when many students are available for courier duty. If you want to make

Low-Cost Factory Tours

Los Angeles Times
(Los Angeles, 213-237-5757, www.latimes.com)
See the original editorial plant and printing press. No children under age 10 allowed.

Wild Turkey Distillery
(Lawrenceburg, KY, 502-839-4544)
Find out how bourbon is made during this free tour.

Hershey's Chocolate World
(Hershey, PA, 717-534-4900, www.hersheychocolateworld.com)
Get a free tour of Hershey's Chocolate World simulated factory, and get a free sample.

Hill & Valley Cheese
(Cashton, WI, 608-654-5411, http://oldcountrycheese.com/default.htm)
Preserve the tradition of Amish cheese production, culture and traditions. Amish crafts, candy, maple syrup and cheese are for sale.

Ben & Jerry's Ice Cream
(Waterbury, VT, 802-846-1500, www.benjerry.com)
Children under 12 can go for free.

Best Time of Day to Call a Ticket Agent

If you're calling the airline directly, try calling after 7 pm or on weekend mornings, when agents receive the fewest calls.

Bonus: You'll wait a shorter time before being helped, and the agent will have more time to find you the flight with the best price.

a reservation in advance, try calling early in the morning at the beginning of the month—you stand a better chance of getting a good deal.

Be sure to let the courier company know if you can fly on short notice and aren't picky about your destination.

The Drawbacks

There are quite a few restrictions on traveling as a courier. Make sure you are comfortable with these limitations before you buy your tickets. And always ask the company when you will receive your actual ticket. You may not get it until you meet the courier agent at the airport on the day of your flight, a condition which makes some travelers rather nervous.

Unreliable Schedules Courier flying is only for people with flexible schedules, since it is practically impossible to book a courier flight more than one month in advance. Most flights have a mandatory one- or two-week stay, although it is sometimes possible to make other arrangements.

One-Passenger Travel Only one courier is sent per delivery, so you must travel alone—although you can sometimes arrange with a friend to be couriers on consecutive days (or on the same day with another courier company).

Baggage Limits You must travel light (often with only one carry-on bag) because couriers usually have to forfeit their right to check any bags since the space will be taken up by the package they are escorting.

Extra Fees In addition, courier companies often charge extra if you pay by anything other than money order and tickets are non-refundable and nontransferable.

Locating a Courier Company

Once you've decided you want to be a courier, you need to find a courier company that flies out of an airport near you.

Cities with the most courier flights: New York, Los Angeles, San Francisco, Miami and Chicago. Your departure point will determine your destination options. Flights from the East Coast, for example, fly mostly to Europe, while those from the West Coast fly mostly to Asia and Australia.

Some flights require you to escort a package on the way home as well. If you're not a courier on the return leg of the trip, you're free to check your luggage.

Jupiter (310-670-5123, www.jupiterair.com) arranges courier flights from the West Coast to Seoul and Bangkok on Japan Air. There is a $35 registration fee. Most flights are for up to one-month stays.

Now Voyager (212-459-1616) provides lists of courier flights as well as its own charters, which are sometimes less expensive. They list flights with American couriers originating in New York, New Jersey, Detroit and Los Angeles. Flights to Europe require an additional $28 airport departure tax. You can pick up your tickets in their Manhattan office or get confirmation information via fax.

The Air Courier Association (ACA) (800-282-1202, www.aircourier.org) offers members information on courier flights, wholesale travel and other discounts. ACA offers a variety of membership programs.

International Association of Air Travel Couriers (IAATC) (352-475-1584, www.aircourier.co.uk) charges members $45 a year for access to up-to-date courier flight information. Members receive a bimonthly bulletin of international travel opportunities, tips and bargains from courier agencies around the country. IAATC itself sells no tickets. You can get a list of last-minute courier flights (updated twice daily) 24 hours a day via fax or the Internet.

Know the Code

Use on-time performance codes to choose between similar flights. A flight's on-time performance code is a number between zero and nine that indicates how frequently that flight arrived on time during the past month. Flights rated nine arrive like clockwork, but you'll be lucky to arrive at all on a flight rated zero. You can find a flight's on-time performance code by asking the reservations agent.

How Seniors Can Fly for Less

For travelers—especially those age 62 and older—there are many kinds of bargains to investigate before buying tickets. Do your research to find the best deals.

Senior Airfare Breaks

Coupon Booklets Most airlines offer seniors booklets with four coupons that can save a lot of money.

Only one coupon is needed for a one-way trip between any two cities in the continental US (two coupons each way for Alaska or Hawaii). So you pay the same rate to fly 300 or 3,000 miles. There are no minimum or maximum stays required.

Typical cost: About $675 for four coupons.

While most senior coupon programs are similar, some offer better conditions or fly to more cities.

Advantages:

• You lock in the current senior ticket price for one year.
• America West and USAirways allow up to two grandchildren (ages two to 11) to travel with a senior using the same coupon booklet.
• Coupons are refundable if not used (but once you use one coupon, the rest become nonrefundable).
• To have confirmed seats using senior airfare coupons requires booking at least 14 days in advance—but immediate travel is possible on a standby basis.

Airline Secret

When a domestic and overseas airline *code-share* a flight—both book seats on one airline's plane—they may charge very different amounts for seats. One carrier may have sold all less-expensive seats, while the other may have some left. The difference can be hundreds of dollars.

Strategy: When booking tickets, always ask if a flight is a code-share. If it is, check ticket prices with both airlines.

Upscale Traveler, 4521 Alla Rd., Marina del Rey, CA 90292.

• Senior coupon flights can even earn frequent-flier miles.
• Coupons let you fly one-way or round-trip—there are no minimum/maximum stay limits.

Disadvantages of coupons:

• During special airfare promotions, tickets could cost less than coupon prices.
• Shorter flights could be cheaper with an individual ticket.
• Some Internet fares may be cheaper.

Flat Discount Except for most deeply discounted promotional fares, seniors and a companion can routinely get 10% off many domestic and international airfares.

Many foreign airlines offer 10% discounts at age 60 or 62, so always compare fares.

Caution: You must tell the travel agent or airline your age and provide a photo ID at check-in to get the discount.

A companion of any age traveling with a senior can also routinely get the 10% discount.

Southwest Airlines Senior Fares

Southwest Airlines (SWA) has attractive senior fares. They are unrestricted and fully refundable, but you must be 65-plus to get SWA senior fares.

SWA flies to 29 states and has a high customer satisfaction rating.

Other airlines will usually match SWA's fares—even their senior fares—for cities where they compete, so, again, check.

SWA senior fares can't be booked on-line—you must call 800-435-9792, www.southwest.com.

Senior Travelers' Clubs

Continental Airlines has a club for seniors that offers discounts of 15% to 20% to people age 62 and older. These fares also earn frequent-flier miles. *More information:* 800-441-1135, www.conti nental.com.

United's Silver Wings Plus is open to those age 55-plus.

Caution: If you are 65-plus, other airline senior deals are better.

Jens Jurgen, editor, *Travel Companion Exchange*, Box 833, Amityville, NY 11701.

Winning with Frequent-Flier Programs

The airlines launched the first frequent-flier programs in the mid-1980s as a way to encourage customer loyalty. The airlines want you to spend more money. Your goal is to make frequent-flier programs work to your advantage.

How It Works

After you sign up to be part of an airline's frequent-flier program, you earn mileage points every time you fly with *that* airline. When the points add up to a certain number (often a minimum of 25,000), you can redeem them for free flights, upgrades and other rewards. *Downside:* You must fly with a particular airline to earn points in its program, so you might be missing out on a better deal on a different airline.

Choose the airline with the following qualities to be your primary carrier:

- Flies in and out of your local airport.
- Has frequent flights with reasonable rates to the cities you visit most frequently.
- Offers high mileage points for the trips you plan to make.
- Has tie-ins to earn extra points with credit cards, car rental agencies and hotels you already use.
- Has tie-ins with other domestic and international carriers you already use.
- Has no expiration date for miles (there are fewer and fewer plans like this).
- Requires the least miles for the most benefit.

Earning Mileage Points

There are many ways to earn frequent-flier miles without getting on an airplane. You can earn extra miles from companies the airline has arranged tie-ins with—car rental companies, cruise ships, long-distance phone companies, credit cards, dining cards, florists, ski resorts, hotels and even stock brokerages and car-buying services. Many major airlines are also making deals with smaller, regional airlines so that your miles from both go to the same account.

Caution: All these deals are constantly changing, so always ask if the mileage offer is still good when you call. Also ask if you're getting the best deal. There are sometimes multiple offers available at the same time for the same service. For example, your frequent-flier newsletter might include an offer of 2,000 bonus miles for signing up with MCI, while an MCI advertisement may offer 5,000 miles on the same airline.

Be Wary of Classified Ads

People who buy nonrefundable airline tickets they can't use sometimes sell them through the classified ads. These tickets are nontransferable. If you buy one, you will have to fly using that person's name, which will obviously be a problem if you have to show a passport or other form of identification before boarding (as is now required on most domestic as well as international flights).

For Those Complicated Trips

On-line travel bookings may cost more in time than they save in cash. Even when they charge fees for their services, travel agents can often come up with cheaper packages than travelers can find for themselves on the Web.

If you have a simple booking—just an airline flight, for instance—you may be able to do it quickly on-line and save money. But the more complicated your trip, the longer you will spend working out the details. A good travel agent is usually able to do all the work for the same price—or a little more.

Bottom line: Decide how much you value your time before trying on-line bookings.

Tom Parsons, editor, *Bestfares.com*, 1301 S. Bowen Rd., Arlington, TX 76013.

Reaping Your Rewards

The number of restrictions on frequent-flier miles has been creeping steadily higher. But if you keep your eyes open and plan ahead, it's still possible to find a good deal.

Get the most for your money by using your miles to buy the most expensive tickets you can. For example, if you're planning to take two domestic round-trips this year and only have enough miles for one free flight, plan to use the miles for the flight you expect will cost more.

Airlines sometimes send out merchandise catalogs featuring items you can purchase with your miles. The merchandise usually requires far fewer miles than the least expensive plane ticket. If you don't have enough miles for a plane ticket and the expiration date is approaching, you might consider the items in the catalog.

Flier Beware

Airlines count on most people never redeeming their frequent-flier miles, and continue to make it harder to cash them in. Here are a few of the problems you may encounter:

1. Expiration Dates Most airlines put a time limit on their frequent-flier miles of two to five years. *Solution:* If time is running out, you can usually get the miles you need from a credit card or other tie-in, or make up the difference in cash.

2. Blackout Dates Airlines have many blackout dates—times when it's impossible to use your miles for a free ticket. These occur especially during the Thanksgiving and Christmas holidays. *Solution:* Make sure you can use your miles when you want to.

3. Sold-out Flights There are usually a limited number of seats available on each flight for people using frequent-flier rewards. *Solution:* Plan ahead and book flights well in advance. If there are still no seats available for frequent-fliers, ask to be put on a waiting list and look for another flight. You can use your miles for a companion fare or upgrade. Or pay your airfare and use your miles to pay for a car rental and accommodations.

4. Missing Miles Sometimes miles you've earned don't show up on your statement. *Solution:* Always save the bottom sheet of your ticket and all your boarding passes until you're sure you've been credited for the correct number of miles.

5. Spending Too Much for Too Little Don't get so caught up with mileage bonuses and tie-ins that you spend more money accumulating miles than they are worth. *Solution:* Always shop around for the best deal.

Selling Your Miles

The airlines will usually only agree to issue your frequent-flier awards in your name or the name of an immediate family member.

It is not actually illegal to buy and sell frequent-flier flight coupons, but most airlines don't allow it. If you use an award issued in a different name and the airline finds out, your ticket could be confiscated and the program member's account penalized.

If you're a risk taker looking for a good deal, consider buying flight coupons from a broker or from FlyerSource (888-318-4287, www.smartflyer.com) on the Internet. To post or view FlyerSource ads, you must register at a cost of $10 for 30 days.

Drive One-Way

Consider flying one-way and driving the other. You can often save up to 50% on a rental car when the companies have a directional imbalance. This means they have a number of cars in New York that really belong in Washington, and vice versa. Call or stop by local car rental offices to compare deals and prices.

Don't Pay Full Price For That Room!

There are plenty of ways to find a hotel room for less than the listed price. Here are some suggestions from travel experts and in-the-know travelers.

Ask Your Travel Agent

Start by asking your travel agent about any unpublicized sales going on in hotels in the area you're planning to visit. Travel agents often have good tips on how to pay less at resort and business hotels.

Travel During the Off Season

Hotel prices drop significantly during the area's off-season. Weekend rates are usually much lower than weekday business rates. And try not to stay in a city during a major convention, when hotel prices go through the roof.

Request a Status Discount

Most hotels offer 10% discounts for people over age 60, and the discount increases for members of AARP, National Alliance of Senior Citizens or Silver Keys. Many hotels will also give you a discount for being a student, veteran, young adult or a member of AAA, a business organization or other group.

Call Hotel Chain Toll-Free Numbers

Before you make your reservations, you can call a few of the larger hotel chains to find out if they have hotels in the area, how much they charge and whether they have any current sales or discounts.

Call the Hotel Directly

You'll almost always save money by calling the hotel directly instead of booking through the chain's toll-free number. Book your room well in advance, so the hotel agent knows you have time to shop around. And don't accept the first rate offered to you. Many

About On-Line Reservations

When making or canceling reservations on-line, keep careful records. It is not always clear from a Web site that your request was completed. You may want to call the airline or hotel to make sure. When discussing a booking with an agent by phone, give your confirmation number or record locator number from the Web site. That will help the agent track down the reservation—and prevent double bookings.

William McGee, editor, Consumer Reports Travel Letter, 101 Truman Ave., Yonkers, NY 10703.

hotels have a fallback rate that they will quote if, and only if, a customer is reluctant to accept the standard rate.

Pay Cash

Some hotels will give you a discount for paying cash instead of using a credit card.

Book Through Your Airline

If you're traveling overseas, consider booking your hotel through your airline. Many international carriers have established relationships with foreign hotel chains that can save you money. For example, American Airlines (800-832-8383, www.amrcorp.com) sells vouchers for 20% to 30% off at several hundred Best Western hotels in Europe, while British Airways (800-359-8722, www.british-airways.com) offers 50% off at more than 60 London hotels (and more in other European cities). Check with your airline to see if it has a similar program.

Join a Discount Club

There are several discount clubs that offer card-carrying members up to 50% off the list price of mid-range hotel rooms across the country and around the world. Request a club's list of hotels to see where they are and what type they are, before you join. The details of these programs change frequently, so be sure to read the small print before you sign up.

- **Encore Preferred Traveler** (301-459-8020, www.virtual-encore.com) lists hotels around the world at varying discounts for an annual $59.95 fee.

- **Hotel Express International** (www.hot-ex.com) Frequent travelers might find it worth the $150 annual membership for access to 50% discounts on hotels throughout the world.

- **Traveler's Advantage** (877-259-2691, www.travelersadvantage.com) offers 50% off at over 4,000 hotels, plus a one-time free-room certificate, airline-savings vouchers, rebate travel agent services and other frequently updated services for around $60 a year.

Call a Hotel Consolidator

Consolidators, also called discounters, book blocks of rooms months in advance—and at steep discounts. In exchange for agreeing to buy rooms on slow nights, consolidators get their pick of rooms when the hotel would otherwise be sold out. Unlike discount-card companies, consolidators deal primarily with deluxe properties, but agree not to heavily advertise their names.

Here are some hotel consolidators and the areas they cover:

- **Accommodations Express** (800-277-1064, www.accommodations express.com). Major US convention and resort cities, including Boston, Las Vegas and Chicago.

- **Capitol Reservations** (800-847-4832, www.capitolreservations. com). Washington, DC.

- **Central Reservations Service** (800-686-6836, www.reservation services.com). Boston, Atlanta, Orlando, Miami, San Francisco, New Orleans and New York City.

- **Express Hotel Reservations** (800-407-3351, www.express-res.com). New York City and Los Angeles.

- **Hot Rooms** (800-468-3500, www.hotrooms.com). Chicago.

- **Hotel Reservations Network** (800-364-0801, www.180096hotel. com). New York City, Chicago, San Francisco, Los Angeles, New Orleans, Orlando, Washington, DC, London, Paris and more.

- **Quikbook** (800-789-9887, http://quikbook.com). New York City, Washington, DC, Atlanta, San Francisco, Boston, Los Angeles and Chicago.

- **San Francisco Reservations** (800-677-1500, www.hotelres.com). San Francisco and surrounding areas.

- **Washington, DC Accommodations** (800-554-2220, http://dc.yahoo. com/external/fodors). Washington, DC.

Hotel Savvy

For much better hotel (or cruise) service, leave a tip for the hotel maid or cruise cabin steward on the first day of a multiday stay.

Little-Known Hotel Discounts

- Shareholder rates may be available if you own stock in the company that owns or manages the hotel.
- A frequent-flier rate may be available if you fly on an airline with which the hotel has a partnership.
- Emergency-situation rates are given to people traveling because of family illness or stranded by natural disasters.
- Family package rates, often available at resorts, include breakfast or recreational discounts.
- Corporate rates are often available if you have a business card, even if you are not traveling on business.

Questions to Ask Before Booking a Room

- Can I cancel my reservation, or check out a day early, without penalty?

Save on Car Rentals

If you're renting for less than one week, you'll get the best rate at a major company—**Avis** (www.avis.com), **Budget** (www.budget.com), **Hertz** (www.hertz.com), **National** (www. nationalcar.com) or **Thrifty** (www. thrifty.com). *For rentals of one week or longer:* You may do better with a small, local company

- Ask about discounts for members of national organizations (such as AAA or AARP)...frequent-flier programs...or credit card affinity programs.
- See if your employer has negotiated a corporate rate that you are entitled to use.
- Beware of fees for an extra driver and one-way rentals with exorbitant drop-off charges.
- Check the basic rental rate against advertised discounts.
- If you're forced to take a compact when you reserved a sedan, ask for a 10% discount.
- Pick up the car downtown to save on airport surcharges.
- Don't take Collision Damage Waiver (CDW) insurance if your personal auto policy or major credit card covers it.
- Return the car with a full tank of gas.

Herbert J. Teison, editor, Travel Smart, 40 Beechdale Rd., Dobbs Ferry, NY 10522.

How to Avoid Getting Bumped

If you definitely don't want to be bumped, here are a few precautions you can take to make sure you're on-board when your plane takes off:

1. Check with the Department of Transportation. Find out which airlines flying your intended route have the best record for not bumping passengers. Be aware that the statistics include involuntary bumping only.

2. Take the least crowded flight possible. The less likely your flight is to be overbooked, the less likely it is that anyone will be bumped.

3. Make sure you have a confirmed ticket. The status box on your ticket should read "OK" not "Standby." Check the status box as soon as you purchase your ticket.

4. Get to the gate on time. Do this even if you already have a seating assignment and a boarding pass. If you're not there by the official check-in deadline, the airline assumes you're not coming and can give your seat to someone else. And, even if you are on time, the last passengers to check in are the first ones to get bumped.

- How late can I arrive without having paid for my room in full?
- Is there room service, and if so, during what hours? (Some hotels have reduced the hours for room service or cut it out entirely.)
- Does the quoted rate include tax and service charges…break-fast…parking?

Biggest Weekend Booking Mistake

Always insist that your weekend reservation be classified as "leisure." If you say it's for "business," there's a good chance the rate will be significantly higher.

Jens Jurgen, editor, *Travel Companion Exchange*, Box 833, Amityville, NY 11701.

Alternate Accommodations: When You Don't Want to Pay Hotel Prices

Hotels aren't the only places you can spend the night while you're on vacation. Consider these money-saving alternatives:

Vacation Rentals

Renting a house, condo or apartment can really cut the cost of your vacation, especially if you make your own meals. Most rentals are on a weekly basis and you may have to follow the traditional Saturday-to-Saturday rental cycle, although deals can usually be arranged during off-seasons. *Example:* Vermont and Colorado ski areas in the summer.

For information: Ask your travel agent, check out your local news-paper or the classifieds in cultural or travel magazines. You can also contact a real estate agent in the town you're interested in or get a copy of the local paper.

Hostels for All Ages

Hostels are generally the least expensive accommodations available. Guests sleep in rooms with other members of the same sex, often in twin or bunk beds. You also share any additional facilities—kitchens, bathrooms, common areas. You give up a little luxury, but often pay less than $10 a night.

Consider joining Hostelling International-AYH (733 15th St. NW, Ste. 840, Washington, DC 20005, 202-783-6161, www.hiayh.org). Annual membership is free for those under 18 years of age, $25 for ages 18 to 54, $15 for ages 55 and up, and $250 for a lifetime membership. Membership includes a membership card entitling you to a variety of travel discounts, and a listing of 125 hostel facilities throughout the United States. Listings of nearly 4,500 more hostels in over 70 countries including Europe and the Mediterranean, or Africa, Asia, Australia and New Zealand are also available.

Home Swaps

One great way to save money on accommodations, especially for a large family, is to find someone who has a home in the place you want to visit and agree to trade a vacation at their home for one at yours. If you arrange a swap with someone who has a home comparable to yours, you'll get the comfort you are used to at little or no cost, saving yourself a bundle on hotel fees. Most home exchanges last at least a month, particularly for retirees and Europeans who receive five or six weeks of vacation a year.

Look into joining one of the vacation-exchange clubs that list thousands of homes all over the globe. Most clubs cost only $65 a year to join, a small price to pay for free accommodations.

Once you find a potential home exchange, make sure you and the other owner agree on the terms before you make the trade. Decide whether you also want to swap cars, whether you're willing to take care of plants or pets and whether you'd like to introduce your guests to some of your friends.

Finding a Home-Exchange Club

These organizations offer different ways to find potential home exchanges around the world:

HomeLink Box 650, Key West, FL 33041 (800-638-3841, www.homelink.org).

Intervac U.S. (800-756-HOME, www.intervacus.com). Intervac offers two types of memberships: Web & Photo ($68), or Web-only ($50) for a one-year listing on-line and in the big *January Book* (Web-only members do not receive *Home Exchange Books*); and Book & Web ($99) or Book, Web & Photo ($117) for a listing in the big *January Book* and on-line for a year and copies of *Home Exchange Books*. Homes are primarily located in the US, Western Europe and Canada, with a few in Eastern Europe, South America and Asia, as well.

The Invented City 41 Sutter St., Ste. 1090, San Francisco 94404 (800-788-2489 or 415-252-1141, www.invented-city.com).

Trading Homes International Box 787, Hermosa Beach, CA 90254 (800-877-8723, www.trading-homes.com). Locations include South Africa, the Caribbean, Australia and New Zealand, as well as Europe and North America.

Single Travelers

Consider a "guaranteed share" when booking a cruise. Almost all cruise fares are double occupancy. But some cruise operators—including Carnival, Holland America and Norwegian—offer to find same-sex roommates for single travelers. If none is available, you will get a private room for the double occupancy rate.

Odds: Male travelers are much more likely to get a room to themselves than are females, because on the average cruise there are roughly 12 single women to every single man.

Consumer Reports Travel Letter, 101 Truman Ave., Yonkers, NY 10703.

Much Happier Bed-and-Breakfasting

B&B owners pride themselves on the individuality of their accommodations. Be sure to express your needs when making reservations.

❏ **Room:** Do you prefer a room with a view? A quiet room? A large one? (These often face the road.)

❏ **Bed:** What size do you prefer? Can you tolerate a footboard?

❏ **Bath:** Do you require a tub?

❏ **Breakfast:** Is it a full breakfast? A simple Continental one? Will you be eating at a table with other people or by yourselves?

Other considerations: Will renovations be in progress during your stay? Will other guests include any groups such as family reunions or tours? Do they take credit cards or checks? Are there any special packages, off-season rates or last-minute discounts?

Sandra Soule, travel writer based in Riverside, Connecticut, and editor of *America's Favorite Inns, B&Bs and Small Hotels* (St. Martin's Griffin).

Great Deals on Top-Notch Cruises

Cruises aren't only for the rich. In fact, if you know how to go about it, you can probably pay less for a cruise than almost any other vacation.

Never pay the price listed in the cruise brochure. Hardly anyone does. Cruise companies are known for selling a large number of cabins at discount prices through travel agencies and cruise consolidators, so you should expect a discount of at least 25%. And if you have a flexible schedule, you can sometimes save up to 75% by filling empty cabins at the last minute. Two-for-one deals are also good bargains, particularly if they include round-trip airfare.

Your best source of discounts is one of the many cruise-only travel agencies that make a business of selling deeply-discounted cabins. Savings are always greater in the off-season, so consider traveling to Alaska or the Caribbean in the spring or fall. You'll save even more if you don't have your heart set on a particular ship or destination, and if you're flexible about when you embark.

Cruises are usually all-inclusive, so that one price covers your accommodations, meals and most entertainment. Find out about additional costs (such as alcoholic beverages or special island excursions) ahead of time so you can estimate your total cost.

Find the Best Cruise for You

Here are some of the larger travel agencies that specialize in cruises, good bets for finding a great cruise at a low price:

Cruises of Distinction (800-434-SHIP). Get on their mailing list to receive catalogs of cruise discounts four times a year. You can also request last-minute cruise specials via E-mail.

Cruises International, Inc. (800-255-7447, www.cruisesinternational. com). They pride themselves on their customer service, creating custom client profiles to find the best cruise match within each client's budget. Get on their mailing list for their seasonal catalog, their magazine, *Cruise Trends*, and their six annual *Cruise Savers Guides*, each of which focuses on a different cruise line.

Spur-of-the-Moment Cruises, Inc. (800-343-1991, www.spurof.com). Calling itself "America's clearinghouse for last-minute and unsold cruises," Spur-of-the-Moment offers discounts of up to 80% on cruises for travelers with flexible schedules.

Travel Services International, one of the largest full travel service agencies, incorporates The Cruise Line (888-721-5200) and Cruises Only (888-278-4737). All can be reached on-line at www.mytravel co.com/cruises. They offer seven-day-a-week service, cruise deals and expert cruising advice, coupled with large savings on cruises and last-minute bookings all over the world.

Savings Especially For Singles

Single persons often face exorbitant supplement charges when they try to book travel on a cruise or tour. That's because most travel accommodations and fares are offered for two people or more.

Useful: Singles travel services locate trips designed for singles and help compatible travel companions find each other for double occupancy trips. Resources:

- *Travel Companion* newsletter and exchange, Box 833, Amityville, NY 11701 (800-392-1256, www.whytravelalone.com). Thousands of match-up listings and many bargains also available by joining for $159/year. Includes a subscription to the newsletter.

- **Connecting: Solo Travel Network**, 689 Park Road, Unit 6, Gibsons, British Columbia V0N 1V7, Canada (800-557-1757, www.cstn. org). Internet-based membership, $25/yr.; mail-based, $35/yr.

- **Grand Circle Travel**, 347 Congress St., Boston 02210 (800-955-1034, www.gct.com). Offers free single supplements on many of their tours—and newsletters to those who travel with them.

- **Going Solo Travel Club**, 629 11 Ave. SW, Calgary, Alberta, Canada, T2R 0E1, Canada (888-446-7656, www.goingsolotravel.com).

- **Loners on Wheels, Inc.**, Box 1060-WB, Cape Girardeau, MO 63702 (888-569-4478, www.lonersonwheels.com). For singles with recreational vehicles, it organizes rallies and campouts nationally.

Arthur Frommer's Budget Travel Online, www.frommers.com.

Hitchhike Your Way to Europe, The Caribbean...

If you have a flexible schedule, consider hitchhiking your way onto a plane flying to Europe, the Caribbean, Mexico or any one of the 50 states. **Destiny Travel** (888-829-9115, www.destiny standby.com) and **Air Tech** (212-219-7000, www.airtech.com), give you access to last-minute empty seats for very low prices.

You choose a departure city, one or more possible destinations, and a three- to five-day window of time during which you are willing to depart. Then you receive a voucher to exchange at the airport for boarding passes. On the eve of your multiple-day window, you contact the company to find out what flights are available. Travelers get their first-choice dates and destinations more than 70% of the time.

These low-price fares are hard to beat, but fare wars have been known to drop prices for round-trip tickets to London down to almost nothing, so be sure to check around before you buy.

Shop Duty Free

If you find great deals on art or antiques in your travels, you should be aware of US Customs rules. Two import specialists give us the inside information.

Art

Artworks can be brought through US Customs duty free from abroad.

Snag: "Artworks" are what the US Customs office says they are. This includes original paintings, drawings, pastels and collages—as long as they were made entirely by hand—plus other art objects if the creator was trained as an artist, graduated from a recognized art institution or has exhibited his/her works in galleries or museums. So, you may need to be able to prove the status of the work's creator.

Frequent-Flier Savvy

Free Flights From Your Job

Business travelers get more out of frequent-flier programs than anyone else, particularly if their company pays for their tickets. Since they tend to travel long distances frequently and pay high prices, business travelers rack up miles quickly and are treated very well by the airlines.

If you travel for your company, you can probably keep the frequent-flier miles from your trip—even if your company pays for your tickets. Ask your supervisor for more information.

Pool Your Frequent-Flier Miles

Consider pooling your frequent-flier miles with other people to make a free trip possible, even if your own mileage falls short. **British Airways** (800-955-2748, www.british-airways.com) lets up to four household members add their miles together. **Japan Airlines** (800-525-3663, www.jal.co.jp) lets family members enrolled in the Family Club combine miles. Rules change frequently, so check with your airline for an update. Combined miles can be redeemed on partner airlines even when those airlines do not allow pooling of miles.

Trap: Fine works created by craftsmen, such as glass works, don't necessarily qualify as artwork—although they are often sold as "duty free." If you are considering acquiring valuable works while traveling abroad, contact the nearest Customs office before leaving on your trip to learn the rules.

Shelly Meyers, US Customs senior import specialist, Los Angeles.

Antiques

Antiques can be brought through US Customs *duty free* from abroad. By US Customs definition, an antique is any object more than 100 years old.

Best: Whenever possible, bring the items you acquire with you when you return through customs rather than ship them separately. Have documentation of age.

Your presence will expedite their passage through customs… save time and money…and assure that delicate or breakable items are handled properly.

It can be well worth it to pay excess baggage charges to have items accompany you.

Cathy Roe, US Customs import specialist, 11099 S. La Cienega Blvd., Los Angeles 90045.

14

Save on Education for The Whole Family

College Savings Plans Are Better than Ever

The hottest thing in college savings today is the Section 529 plan, a tuition-savings plan for a child or grandchild. Once in the plan, assets build up tax free until they're withdrawn.

Under the *2001 Tax Relief Act*, which started January 1, 2002, withdrawals from state 529 plans are tax free if the money is used to pay tuition and other college costs.

Red flag: Make sure you aren't risking financial aid for your child by contributing to a state 529 plan. Families with incomes of as much as $90,000 may qualify for need-based aid—up from the old ceiling of $60,000.

The higher your income, the more attractive a 529 plan is. If you have several kids in college at the same time, the income threshold may be higher, depending on the cost of each school. Higher-income families are *unlikely* to qualify for financial aid unless they have at least two children in college at once.

Ways to Pay

State-Sponsored Tuition Plans Families can use a qualified state-sponsored tuition plan to pay for a state college or university. These programs let you pay your child's tuition now, at today's rates, and guarantee that your costs will be covered when the time comes to enroll, even if it's years away. The programs also guarantee your child's admission to at least one of the institutions covered by the agreement.

Deferred-Payment Options Many colleges also offer optional monthly payment plans to help you spread out your expenses. Two plans widely used by universities are offered by **Academic Management Services** (800-635-0120) and **Key Education Resources** (800-KEY-LEND; www.key.com/educate).

How the Plans Work

Specific plans vary by state. All plans allow for a large initial contribution—generally up to $100,000. Unlike assets in a Uniform Gift to Minors Act or Uniform Transfer to Minors Act account, you keep control of the money in a 529 plan. You can take it back if you feel the person will misuse it, but there is a plan penalty of up to 15%.

Anyone can open a state 529 plan for a child—you do not have to be a relative.

Tax Advantages

There is no up-front federal tax deduction for money put in a 529 plan, although many states allow you to deduct contributions on your state tax return. Money builds up tax sheltered until withdrawn to pay tuition bills. Thanks to the tax law, withdrawals from state 529 plans will be completely tax free.

Provisions expire after 2010. Congress could start taxing withdrawals again after that. Even if it does, it's a good bet that tax-free withdrawals will be permitted for money already contributed.

Gift tax benefit: The normal limit on tax-free gifts is $11,000 per gift per year. Section 529 allows you to bunch five years of tax free gifts into one year. Each donor can give $55,000 tax free to fund a 529 plan—$110,000 in total from a married couple—every five years.

Choosing a Plan

Investment Options Money in a state 529 plan is invested by a manager selected by your state—typically a mutual fund company. Because withdrawals not spent on college costs could trigger tax liabilities and penalties, you should be satisfied with your investment options and the manager's performance record before committing your money. If you don't like the way a state 529 plan is managed, you can transfer money, without tax or other penalties, to another state's plan.

Look at investment return figures before signing up. Because the oldest of these plans has been around only since 1997, there are no long-term performance figures. Check the newspaper to see performance of the fund company's publicly available funds. Would you invest in its funds outside of the state 529 plan?

Helpful resource: www.savingforcollege.com (800-400-9113) has comparisons of investment returns and other features of the various state plans.

State Tax Breaks If your state offers tax breaks, its plan may make the most sense financially, even if its performance lags that of another state.

Example: New York's plan allows a husband and wife to each deduct contributions of up to $5,000 a year on their state income tax. *Bonus:* Its manager, TIAA-CREF, boasts high returns and low costs.

Designating Beneficiaries Structure the plan so ownership passes to your spouse or another adult until it is used to pay school bills. Otherwise, if you die before money is withdrawn and allow the money to pass to the youngster, he/she may not use the money for college.

Note: Private institutions can offer prepaid *tuition* plans, but not savings plans. Withdrawals from these plans will be tax free starting in 2004.

Financial planner Raymond Loewe, CLU, ChFC, founder, College Money, which does college financial planning for clients, 112-B Centre Blvd., Marlton, NJ 08053. www.collegemoney.com.

Getting Into the Top Schools

Help kids get into the best colleges by making the right moves while they are in high school. Here's what you should be doing month by month:

Freshman Year

September Encourage the student to focus on one or two key extracurricular pursuits—the more unusual, the better.

October Assess chances of receiving financial aid. Consult college finance guidebooks for formulas—or hire an independent financial aid consultant.

January When the child turns 14, reassess your investments. If you will be eligible for aid, diminish savings in the child's name. If you won't be eligible, take advantage of the child's lower tax rate by gifting appreciated stocks, funds, etc.

Sophomore Year

September Student should start looking at college guidebooks.

October Student should take practice PSAT. The real one will be given the following year.

November Start your financial-aid planning now. For example, be careful about selling shares of stock after January 1 of the junior year as this will reduce aid eligibility.

Junior Year

October Student takes PSAT test.

January Student should take an SAT review course.

April–June Student takes SAT test. Sign up more than five weeks before the test date. The last test is given in early June. Students

College Admissions— The Big Myths Debunked

Myth: The well-rounded student is the most desirable.

Reality: Colleges like students who have focused on one or two areas and developed excellence and leadership in them.

Myth: The admissions essay matters only in close decisions.

Reality: It almost always counts heavily. It is read very carefully at small schools and almost as carefully at medium-sized and large ones. Only the biggest universities focus more on numbers than on essays.

Myth: The student should not seem too eager to attend, except when applying for early decision.

Reality: Colleges want enthusiastic students. They favor applicants who make it clear that they want to attend —and explain why.

Myth: If you know the right person, you can get in easily.

Reality: This works in perhaps 1% of cases—if you know someone who has made enormous donations. Otherwise, acceptances are based on merit.

Schools do value legacies, however. Sons and daughters of graduates are often in a separate "legacy" pool, which may double their chances.

Frank Leana, PhD, educational counselor in New York City.

Save Thousands With Advanced Placement

You can save thousands in college costs with advanced placement. There are 33 Advanced Placement (AP) tests, in 19 subjects, given in mid-May every year. Course work is not required to take AP tests—a student can study on his/her own. Students scoring at least four out of a possible five get college credit for their knowledge.

Surprising: You need answer only 50% to 60% of questions correctly for a score of four.

Savings on college costs can be significant—one-third of the latest Harvard entering class had enough AP credits to start as sophomores or above... saving at least one year of tuition.

Adam Robinson, education consultant based in New York City, cofounder of The Princeton Review and author of What Smart Students Know (Crown).

applying to highly selective schools should sign up for SAT II tests in specific subjects.

Senior Year

September Visit schools the student is considering. Make sure he/she has taken all courses required for admission to each school. Determine financial-aid filing requirements for each college. *Note:* Rushing won't get you more money, but missing deadlines will shut you out.

December–January Meet all financial-aid and admissions deadlines.

Kalman Chany, president of New York–based Campus Consultants Inc., a financial-aid consulting firm. He is author of *Paying for College Without Going Broke* (Princeton Review).

Helping Your Child Pick the Right College

When helping a child choose a college, don't just look at the school's academic or sports reputation. Consider how a school can help jump-start his/her chosen career.

Step One: Define a Career

Few high school students know what they want to do when they grow up. But they usually know what broad areas interest them.

Useful resources to find careers that match those interests:

- *Barron's Profiles of American Colleges* (Barron's Education Series).
- *The College Board's Guide to 150 Popular College Majors* (College Entrance Examination Board).
- *The College Board Index of Majors and Graduate Degrees* (Henry Holt).

Web Resources

In addition to the College Board's Web site, www.collegeboard.com, which has a self-diagnostic test to point students toward possible career options, here are other Web sites I like:

- *Princeton Review* (www.review.com) has a very clever and interactive site that covers much of the same territory.
- *Petersons* (www.petersons.com) is good for those interested in culinary arts, business, information technology, graphic arts and visual communications.

Consider Co-Op Programs

Cooperative learning can give students a leg up on their careers. Generally, a student in one of these programs spends four terms in

a paid internship. When he graduates, he has highly relevant work experience, important contacts and—ideally—excellent references.

A few colleges and universities offer co-op programs, including Northeastern University in Boston, Drexel University in Philadelphia and Kalamazoo College in Michigan. More information is available at www.collegeboard.com.

Frank Leana, PhD, educational counselor in New York City. He is author of The Best Private High Schools and How to Get In *(Random House/Princeton Review).*

Ben Kaplan, Founder of ScholarshipCoach.com Won $90,000 in College Cash— and You Can Too

The average cost of attending a top university today is more than $120,000 for four years—and that figure is increasing. College financial-aid departments can help...but this help can be limited. Many families are forced into assuming enormous student loan burdens.

Merit-based programs, which award college money that doesn't have to be paid back, are an alternative. These scholarships are available to high school, college, graduate and returning students as well as to children under age 14. And you don't need top grades to win these awards.

Getting Started

Go On-line The Internet is a great place to start the scholarship hunt. More than a dozen scholarship databases help students identify appropriate programs.

To use these databases, you generally fill out on-line questionnaires and the databases match you with scholarships based on your submitted profile. No one site is comprehensive—so try all of them.

For links to these databases and a special interface for optimizing your search, visit www.scholarshipcoach.com and click on the "Scholarship Surfer" button.

For detailed ratings of the strengths and weaknesses of each database, see my book *How to Go to College Almost for Free* (HarperCollins).

Finding the Right Scholarship

- ***How to Go to College Almost for Free*** by Ben Kaplan (HarperCollins).
- ***The Scholarship Scouting Report*** by Ben Kaplan (HarperCollins).
- ***College Scholarships and Financial Aid*** by John Schwartz (ARCO/Macmillan).
- ***The Complete Scholarship Book*** edited by Fastweb.com. (Sourcebooks, Inc.).
- ***Directory of Financial Aids for Women*** by Gail Ann Schlachter (B. Klein Publications).
- ***Financial Aid for African Americans*** by Gail Schlachter et al. (Reference Service Press).
- ***Financial Aid for Asian Americans*** by Gail Schlachter et al. (Reference Service Press).
- ***Financial Aid for Hispanic Americans*** by Gail Schlachter et al. (Reference Service Press).
- ***The Scholarship Book*** annual by Daniel J. Cassidy & Michael J. Alves (Prentice Hall).
- ***Scholarships*** annual by Gail Schlachter et al. (Kaplan).

Ben Kaplan's Tips for Using ScholarshipCoach. com

When you click on the "Coach's Interview" button, the virtual Scholarship Coach will ask a series of questions. Based on your responses, the Scholarship Coach can give you advice unique to your circumstances.

Using the "Sample Winners" link, you'll be able to read actual winning scholarship entries, and you"ll learn to play the scholarship game from those who have been successful. The Web site also offers a "Weekly Briefings" page to get the inside scoop on each week's featured scholarships. Knowing the insider's perspective gives you an edge over other applicants.

Search your area of interest in different ways. A scholarship for students who are interested in studying biology might not be cross-listed under science.

Start Early...and Stick With It The scholarship hunt is not solely for high school seniors. Start your scholarship hunt in seventh or eighth grade and continue through college.

Different programs are aimed at different age brackets. Scholarships awarded to younger students are either held for them until they enter college or awarded in the form of U.S. savings bonds, or are given as outright cash. An early start:

- Increases the number of potential scholarships available to you because the applicant pool is often smaller.
- Helps you position and prepare yourself for opportunities.
- Gives you a chance to perfect your application skills.

Think Local Large national scholarships get attention, but local scholarships are well worth seeking out. Although prizes are often smaller, the competition is lighter—so you have better odds.

Call or drop by local clubs and organizations to ask if they offer any scholarships.

Possibilities: American Legion Posts, Elks Clubs, Key Clubs, Kiwanis Clubs, Knights of Columbus, Lions Club, VFW, YMCA/YWCA, 4-H Clubs.

Also look into local unions, small local banks, savings and loan institutions, credit unions and parents' employers and unions. Scholarships often are available even to those who don't belong to particular clubs or who don't have accounts at specific banks.

Target Scholarships Tailored to Your Strengths Some scholarships are academically focused, but many others don't require you to submit grades or test scores.

Scholarships may be awarded based on success at a single task, like drawing a picture or delivering a speech, or criteria such as community service or overcoming obstacles.

If you have a specific career goal or hobby, contact organizations in these areas and ask if they offer any scholarships.

Useful resource: *The Scholarship Scouting Report* features in-depth profiles of the nation's top scholarships, as well as sample winning entries and interviews with scholarship winners and judges.

Winning Applications

Paint a Portrait Scholarship judges award money to people, not résumés. Focus on who you are, not just what you've done.

Don't Make Excuses for Blemishes on Your Transcript Instead, treat them as obstacles that you have overcome. One scholarship winner, who had gangs and drugs in his past, described what he had learned and how he was trying to turn his life around.

Many applications require a short essay. *Strategies:*

Make It Personal Don't submit an essay that anyone could have written. Include plenty of unique experiences, perspectives and details.
Keep It Snappy Concise, interesting essays will be noticed.

Recycle Essays from class work and other applications whenever possible.

Some Interesting Scholarships

- **Prudential Spirit of Community Awards** (800-843-7625, www.prudential.com/community/spirit). Rewards students ages 11 to 19 who have started volunteer community service programs in their region. Scholarships range from $1,000 to $5,000.

- **The Scholastic Art & Writing Awards** (212-343-6493, http://scholastic.com/artandwriting). More than 1,000 prizes awarded in a wide range of art and writing categories. Prizes start at $100 and can climb as high as $20,000.

Ben Kaplan won $90,000 in scholarships—enough to cover virtually the entire cost of his Harvard education. He is the best-selling author of two books, *How to Go to College Almost for Free and The Scholarship Scouting Report* (HarperCollins), and is the founder of the ScholarshipCoach.com Web site.

Scholarship Warning

If your child wins an outside award from a fraternal association, union or private foundation, many schools reduce your aid package by the amount of the scholarship. Try to convince the school to reduce the loan and work-study portions of the package rather than grant money dollar for dollar.

Kalman A. Chany, president, Campus Consultants Inc., financial-aid consulting firm, New York, and author of *Paying for College Without Going Broke* (Random House/Princeton Review).

National Merit Scholarships

More than 7,900 students (finalists) receive National Merit Scholarships each year, in amounts ranging from $500 to $10,000.

1. About 2,000 receive a one-time award of $2,000 directly from the National Merit Scholarship Corporation every year.

2. About 1,200 finalists receive awards provided by corporations, company foundations and other business organizations. These corporate-sponsored awards range from a single payment of $2,000 to $5,000 to a renewable, yearly stipend of between $1,000 and $5,000 (totaling up to $20,000).

3. About 4,000 finalists receive renewable awards from $250 to $2000 per year from colleges and universities. College-sponsored awards must be used at the college or university that financed it.

National Merit Scholarship awards are based on a combination of financial need and student scores on a national examination, the Preliminary Scholastic Aptitude Test/National Merit Scholarship

Your State College Or University May Be Your Best Deal

For in-state residents, state colleges and universities offer some of the best deals in education. The tuition will probably be far less than at a comparable private institution. For example, the University of California charges California residents as little as $0 in tuition (but almost $3,000 in mandatory fees), while Stanford University—a private California university—has tuition that runs to $25,917. *Added bonus:* State colleges and universities favor in-state residents for financial aid.

Warning: If your child is looking at a state college or university outside your home state, be aware that the tuition could be as costly as at private institutions.

Contact your child's high school college adviser for more information. If you still have questions, call the National Merit Scholarship Corporation at 847-866-5100.

Scholarship Scams

Most scholarships can be researched in the library and on the Internet at little or no cost. But if you have neither the time nor inclination to do the work, scholarship services will save you from doing the research on your own. *Warning:* Be sure to use a service that is legitimate.

One of the first, key signs that a scholarship offer could be a scam is if the service says it can guarantee a scholarship or grant. *Remember:* Scholarships can never be guaranteed. And paying an advance fee will not secure you a financial award. Most likely, if you do pay a fee for a scholarship, even under a money-back guarantee, you won't receive the scholarship *or* your refund.

Here are some things to watch out for:

- Don't believe companies that tell you you can't get the same information anywhere else.

- Don't pay for lists of sources before you do your own research.

- Beware of companies that say you need to give them your credit card or bank account number so they can hold a scholarship or grant for your child. Legitimate scholarships will never require this.

- Avoid companies that say they'll do *all* the work for you. You will always have to fill out any legitimate scholarship paperwork yourself.

- Watch out for companies that tell you the scholarship will cost you money. Scholarships and grants are created to *save* you money and should never have a fee attached.

- Never believe companies that call you to tell you that your child has been selected as a finalist in a contest he/she never entered. Legitimate scholarship and grant organizations do not solicit you. You must go to them.

For more information on scholarship fraud, contact the Federal Trade Commission at 202-326-2222, www.ftc.gov.

Consider a Community College

To save money, your child should consider getting a two-year associates degree, or taking the first two years of classes at a community college and then completing a four-year degree elsewhere. Community colleges are partially funded by local and state tax revenues, so their classes usually cost far less than those at four-year schools.

Most community colleges provide the same course of study as the first two years of a four-year college. *Warning:* If your child begins at a community college and plans to continue on to complete a bachelor's degree, make sure he/she takes courses with credits that will transfer to a four-year school.

How You Save

Varied Tuition Costs   A local community college might cost less than one that's further away. In some states, like New Jersey, the tuition at a community college is less expensive for students from the county or area of the school. In other states, like New York, all state residents pay the same tuition.

Savings on Room and Board   Community colleges do not have dorms, so students may save on room and board by living at home. The cost of commuting is usually minimal.

Establish Residency in A New State

The least expensive way to attend a state college or university outside your home state is for your child to become a resident of that state.

Each state has its own way of determining who is an in-state student. *What your child needs:* A driver's license in the state for six months to a year or more; a car registered in the state; established bank accounts; a permanent address; and that he/she be registered to vote. If feasible, your child should move to the new state and work there for a year before starting college.

The state college or university your child is interested in attending should be able to tell you the quickest way to establish residency.

Working for a Low-Cost Education

The federal government and the armed forces offer a variety of programs in which college students work or provide military service in exchange for financial aid.

Federal Work-Study Programs

Federal work-study (FWS) programs provide part-time jobs for undergraduate and graduate students who demonstrate financial need. These programs encourage community service and work related to a student's course of study.

Most FWS jobs are on-campus in one of the school's service departments. For example, students may work in the cafeteria, financial aid office or research library. FWS payment is dependent upon individual school policy, and is either paid to students or applied directly to their college cost. For information on how to apply call 800-433-3243, www.fafsa.ed.gov.

Overseas Bargains

College abroad can be a great education at reasonable cost. US students who matriculate in other countries often find they learn as much from simply living elsewhere as they do in classes. Tuition at top universities is surprisingly affordable.

Example: Oxford University in England costs one-half to two-thirds as much as Harvard—and room and board costs less, too. McGill University in Canada can cost one-fourth as much as Harvard.

Financial aid is available through the Stafford Loan program.

Kalman A. Chany, president, Campus Consultants Inc., financial-aid consulting firm, New York, and author of *Paying for College Without Going Broke* (Random House/ Princeton Review).

AmeriCorps

AmeriCorps is a federal work-study service organization with more than 450 different national service programs around the country. Workers earn education vouchers in exchange for one to two years of national service. *The awards:* One year full-time service (1,700 hours) $4,725; one year part-time service (900 hours) $2,362.50. Money may be used to help pay back student loans or finance college, graduate school or vocational school tuition. *Warning:* Your child may be able to make more money for college working at a regular job.

AmeriCorps members receive a modest living allowance of approximately $150 a week—it varies by location. Members must cover their own housing and meal expenses using this allowance. Health insurance is also provided, and some members may receive child-care assistance.

Service opportunities are available in the areas of education, public safety, human needs and the environment. Contact:

- **AmeriCorps** at 800-942-2677, www.americorps.org.
- **AmeriCorps National Civilian Community Corps** at 202-606-5000, www.americorps.org/nccc.

The National Civilian Community Corps is AmeriCorps' residential national service program for 18- to 24-year-olds. The program is full time only and runs for 10 months. Members receive a modest bi-weekly allowance, and live in dormitory-style housing and receive meals. Five campuses participate in this program.

The award: After the full 10 months are completed, members receive $4,725 to help pay off their student loans or to pay for future educational expenses. Health insurance is part of their membership. *Contact:* 800-942-2677.

ROTC

The US Armed Forces sponsors the Reserve Officers Training Corps (ROTC), a federal, merit-based scholarship program available at many colleges and universities. *Note:* ROTC programs are highly competitive and preference is sometimes given to students studying nursing, engineering, science or business. Scholarships pay up to $16,000 a year of college tuition, plus money toward textbooks and a small yearly stipend.

In addition to their regular classes, ROTC students must attend special classes sponsored by the US Armed Forces. Upon graduation, they are committed to serve as active-duty officers for four years in the branch of service that sponsored their ROTC program.

For information about available programs, contact military recruiters, look in your college catalogs or call 800-USA-ROTC, www.armyrotc.com. The Navy ROTC program also offers a special two-year program for college juniors and senior. For information call 800-USA-NAVY, www.cnet.navy.mil/nrotc/nrotc.htm.

How to Get Federal Financial Aid

There are government grants and loans, as well as campus-based federal programs, that may be able to assist you in paying for your child's college education.

To be eligible for federal financial aid, a student must:

- Be a citizen of the US.
- Have a high school diploma or General Education Development (GED) Certificate.
- Be working toward a degree or certificate in an eligible educational program.
- Have financial need (except for loan programs).
- Not be in default on a previous federal loan or owe a refund from a previous federal grant.

Defining Financial-Aid Eligibility

Most financial-aid programs provide funds only to those who are considered *dependent* by federal law and *in need* of federal assistance.

What Is Dependency? According to the law, students are considered dependent if they:

- Are 22 years old or younger.
- Are not veterans of the US Armed Forces.
- Are not enrolled in graduate or professional programs.
- Are not married.
- Are not or were not orphans or wards of the court until age 18.
- Do not have legal dependents.

What Is Financial Need? The federal government determines dependent students' financial need by looking at both their own and their parents' income and assets. They consider 5.6% of parental assets and 35% of the student's assets to be available to pay for tuition. *Caution:* Don't put too many assets in your children's names.

Independents Are Not Ignored Students not considered dependents can receive financial aid. Federal student aid for independent students does not take parental assets into account at all. Check your child's options out with the aid administrator at the schools to which he/she is applying.

Applying for Federal Financial Aid

To apply for federal financial aid, your child must file a Free Application for Federal Student Aid (FAFSA). You can get an application from your child's high school or contact the Federal Student Aid Information Center, Box 84, Washington, DC 20044, or call 800-433-3243, www.fafsa.ed.gov.

Campus-Free Programs

Here are a few colleges and universities that offer college degree programs through long-distance learning:

- **Bemidji State University,** Center for Extended Learning, 1500 Birchmont Dr., NE, Bemidji, MN 56601-2699, 218-755-3924; www.bemidji.msus.edu. Accredited by the **North Central Association of Colleges and Schools.**

- **California College for Health Sciences**, 2423 Hoover Ave., National City, CA 91950, 800-221-7374 or 619-477-4800; www.cchs.edu. Offers BS degrees in health services and business. Accredited by the **National Home Study Council** and **Career College Association**.

- **Central Michigan University Distance and Distributed Learning**, 802 Industrial Ave., Mount Pleasant, MI 48858, 800-688-4268; www.cmich.edu. Offers BS degrees in business. Accredited by the **North Central Association of Colleges and Schools.**

- **Indiana University**, School of Continuing Studies, Owen Hall 001, 790 E. Kirkwood Ave., Bloomington, IN 47405, 800-334-1011; www.indiana.edu. Offers BA degrees in general studies. Accredited by the **North Central Association of Colleges and Schools.**

Free College Is Not Just a Fantasy

- **Berea College,** Admissions Office, Berea, KY 40404, 800-326-5948; www.berea.edu. Offers a wide variety of liberal arts majors, such as agriculture, art, classical languages and mathematics.

- **Cooper Union for the Advancement of Science and Art**, Office of Admissions, 41 Cooper Square, New York, NY 10003, 212-353-4120; www.cooper.edu. Specializes in top-quality architecture, graphic design, engineering and fine arts educations.

- **Williamson Free School of Mechanical Trade**, Office of Admissions, 106 S. New Middletown Rd., Media, PA 19063, 610-566-1776; www.williamson school.org. Offers degrees in horticulture, carpentry, brick masonry, machine shop and other mechanical trades.

Qualifying for Federal Financial Aid

Within a month of filing a FAFSA, your child will receive a Student Aid Report (SAR) stating your expected family contribution (EFC). This will determine how much you're expected to contribute to your child's college education, and whether your family qualifies for aid. Your child's financial need is determined by subtracting your EFC from the cost of attendance.

If you have not heard anything for more than a month, you can check on the status of your child's FAFSA. *Contact:* Federal Student Aid Information Center, 319-337-5665.

Watch Out for Deadlines

The FAFSA has a strict deadline for applications. Students cannot apply for aid before January 1 of the year they want to attend school but should apply as soon after this date as possible.

Each college and university sets its own deadlines for school-administered financial aid. Deadlines are often early in the calendar year, and students must meet them in order to receive funding. Get the deadline date from the financial-aid administrator at each school.

Getting Four Full Years of Aid

Theoretically, as long as your child stays in the same school, and the school's budget does not change dramatically, you should receive the same amount of aid each school year by resubmitting a FAFSA.

If your child changes schools, federal financial aid doesn't automatically follow. Check with the new school to find out what steps you must take to continue receiving aid. *Good news:* If your child transfers to a more expensive school, the amount of federal aid you receive may increase.

On-Line Help

The US Department of Education's Web site, www.ed.gov, offers financial-aid applications and guidance. The National Association of Student Financial Aid Administrator's Web site, www.finaid.org, has links to financial-aid offices at many universities and colleges.

Money for College from the Federal Government

The federal government has several programs that can save you money on college tuition. Eligibility, availability and funding may change from year to year.

Pell Grants

Students who demonstrate the greatest financial need based on federal standards are eligible for Federal Pell Grants of up to $2,700 a year. The amount of the grant depends on a combination of your expected family contribution and the tuition at the college where your child enrolls. Part-time students are eligible, although the amount of the grant will be less than that for full-time students. Pell Grants are particularly useful for older students who are beginning or returning to college while also managing a profession and a family.

Pell Grants are awarded by the government, but disbursed by individual colleges. Grant funds may be applied directly to your child's school costs, paid to your child directly by check or distributed through a combination of these methods. Make sure that the school tells you in writing how and when your child will be paid, and how much the award will be.

It is important that your child knows how much money to expect and when to expect it. Funds must be paid out at least once per term (semester, trimester or quarter). Schools that don't use the traditional terms must distribute funds at least twice during the academic year.

Federal Supplemental Educational Opportunity Grants

Federal Supplemental Educational Opportunity Grants (FSEOGs) are gift aid for undergraduates with exceptional financial need. They are federal grants administered directly by the financial aid office at each participating school. FSEOGs are awarded only to undergraduate students who have not yet earned a bachelor's or professional degree.

Federal Pell Grant recipients are given preference for FSEOGs. Unlike Pell Grants, which are administered by the government and guaranteed to all eligible students at a participating school, FSEOGs are only available to recipients selected by each college, and awards are based on the availability of funds at each school.

How much aid students receive depends on their financial need, the amount of other aid they are offered and the availability of funds at their school. Your child could get between $100 and $4,000 a year.

FSEOG funds may be applied directly to school costs, paid to your child by check or distributed through a combination of these methods. Schools must pay FSEOG money to students at least once per term (semester, trimester or quarter).

Federal Student Loans

Stafford loans provide students with low-interest loans to help them meet the costs of attending colleges, universities and vocational and technical schools. Loans, unlike grants and scholarships, must eventually be paid back. In cases where there is proven financial need, the government will pay the interest due on these

Not Just for Undergraduates

Vista is the **AmeriCorps** program for college graduates. Like in the regular AmeriCorps, Vista workers receive a living stipend and money to repay their college loans in return for working at one of a variety of service jobs around the country. Call 800-942-2677 for more information.

Pay Less for Graduate School

One of the most cost-efficient ways to go to graduate school is to become a teaching assistant. Most PhD candidates compete for jobs as teaching assistants to fund their degrees. As a teaching assistant, your course work will be paid for by the university, you will probably receive a living stipend and the work you do is often complementary to your course of study.

loans so long as students remain in school at least half-time and make satisfactory progress. Once students have graduated, however, they are responsible for paying the interest themselves.

Eligibility for Stafford loans is based on federal financial-aid requirements. Students must also sign a statement of educational purpose that says they will only use the loan money for educational expenses. The application deadline for a Stafford loan is determined by your loan agency and the college your child attends.

Virtually all college students qualify for Stafford loans. But not every school participates in this program, so check with your school's financial administrator to find out whether you can apply.

Federal Parent Loans

Parent Loans for Undergraduate Students (PLUSs) allow you to borrow the total cost of tuition less the amount of financial aid your child is already eligible to receive.

To be eligible for a PLUS, you will be required to pass a credit check. If you fail the credit check, you can still receive a loan for your child if a friend or family member endorses the loan, promising to repay it if you fail to do so.

PLUS eligibility is not determined by financial need, but you must meet some general requirements such as having US citizenship. As with the Stafford loan, the college or university you are interested in will tell you how to borrow the money. Unlike the Stafford loan, however, the PLUS has interest payments that cannot be deferred until a later date.

Cutting the Cost of College Incidentals

Tuition is not the only cost involved in going to college. You'll also need to take into account the cost of school fees, books, room and board, travel expenses and general costs of living. But there are ways to save on these add-ons.

Room and Board

Many colleges and universities require students to live on campus during their freshman year and require freshman to have a meal plan as well. Other students may have these options:

Campus Dormitories They usually come with a five- to 21-meal plan (sometimes optional) and on-site security.

Campus Apartments They usually include a kitchenette and may have some campus security.

Off-Campus Housing or Apartments They often have a kitchenette, but offer no campus security. Depending on the college or university's location, even a 12-month lease may be more cost-efficient than on-campus housing. If your child wants to stay in the apartment over the summer (he/she may be working or attending summer school), one-year leases are appropriate. If not, look into nine-month leases or subletting the apartment during the summer.

Computers

On-campus computer stores frequently offer students discounts of around 10% on new computers, but check to be sure you're getting the best price. *Warning:* Don't choose a model until you have checked with the college's computer center and found out which system the school uses.

Consider investing in a laptop—it costs more, but can be brought along to lectures or the library.

Books and Textbooks

Most campus bookstores sell used books and they are always sold at a reduced price. *Caution:* Be sure to flip through the book to make sure the text can be clearly read. Some students highlight and heavily mark their books. Students can save even more money by selling books back to the bookstore when they are no longer needed.

Don't depend solely on the campus bookstore. Most college towns have more than one bookstore, so it's a good idea to shop around and compare prices. *Another source:* Enterprising students sometimes purchase bulk orders of their school's most popular textbooks and sell them to fellow students at better prices than the campus bookstore. Check out bulletin boards around campus or ask upperclassmen to find out any available deals.

Financial-aid offices are frequently willing to make adjustments to student budgets if students can document that their books and supplies cost more than average. Save your book receipts and don't be afraid to ask the financial-aid department for help if you think your book costs are excessive.

Alternatives to Expensive Private Schools

If you can't find the kind of education you want for your child in traditional public schools, there are other low- and no-cost options. See if your community offers:

More on Stafford Loans...

To get the best deal on Stafford student loans, it pays to shop around for a lender. Many offer incentives that can reduce the borrowing cost. These may include a 0.25% discount on the interest rate if your monthly payments are automatically deducted from your bank account...or a 2% rate reduction on the remaining portion of the loan after making 48 consecutive monthly payments on time. But even one late payment can wipe out this break.

Trap: Some colleges participate in the direct lending program for Stafford loans. If this is the case, you'll borrow directly from the government through the school's financial-aid office and will not be eligible for these incentives.

Kalman Chany, president, Campus Consultants Inc., 1202 Lexington Ave., New York 10028.

Housing that Pays for Itself

Save on boarding costs and even make a profit! Look into purchasing an apartment or small house near campus for your child to live in. Then hire your child as the building manager in exchange for free rent, and rent out the extra bedrooms.

Rental income should offset your maintenance costs. Plus, your mortgage payments will give you equity in an asset of value while payments for a dorm or apartment would not. You can then sell the house after your child graduates and get back some or all of your original investment, or possibly even make a profit.

Managing a house is not always an easy thing to do, however, so this option works best with mature, responsible students.

Magnet Schools

Magnet schools are free public schools that emphasize particular subjects and try to retain economic and cultural diversity. Students from the same school district compete for places at their area magnet schools. Areas of study may include science, the arts, languages.

For information about magnet schools: Magnet Schools of America (202-824-0672, www.magnet.edu). They will usually give you information on schools in your area over the phone, or you can buy their directory of more than 4,000 magnet schools in 43 states.

Charter Schools

Charter schools—grades K through 12—use alternative teaching methods not usually found in traditional classrooms. They're funded by the federal government and do not have enrollment restrictions. A charter school will be closed if it does not achieve federally mandated educational results. Almost all states require that these schools abide by health, safety and civil rights laws.

For information about charter schools: The Center for Education Reform (800-521-2118, www.edreform.com) or the US Charter School Web site (www.uscharterschools.org), which maintains a detailed glossary of charter schools listed by state, as well as links to other charter-school Web sites.

Parochial Schools

Parochial schools often offer a lower-cost alternative to private schools. In addition to a general education, they teach students the values of the particular religious organization that maintains the school. Your child need not belong to the religion espoused by the school, but he/she may receive instruction in that religion. Parochial schools use discretion over whom they will accept. Throughout the US, parochial schools are maintained by Roman Catholic parishes, a variety of Protestant churches and Jewish organizations.

Bargains in Top-Notch K–12 Educations

Whether you want to finance your child's private elementary or high school education, or pay for after-school or weekend activities, there are plenty of ways to save.

Corporate Financial Aid

Your own employer may offer financial aid for your child's pre-college education. Corporate giving guidelines describe the amount of funding allocated to education grants. Some corporations offer no-strings-attached cash grants while others give on a matching basis. Matching basis funding means you have to match

a certain percentage of the amount you receive from the company (or find another source to match it).

To find corporate/employee programs that offer educational funding, look in Laurie Blum's *Free Money for Private Schools* (published in 1992 by Simon and Schuster and now out of print) at your local library. Once you locate a corporation that provides grants for education, get a copy of their *Programs and Guidelines* brochure or annual report. Send your request for more information with a self-addressed, stamped envelope to the Foundation or Fund department.

A few corporations that offer grant assistance both locally and nationally are American Honda Motor Company in California, General Electric Company in Stamford, Connecticut and Hitachi Foundation in Washington, DC.

Private School-Sponsored Financial Aid

Private schools offer their own financial aid to students from a variety of income levels. Ask a school's financial-assistance office for further information about qualifications, application procedures and deadlines. Schools often give financial awards based on athletic or artistic merit, academic merit and financial need. Most private schools give partial scholarships to assist in paying expensive tuition costs, and partial assistance can really make a difference.

Summer School Can Save Time And Money

Students who want to save money should consider taking summer classes at their local community college.

Taking summer classes at a less expensive school will not only reduce your costs, but may also allow your child to graduate sooner. Summer classes are also a great way to alleviate some of the pressure of an overloaded semester. They tend to be a little more lenient academically and smaller in size, which means that the professor is more accessible for one-on-one discussions and questions.

Students should always make sure that any course credits are transferable to their primary school before they enroll in a summer class.

Free (and Almost Free) College for Senior Citizens

More than 300 colleges and universities across the country have special programs for seniors who are interested in going back to school.

This usually means free or low-cost tuition. Sometimes there are also discounts on school fees, books and even housing. The tuition and basic fees for seniors are the lowest charged to any student.

Some essentials like books aren't always discounted, and health insurance, parking and fees for degree-seeking candidates may also be full price or unavailable. Contact the school you wish to attend and ask how to apply for a discount or waiver.

Listen in for Free

At some schools, seniors can audit classes for free. You won't receive academic credit, but you can brush up on your knowledge of history, learn how to use the Internet or take that poetry course you've always dreamed of without making a dent in your wallet. You usually need to get permission from the professor or the department that schedules the class, but permission is rarely denied.

After-School Programs

You don't have to spend a fortune to send your children to after-school activities that will enhance their lives and not empty your wallet.

School-Based Programs

Most public schools offer no-cost after-school programs for five- to 13-year-olds. Check with the school guidance office to see what free programs are available in your town.

Community-Based Programs

Check out your local community center, Y or JCC—they may offer children's programs either free or at low cost.

Most auditors are asked not to engage in class discussions so that they don't reduce the time available for paying students. Auditors are also not required to take any tests or examinations, and they do not receive a class grade.

Finding the Right Program for You

State universities are your best bet for special senior programs.

At least 30 state colleges across the nation have programs and discounts for senior auditors. Most schools require that you be age 60 or older to receive free-course privileges. Some schools restrict the privileges to residents of their own state. For example, the University of Colorado at Boulder (303-492-8484, www.colorado.edu) allows Colorado citizens ages 55 or older to audit classes for free.

Some schools, like the University of Arkansas (479-575-2000, www.uark.edu), allow persons 60 and older from any state to take or audit classes free of charge. They also offer campus housing and meal plans to senior students taking a full course load (usually at least 12 credits or four classes). Boston University (617-353-9852, www.bu.edu) permits people 60 and older from any state to audit courses for $35 a course year-round, and offers some university housing in the summer.

To find out about senior programs at a college or university near you, call the school's admissions office.

15

Cutting Insurance Costs

Most People Fail to Insure Their Most Important Asset

The odds are one in four that a 35-year-old man will miss more than 90 consecutive days of work due to an illness or injury.

The right disability insurance protects you and your family against the loss of your income in such situations. To get the most for your money:

Don't Count on Your Employer

Purchase your own individual disability insurance rather than settling for the coverage provided through your employer.

A privately purchased policy gives you far stronger rights and outstanding remedies against your insurance company if it denies your claim or fails to pay benefits promptly. Other advantages:

- You can obtain more and broader coverage than employer-provided policies typically provide.

Comparison Shop For Insurance

Comparison shop for insurance at www.answerfinancial.com...www.insurance.com...www.insweb.com...and www.pivot.com. Insurance sites have different companies as partners, so no one site gives you a full view of what is available.

Also: Contact your state insurance department for a list of carriers licensed to sell the product you want—and details on complaint records on insurers.

To locate your state insurance department: www.naic.org.

Business Week, 1221 Avenue of the Americas, New York 10020.

- Any benefits you receive are tax free if you pay premiums personally. Benefits from employer-provided insurance are taxable.
- Your company-sponsored insurance plan will offset whatever benefits you qualify for by subtracting payments under your state disability insurance, workers' compensation and Social Security disability.

Result: The disability payments you receive under a company-paid policy can be pitifully small—sometimes as low as $50 a month.

The Best Policy

Buy the maximum amount of individual disability coverage you can afford. That amount is determined by your annual income and will generally replace no more than 60% of your earnings. So if you make $100,000 a year, your maximum annual benefit would be $60,000.

Be prepared to provide income tax returns for the last three years to document your past earnings.

If you are self-employed, your benefits will be based on net earnings after business expenses, rather than gross business earnings.

Key requirements of any individual disability insurance policy:

Noncancellable The insurance company can never pull out of your state, regardless of how many of its policyholders later become disabled and file claims. The only way that you can lose this coverage is if you don't pay your premium within the policy grace period.

Guaranteed Renewable to Age 65 The insurer can never increase your original premium, no matter how many policyholders become sick or injured...and no matter how much money the company is losing on its disability business.

Covers Inability to Work at Your *Own Occupation* You will receive benefits if you can no longer do the important duties of your occupation at the time you became sick or injured—even if you could work full-time in a different occupation.

Example: A heart surgeon develops a tremor in his hands. If he has "own occupation" coverage and can no longer perform surgery, he would receive total disability benefits—even if he could work full-time as a general practitioner.

Avoid *Any Occupation* Coverage Although this type of protection is much cheaper, it pays benefits only if you are unable to perform *any* occupation for which you have been trained or educated...or are suited.

Example: The heart surgeon would not qualify for benefits if he could work as a high school science teacher.

Obtain the Longest Benefit Period in Your *Own Occupation* for as Long as Possible You want this coverage to last your lifetime...or at least until you reach age 65. But be prepared to negotiate. Insurance companies may initially offer it for no more than two, five or 10 years—and sometimes for as little as one year. However, any period for which you are protected in your own occupation is better than having to meet Social Security's stricter standard of "any occupation."

90-Day Wait (*Elimination Period*) Before Collecting Benefits Have enough financial reserves to weather four-and-a-half months without any income. It will likely be that long before you receive your first disability benefit payment.

Since benefits are paid retroactively—and on a monthly basis—you must be disabled at least 30 days in addition to the 90-day elimination period before benefits begin. It usually takes two weeks to process your first check, so the total wait before receiving any money is about 135 days (90 plus 30 plus 15). Extending the elimination period to 120 days or longer can cut premium costs, but the savings usually are not worth the longer wait.

Include residual coverage as an option—so if you become able to resume some but not all of your duties and have some loss of earnings, you will be entitled to partial disability benefits.

Avoid Policies that Have a *Fraud Exception* This allows an insurance company to cancel your policy if it discovers at any time that you fraudulently misstated any answer that affected its risk of insuring you.

Look for policies with a two-year contestability period. Then, after two years, the company can't cancel your policy even if there is misinformation. Options on the fraud exception vary by state.

Fraud exception or not, answer application questions honestly. Don't overstate income or conceal medical problems. Make sure you read the occupational, medical and financial questions yourself. A company with a two-year contestability clause has the right to rescind a policy within the first two years if it discovers you have made material misstatements.

Cost-of-Living Adjustment If you are young and expect to earn a lot, paying extra for this benefit is money well spent. If you become disabled at age 40, cost-of-living adjustments will keep you ahead of inflation for the next 25 years.

What You'll Pay

Premiums can equal or exceed those of life insurance.

Example: A 40-year-old white-collar professional earning $75,000 a year would pay an annual premium of $1,956 for an "own occupation" coverage. The policy would provide $3,900 per month in benefits ($46,800 a year), replacing a little more than

How to Complain About Or Choose an Insurance Policy

- If you have complaints, concerns or queries about your insurance policy, call the **National Insurance Consumer Helpline** at 800-942-4242.

- ***Best Insurance Reports***, the publication of **A.M. Best Company**, a leading financial rating organization, ranks many insurance products and is a terrific source for consumers. It is available at most public libraries and at the company's Web site, www.ambest.com.

Variable-Life Insurance Trap

Costs may go up—or the policy may not last as long—when investment values go down. In a level-death-benefit policy, a rising account value lowers the "amount at risk"—the difference between the death benefit and the account value—which, in turn, lowers insurance charges. Conversely, a falling account value increases insurance charges, which can have a snowball effect if prolonged.

Better for most people: Term insurance and mutual funds rather than a variable policy.

James Hunt, a life insurance actuary for Consumer Federation of America, 1424 16 St. NW, Ste. 604, Washington, DC 20036. www.consumerfed.org.

60% of his/her earnings, up to age 65. If he added a 3% cost-of-living adjustment, the premium would jump about $300 to $2,250 a year.

Where to Buy

Purchase disability insurance from a licensed agent who has shopped the lowest rates and provided you with the most generous coverage available. Your agent can be helpful should you ever need to upgrade your coverage or file a claim.

Start by finding out who are the licensed and appointed agents in your area from these leading insurers:

- **Berkshire Life** (800-819-2468, www.berkshirelife.com)
- **Guardian** (800-933-3303, www.glic.com)
- **MassMutual** (800-272-2216, www.massmutual.com)
- **Northwestern Mutual** (414-271-1444, www.northwesternmutual.com)
- **UnumProvident** (800-421-0344, www.unum.com)

There are no Web sites that compare the rates of individual disability coverage from insurance carriers. Contact the agents or the companies individually. You can also get this insurance through professional and trade associations.

Frank N. Darras, managing partner in the law firm of Shernoff, Bidart & Darras, 600 S. Indian Hill Blvd., Claremont, CA 91711. He has been involved in more than 5,500 disability insurance cases and is considered the nation's leading expert on the subject.

When Term Insurance Is Right for You

Term insurance is appropriate for almost everybody—even people in their 60s can find good rates these days. Intense competition among life insurance companies means that many policies cost less than half what they did six or seven years ago. And toll-free phone numbers and the Internet have made it much easier and less time-consuming to compare the rates of one company with those of another.

Understanding Term Insurance

Unlike a cash-value policy, which has an insurance portion and an investment portion, a term policy is pure insurance coverage.

The annual premium you pay covers the cost of your insurance benefit—which is the face value of the policy. Once you pass the physical exam and qualify for an insurer's term policy, you never have to take another exam.

Your policy can usually be converted into a cash-value policy later in life—if you decide you need the other type of insurance.

Important: Term insurance lets you keep your options open to switch to a cash-value policy later. But if you start with a cash-value policy, you can't switch to term without paying a surrender fee.

The two types of term insurance:

Annual Renewable Term covers you for a 12-month period. It charges premiums that increase every year. To make the arrangement more affordable, companies typically charge bargain-basement rates during the first few years and then sharply increase the premiums after that.

Level Premium Term charges the same fixed annual premium for set periods—usually 10, 15 or 20 years. Even though their initial premiums are usually higher than those for annual renewable term, level-term policies usually cost less over the long term.

These days, the best deals are 20-year, level-term policies.

Meeting the Requirements

You will be charged a lower premium if you qualify for "preferred risk" status. This status typically covers nonsmokers who have no medical problems and come from healthy families. For you to qualify, most insurers insist that neither parent has died of cancer before age 60.

Expect the insurance company or agent to ask what seems like a lot of intrusive personal questions at the outset. This means they are being thorough about screening applicants.

Also, don't expect to qualify for the best rates if you are fond of dangerous sports. Scuba diving, private airplane flying, bungee jumping and hang gliding will place you in a higher-risk—and higher-cost—category.

If you lie about your activities on the application, the insurer may challenge a death claim later. If you have a chronic health problem—such as diabetes or epilepsy—it is beneficial to submit applications to several different insurers. Each insurance company takes a different approach to chronic illnesses. One insurer may approve someone with a particular health problem, while another carrier may reject the same person. Often this type of underwriting analysis is done on a case-by-case basis.

If there are reasons why you believe your condition is not as grave as it may seem, let the insurer know. It is possible that after checking with your physicians, the insurer could accept you anyway.

Comparing Costs

Because the life insurance landscape is changing so rapidly, it is beneficial to periodically compare the cost of your current policy to new ones in the marketplace. Reevaluate your policy at least every five years.

Whole-Life Insurance: Yes? No?

Whole-life insurance makes sense under certain circumstances if you consider it a long-term *investment* vehicle.

Return on whole-life policies is based on what the insurer earns on its own portfolio. Returns vary over time—but are tax free if you hold the policy until you die. So if the insurer gets good, steady returns for several decades, total return may be better than you would get by buying term insurance for less than the whole-life premium and investing the rest yourself.

If you want to cancel a whole-life policy: Consider a tax-free exchange for a low-load variable annuity—an insurance vehicle in which you choose the investments—since cashing out a whole-life policy is a taxable event. Choose an annuity with low expenses and no surrender charge.

Glenn Daily, fee-only insurance consultant, New York. www.glenndaily.com.

Group Coverage

Before purchasing an individual policy, see if any clubs, fraternities, alumni groups or professional associations you belong to offer group insurance plans. Group plans are usually considerably less expensive than individual plans.

Shopping Around

You can probably complete your comparison shopping in less than an hour.

Getting started: Contact Ameritas (800-552-3553, www.ameritas direct.com), a leader in low-cost term insurance products, to get a baseline figure. Its policies are also convertible to low-load, cash-value policies.

Two insurers with low-cost policies sold by agents are:

- **First Colony Life,** a subsidiary of GE Financial Assurance (888-325-5433, www.gefinancialassurance.com).

- **Lincoln Life** (800-454-6265, www.lincolnlife.com).

Also contact one or more Internet brokers, such as Quotesmith. com (800-431-1147, www.quotesmith.com).

Avoid Most Bells and Whistles

Most of the extras that can be attached to a term policy aren't worth it.

Example: Avoid buying an accidental-death-benefit rider. Ask yourself why your beneficiaries would need more money if you die in an accident rather than as a result of an illness. Usually, there is no good reason.

However, there are a few policy provisions that can be helpful. They include:

Waiver of Premium If you don't have good disability coverage at work, this pays insurance premiums if you become disabled and have trouble paying them.

Accelerated Death Benefit This pays a portion of the death benefit before you die and can help if you have a few months to live and need money to pay medical bills…to stay home…or to take a last vacation. There is usually no charge for this rider.

Glenn Daily, one of the country's top life insurance experts and a fee-only insurance consultant, New York.

Save on Car Insurance

Some features of auto coverage are required, some are desirable and some are a waste of money. By putting your money only in the coverage that makes sense for you, you can shrink your auto insurance premiums dramatically.

Caution: Don't cut back to the point where your family—and your assets—are inadequately protected.

Required Coverage

Most states require "bodily injury liability insurance." This covers medical treatment for injury caused by you to your passengers, as well as to other drivers and their passengers—even pedestrians. Some suggestions:

- **At least $100,000 per person per accident of bodily injury coverage.**
- **Property damage coverage.** This covers repairing or replacing other motorists' cars and property.
- **Collision coverage.** If you lease or finance your car, you are required to carry coverage to handle damage to it.

  You can *choose* to carry collision coverage if you own your car outright.

- **Comprehensive insurance.** Covers theft of your vehicle and damage to it (other than by way of accident). Again, if you lease or finance your car, you're required to carry comprehensive coverage. It's optional if you own the car.

Savings Strategies

Insurance premiums vary from company to company...and from policy to policy. It's essential to comparison shop.

Several Web sites show sample rates to assist you. It's best to see if your state insurance department Web pages list this information—most do.

Other cost cutters:

Increase your deductible If you carry collision and/or comprehensive coverage, raise your deductible. Decide how much you can afford to pay out-of-pocket.

Example: Increasing the deductible from $200 to $500 on collision and/or comprehensive coverage can lower the cost of this coverage by almost 30%.

Drop Collision Coverage If your car is worth less than $3,000, you'll pay more in premiums over time than you would ever collect, even if the car were totaled. To determine your car's value, check the *Kelley Blue Book* in your library or at www.kbb.com.

Buy a Car that is Unlikely to Be Stolen Or one with low repair costs. Cars with high theft rates or which are expensive to repair have high insurance costs. Ask your insurance agent before buying.

Drop Towing Coverage This only pays if an accident renders your car undrivable. If you're a member of an auto club, such as AAA, you don't need this coverage, since they provide this service. Basic AAA membership costs $55 to $70 a year. www.aaa.com.

Drop Glass Coverage This feature covers the full cost of replacing broken glass, without a deductible. Sometimes it's built in to the comprehensive premium. If not, it can add 20% to auto insurance costs.

Car Insurance · Scam

Some sophisticated crooks have a scam which involves breaking into a car with out-of-state plates and stealing the insurance card. They call up the insurance company taking responsibility for an accident, and then call again posing as the victim. The thief brings a damaged car to the adjuster and gets a check. Your premiums go up. Avoid this by keeping your insurance card with you at all times instead of in the glove compartment.

Maximize Your Discounts

Most insurance companies offer various discounts. *But beware:* Some insurance companies with the highest prices offer the largest discounts—but still end up high in overall price. Make sure you get all the discounts you are entitled to, but shop around for the lowest price *after* discounts are applied. You're eligible if you:

- **Drive less than 10 miles to work.** Allstate, for example, discounts if you drive less than 7,500 miles annually. Other companies differ, so check with your insurer.
- **Drive a car that has safety equipment**—such as automatic seat belts, air bags, antilock brakes.
- **Have had no accidents or tickets within the last three to five years.** Taking a driver training course can also result in savings if you're under age 25—one course may cut premiums for several years.
- **Insure more than one car on your policy**—or insure your home with the same insurance carrier that insures your car.
- **Are in a special category.** You're eligible for discounts if you fit a certain profile, such as:

  - ☐ **Age 50-plus and belonging to AARP.** The Hartford's AARP Auto Insurance Program, http://aarp.thehartford.com, offers AARP members discounts of up to 40%. But shop around—their rates are frequently not the lowest.
  - ☐ **Teachers who belong to a state education association or the National Education Association** (www.nea.org) can get a discount from Horace Mann Insurance Company (www.horacemann.com) in most states.
  - ☐ **Individuals with a college degree in certain engineering or science-related fields** in some Western states. These people can get a discount from the 21st Century Group (www.i21.com) and Argonaut Insurance Company (www.argonautgroup.com).
  - ☐ **Active and retired armed services personnel.** They can save by going to USAA (www.usaa.com).

Bonus: If you buy insurance on-line through Progressive Insurance Co. (www.progressive.com) or Reliance Direct Insurance Co. (www.reliancedirect.com), you'll get a nominal discount in addition to any others.

Robert Hunter, former Texas insurance commissioner and an insurance actuary with the Consumer Federation of America, 1424 16 St. NW, Ste. 604, Washington, DC 20036.

Ways to Bring Down Your Premium

Your Choice of Car

Although it might sound a little strange to start shopping for insurance before you even have a car, it's not. Different makes of cars have very different insurance costs, and choosing a car that's less expensive to insure can save you a lot of cash. For example, sports cars and sport-utility vehicles cost more to insure, while cars with excellent safety records are cheaper. In addition, safety features such as air bags, automatic seat belts and, in some cases, antilock brakes, can get you a discount on your premium.

Teenage Drivers

A teenage driver can add a considerable amount to your insurance costs. You can reduce your premium, however, by only insuring your teenager to drive your least expensive car.

Also, encourage your teen to study. Most companies give a discount to teen drivers who maintain higher than a B average. And if you send your child to a college more than 100 miles away from your home (without a car), you can get an even bigger discount on your premium.

Good Driving

If you haven't been at fault for an accident in more than 10 years, you're probably eligible for as much as a 20% discount on medical and collision coverage. You can get a smaller discount for three or more years of clean driving. Also, companies award a 10% discount on the premium to drivers who pass a driver's safety training course. This discount could be void if you're over 65, however.

Older Drivers Only

The AARP 55 Alive Driver Safety Program is the nation's largest classroom driver improvement course designed for motorists age 50 and older. The eight-hour course is taught in two four-hour sessions spanning two days and costs $10. There are no tests and it is open to AARP members and nonmembers. Graduates may be eligible to receive a state-mandated multiyear discount on their auto insurance premiums.

Antitheft Devices

Buying a car with an antitheft device, or installing one yourself, can reduce your premium. In most cases, it will save you 10% on your premium, but certain devices, such as the kill switches installed in many Ford and GM cars, may cut your costs up to 25%.

When to Stay Put

If you've recently received a few traffic violations, consider staying with your old insurance company instead of looking for a new policy. Tickets will immediately affect the pricing of a new policy by a new company—but they often take longer to affect the price of your current one.

Car Pool Insurance

Most auto insurance policies provide liability protection if you have an accident while driving a work car pool. But some policies consider car pool driving a business use and require extra or different coverage. Rules vary by company and region—ask your agent.

Even if you are covered: Consider boosting medical-payments coverage from the standard $2,000 to $5,000 per person. This pays for injuries to passengers no matter who is at fault—and covers injuries when someone is getting into or out of your car.

Madelyn Flannagan, vice president, research and education, Independent Insurance Agents of America, Alexandria, VA. www.independentagent.com.

Multiple Cars

Insurance companies provide discounts when you put more than one car on your policy. In such cases, RVs and even trailers count as cars. Also, companies often reduce your premiums if you use them for more than one kind of insurance. So find out what your life insurance or health insurance company charges for car insurance.

Drive Less

A car that is used every day for business costs more to insure than a car used only for pleasure. Consider declaring your car a pleasure vehicle and taking public transportation to work to cut your premium costs. Or, if you have to drive to work, join a car pool. Putting less than 7,500 miles a year on your car can also qualify you for a discount.

If you're planning on not using your car for a month or more, inform your insurance company. They'll deduct your collision coverage for the time your car is not in use.

Garaging It

Drivers who live in certain urban areas are forced to pay a larger premium because of the risk of theft and break-ins. Putting your car in a garage can significantly lower your payment. Even in a suburb, garaging your car reduces wear and tear, and will get you a lower rate.

There's a Price for Value

Just because you're getting the best price for a premium doesn't always mean that you're getting the best deal. When shopping for premiums, talk to other policyholders about collecting claims, customer service and repairs. If they have had any problems, consider trying another company. Also check the state insurance department complaint record on the company.

Check for Gaps in Home Insurance Coverage

Replacement Value Coverage Items you own drop in value greatly as soon as they become "used." If your insurance covers only their market value, it won't pay enough to replace them. Make sure your insurance provides "replacement value" protection.

Key: If you live in an older house, have replacement value coverage sufficient to bring the house up to current building code standards if you have to rebuild. If your insurer doesn't offer replacement value coverage, put an inflation rider on your policy to ensure adequate protection.

Excluded Items Standard homeowner's policies don't cover jewelry over $5,000 in value, furs, antiques, art works or boats above a specified size. Get separate riders to cover such items.

Absentee Coverage Some policies provide little or no coverage when you are away from home for more than 30 days. This could be a problem if you spend winters or summers in a separate vacation residence. You may need to modify your coverage if necessary.

Homeowner's Association Assessments It's possible for a homeowner's association to assess an individual for damage to community property. If you are a member of a homeowner's association, you may need a rider to protect against this.

Home-Office Liabilities Homeowner's policies generally don't cover business-related liabilities. So you may need either a rider to your homeowner's policy or separate coverage to protect against the loss of business property kept at home or the risk of liability to business visitors.

Lee Slavutin, MD, CPC, CLU, chairman, Stern Slavutin-2 Inc., an insurance and estate-planning firm, 530 Fifth Ave., New York 10036, www.sternslavutin.com.

How to Fight Your Insurers…and Win

Rely on Your Agent When you are shopping for auto or homeowner's insurance, one downside of buying through a discount direct-sales arrangement is that you won't have an agent in your corner.

An agent might be affiliated with the insurance company. But since he/she is paid in commissions, his loyalties lie with customers. The more successful the agent, the more powerful an advocate he is. The last thing the company wants to do is anger one of its revenue generators. If you run into any static, get help early. One call from an agent saying, "This is a good customer" or "I told him this was covered" goes a long way.

Don't Get Scared Off by Technicalities Meet deadlines and know precisely what your policy covers. But don't panic if you are denied a claim because of a missed deadline or misinterpretation of complex contractual language. Courts have consistently sided in favor of policyholders in these situations. A technicality should not be enough to prevent a legitimate claim.

Fight Even the Small Things If you believe your insurance company is trying to cheat you, it might be worth fighting over even minor problems.

Lowering the Cost Of Homeowner's Insurance

- **Increase your deductible.** By raising your deductible, you might be able to save as much as 25% on premiums.

- **Take more than one policy out with the same company.** For instance, use the same company for your auto or liability insurance as you do for your homeowner's policy.

- **Buy a new home.** Newer homes are generally in better structural condition than old fixer-uppers, so you may get lower premium rates.

- **Improve the security of your home** with new smoke detectors, alarms and similar devices.

- **Be a loyal customer.** Some insurers reward customer loyalty with lower rates if you've had a policy with them before.

- **Don't smoke.** There is a higher incidence of fire in the homes of smokers. Nonsmoking families may be able to get lower rates.

- **Ask about senior discounts.** If you're over age 60, the company may offer you a better deal.

The Truth About Mortgage Insurance

Home owners pay $1.3 billion a year for unnecessary mortgage insurance.

Key: Home buyers who make a down payment of less than 20% generally have to buy private mortgage insurance at an annual cost of $500 or more. But if the equity in your home has increased to 20% or more of the home's value, due to either loan payments or appreciation in value, you can ask to have the insurance canceled. Call your lender to see if you still need to carry this insurance.

Robert Hunter, director of insurance, Consumer Federation of America, 1424 16 St. NW, Ste. 604, Washington, DC 20036. www.consumerfed.org.

Example: A client who fought a $48 claim refusal wound up winning a $4.5 million judgment. The jury wanted to punish the insurer for its lack of ethics.

This is extreme, but anyone who feels an insurance company is doing him wrong should consider standing up to it.

Contact Your State's Department of Insurance Before You Go to Court— but don't be surprised if it sides with the insurance company. Every state has an office that handles consumer insurance problems— the phone numbers are listed in your phone book's state government listings.

Advice is generally free. Unfortunately, many state insurance commissioners go on to high-paying jobs with insurance companies, so that's where their sympathies lie.

California, Illinois and New York have slightly better records. But even in these states, there are problems.

Get Everything in Writing In order to contest an insurance company's decision, you need the specific reasons for that decision on paper.

Move Up the Ladder Send a summary of the problem, with *copies* of relevant documents—not originals—to the insurance company's claims department manager. Send letters by certified mail, with return receipt requested.

In most states, insurance companies are required by law to respond to complaints. If you don't hear back within three weeks, send a second letter with copies of everything you initially sent.

If that doesn't get you satisfaction, write to the insurance company's president—you can find the address in A.M. Best Company's *Rating Book of Insurance Companies*, available in public libraries or at www.ambest.com.

If you still can't resolve your problem, consult a lawyer on a contingency basis. In most states, the insurance company may have to pay punitive damages if you can show its conduct was flagrant.

Helpful: Even if you can't bring the insurance company around to your way of thinking, it might provide further explanation for its decision. These details could prove useful if you eventually take the insurance company to court.

William Shernoff, senior partner, Shernoff Bidart & Darras, a law firm specializing in bad-faith insurance litigation on behalf of consumers, 600 S. Indian Hill Blvd., Claremont, CA 91711. He is author of Fight Back & Win: How to Get Your HMO and Health Insurance to Pay Up (Capital).

Dental Insurance Plans

Most dental coverage is the result of an existing insurance package that employees receive from their employer. Employee dental plans vary. Some employers offer more than one dental plan. In fact, in some states, the right to choose

between two plans is the law. If you have a choice, the types of coverage are generally grouped into the following categories:

Direct Reimbursement Programs reimburse patients a percentage of the dollar amount spent on dental care, regardless of the type of treatment. This plan usually does not exclude particular types of treatment, and lets patients go the dentist of their choice.

Usual, Customary and Reasonable (UCR) Programs usually allow patients to go to the dentist of their choice. These plans pay a percentage of the dentist's fee or the administrator's reasonable or customary fee, whichever is less.

Table or Schedule of Allowance Programs offer a list of covered services with assigned dollar amounts. The dollar amounts represent just how much the plan will pay for those services that are covered. Most often, the dentist's full charge is not covered for each service. The patient pays the difference.

Preferred Provider Organization (PPO) Programs are plans under which contracting dentists agree to discount their fees as a financial incentive for patients to select their practices. A patient must choose a dentist in the plan to receive a reduction of benefits.

Capitation Programs pay contracted dentists a fixed amount (usually on a monthly basis) per enrolled family or patient. The dentists agree to provide specific types of treatment to the patients at no charge (some treatments may require a patient co-payment).

Dental Plan Exclusions

Some dental plans exclude treatments such as sealants, adult orthodontics, preexisting conditions, specialist referrals and other dental needs. Some also exclude treatment for family members.

The American Dental Association highly recommends that patients not let the exclusions and limitations in their dental plans determine their treatment decisions.

Individual Dental Insurance

Although dental insurance can help pay a portion of dental costs, experts do not recommend purchasing individual dental coverage. Dental coverage is not economical for those in individual plans because the premiums you pay are often more expensive than the cost of the dental treatment you receive.

However, a few companies offer dental benefits for individuals. Most of these plans are referral plans or buyers' clubs. Under these types of plans, an individual pays a monthly fee for access to a list of dentists who have agreed to a reduced fee schedule. Payment is made from the patient directly to the dentist.

The Truth About Rental Insurance

Not all renter's insurance policies are alike. With the less-expensive *actual cash value policies*, you recover what items were originally worth minus depreciation. That can be much less than it would cost to replace them today.

Better for most people: A replacement cost policy, which covers the cost to purchase new items. These policies cost an average of 15% to 20% more than actual cash value policies but are well worth it.

Richard J. Roll, president, American Homeowners Association, Stamford, CT.

Rental insurance is a must for people who live in apartments. Many people believe that a building's insurance covers their belongings in case of fire or other catastrophe. But that is not true —even in condominiums or co-ops. The only way to protect what you own, no matter where you live, is to have your own insurance policy.

And: Apartment owners need insurance even if they rent out the apartment.

Robert Irwin, real estate investor and broker, Los Angeles, and author of The 90-Second Lawyer (John Wiley & Sons).

Insurance for Your Pet

Pet insurance is increasingly worthwhile because of rising veterinary bills —especially for animals that are very young or old.

Ask your veterinarian to estimate typical medical expenses for a pet like yours—and if he/she recommends any particular policy. Basic plans cover illness and injury. More expensive policies cover dental and wellness services, including annual checkups and immunizations.

Leading insurers: Petshealth, 800-807-6724, www.petshealthplan.com... Premier Pet Insurance, 877-774-2273, www.ppins.com/index.asp...Veterinary Pet Insurance, 800-872-7387, www.petinsurance.com.

To evaluate plans: Ask which services are included and excluded... costs of premiums, deductibles and co-payments...timing and size of surcharges as pet's age...coverage for preexisting conditions...multiple-pet discounts.

Jay Tischendorf, DVM, associate veterinarian, Metzger Animal Hospital, State College, PA.

Do You Have the Best Insurance?

Health insurance may be one of the most economical investments you make. Without health insurance, every cent you save could be exhausted by a serious illness. Most health insurance plans cover hospital care and medical treatments, including visits to the doctor, medical tests and similar expenses.

Group vs. Individual Plans

Group insurance plans cost, on average, between half and two-thirds of what an individual plan costs. Many types of group plans are available. The most common ones are those offered by your employer. Religious organizations, labor unions and private organizations frequently offer their members group insurance plans as well.

If you don't have access to a group plan, your alternatives are buying an individual policy or joining a managed health-care plan, such as an HMO.

Choosing a Higher Deductible

Health insurance is vital to maintaining economic stability and a sound financial future, but it's generally rather expensive. There is a way, however, to cut your costs.

In most cases, choosing a higher deductible lowers your insurance costs. A deductible is a dollar amount you must pay before the insurance kicks in (a typical deductible is $300 a year per individual).

If you have a choice of several deductibles, you may want to opt for the highest one you can afford, say $1,000. This way you can use the insurance as a protection against major expenses rather than as a way to pay for everyday health care. Be sure, however, that the deductible is applied to the annual total of your expenses, not against each individual expense.

Indemnity Plans

Don't fall prey to what seems like the cheap cost of indemnity plans, because they may not be the best value for your money.

Indemnity plans guarantee that they'll pay a specific amount per claim (for example, $100 for every day you're in the hospital), but in general they are not a smart use of your insurance dollar. The amount they pay often covers only a fraction of the actual cost of any care you receive. And once you buy the policy, you may find hidden restrictions.

Is Your HMO a Better Value than the More Expensive Plan?

Managed care has become the preferred solution to expensive health-care costs, and HMOs are the leading type of managed-care organization.

Instead of charging for each service or visit to a doctor or hospital, health maintenance organizations (HMOs) charge you an annual fee that covers all the care you receive. A big plus of prepaid care is that you never have to remember to file insurance claims or wait to be reimbursed for money you've paid out for treatment. And an even bigger benefit is that all the care you get is covered, so you won't be faced with an enormous bill for medical care you can't afford.

Types of Managed Care

Get to know the other types of managed-care plans:

Preferred Provider Organizations (PPOs) PPOs are networks of doctors that provide discounted care to members of a sponsoring organization, such as an employer or union. If you use a participating doctor, you pay a small co-payment at the time of your visit (approximately $10 or 10% of the bill).

But if you go to a nonparticipating, out-of-network doctor, your share of the bill jumps dramatically.

Open-ended HMOs Open-ended HMOs cover visits to the doctor of your choice. You will probably have to pay a larger premium (monthly fee) for this option, but you may want the flexibility to use a particular practitioner.

Questions to Ask Before Choosing

Choosing a managed-care plan will cost you less than buying a traditional fee-for-service policy. But if you are trying to decide among various plans, it pays to ask a few questions about each before selecting one:

- Can I choose which doctor I want to see, or are they assigned by availability?
- How long is the average wait for an appointment?
- Can I see doctors outside the network? How much will it cost?
- Is there a cap on the total coverage the plan will provide?
- How much will each visit cost? Is there a limit to the number of visits?
- Is there a co-payment?
- If a specialist is needed, will consultation be paid by the plan?

Insurance You Don't Need...

- **Mortgage protection insurance:** It is cheaper to buy term life insurance to pay off your mortgage and other debts.

- **Funeral insurance:** Expensive and inefficient. Again, term life insurance is better because you can buy many times as much coverage for the same cost.

  Worth considering:

- **Trip-cancellation insurance**—if you pay up front for an expensive vacation.

- **Flood and earthquake insurance**—if you live in areas in which these natural disasters are likely.

  Robert Hunter, director of insurance, Consumer Federation of America, 1424 16 St. NW, Washington, DC 20036. www.consumer fed.org.

Tax-Free Medical Funding

Many companies give you the opportunity to set aside pretax income to pay for medical expenses your insurance doesn't cover. You have to use the amount you've set aside within the year, or you'll lose it. But if you have a sense of the minimum you're likely to spend each year on deductible or uncovered expenses (such as contact lenses), it can be a smart move.

Check with your employer or the human resources department of the company you work for to find out whether this is an option for you.

- Can I be dropped if I need lots of care or make frequent visits to the doctor?
- Are medications paid for? How many times can I refill them? Can I buy in bulk? Do I co-pay each time or just for the first prescription?
- What hospitals can I use? Are there any limitations on the length of hospital stays?
- What are emergency hospital care costs?
- Are there any health services for home nursing?
- Are orthopedic shoes, eyeglasses, syringes, blood-glucose meters and similar equipment covered?
- Are health classes, weight-reduction seminars, exercise clinics or special services reimbursable?
- Are there discounts for nonsmokers or people involved in fitness programs?

Avoid Common HMO Traps

Since HMOs are increasingly common sources of health insurance, it's good to know how to avoid any traps that can increase your costs.

Traps and Solutions

Trap: Not realizing you can change primary-care physicians only at specified times.

Every plan has its own rules, but generally you can only switch doctors at certain times or frequencies. Some plans allow you to change once a quarter, others three times a year. With some plans, you can switch only at the beginning of the month—while with others you can change only at the end of the month, even if you move or your doctor relocates, or if your doctor is away or unavailable.

Possible solution: First, check the language of your contract to make sure you are making the change at the right time. Otherwise, you may be disqualified from coverage and have to foot the bill yourself. You may be better off staying with your old doctor for the time being.

Trap: Slow referral procedures.

Because you must obtain a referral in order to get a specialist's care paid for by an HMO, the process can sometimes be agonizingly slow and result in a delay in diagnosis.

Possible solution: If you believe that it is urgent for you to see a specialist and your doctor disagrees, ask for a written explanation of why your condition is not urgent. If the doctor turns out to be wrong, you'll have documentation for bringing a legal case. Putting the opinion in writing may also cause the doctor to think twice.

Beware: If you pay for a visit to a specialist yourself without your HMO's approval and you cannot prove it was an emergency, you will probably not be reimbursed.

Trap: Allowing your physicians to make benefits decisions, rather than medical decisions, on your behalf.

This may seem like quibbling, but there's an important difference.

Solution: To protect yourself, ask your doctor to explain to what extent a decision is being influenced by contracts with your health plan. The key is making the distinction between decisions about payment and decisions about health and well-being.

If your doctor is overly influenced by HMO policy, you should be concerned about decisions affecting your health and well-being. So in every situation, ask your doctor this question. If the doctor's decision is based on policy instead of your health, ask what your next step should be to receive the best care.

COBRA Insurance

If you leave your job, you don't have to worry about paying for the expensive costs of an individual insurance plan right off the bat.

COBRA (Consolidated Omnibus Budget Reconciliation Act of 1985) gives you the right to continue your group insurance for 18 months after you leave a job, whether you quit, are laid off or retire (and for 29 months if you're disabled). The general rule is that you can buy coverage for 102% of your employer's cost.

Your employers cannot deny you coverage, except by ending health insurance for all employees.

How to Get the Most Out of Managed Care

Health care is big business. In fact, it is the country's number-one form of commerce. But patients face a stacked deck. Health-care providers, such as doctors and hospitals, want to make money. Managed-care organizations want to save money.

Your personal health comes third.

The key to getting quality medical care is to be assertive. You cannot entrust this crucial issue to anyone else.

Here's how to get the most out of your managed-care plan:

Know What's Covered

Carefully read the plan documents provided by your employer or insurer to find out what is covered. Don't wait for a medical emergency to do this important fact-finding.

Publications don't cover everything...and there may be gray areas that need clarification, such as care when traveling and some medications.

If you or someone in your family has a medical condition that doesn't seem to be covered, call the insurer's customer service number or emergency hotline. Ask what treatment options are covered.

Get the answer in writing before proceeding with any treatment. Otherwise, you may end up paying for it yourself.

Example: For mental illness, many plans will pay for a certain number of days of care in the hospital and a certain number of outpatient visits with a psychologist. But many people with mental illness are now being treated on a "partial hospitalization" basis, spending six hours a day in the hospital and going home at night.

Before You Retire Early, Check the Small Print

Before taking early retirement, check to see if your company can cut retiree health benefits. More and more firms are reducing them as cost-cutting pressures increase. Even companies that promise to provide retiree health benefits often include reservation clauses stating that they reserve the right to make benefits changes. Consider negotiating guaranteed health coverage as part of your retirement package.

Retirees age 65 and older can rely on Medicare, but that does not cover spouses under 65 or children.

Challenge Bad Rulings

Your physician may advise against a certain procedure simply because it isn't covered by your plan. Don't automatically accept that. Your medical options should be determined by what is best for you—not by what your doctor thinks the plan will pay for.

Get a second opinion to determine which procedure is best.

If there is a conflict between two doctors about a serious condition, seek a third opinion.

Important: Never tell the physician from whom you are seeking a second opinion what the first physician said. That may influence his/her opinion—he may not want to disagree with a peer for fear of losing future referral business.

Use Special Programs

If you have a chronic health condition—asthma, arthritis, high blood pressure, diabetes, etc.—participate in your plan's disease-management program.

This is a multidisciplinary team approach that includes physicians, nurses, social workers and pharmacists. *Aim:* To prevent acute episodes that result in hospitalization.

Patients may receive special education about their conditions, frequent telephone monitoring and regular home visits by nurses.

Example: After one plan started a diabetes-management program, patients' emergency room visits dropped by 75%...hospitalizations dropped by 70%...and lost workdays declined by 63%. The annual savings amounted to about $1,500 per patient.

Ask if your plan has contracts with any *centers of excellence*. These are special facilities, such as the Mayo Clinic, the Cleveland Clinic and Memorial Sloan-Kettering Cancer Center, that are known for treating certain conditions, such as advanced heart disease or cancer.

Because they specialize in specific disorders, their staffs know better how to proceed without wasting time and money. They generally don't order unnecessary tests or perform procedures that are not needed.

Choose Your Hospital

Find the best hospital for your procedure. Don't automatically accept the facility that your plan routinely uses.

The medical support system at a specialized facility—nurses, technicians and other specialists—plays at least as big a role in your recovery as the surgeon.

Medical Care for Children

If your child has a serious illness, insist that he be seen by a pediatric specialist. Children have very different medical needs than adults. A doctor who sees only adults may not provide the best treatment for your child.

Follow Emergency Rules

Carefully follow the rules about emergency health care while traveling. Denials of such claims are a frequent source of consumer complaints, although many plans are relaxing their stance.

If you must go to an emergency room or be seen by a physician while away from home, get the following:

- Detailed bill, including the diagnosis, a list of services provided and charges.
- Names, addresses and phone numbers of all health-care providers, as well as the medical license number of the doctor who treated you.
- Copy of the medical record of your care.
- Letter from the doctor or hospital stating that the treatment could not have waited until you returned home and that transferring you to another facility would have adversely affected your health.

Keep Good Records

At the first sign of a problem regarding your medical treatment—say, your plan refuses to refer you to a specialist when you believe you need one—start keeping notes.

Document each interaction with your physician or plan employees, noting the names of those with whom you spoke, the date of each conversation, what was said and by whom. This documentation is crucial if you later challenge the plan's decisions.

Appeal If Not Satisfied

Many denials are later reversed, so file an immediate written appeal if you disagree with your plan's initial decision.

Contact the claims examiner for your case, and explain why you feel your benefits were wrongfully denied. Also state what action you want your plan to take.

If your appeal is denied, ask the claims examiner to explain in writing why the plan rejected your claim. Then move up the chain of command and speak with the examiner's supervisor. Again, ask for the plan's decision in writing.

If you're still not satisfied, ask to have your case reviewed by the plan's medical director. Sometimes it may be necessary to contact your state regulatory agency or a private attorney.

Best line of defense in appeal: Your health-care providers' opinions. Ask your doctor to write to the plan explaining why he feels certain tests or treatment are necessary. If medical research or second opinions support his view, be sure to include them as well.

Charles Inlander, president of People's Medical Society, a nonprofit organization that helps consumers make informed decisions about health care, 462 Walnut St., Allentown, PA 18102. He is author of many books, including This Won't Hurt (And Other Lies My Doctor Tells Me) *(People's Medical Society).*

Don't Trust The List

Don't assume that doctors are in an HMO just because their names appear in the plan's list. Call the doctors directly and ask if they are in the plan, and if they are accepting new plan patients.

An HMO's list of doctors may be inaccurate or out of date. Doctors may have died, quit the plan after the list was printed or been dismissed right after the sign-up period for new members.

How to Check the Quality of an HMO

Before you join an HMO, you should consider checking whether it has been accredited by the **National Committee for Quality Assurance** (NCQA, 888-275-7585, www.ncqa. org). NCQA is an independent nonprofit organization that rates HMOs on their medical treatment, physicians' qualifications, preventive health services, record keeping and more. At least 50% of all HMO enrollees have been rated. You can call NCQA for a free **Health Plan Report Card**, which is updated on the 15th of each month.

Best Ways to File Claims

Getting the money your insurance company owes you may just be a matter of filing a claim properly the first time. To do so, you've got to pay attention to detail.

Filing a claim is so complex that it provides many opportunities for errors and misunderstandings. When mistakes occur, insurers, already under pressure to hold down costs, are likely to question, deny or reduce the amount you're claiming.

In response, a new type of service has emerged to help people file claims and battle insurers.

Claims assistance professionals (many of whom formerly worked for insurance companies as claims administrators), charge anywhere from $25 to $90 per hour, and with their help, an estimated 50% of the claims that are challenged end up being paid by insurers.

Here are the effective strategies of claims assistance professionals that you can use yourself instead of spending the money to hire one.

Avoid Clerical Errors

A significant number of claims are rejected because of clerical errors. When you send in your claims, clerks may have to key them into computer systems, raising the risk of error. Even electronic claims can be problematic. Insurance group or Social Security numbers can be transposed.

These days, every diagnosis and procedure performed by a doctor is given a code number. Insurers look to the codes to decide if the doctor overcharged or used an inappropriate treatment, so if the numbers are wrong, claims will remain unpaid.

Your insurer should tell you why a claim is denied or reimbursed at a lower level, so that you can correct any claim error that may be the cause. If the insurer says that treatment was not related to the diagnosis or was inappropriate, it could be a sign that the codes are wrong.

Keep Detailed Records

When challenging your claim, do it in writing and keep careful records of all contacts with your health insurers. Send copies to your doctor or hospital and the insurance company, and keep a copy for yourself. Keep notes about any telephone conversations you've had with the insurer detailing with whom you spoke, when you had the conversation and what was said—in case you need to refer to those conversations at a later date.

Enlist Your Doctor's Help

Enlist your doctor's help if your insurer won't pay what your doctor is charging. An insurer may feel the charges are more than the usual, customary and reasonable fees.

It's in doctors' best interest to prove that their tab isn't out of line, and they should be willing to send a letter to your insurance company detailing the facts.

In other cases, the doctor may need to submit a more detailed explanation of treatment and services. The procedure you received may be more complicated than the insurance company realizes.

Provide More Information

Provide more information about your symptoms if your insurer says the treatment wasn't medically necessary. Additional details may help to explain why you needed the treatment.

If your insurer protests that your treatment was experimental and not eligible, have your physician write a letter. Or, if you write it, have your doctor add to it citing medical studies or discussing how commonly the treatment is used.

Keep Track of Policy Changes

Keep careful track of policy changes and of what you've spent that qualifies against your deductible. Carefully read any memos and booklets from your employee benefits department or health insurer.

How to Fight Your Health Insurer...and Win

Don't throw up your hands if your health, auto or home insurance company denies a claim. There are ways to fight back.

More than half of all Americans will have a disagreement with their medical insurers some day. Problems often develop when you're not able to use a specific health-care provider...or obtain approval for a specific treatment...or when a bill is "kicked back" —unpaid—from the insurance company after treatment.

When a claim is denied, the patient's health-care provider normally handles the first stage of the appeals process. If the appeal is rejected, the patient needs to play an active role in further appeals.

Find Out Why the Claim Was Rejected

It is usually because:
- The treatment was not preauthorized, as required by the plan.
- The claim was coded incorrectly by the provider.
- The insurance company believes the treatment was not medically necessary.
- The insurance company regards the treatment as experimental.
- The insurance plan specifically excludes that treatment.
- The health-care provider is not included in the plan.

Ask Questions Before Switching Your HMO

While low out-of-pocket costs make HMOs attractive, you still need to ask hard questions before switching from one plan to another.

Here are some key questions you may want to consider asking before you sign on the dotted line:

- Will the HMO physician you want to use as a primary-care doctor be able to see you as a new patient?
- If you have a chronic condition, how does the HMO handle it?
- How easy is it to get appointments and referrals to see specialists?
- Can you get a standing referral to see a specialist without having to go through a primary physician each time?
- Will the HMO allow a specialist to be your primary physician? If so, will the specialist be able to see you for ailments and checkups unrelated to the specialty?
- Does the HMO offer a variety of benefit packages?
- How far will you have to travel to see a primary-care physician or specialist?
- How does the health plan cover an emergency? Does it require prior authorization for an emergency visit? What is its definition of an emergency?

Find the Person In Charge

Take the matter to a higher authority if you're not satisfied with what your insurer's customer service representative tells you. That person has a supervisor who may be able to help you.

If you feel you are being wrongly denied care by an HMO, ask for a medical director, a customer relations vice president or someone whose job it is to oversee such problems. Most HMOs are required by law to have an appeals process.

If your medical insurance is provided by your employer, complain to your company's employee benefits people. Since they're the ones who choose and pay for the health insurance coverage, they may have more clout with the insurer than an individual employee does. Insurance company executives should be notified if employees are getting poor service.

If you still can't get satisfaction, try your state insurance commissioner's office. Most allow that any claim can be challenged as long as it is done in writing. Just threatening to contact the state insurance commissioner's office will likely cause your insurer to review your claim.

If you did not receive written notice of the denial, call the insurance company and request one. Without such documentation, you will have no foundation for an appeal.

Get a Copy of Your Health Insurance Policy

An estimated 40% of people facing rejected claims do not have this document. Request a copy from your employer's human resources department.

Enlist Help

With the written denial and health-plan documents in hand, it is time to seek professional help. Our nonprofit organization, Patient Advocate Foundation, can provide references (800-532-5274)...or check our Web site for a list of resources in your region (http://data.patientadvocate.org).

Keep an Eye on the Calendar

Every insurance policy has a limited window for filing appeals, generally 30 to 90 days from the date of rejection. After the deadline, it becomes substantially more difficult—or even impossible—to appeal.

Address the Reason for the Insurer's Rejection in Your Appeal

- If the insurer says a procedure is medically unnecessary—find statistics showing the procedure may extend or improve quality of life. Also provide encouraging statistics from clinical trials.
- If the insurer claims that a medical procedure is experimental—you, your health-care provider or your lawyer must prove otherwise, by citing studies on the subject published in well-regarded, peer-reviewed medical journals. Enlist the help of your health-care provider.
- If the insurer excludes the procedure—file a *compassionate appeal* and cite facts to support exceptions.

Important: Doctors' appeals of rejected claims are most likely to fail when they focus on medical ethics and opinion and neglect what the insurance companies like—hard proof.

Nancy Davenport, founding executive director, Patient Advocate Foundation, a nonprofit organization that acts as a liaison between patients and their insurers and provides insurance counseling to consumers, 753 Thimble Shoals Blvd., Ste. B, Newport News, VA 23606. www.patientadvocate.org. This organization publishes two books on insurance, *The Managed Care Answer Guide* and *Your Guide to the Appeals Process.*

Medigap, the Supplement To Medicare

Medigap policies cover a variety of services, including nursing home co-payments, foreign-travel emergencies and prescription drugs. The best time to buy Medigap insurance is within the first six months after you begin your Medicare coverage. Otherwise, it may be more expensive.

Getting Free Advice on Medigap

You can get free advice on your insurance options and answers to your Medigap questions through your state's insurance counseling office. You can find the number in your telephone book or in the Health Care Financing Administration's *Guide to Health Insurance for People with Medicare*, which is available from your local Social Security office.

Another option is to check with the agency in your state that coordinates information and services for older residents, such as the Department of Aging. You can find its number in the *Guide to Health Insurance*, in the telephone book, and from groups such as the United Seniors Health Cooperative.

Remember that each state's insurance rules are a little different, so if you move after you retire, you may need to revise your Medigap coverage.

Medicare Opportunity

Many HMO insurers are working to provide in-network medical care to retirees that's much cheaper than regular Medigap coverage. If retirees are willing to commit themselves to visiting only network physicians, they won't need to purchase Medigap coverage. Instead, they will pay only $10 per doctor's visit and Medicare will reimburse other expenses. If this is an option open to you, it's worth considering.

Pay Attention to Your Medicare Treatments

When you get **Medicare** treatments, keep a log of all your medical visits and any procedures that are done. This will help you check if you are billed incorrectly, and make it easier if you have to file an appeal for additional payment.

Review every bill carefully. Medicare bills from hospitals and doctors often contain errors.

Also, it usually takes 35 to 45 days for Medicare to pay a claim. If you do not get an explanation of Medicare payments within 45 days, contact the Medicare carrier in your region.

Before traveling outside the US, find out what Medicare covers you for while abroad.

At-Home Nursing Care

Only the very rich can afford not to be concerned about the likelihood that some day they will need home care or nursing home care.

But the rest of us do have to worry about becoming incapacitated. And most of us would prefer to be cared for at home. Questions we all have:

- How much does home care cost?
- Will Medicare pay for some of it?
- What quality of care can one expect from the government?

Medical Mistakes And Medicare

Medicare patients are entitled to information about doctors' mistakes, says a new court decision.

After a woman died of cancer, her husband alleged that her death was caused by doctors who misdiagnosed her condition as an abscess, appendicitis, bladder infection and "old woman's pain." The government investigated, but—citing Medicare regulations—refused to tell the husband what it found. He sued.

Court: The regulations are invalid. Medicare must disclose the results of the review and of all other reviews held in cases in which a patient or family member claimed medical mistakes or poor care.

Public Citizen v. Dept. of Health and Human Services, DC, Dist. of Columbia, No. 00-0731 (ESH).

- Do I need a Medigap policy?
- What about a long-term-care insurance policy?

Medicare

Medicare generally covers a very limited portion of the cost of care provided in the home. Although home care typically follows a hospital stay, Medicare does not make hospitalization a prerequisite for coverage.

As long as the care is necessary for treatment of an illness or injury, Medicare coverage applies. This coverage, however, includes only the items defined as "home-health-care benefits." These include:

- Medical social services.
- Nursing care (part-time or intermittent).
- Medical supplies/equipment.
- Physical therapy.
- Occupational therapy.
- Speech therapy.
- Home health aides (part-time or intermittent), but only if a skilled service—such as therapy—is provided also.

The benefits *must* be prescribed by a doctor and provided by a home-care agency that has been certified by Medicare.

Your share: You pay an annual $100 deductible and co-payments for benefits under Medicare Part B. You must also make a 20% co-payment for medical supplies—hospital beds, walkers, wheelchairs, etc.

Exception: People under a managed care type of Medicare do not have to make a co-payment for benefits received under Medicare Part B.

Medicare Does Not Cover Everything For instance, Medicare limits coverage for part-time or *intermittent* home care—fewer than five days a week on an infrequent basis—to 35 hours per week. If continuing care is needed—care for a period of up to 21 days—then coverage can be for up to seven days a week, but only for up to 56 hours a week.

If a home health aide and nursing services are needed, the amount billed must be kept under 35 hours a week to be considered intermittent.

Medicare Does Not Cover the Cost of Long-Term Care or Personal Assistance Care These are considered custodial-type care rather than medical care. This kind of care applies to those with chronic conditions, such as Alzheimer's disease, Parkinson's disease, etc., who need assistance with daily living activities (eating, bathing, getting in and out of bed, going to the bathroom, etc.).

Medicare Does Not Cover the Cost of Housekeeping This is often needed by a person with a chronic condition.

Medigap Coverage

Supplemental Medicare insurance—Medigap insurance—picks up only the amounts of Medicare *covered expenses* that Medicare does not pay for, such as co-payments and deductibles.

Medigap *does not* cover the cost of long-term care, since Medicare doesn't provide this coverage.

Medicaid

The cost of custodial care provided in the home may be covered by Medicaid in a few states.

Medicaid is designed to pay only for those who are "poor." So, to be eligible for Medicaid, a person's income and assets must be below limits set by law. Only a few states have a broad home-care program.

Loophole: In most states, people who transfer assets so that Medicaid will pay for *in-home care* are *not* subject to the federal government's 36-month look-back rule. That rule disqualifies people who unload assets within that time period from getting Medicaid to pay for their stay in a nursing home.

Beware: Individual states may impose look-back rules that bar people who transfer assets from getting Medicaid to pay for in-home care.

Tax Incentives

The tax law now provides breaks that defray some custodial care costs. A person needing home care can take an itemized deduction for "qualified medical expenses" to the extent that total expenses exceed 7.5% of Adjusted Gross Income (AGI). Deductible medical expenses include:

- Out-of-pocket medical costs, including out-of-pocket payments to home health aides.
- Medicare co-payments and deductibles.
- Long-term-care insurance premiums up to a dollar limit (depending on age).
- "Long-term-care services"—up to any amount—provided to a person who is chronically ill. The meaning of "long-term-care services" is liberally interpreted to include rehabilitative services and personal care services. This is so even though personal care service probably would not qualify as a deductible medical expense were it not a *long-term-care* service.

Taxes: Some part of the benefits provided under a long-term-care policy may be taxable.

Peter J. Strauss, Esq., a partner in the law firm Epstein Becker & Green, PC, 250 Park Ave., New York 10017. He is a fellow of the National Academy of Elder Law Attorneys and coauthor of *The Elder Law Handbook—A Legal and Financial Survival Guide for Caregivers and Seniors* (Facts on File).

Long-Term Care... New Option

A problem with obtaining long-term care insurance is that most people won't need long-term care, in which case the expensive premiums are wasted.

But new combined life insurance/long-term-care policies address this problem. The policies pay a standard life insurance benefit, but should you need long-term care, you can tap the policy benefit tax free. The life insurance benefit may be reduced by amounts spent on care needs. Whether you eventually need care or not, your premiums will earn a return. Ask your insurance adviser for details.

Lee Slavutin, MD, CPC, CLU, is a principal of Stern Slavutin-2 Inc., insurance and estate planners, 530 Fifth Ave., New York 10036; www.sternslavutin.com.

How to Ensure Lifetime Care For a Child with Special Needs

Three-pronged strategy for the best possible lifetime care of a disabled child...

- **Create a *special needs* trust** under your will to pay for things above what government programs provide. Fund the trust from your estate—rather than when you are alive—to avoid tax complications.

- **Give money to family members** with a *nonbinding* request that they use it to help the child. Their help can get around restrictions on what can be done with the special needs trust.

- **Contact charities** involved in the child's disability. Many have programs to help with lifetime-care issues.

Martin Shenkman, CPA, attorney in private practice in New York. www.laweasy.com.

Is Nursing Home Insurance Right for You?

The risk is real...about 11% of those turning age 65 can expect to spend a significant amount of time in a nursing home. The average cost for a year's stay is about $40,000 today—but in a number of areas in the country, it can top $100,000.

How are you going to cover such a huge expense if the need arises? The answer depends on your income and net worth:

- The "poor"—and those who spend down their assets to become poor—can rely on Medicaid to cover the cost of a nursing home stay.
- The "wealthy" can afford to use their incomes to pay for such care without affecting their assets or the standard of living for other family members.
- Those in the middle—individuals with a net worth, say, of between $500,000 and $5 million—should consider buying a long-term-care policy.

Here are some factors to weigh in deciding whether to buy a long-term-care policy, and when:

Can I Afford It?

Premiums for long-term-care policies aren't cheap. They can run between $2,000 and $10,000 a year for those under age 70, and as much as $15,000 or even $20,000 a year for those 70 and older. Like life insurance policies, the younger you are when you take out the policy, the lower your premiums will be.

Caution: Premiums for long-term-care policies are considered "level premiums"—that is, they don't increase as you age. *However* —the insurance company has the right to increase the premiums for a whole *class* of policies. This could happen with long-term-care policies as insurance companies gain more experience and find they've underpriced them.

Cost of the premium depends on:

- The person's age when the policy is first purchased.
- The benefit per day.
- The period for which benefits will be paid—three years, five years, life.
- The "elimination period"—the time before benefits will start.
- Other factors, such as a cost-of-living adjustment to the daily benefit.

Today, the people who can afford it are taking the maximum daily benefit available ($250 to $300 a day) and are choosing life-time policies (instead of those running for three, five or 10 years).

Types of Policies

The type of policy you buy really depends on what you can afford.

The best of policies: Lifetime coverage for the maximum benefit ($250 to $300 a day, depending on the company)…with a short elimination period.

But if you find the cost of such coverage prohibitive, consider a more modest policy, say $150 to $200 a day, for a shorter period than life, or with a longer elimination period.

In comparing policies offered by different companies, there are nuances to consider that can affect your choice.

Example: Be sure you understand how each company counts days of care for purposes of the elimination period. Say someone needs three days of care per week. Does this count as an entire week for the elimination period or will it take seven calendar days to equal one week for the elimination period?

Get Professional Help Use an insurance professional who can guide you through the intricacies of long-term-care insurance.

Experience Counts Stick with an insurance company that has experience with long-term-care policies, such as GE Capital, Travelers, John Hancock, Fortis and Unum.

Tax break: A portion of the premiums can be treated as a deductible medical expense based on your age, thereby offsetting some of the cost for those who itemize their medical expenses.

Note: There have been proposals in Congress to make long-term-care insurance premiums fully deductible. That would further reduce out-of-pocket costs.

Can You Afford Not To?

If you are in the middle—not rich and not poor—you may not accumulate enough through savings to pay for nursing home care. If you are in this situation, you should consider buying a long-term-care policy.

Example: At age 60, you buy a $100-per-day benefit at a cost of $519 per year—a three-year policy with a 90-day elimination period.

Then assume at age 80, you require nursing home care. You would have paid $10,380 over the 20 years of coverage.

Had you used that same $519 each year to invest for an after-tax return of 6%, you have only $20,237 after 20 years.

This would cover just 203 days in the home (at $100 a day). The policy would cover 1,095 days.

When to Buy a Policy

Those who are 55 years old or older should start to look seriously at long-term-care policies.

Note: An increasing number of employers are offering this coverage as an employee benefit.

Do the Research

Every state has a long-term-care ombudsman who acts as an advocate for nursing home residents and helps prospective residents evaluate specific facilities.

For a free referral to the ombudsman in your area, contact **The National Citizens' Coalition for Nursing Home Reform**, 202-332-2275, www.nccnhr.org.

Ellen Hoffman, retirement columnist for *Business Week Online* and author of *Bankroll Your Future: How to Get the Most from Uncle Sam for Your Retirement Years* and *The Retirement Catch-Up Guide* (Newmarket).

Compare Nursing Homes

Visit the home to get an impression of administrators, nurses and residents. Ask to see the **Centers for Medicare and Medicaid Services (CMS)** annual inspection report. It details complaints and violations of federal standards. Or access this on-line at www.medicare. gov. Click on "Nursing Home Compare."

Ellen Hoffman, retirement columnist for Business Week Online and author of Bankroll Your Future: How to Get the Most from Uncle Sam for Your Retirement Years and The Retirement Catch-Up Guide (Newmarket).

If you don't have employer-provided coverage, then look into individual coverage. The younger you are when you start the policy, the lower your premiums will be.

But if you buy at 55, won't you be paying premiums for 20 or 30 years before needing benefits, if ever? Does that make sense?

While your chances are better than 50% that you'll never put in a claim, should you need to do so, you're likely to come out ahead financially if you have a policy.

Suppose a 55-year-old buys a policy to provide $250 a day for a lifetime if needed (with a 90-day elimination period). She would pay $3,452.20 a year in premiums.

Example: If she should need long-term care after just *one year* of paying premiums, she would recover her entire outlay in just 14 days in a nursing home of average cost.

Five years of premiums would be recovered in 69 days, 10 years in 138 days. And—20 years in 276 days.

Even if this 55-year-old were not to need any benefits until age 85, her 30 years of premiums would be recovered in 414 days.

Lee Slavutin, MD, CPC, CLU, a principal of Stern Slavutin-2 Inc., insurance and estate planners, 530 Fifth Ave., New York 10036; www.sternslavutin.com.

Assisted Living Resources

Administration on Aging (330 Independence Ave. SW, Washington, DC 20201, 800-677-1116, www.aoa.dhhs.gov). Operates more than 660 agencies that provide information on local care options.

American Association of Homes and Services for the Aging (2519 Connecticut Ave. NW, Washington, DC 20008, 800-508-9442, 202-783-2242, www.aahsa.org). Not-for-profit organizations that provide health care, housing and community services to the elderly.

Assisted Living Federation of America (11200 Waples Mill Rd., Ste. 150, Fairfax, Virginia 22030, 703-691-8100, www.alfa.org). Represents more than 7,000 member businesses. Free on-line publications to help you choose an assisted-living residence.

National Association for Home Care (228 Seventh St. SE, Washington, DC 20003, 202-547-7424, www.nahc.org). More than 22,500 agencies, including home-care providers, hospices, home-care aide organizations.

Barbara Weltman, an attorney practicing in Millwood, NY, www.bwideas. com, and author of The Complete Idiot's Guide to Making Money After You Retire (Macmillan).

Index